ACTON SOCIETY STUDIES: 1

Direct Action and Democratic Politics

ACTON SOCIETY STUDIES

Direct Action
and Democratic
Politics

edited by
ROBERT BENEWICK and TREVOR SMITH

LONDON. GEORGE ALLEN & UNWIN LTD
Ruskin House   Museum Street

First published in 1972

© George Allen & Unwin Ltd 1972

ISBN 0 04 350040 4 hardback
      0 04 350041 2 paperback

Printed in Great Britain
in 10 point Plantin type
by Alden & Mowbray Ltd
at the Alden Press, Oxford

CONTRIBUTORS

ROBERT BAXTER
is Lecturer in Government and Political Theory at the University College of Wales, Swansea. He is currently conducting a survey of political attitudes in East Belfast and is editor of a forthcoming book on city politics.

ROBERT BENEWICK
is Reader in Politics in the University of Sussex. He is the author of *Political Violence and Public Order* and co-editor with Robert Dowse of *Readings on British Politics and Government*.

PETER CADOGAN
is General Secretary of the South Place Ethical Society. He has been Secretary of the Committee of 100 and of the Save Biafra Campaign, as well as a member of the National Council of CND. He has also written articles for a number of periodicals.

GEORGE CLARK
has been instrumental in the formation of several community action groups in North Kensington, and has recently founded the Committee for City Poverty. In addition to his involvement in such projects, he has been closely associated with CND, and was a founder member of the Committee of 100.

GAVIN DREWRY
is a Lecturer in Government in the Department of Sociology, Bedford College, London University. He has been involved in a research project on the House of Lords in its judicial capacity, and is currently collaborating on a study of law reporting and the legislative process.

NICHOLAS GARNHAM
has worked for several years in television as a film editor and documentary director. He is co-author with Joan Bakewell of *The New Priesthood: British Television Today* and author of *Samuel Fuller* in the Cinema One series.

PETER HAIN
is at present studying Economics at Queen Mary College, London University. He was Chairman of the Stop The Seventy Tour Committee and is now Chairman of the Young Liberals. He has published *Don't Play With Apartheid*.

CONTRIBUTORS

ROBIN JENKINS
has been Research Fellow at Essex University, the
Institute for Peace and Conflict Research in Copenhagen
and the Institute of Race Relations. His books include
Exploitation and *The Race Relations Industry* (forthcoming).

VICTOR KIERNAN
is Professor of History at Edinburgh University. Among
his numerous publications are *British Relations with China
1880-1885* and *The Revolution of 1854 in Spanish History*.
He is currently working on a volume of translations from
Faiz, the leading Urdu poet, and is writing on Indian
history and the application of Marxist theory to history.

ALEXANDER KIRBY
is the editor of *Race Today*. He was formerly assistant
curate (Anglican) in the Isle of Dogs, East London, and
was community relations officer for the London Borough
of Newham.

BRIAN MACARTHUR
is the editor of *The Times Higher Education Supplement*.
After leaving Leeds University, where he was President
of the Union, he worked as a university correspondent
with three newspapers before becoming the Education
Correspondent of *The Times* in 1967.

ROBERT MAST
has been on leave from the Department of Sociology,
University of Pittsburgh, to the Institute of Race Relations
where he is Associate Director of the International Race
Studies Programme. He has contributed a number of
articles to professional journals.

PETER MOODIE
is Lecturer in Law at Birmingham University. His current
research interests centre on a socio-legal study of police
powers.

BHIKHU PAREKH
is a Lecturer in the Department of Political Studies at
Hull University. He is co-editor with Preston King of
Politics and Experience, with R. N. Berki of *The Morality
of Politics* and editor of *Dissent and Disorder*.

HANNAN ROSE
is Lecturer in Interdisciplinary Studies in the Faculty of
Social Sciences, University of Kent. He is researching into
voluntary local liaison in race relations.

TREVOR SMITH
is Senior Lecturer in Government and Political Science
at Queen Mary College in the University of London.
He has taught at the Universities of Exeter, Hull and York,
and is the author of *Anti-Politics: Consensus, Reform and
Protest in Britain*. He is also Research Adviser to the
Acton Society Trust and the Joseph Rowntree Social
Service Trust.

TONY SMYTHE
has been General Secretary of the National Council for
Civil Liberties since 1966. Formerly active in the Com-
mittee of 100 and General Secretary of the War Resisters
International, he is also a committee member of the Joint
Council for the Welfare of Immigrants and the Immigrant
Advisory Service.

ELIZABETH VALLANCE
is Lecturer in Political Science, Queen Mary College,
London University. She is currently editing an Acton
Society Study of the Limits of State Regulation
regarding Self-destructive Acts.

DAVID WILLIAMS
is Senior Tutor at Emmanuel College, Cambridge
University. He has published *Not in the Public Interest*
and *Keeping the Peace*.

CONTENTS

INTRODUCTION

Direct action is a traditional and legitimate form of political behaviour in a democratic State. Ruling groups have rarely released or shared their power with others voluntarily. Institutional changes have seldom occurred in the absence of pressure. New policies and programmes have been introduced frequently by means outside the conventional boundaries of Parliamentary politics. As new demands and needs arise, their advocates have resorted to direct action in order to achieve recognition, participation and acceptance in the political system. When more established groups perceive the system as unresponsive or ineffective, they may well adopt more militant tactics to articulate their grievances. And although it is sad commentary, it is often through forms of direct action that the moral basis of politics is kept before the government and the public.

The political and industrial development of Britain, even though it has been more continuous and less cataclysmic than most nations, provides an impressive illustration of the role of direct action. It also makes clear that government resistance is to be expected. However, the way in which a government views this form of political activity can further or restrict democratic politics. Fundamentally, a commitment and determination to come to grips with the structural defects of society will be its most effective deterrent. Short of this, the response will be contingent upon the purpose and methods employed by those groups that undertake direct action. That is, whether the issue is considered resolvable within the existing system, necessitates changes in the system or demands its abolition. Thereafter, assuming the absence of a revolutionary situation, the choice among the options available to a government is dependent upon the ideological predispositions and political priorities of both the government and the direct actionists.

The wave of political unrest in recent years has inclined the British government in a restrictive direction. This, like direct action itself, has been encouraged as much by events abroad as by those at home. It also suggests an interpretation of democracy which discounts conflict and places it on a parity with efficacy and stability. For a nation so bound up in traditions, it is ironical that one of its most distinctive features can so easily be ignored. Part of the explanation lies in the technocratic and consensual approaches to politics, also borrowed from abroad in the late 1950s and early 1960s. The divisive features of British society were seen as disappearing, class conflict was dismissed as a relic of history, and party disputes were treated more as matters of personalities and images rather than of policies. With increasing confidence gained from the availability of intellectual skills and technocratic hardware, politics was viewed as a process for making adjustments to commonly accepted policies, for tinkering with institutions and for mopping-up marginal areas of deprivation. Economic growth, Parliamentary reforms, and progress in general were questions of technique. Ideology was deemed to have been replaced by consensus in domestic politics and by a growing convergence in international politics.

The response to the Campaign for Nuclear Disarmament, particularly on the part of political scientists, was indicative of this phenomenon. Rather than exploring the implications of its affinities with the nineteenth-century mass movements, the Campaign was regarded as a deviant case in contemporary political behaviour. Since its demands could not be accommodated within the realm of conventional pressure group politics, it was treated as a paradigm of a cause having no influence and thereby forced to rely on the mass demonstration. (We now know that the Aldermaston marches made it possible for serious discussion to take place in Whitehall.) Little attention was paid to the nature of the issues raised and the currents of thought represented, so that the possible inferences that could be drawn about the morality as well as the realities of a democratic political system were ignored.

It has become increasingly obvious that Britain along with other industrial nations is neither the technocrat's nor the social scientist's paradise. The government has been confronted with a succession of demands presented by means of direct action. Moreover, many of the groups involved cannot conveniently be placed at the extremes of a political spectrum. Government reaction has been more than a reflex to the breakdown of consensual politics and the shortcomings of the technocratic approach. The argument here is that the postulation of a newly-styled politics appropriate to advanced industrial nations was invalid in the first place. Consequently, perspective has been distorted which may engender over-reaction. This is compounded by confusion among the levels of direct action. Parochial demands that can be reconciled within the prevailing system are dressed-up in revolutionary language while fundamental conflicts are handled as problems of law and order. The stakes are thereby raised, positions polarized and distinctions among groups and among their goals obscured. Violence adds another, although by no means new, dimension. It is important to distinguish between direct action that is deliberately violent and that which becomes violent. A question of enduring relevance, however, is how necessary and how effective is violence?

The present volume was originally conceived in 1970. It was prompted by the growing recourse to direct action and in anticipation of restrictive legislation. The Conservative party, then in opposition, had committed itself to the issue of law and order for a general election campaign and the Labour party also felt compelled to include a statement in its election manifesto. It was our conviction that by placing in historical and comparative perspective what was generally considered an upsurge in the direct prosecution of claims upon the government as well as in the militant expression of dissatisfaction and disaffection, a sense of proportion could be restored. The enterprise was initiated in the spirit of concerned research rather than for motives of influencing policy.

The Conservative government was returned to office in June 1970 and although there has been no legislation it is reasonably clear that if an occasion is presented, the government is prepared to act. There is, then, no cause to relax our efforts. It is apparent that the government for the present is content to rely on existing legislative judicial and administrative sanctions and can claim considerable satisfaction. The Cambridge Garden House riot trial, the Dutschke case and the use of the Criminal Damage Act to raid the premises of left wing groups leave little doubt about the government's credibility on the issue of law and order. All three instances raise questions about the impartiality of British justice, the infectious influence of governments who almost everywhere fear protest and dissent, and the lowering of the threshold of violence which is discussed in Chapter II.

We have deliberately refrained from imposing definitions of direct action or democratic politics. It would be difficult, if not impossible, to obtain agreement from any group of contributors. This proved to be the case at a conference held in association with this volume at the National Liberal Club in May 1971. Hence V. G. Kiernan in Chapter I includes direct action on the part of the State but in a way that differs from that of Inspector Reg Gale of the Police Federation who at the conference viewed it as a method of solving social problems before they become occasions for militant forms of dissent. Gavin Drewry suggests another approach in Chapter XVI. He sees direct action as a negation of conventional party politics and a rejection of the *status quo*. What did emerge from the conference was that much depends on who defines direct action and how it is defined. It can be used as a term to connote approval or disapproval. Militants may see it as an expression of democratic participation, while authorities may apply the label to denigrate something that they do not like. A number of the contributors refer to the language problems and Elizabeth Vallance examines them in detail in Chapter IV.

Similar problems occur in discussions of democracy. It is viewed in both conventional and radical terms in the present volume. Some of the contributors write from the standpoint of Parliamentary democracy while others look to forms of direct democracy. However, the obstacles to obtaining agreement are not foremost in our minds. What we wish to convey by including a variety of views and approaches is the substance as well as the nature of direct action. The contributors accept direct action as a legitimate form of political expression in a democratic polity, describe its manifestations, discuss its causes and effects, its uses and abuses and estimate its significance.

Among our main concerns in regard to bias is the selection of topics and the limitations of space. Systematic evaluation suffers to the extent that it is abstracted from the historical, cultural, economic and social as well as the political context. Choice rested on critical considerations and representativeness rather than upon predetermined variables. The emphasis may be disputed and there are important omissions, including industrial strife, Celtic nationalism, women's liberation and extensive treatment of community action. The rule of the law and the position of the judiciary also merits more intensive study than is possible in this volume. An attempt has been made to avoid viewing direct action from the top down. A proper understanding would be incomplete without the insights of those who have actually participated or are currently involved. At the same time, attention is focused on the active role of institutions in an effort to stimulate further research in this direction.

A number of general themes are developed in Part One. V. G. Kiernan in a broad historical sweep covers industrial and political progress in Britain. The idea and reality of progress was one of several factors that contributed to the growth of a peaceful political style. Direct action, violence and virulent class conflict cannot be discounted, however. Reference has already been made to direct action on the part of the ruling class which forms an integral part of Professor Kiernan's thesis. He notes, however, that if the British ruling class is unable to subdue an opposition by a single blow, its instinct is not to escalate but to seek out alternatives. Robert Benewick's discussion of how the government and the police viewed Fascist and anti-Fascist violence in the 1930s is in part a micro-example of Kiernan's macro-study. More important is the attempt to describe a threshold of violence. He argues that this has now been lowered as much by the government as by the militants. The consequences for democratic politics are both immediate and long term.

The view that violence is not justified in a liberal democracy which provides opportunities for peaceful change is challenged by Bhikhu Parekh. He contends that the language and practices of liberal democracy may occasionally provoke violence. For Parekh, the question of violence is ultimately a political rather than a legal one, and it is on this level that it must be judged. Elizabeth Vallance would dispute Dr Parekh's approach and some of his assumptions. Where Parekh is interested in extreme manifestations to direct action, Mrs Vallance's framework includes its many forms. By comparing and contrasting the language of democratic politics with that of direct action, she shows the weaknesses of the latter *vis à vis* the former in terms of both accommodation and confrontation.

In the United States, violence has reached proportions unknown in modern Britain with the notable exception of Northern Ireland. This has prompted numerous studies, the most comprehensive of which are perhaps the Task Force reports to the National Commission on the Causes and Prevention of Violence. A prominent assumption in the writings of social scientists is that the study of violence is the study of behaviour. This assumption has scientific, political and policy implications, and these are discussed critically by Robin Jenkins. He attacks them on the grounds that the approach adopted views society through the eyes of the ruling élites. Robert Mast explores the dimensions of the concept 'law and order', drawing largely from American experience. These dimensions include the concepts of freedom, justice, democracy and equality and the separate concepts of law and order. When the two separate concepts, law and order, are combined they become 'a slogan and strategy for repression'. He concludes, however, that although this is a negative response to change, it does have positive implications.

Part Two comprises a number of specific studies that convey the pattern of direct action in contemporary British politics. Northern Ireland is to a limited extent England's Vietnam. The public has been exposed through the media to endless reports of continuous and extensive violence. These reports have begun to lose their shock value for the violent conflict appears to be both remote and routine. There has been no shortage of proposals for the containment of violence either by officially-sanctioned counter-violence (the use of troops) or by 'acceptable' reforms or concessions. And like Vietnam, the end is not in sight. There is an awareness but little understanding of how deeply rooted are the antagonisms. Robert Baxter makes it clear that the historical and structural problems of society raise questions fundamental to the State. He argues that the need is not to bring the Catholic and Protestant communities together but to allay their fears of cultural imperialism.

The notion of privilege is implicit in the British political culture and traditionally associated with prerogatives of élite groups. In the struggle to retain or abolish privilege and to resist or obtain rights, there has been frequent recourse to direct action. The extension of the franchise and the rise of the Labour movement illustrate this. The struggle against privilege persists although it is no longer exclusively directed towards traditional élites. Women's liberation is a straightforward example. Hannan Rose notes how race relations came to be defined as a problem of immigration control. One could add to his analysis the argument that the government's burden was shifted from securing the rights of immigrants by improving economic and social conditions to granting or withholding privileges. Much of the public displeasure against university unrest springs from a view of students as a privileged minority. Brian MacArthur shows that student violence can be attributed to the slow response of university administrators to reformist demands; indeed, it could be inferred that the thought of students possessing rights was only seriously entertained by university authorities where their own privileges were not threatened.

Hannan Rose surveys the politics of race relations since the 1950s. He demonstrates how the liberals were out-manoeuvred and explains why efforts on behalf of the coloured minority were ineffective. The immigrant groups themselves have been only marginally political and their objectives have been limited. This period of quiescence may be deceptive in terms of the future, and he predicts the possibility of militant action. This could take the form of Black Power. It is amorphous both as a concept and as a movement. Alexander Kirby discerns three distinct aspects and describes its manifestations in Britain. He believes that at present Black Power has little meaning for the coloured community but that it has potential for the future.

Brian MacArthur was a university correspondent with four newspapers during the 1960s. From this unique vantage point, he argues that there is a somewhat higher proportion of students than before who are willing to resort to violence. In other words, the universities have not been under siege by a violent mass of students. In analysing the causes of student violence and its subsequent decline, it becomes apparent that, despite the impact of events abroad, conditions peculiar to Britain are the vital considerations.

Peter Cadogan was Secretary of the Committee of 100 and a member of the National Council of the Campaign for Nuclear Disarmament. George Clark was also closely involved in CND as well as being a founder member of the Committee of 100. At present he is devoted full-time to the promotion of community action projects. Peter Hain was Chairman of the Stop The Seventy Tour Committee and at twenty-two is Chairman of the Young Liberals. All three write from explicitly committed viewpoints and in doing so add more than just flavour, atmosphere or descriptive character. They contribute a positive dimension to direct action without which any study or understanding would be artificial.

For Peter Cadogan, the common denominator of civil disobedience is the injection of personal responsibility into political activity. He discusses the circumstances in which civil disobedience re-emerged in Britain in the late 1950s, its character and its strategies. The evolution from civil disobedience to confrontation is described and according to Cadogan both suffered from similar disabilities. He offers a critical analysis based on his own involvement rather than a series of categorical solutions. What he does countenance is the need for ideas – but only those freed of the rigidities of traditional ideologies.

George Clark's account is largely autobiographical at the request of the editors. The result is a portrayal of why an individual turns to direct action and how he is able to sustain his involvement. Clark discovered that belief in the need for changes in the structures of society is contingent upon changes in personal behaviour. His approach derives from a firm conviction in non-violent methods. There is a qualitative link between the levels at which direct action occurs, because large issues are embodied in its most simple forms. He concludes with an eloquent plea to begin working at the bottom of British society.

The campaign to stop the South African cricket tour in 1970 can claim unqualified success in achieving its objectives. Critics and sceptics take comfort in that apartheid remains firmly entrenched in South Africa. This underestimates the significance of the Stop The Seventy Tour Committee. As Peter Hain makes clear, the British position on South Africa and race was exposed. Public opinion was mobilized and the government was forced to intervene in the interests of social justice as well as for the maintenance of public order. Hain evaluates the immediate consequences and spells out the future implications for protest politics.

Part Two is concerned with the views and strategies of those who resort to direct action. But how is the State affected? Direct confrontation with the State is not new nor is it static, for circumstances and conditions change. What are the views of the decision-makers and of those committed to participation in the political system? What options are available and what influences choice? How well adapted is the law and can the present institutions cope with new demands and the increasing number of claims? What are the means, aids and alternatives available for the presentation and processing of grievances and reforms? Are there sufficient checks on the power of the State and the police? These questions are considered in Part Three.

David Williams explains the importance of protest in democratic politics and the democratic importance of free speech and assembly. Governments in Britain and the United States have attempted at least initially to respond to the new forms of direct action within these guidelines. More specifically in Britain the approach appears to be cautious in regard to enlarging the powers of the police, changing the law or applying it too stringently in the courts. At the same time, there has been a willingness to entertain grievances and to consider institutional reforms. This is not a complacent view but an effort to show the difficulties that a government faces in reconciling dissent with democratic procedures.

It is difficult to conceive of a revolution that will abolish the police or the need for policing. Whatever one's view of democratic politics, the problem of police control is of the utmost importance. Peter Moodie examines police behaviour and the present structure for its review. The examples he cites raise serious questions about the nature of police activity and control. Moodie concludes with a critical survey of the proposals for reform.

Gavin Drewry looks at the attitudes of the Conservative and Labour parties towards direct action and at the dilemmas posed for individual Members of Parliament. Neither party adopts a monolithic approach for the issues are too complex. There is general consensus on the sanctity of civil liberties but as Drewry notes there is no firm agreement on what freedom of assembly, for example, means in practice. Their respective histories help to shape their positions as with the Labour party – committed to Parliamentary democracy yet born out of militancy. One of the parties may be singled-out as a target for pressure applied through direct action. A major party or section of it may share some or all of the goals of a direct action campaign. An MP may be caught between loyalty to his party and the political system and involvement in a movement or a cause. These considerations and others coalesce when direct action threatens the maintenance of public order.

The National Council for Civil Liberties is engaged in continuous confrontation with the dilemmas of direct action and democratic politics. No one is in a better position than Tony Smythe, its General Secretary, to discuss what he characterizes as 'the curious no-man's land' occupied by the NCCL. A commitment is inherent in its role yet it must act impartially as an intermediary. A style of militancy is demanded while at the same time it must retain its credibility. The NCCL seeks to preserve and further the climate of political freedom and to defend civil liberties from the incursions of over-zealous authorities or of an outraged public.

The influence of the media in shaping direct action is receiving increasing attention. Again the editors have turned to someone directly involved and with considerable experience, the independent television producer, Nicholas Garnham. His thesis is that television is not the helpmate of those who believe in direct action. Its bias is both historical and structural. As for its liberating potential, there are ideological and political limits. Garnham is particularly critical of the myth of impartiality which he sees as having serious consequences for direct action and democratic politics.

Finally, Trevor Smith critically analyses the new wave of protest and discusses it in relation to the ideal of democratic politics.

R.B.

ACKNOWLEDGEMENTS

The editors wish to thank Mrs Susan Rayner of the Acton Society Trust's staff for organizing the conference at which the contributions to this book were discussed, and for undertaking a good deal of sub-editing with care and skill. They also acknowledge the assistance of Mrs Angela Thomas who helped with the sub-editing at an earlier stage, and Miss Jackie Eames, who typed the manuscript for publication.

PART ONE

Theoretical and Historical Perspectives

I Patterns of Protest in English History

V. G. KIERNAN

'Direct action' is a phrase that has come rapidly into circulation in recent years. What it connotes is hard to define, since the boundaries that it crosses depend on what happens to be law, and on more quickly fluctuating opinion and convention. It may manifest itself in any shape from boycott to bomb; it may rely on moral coercion, like one of Gandhi's fasts or a suicide in Japan on an opponent's doorstep, or on physical force, which may be employed against buildings or other property, or against life or limb. Its extremist and most socially acceptable form is war. It may be concerned with political objectives, or with others, but here again the dividing-line is a fluid one, and political behaviour is influenced by habits belonging to other departments of life. For example, the English upper class clung less tenaciously than any on the Continent to the privilege of the duel, that vestigial right of blue blood to ignore the law; and it was also less prone than most to poke its sword into affairs of State.

There has always been direct action of one sort or another in practice, but as a principle, a deliberate procedure, it could only emerge in a society long familiar with other, more 'constitutional' methods, and as an expression of dissatisfaction with them. In Tsarist Russia, or in Asia at large, malcontents took to plotting, assassination and insurrection as naturally as M. Jourdain talked prose, because they knew of no other way to express their feelings. It was in the English-speaking world that direct action as a concept originated and found a name, like so many political things before it that have passed into currency everywhere. It was talked of in the USA before 1914, and in Britain before the end of 1918, and again in 1926 during the General Strike. A decade later it was afloat in India, in the wake of the Congress civil disobedience movements, and it was there that it had a first dramatic baptism of fire and blood in the Direct Action Day proclaimed by the Muslim League on 16 August 1946. Lately, other languages in and out of Europe have been either borrowing the English phrase, or making literal translations of it.[1]

In Britain or America it would have been more exact to call it *directer* action, for in reality their political life always directly involved

25

large numbers in the management of national or local affairs, gradually transforming their people into that peculiarly English entity, the *public*. 'Of all societies since the Roman Republic', Morley could assert, '. . . England has been the most emphatically and essentially political', by virtue of its mode of 'government by deliberative bodies, representing opposed principles and conflicting interests'.[2] In medieval times, a ruling class formed by the Conquest, in a country just small enough to be managed by consensus of those strong enough to have a voice, acquired an exceptionally clear sense of itself as a collective body or estate. Violence was, as elsewhere, undeniably endemic – forcible self-help in the shape of private conflicts between barons, risings of baronage against Crown, struggles of towns against overlords, of peasantry against landowners; while interdicts to enforce rights of Church against State might be called an early version of non-violent non-cooperation. But all such contests had, in a higher degree than in most other regions, more or less of an institutional character, or took place within a framework of law or custom. Complexities of feudal property and obligation were too great for the most turbulent baron to rely on the right of the sword pure and simple, as a robber-knight beyond the Rhine might do. The *Magna Carta* came about in 1215 because King John's arbitrary demands for contributions upset 'the carefully balanced medieval society with its strong corporate sense and strict counterpoise of privilege and responsibilities',[3] and because, as in many later reform struggles, a 'moderate' or 'constitutional' leadership was able to profit by the pressure of more extreme factions on the government. In sum, the result was a surprisingly wide-ranging survey and definition of the rights of all entitled to claim them. Even peasants could find in manorial custom something like the warrant that the barons at Runnymede claimed in feudal prescription. In the peasant revolt of 1381, a rational, purposeful character can be seen, instead of a mere *jacquerie*, and despite its defeat it may have helped to avert a return to serfdom.[4] In 1450, the rebels, who were led by Jack Cade and came mainly from Kent, were 'a body of peasants with a very strong leaven of gentry, shopkeepers and craftsmen': also with a distinct political attitude, a reasoned case finding much support in London, on the eve of the Wars of the Roses, against weak and bad government.[5] It is another feature of all these pre-Capitalist movements that diverse classes or sections of them were able to make common cause.

A century later, *A Mirror for Magistrates*, that compendium of Tudor statecraft, despite its bias towards authority could not withhold a grudging tribute to Cade.[6] Sixteenth-century thinking had the same pragmatic quality as Chinese, and like it recognized that in the last resort a bad government lost the mandate of Heaven and deserved to be overthrown; conversely, anyone who tried to overthrow the government and failed deserved to lose his head. Absolute monarchy as represented by the Tudors was relatively easy-going, because it rested less on armed strength than on support (as in other countries) of urban opinion, and on the special support of the chief propertied groups, more effectively organized or self-organizing than elsewhere. With the coming of the Reformation and its great social and economic changes, there was bound to be a moving apart, a friction between the interests that were pushing these on and benefiting by them, and a mass of opinion resentful of change or fearful of losing by it. Resistance inflamed by Catholic conservatism might drift in several directions. It broke out most formidably in the Pilgrimage of Grace in Yorkshire and Lincolnshire in 1536. This must have contained ingredients of feudal insubordination, antipathy to the new centralizing régime. But it can also be considered, it has been argued with reference to Lincolnshire, as an attempt by those who guided the elemental mass not to overturn the government but only to alter some of its policies. At a time when Parliament could not yet be 'the effective conflict-resolving mechanism of the society', riots and manifestos, or seizure of a county town, might be the means by which a region, with a strong regional life of its own, expressed its disgust at maladministration. They were kept nevertheless within 'a framework of form and convention which aimed at limiting the disruptive effects of the movement, and the amount of damage which might result, particularly to the landed governing class.'[7] No wonder a plain man like Bishop Latimer might express, in his sermon against the rebels, some bewilderment as to what was really happening: 'They rise with the king, and fight against the king in his ministers and officers; they rise with the Church, and fight against the Church; . . . they rise for the Commonwealth, and fight against it . . . . Lo, what false pretence can the devil send against us.'[8] He may really have been watching a primitive rehearsal of His Majesty's Opposition.

Something similar may be said of the peasant movement in Norfolk in 1549, led by Ket, which like Cade's in Kent a hundred years before had a sober and public-spirited complexion. A 'keen sense of order . . . permeated the whole undertaking' the occupation of Mousehold was 'a sort of vast sit-down strike'.[9] Though peasants might riot against sporadic enclosures, and had chronic minor grievances, there was no such issue to bind them together and alienate them from the State as the maintenance or reintroduction of serfdom that provoked the great agrarian revolts abroad. Ket was appealing to the government against bad local magistrates and landowners; he organized a substitute county administration – not altogether unlike the councils of action of 1926 – and demonstration only turned into rebellion when the authorities set out to crush it by force.

Outbreaks more fundamentally hostile to the new England that was taking shape were confined now to peripheral areas. There was a Western Rising in 1549 against the new Prayer Book, of rustics led by priests, in Cornwall, still part of the Celtic-speaking fringe of Britain, and Devon. In 1569 the feudal and Catholic Northern Rebellion took place, drawing its strength from the hills and moors of the north country. Subsequently, resistance of this type dwindled to the level of conspiracy, managed by Jesuits and other professional agents, with Guy Fawkes's plot to mark its dead end. Such plottings encountered an increasingly superior technique of counter-espionage, and were fatally compromised by their foreign connections and reliance on foreign backing, as other movements in Britain in later times have been. They were compromised also, perhaps, by a feeling already astir that the strategy of secret plans, disguises, deceptions, was somehow un-English, or alien to a land where some freedom of open debate, however restricted, always had a place; that it was only fit for 'priests, and cowards, and men cautelous', as Brutus says in a great speech that may be felt to embody a national distaste.[10] Possibly sensitive to this, when Essex made his rash attempt in London near the end of Elizabeth's life, appealing to the newer religious minority of Puritans, he went about it in an ostentatiously open, amateurish fashion.

England reached the seventeenth century with a well-formed conviction, proclaimed by Lord Chief Justice Coke long before W. S. Gilbert's Lord Chancellor, that

> The Law is the high embodiment
> Of everything that's excellent.

Respect for law was equally respect for property, whose guardianship was its chief duty, and collaboration among the propertied classes had developed sufficiently to enable Parliament to survive when most similar bodies, like the States-General or Cortes, were fading out. Yet in Coke's day, complex shifts in class interests and relations were preparing a long civil war. Any such social ferment may dissipate itself in mere froth or anarchy, if there is no strong containing channel, as the Wars of the Fronde in contemporary France largely did. Voltaire was to contrast the frivolity of these with English orderliness: like many Frenchmen, he saw history and politics very much in terms of Anglo-Gallic antitheses. 'The English displayed in their civil disturbances as it were a sullen fury and a reasoned frenzy.'[11] Who was on which side might depend a great deal on the still very active and still largely personal politics of each county, but there was enough sense of national destiny to resolve all these into a meaningful confrontation. Religion played an indispensable part in this, and in helping to nerve men for the venture into the unknown that armed rebellion in a land of settled government implies. The paradoxical outcome was that this land of law and lawyers carried out far the most successful revolution of all the many that were essayed in seventeenth-century Europe, as in 1215 it had carried out the most orderly feudal resistance of any in medieval Europe. England was undergoing not a collapse of authority but a collision between two rival authorities. Even the left-wing movement that emerged in defiance of both had a discipline and a rational programme of its own; whereas the only plebeian intervention in the Thirty Years War in progress in Germany was an occasional wild tumult.

Once the left movement failed, or could only take such action as the rising of the Fifth Monarchy men against Cromwell in 1657 (the religious forlorn hope of the revolution still pressing forward when all the rest was receding), Commonwealth politics sank into sterility. Among the Royalists especially there was again a labyrinthine weaving of futile plots, an efflorescence of secret cyphers; again, perhaps, uncongenial to the English temperament, if only on account of its impracticality, if less so to the clerical temperament: one of the most laborious spinners and weavers was a Dr John Barwick, DD.[12] Nothing better came of it than the miserably bungled rising headed by Penruddock in 1655. In 1660, under cover of the Restoration, the divided ruling class moved quietly together again, broadened by coalition with other leading forms of wealth, and with a composite character, and therefore an adaptability and durability which a thoroughbred class is always liable to lack. Again the Fifth Monarchy men, buoyed by millenarian fantasy, rose in vain. More weighty attempts to upset the new balance could come only a quarter-century later, and then only in far-off regions and under the leadership of outsiders, Monmouth in the south-west and Argyle in Scotland, and their risings in 1685 were soon quelled. When James II sought to upset the balance from the opposite quarter, he was able to make a fight only still further away from Westminster, on the banks of the Boyne. From the wild Highlands, his son and grandson could levy war against the Crown as late as 1715 and 1745; but their dependence on this outlandish 'colonial' base only promoted English solidarity, much as Castilian loyalty was always cemented by the perpetual disloyalty of Basques and Catalans.

The Glorious Revolution of 1688 was glorious, for respectable opinion and Whig tradition, because the common people had nothing to do with it, except cheer. It was made for them, as the Reformation had been, by their superiors, men entitled by rank and wealth to take action on the country's behalf. Monmouth's ambitions had led him, very reprehensibly, to recruit peasants and miners. After their taste of Ironsides and Levellers, men of property had no intention of ever again allowing the people to partake in politics. On the other hand, their rival factions, Whig and Tory (the latter in particular as being normally the weaker), were prepared at times to conjure up for their own purposes that caricature of the people, the mob. A crowd running amuck might be destructive, but it presented no real threat of subversion. It could be used by one party against the other, and later on, when a genuine left began to reappear, against this; hence the long history of the 'Tory mob', whose ancestry can be traced back to feudal demagogy, while its descendants come down to the age of Fascism.

To the peaceable citizen, a mob was a recurrent bugbear, and the Riot Act was passed in 1716 to keep it under watch and ward. It was, moreover, 'a creature of very mysterious existence', as Dickens called it in his novel about the Gordon riots in London in 1780, published in 1841 amid forebodings of Chartist outbreaks.[13] In fact, a true 'mob' is seldom, if ever, merely criminal, but is rather a multitude of individuals making a convulsive effort to merge themselves into something bigger, to find a momentary unity and purpose in a society meaningless to them, to achieve a fugitive sense of power and of participation in events.[14] Hence it requires some ideal, or creed, however cloudy, and eighteenth-century Britain found it most readily in some sectarian delusion, residue of the religious fervour of the revolutionary age. This happened in the Sacheverell riots in London in 1710 under High Church watchwords, and in the Gordon riots, anti-Catholic and probably with an anti-Irish but also an anti-aristocratic colouring. Pathetically, the disinherited were seeking to identify themselves with their stepmotherly England, to protect her against imaginary foes; and the populace of a capital city, whether London or Stamboul, always feels a special responsibility for the national welfare. But in 1780 there seems also to have been a hint of a permissive attitude on the part of men in high places, who counted on the disturbances to clear the way for designs of their own.[15] An analogous situation brought about the Porteous riots of 1736 in Edinburgh, flavoured by national resentment against the Union of 1707 with England, lingering on among plebeians long after their betters had succumbed to English gold; and those in Edinburgh and Glasgow in 1779, forerunners of the Gordon riots, when anti-Popery feeling compelled the exclusion of Scotland from a Roman Catholic Relief Bill.

Town mobs must have been swelled by recent incomers, disgruntled or demoralized, from the countryside. The coalition of 1660, inaugurating the age of agrarian capitalism and nascent industrialism, was made at the expense of the English peasantry; the mass of this, isolated by want of any urban ally as it had not been in the past, was being gradually reduced to the status of landless labourers. It may be remarkable that the peasants submitted so tamely to their fate; but it came on them slowly, and they were already divided, the luckier ones rising to be farmers or English kulaks. There was, moreover, to nip any resistance

may be a fundamental difficulty for Socialism that, since it is avowedly a new thing, men cannot walk into it backwards, eyes fixed on familiar landmarks of the past, as they walked into many earlier revolutionary changes. Moreover, the 'croppers' or shearmen who were prominent followers of 'General Ludd' were among 'the aristocracy of the woollen workers',[26] and a better-off class may be likelier to resort to force to avoid deprivation of social status, as well as income, than a worse-off class trying to raise itself from the bottom.

After the wars, the middle-class movement for Parliamentary reform was free to revive, and soon began to draw in working-class discontent behind it. Here could be found an alternative ground for a fight in defence of ancient right, or, Parliament being obviously old and warped, its renewal. Parliament's survival through the ages lent it a venerable aura, freshened by its survival through the wars: an England led by it had, after all, defied the conqueror of Europe, now its captive. Leaders of the reform agitation could both welcome the support of the working class, old and new, and feel that they were doing good service by leading it into the constitutional path. They were gaining strength fast enough to be unafraid of mobilizing the masses, in the spirit of Cobbett's maxim that history is not made by cloistered debate but by the hurly-burly of the streets. It was the authorities that decided to go one better, at Peterloo in 1819, in the spirit of Napoleon's maxim about a whiff of grapeshot keeping the streets clear. The decision emerged from very complex processes of thought and feeling, involving all kinds of men in office, high and low, central and local;[27] but, in sum, it was the ruling class collectively that was resorting to direct action, and this action was one of a long series of similar acts of authority in modern Britain and its Empire. They have been exploratory moves, experiments to test whether an opposition can be crippled by one hard blow. If the blow miscarries, as it did at Peterloo, British ruling-class instinct is not to go on launching heavier ones, but to step back, to find new ground, to try something else; to refrain from pushing things to extremes, for fear of coming off the loser, or with only a Pyrrhic victory. Napoleon might have called it the instinct of a nation of shopkeepers, accustomed to settle everything by haggling; the shopkeepers might have reminded him that his own instincts had landed him at St Helena.

On its own dunghill, the countryside, the ruling class was far less ready for compromise, as appeared when the long-suffering farm labourers at last caught the infection of revolt and embarked on their own desperate course of machine-breaking and rick-burning, the 'Captain Swing' rising of 1830. Farm drudges *must* be kept half-starved and docile if the gentry were to live in luxury, and the mutineers were hunted down ruthlessly; 1,976 arrested, 19 executed, 481 transported.[28]

Still, this unexpected turning of the worm was unnerving, and the landed oligarchy was far less able to cope with the big towns which erupted into rioting in 1831 as the agitation for the Reform Bill intensified – Bristol, for instance, in October, under the eye of the old poet Crabbe, who as a young man had watched the Gordon riots.[29] At such times of excitement, it would seem that some subtle change of temperature, some hint of a relaxed attitude to order in respectable quarters, is enough to give a lower class the signal that the hour has struck. A lawless populace then constitutes the battering-ram that opens the breach for those above it. It is by such a combination of pressures that all 'peaceful' reforms, like that of 1832, came about. Under it, the landowners, themselves already a capitalist class, of the bastard agrarian type, were ready to take the industrial bourgeoisie into partnership and, as Macaulay had appealed to them in the House to do, 'save property, divided against itself'.[30]

Property was saved at the expense of the propertyless, as in 1660 at the expense of the peasantry. Between 1832 and 1848 the working class, cheated of any part of the reward, went on struggling by itself for the vote and – more threateningly – for a Parliament drastically remodelled and made responsive to the popular will. Chartism occupied a halfway period in political evolution, and was more preoccupied with the choice between physical force and peaceful suasion than any other British movement before or since. Indignation at middle-class betrayal, and the obvious effectiveness of recent rioting, gave an initial impetus to thoughts of action. Drilling and arming had started before the Reform Act, with tacit middle-class approval, and went on sporadically afterwards without it. Members of the National Union of the Working Classes brought out a cheap edition of Colonel Macerone's *Instructions* for street warfare: 'The pamphlet was common enough in middle-class hands.'[31] There was a climax in 1839, when a lively expectation of rebellion spread, and Harney, an admirer of Marat and Robespierre, was proposing that the country should elect a new Parliament without waiting to be given votes, and that a million armed men should march on London to instal it. It does not appear that the physical-force men had made any large-scale preparations for any such move. One of them, John Taylor, had five old brass cannons buried somewhere, ready for a resurrection-day. 'Poor men! How little they know of physical force!', wrote General Napier, commanding in the north, himself humanely anxious not to have to resort to it.[32] The brass cannons remained silent, and despite much inflamed talk at mass meetings nothing graver happened than the Bull Ring riots at Birmingham.

After this, revolution was a diminishing prospect, though both friend and foe were slow to recognize the fact. Fiery talk went on.

Often, no doubt, it was only rhetoric, serving to mark individuals out as men of spirit and determination, or to break down apathy and bring in recruits; or it might be a mere blowing-off of steam, or alcoholic vapours. But ordinary Chartists had no commitment to non-violence as a principle, and many who rejected revolution as a national pro-gramme were quite ready to engage in impromptu local affrays or scuffles.[33] Ernest Jones's thinking probably expressed the view of most of those given to thinking; for example, in his poem 'The Factory Town' (one of the best that the movement produced):

> Fear ye not your masters' power,
>   Men are strong when men unite;
> Fear ye not one stormy hour:
>   *Banded millions need not fight.*[34]

His general teaching was that Chartists should not be the first to strike a blow, but they were entitled to strike in self-defence.[35] How they could do this, if attacked as at Peterloo, without making organized preparations beforehand which would be taken to brand them as aggressors, was not clear – as in similar contexts it never has been.

While Chartism rumbled, respectable citizens with uneasy recollec-tions of disorders they had lately winked at were frequently perturbed, though their picture of the mob remained confused and contradictory. In Kingsley's *Alton Locke*, the hero watches a tumult of starving farm labourers with sympathy, but soon notices plundering and discovers 'how large a portion of rascality shelters itself under the wing of every crowd'; he sees, too, how hastily it runs away at the first approach of the yeomanry.[36] Belief in the mingled folly, ferocity and cowardice of all crowds was rubbed deeper into the middle-class mind by every fresh commentator on Shakespeare, as it continues to be to this day. All the same, English political habits provided a safety-valve for unruly passions, in the mimic warfare of election days; passions not seldom shared by the candidates, who might be hereditary rivals for first place in the county and were not squeamish about how they got the better of each other. Crabbe had another brush with Demos soon after becoming Rector of Trowbridge in 1814. 'A riotous, tumultuous, and most appalling mob' besieged his house, to prevent his going to the poll – though in fact it let him pass unmolested.[37] Rowdy election humours furnished novelists with a stock theme. In Eliot's *Felix Holt*, we hear a landowner's agent bribing miners to indulge in some rough play: 'No pommelling – no striking first. There you have the law and the constable against you. A little rolling in the dust and knocking hats off, a little pelting with soft things . . . .'[38] On the great day, party strife degenerates, according to rule, into a farcical drunken turmoil.[39] For the voteless plebeian, such an occasion had the charm of a saturnalia, when he was temporarily licensed to work off his feelings against the quality with insults, or something better. If the contest depicted in Tressell's *The Ragged-Trousered Philanthropists* was at all typical, brawling was still use and wont among enfranchised workers at the end of the century, and kept them harmlessly giving each other, instead of their bosses, black eyes or bloody noses.

Patterns of protest are always partly drawn by the weapons used against them. England's governing class drew some discretion from its lack of armed resources. It had no conscript army, and its professional army, besides being limited and largely required overseas, was recruited from the humblest classes, and might be tempted to fraternize with them.[40] To a great extent, property had to look to its own defence. West Riding manufacturers fortified their mills with an armed garrison, a cannon, a barrel of vitriol.[41] Landowners were well accustomed to self-help. In the winter of 1819 when Northumberland miners and west-of-Scotland weavers were showing 'a spirit of alarming insubordination', Scott and his fellow-lairds on the Borders set on foot 'a legion or brigade upon a large scale, to be called the Buccleuch Legion'.[42] In 1830, Wellington exhorted gentry and magistrates to collect and arm their grooms, huntsmen and footmen, and ride forth against the miscreants. In Norfolk, Lord Suffield 'enrolled his own private army of a hundred men', [43] very much like a feudal landlord in Bengal.

Private enterprise like this, seldom met with in more bureaucratic countries, was growing archaic as industrialism advanced, and had the demerit of turning things too nakedly into a class war, a battle of haves against have-nots. Use of the Yeomanry was only a degree less provocative, as at Peterloo where the Manchester and Salford corps seems to have taken the field bent on teaching the workers a lesson.[44] The new England of the manufacturers, personified by Peel, was working out a new system, a regular modern police. Dublin was the first area to be experimented on, in 1808; London followed in 1829, and the rest of Britain after it, while on the rest of Ireland in 1829 was bestowed the Royal Irish Constabulary. This was a para-military force, akin to the *gendarmerie* in France or the *Guardia Civil* in Spain, and similarly hated. Otherwise the new police were not given fire arms, and this made a vital difference. They were not designed to court popularity, but rather to harass and intimidate, and were in fact for a long time detested. Chartist threats were sometimes a reprisal against their strong-arm methods.[45] Mayhew's costermongers, all keen Chartists, 'could not understand why Chartist leaders exhorted them to peace and quietness', and they hated their new shepherds. 'I am assured that in case of a political riot every "coster" would seize his policeman.'[46] Still, their having only truncheons kept retaliation within bounds, while in the long run their duties, like those of the State, would gradually expand to include all sorts of neutral or even benevolent functions. They enabled government to withdraw from property its rights of private warfare, and to interpose what could pass for an impartial shield between the jarring classes. It became easier besides to tolerate public meetings, as a country like contemporary Spain could not. 'The people have a right to meet', Lord John Russell declared in a speech at Liverpool in 1838; and it formed one of the great British discoveries that the more freedom the public was given to air its views, the more moderate and 'responsible' these became.

'While the English Chartists were debating the right to use physical force, those of Wales took to arms.'[47] Wales shared the preference of the Celtic borderlands, as of most unsophisticated peoples, for direct methods.[48] Chartism was brought to Newport in 1838 by Henry Vincent, an adherent of the force school, and after the rejection of the national petition in 1839 plans for a rising were promptly put in hand. Its miserable failure and its death-roll must have had a disheartening effect on all later thoughts of insurrection. But it was closely followed by a more authentically Welsh trial of direct action, the Rebecca Riots of 1843–4 in Carmarthenshire. These were concerned with tangible grievances that meant more to hill farmers than votes or debates at Westminster, with the new turnpike toll bars as the last straw. Toll bars were pulled down at night by bands of mounted men disguised as women, whose leader was always called 'Rebecca', as the commander of any Luddite operation had been called 'General Ludd': an illustration of the fondness of the folk-mind for eponymous heroes – 'Captain Swing' was another – which suggests a possible family tree for Robin Hood. The element of mummery afforded a rough disguise; it was also a psychological aid to illicit activity, in the same way as Ku-Klux-Klan cowls or hippy costumes, and it could make a special appeal to a hill people stuffed with old-time poetry. (Many Luddites came likewise from small upland villages.) Religion, if the name 'Rebecca' was taken as usually supposed from the Old Testament, was once again nerving men to defy man-made law. Toll bar keepers, unlike their toll bars, were seldom injured. Authority showed less restraint, and suppressed 'Rebecca' with some bloodshed; but her aims were largely achieved all the same (by contrast with those of Newport), as such limited aims often have been.

Little Welsh national feeling seems to have been in evidence.[49] It was very different with the agitations in Ireland. These went through two phases, the campaign for Catholic emancipation won in 1829, roughly analogous with the one that ended in Britain in 1832, and then the broader movement for Repeal of the union with England, which may be compared with – and drew support from, and failed along with – the Chartist movement. In point of tactics, to Irish peasants as to

Welsh (or to London costers) it seemed plain sense to utilize whatever methods came to hand for making things hot for the enemy. Tom Moore heard at Mallow during his 1823 tour of 'a strong feeling among the lower orders, that if they persevere in their present harassing and violent system, the Church must give in.'[50] But in the political leadership O'Connell stood firmly, despite the challenge of Young Ireland, for legalism, and under British prompting the Pope forbade any clerical encouragement of sedition.[51] In 1845–6 famine followed by mass emigration came to prostrate the country, luckily for the government before the tocsins of 1848 were set ringing round Europe.

1848 came and went, and the British Constitution floated securely, a watertight ark, on the flood-waters engulfing Europe. Dramatic events abroad were bound to react on British politics, for the whole Continent was in some ways a single political whole. The defeat and bloodthirsty suppression of the Paris workers in June 1848 must have had a chilling effect on any Chartists spoiling for a fight. In the longer term, conflict abroad might foster partial reform in Britain. Just as 1830 in Paris must have helped to bring about 1832 in London, 1848 in Paris added point to Carlyle's jeremiads, kept up ever since his *French Revolution* in 1837 – his sermons to the ruling class about the need to read the signs of the times. Kingsley pointed the moral in his 1850 pamphlet about London's sweated tailoring workers, when he ended by predicting that increasing misery must sooner or later produce an explosion: 'the boiler will be stretched to bursting pitch, till some jar, some slight crisis, suddenly directs the imprisoned forces to one point, and then –

What then?
Look at France, and see'.[52]

Collective thinking is always a matter of images or symbols more than of logic, and industrialism, familiarity with mechanical processes, and imagery inspired by them, could help to give Englishmen a livelier sense of social realities than philosophers in agrarian Germany ruminating on 'organic' theories of the State.

As a rule, however, when John Bull cast his eye across the Channel he compared himself with his neighbours, greatly to his own advantage. National characters develop by interaction and repulsion. Planted between skipping Frenchmen and lurching Irishmen, he had long been coming to pride himself on his own solid, sturdy, common sense and ballast. Laureates and leader-writers dwelt on the frivolity of the Gallic weathercock, 'the red fool-fury of the Seine',[53] as a warning against such fretful impatience at home. Whatever its brutalities, capitalism fitted in with and strengthened a rational quality already English, of which the word 'businesslike' was highly typical, and businesslike habits of handling affairs, from the House with its Speaker down to the shareholders' or club-members' meeting with its chairman, made bawling and brawling look childish. In Prussia a powerful bureaucracy was moulding a rationality of its own, but of another species. In England the notion of 'the King's Peace' had always had a flavour of voluntary acceptance, distinct from the Continental ideal of Order imposed from above; or if Englishmen thought of order, it came naturally to them to talk of 'law and order' together.

This included, increasingly, the factor of progress. In Russia Zhelyabov the terrorist was complaining that history was frightfully slow, and must be given a shove forward; in Britain it seemed to be moving quickly enough. Even the sensation of travel by railway, faster than human beings had ever gone before, gave a sort of physical corroboration to the sense of progress. This could not be kept confined to miles per hour or tons per year, but must have its place in the political sphere as well: the masses should be admitted by safe degrees into the sacred Parliamentary enclosure, at least into its outskirts. A liberal like Brougham drew from 1848 the lesson that universal suffrage would be fatal among erratic foreigners, but would be far less risky in England; indeed it would be a good thing to give votes straightaway to 'the best and by far the most independent of the lower orders, the Artisans.'[54]

In the meantime, comfort could be found in the fact that bad as many things might be in Britain, abroad they were manifestly worse. Strong nations tyrannized over weak, and respectable England was always ready to sympathize with national (not class) revolt, in Italy or Poland or Hungary, though not in Ireland or India. Patriotic risings there supplied some of the glamour that British politics lacked, and a vicarious sense of participation in heroic events (which the middle classes could also enjoy by reading Carlyle's *Cromwell*, published in 1845). A few individuals did participate, like Byron going to Greece; the host of volunteers of 1914 supposed themselves to be going to Belgium on the same errand. On the whole, feeling was content to express itself in enthusiastic welcomes to famous exiles – an Espartero, a Kossuth, a Garibaldi. Literate workers, who in Chartist days read Byron and Shelley, were drawn into these demonstrations, common ground for them and those above them. Occasionally indignation could find a legitimate vent on foreigners of the stamp of Marshal Hainau, roughly handled by the draymen of Barclay's brewery in September 1850 after his pacification of Hungary. Later on when international Socialism dawned, this sentiment would take on another aspect, less palatable to official opinion.

By and large, England remained an unmilitary country, and this helped to foster peaceful political habits. Its one European war between

1815 and 1914, the Crimean, was fought in the aftermath of the Chartist peril, and helped to divert restless feelings outward; so did the Indian Mutiny in 1857, and the outburst of Gallophobia that led to the Volunteer movement of the years from 1859. Colonial troubles like the Mutiny taught Britain's rulers some lessons, and indirectly promoted better treatment of common people at home. If Coercion Acts were obviously proper for Irishmen, they must by the same token be improper for Englishmen. And they were the less needed because Englishmen, contemplating their Empire through the school-spectacles given them, could see there a grand vindication of the law-abiding virtues. The *Pax Britannica* was the extension of the Queen's Peace to dark continents that knew nothing but despotism or anarchy; the high seas were being added to the Queen's high road, as cherished phrases about 'Britannia policing the seas' emphasized. In the regions growing into Dominions, democracy was coming effortlessly, and this helped to ensure its coming to Britain; though not the transforming democracy that Chartism had dreamed of.

Victorian Britain's self-complacent picture of a sober nation satisfied with a regulated growth of its liberties contained of course a good deal of wishful thinking. Behind it persisted much uncertainty and many forebodings; they found one expression in the spreading mood of religious doubt. In a nation so deeply divided, it was hard to make out how far the masses were coming to accept the picture. But the philosophy of Parliamentarism, the settlement of sectional quarrels by compromise, could not be without an influence on them; ideas and modes of behaviour, like fashions of dress, seep down by a thousand crannies from one social level to another. For those still discontented, steam transport made it easier to choose another way out, a negative form of direct action, emigration. This was an important relief for all European countries: it came easiest to Britain, with its large colonies of settlement and its community of language with America, least easily to insular France. All this helped to bring it about that the barricade, a central fact of political life on the Continent, was almost unknown in Britain. It is noteworthy also that Britain had to borrow another, much newer French word, *sabotage*,[55] even if wooden clogs were as common in Lancashire mills as *sabots* in French. Luddism had become a mere memory, though it had a belated recrudescence in the 'Sheffield outrages' of 1866, when William Broadhead of the Sawgrinders' Union hired men to blow up a factory with new machinery and to make murderous attacks on interlopers; it is tempting to see in them a side-effect of the Volunteer mania and sabre-rattling of the 1860s. Of political terrorism, the thought scarcely spread beyond the trickle of foreign refugees who brought it.

Strict adherence to legality as a principle took hold more quickly at the top of the popular movement than at the bottom, where the plain man's faith in his fists lingered. Muscular energy of an elemental sort might overflow at times into assaults on Irish immigrants, precursors of the – happily few – race riots of the next century. But fists themselves were coming under rule and regulation, which made hitting below the belt one of the deadlier sins. It was indeed in the fantasy-realm of sport that the ideal Victorian pattern of society came nearest to fulfilment. Nothing could be more characteristic of England than the growing cult of sport, the mimic warfare of the playing field, presided over by codes of conduct like the 'laws' of cricket, and by impartial umpires, flesh-and-blood symbols of the impartial State. Most English of all was the Gentlemen *v* Players match, first played at Lords in 1806 and annually from 1819. The Football Association was founded in 1863. Sport brought with it the notion of 'fair play', spreading far beyond its own arena and bringing the expectation – made up as in all such cases of some truth and more illusion – that sooner or later everyone would get his due.

How the Gentlemen were likely to play the game when alarmed for their moneybags was illustrated by the events of 'Bloody Sunday', or 13 November 1887, when the police, with soldiers in support, were turned loose on a mass meeting of unemployed and pro-Ireland demonstrators in Trafalgar Square.[56] A vigorous labour movement was on the march again, tinged now with Socialism. This operation was the Peterloo probe again, with truncheon instead of sabre. Its effectiveness must remain uncertain, as unemployment and discontent receded for some years, and the new imperialism helped to muffle them. English Socialism was too confined to a few intellectuals to revive seriously, in the climate of the later nineteenth-century, the Chartist debate about force and its place in political philosophy. William Morris, a very realistic idealist, did face the problem, and expected force to be necessary to give capitalism the final blow;[57] but that lay too far in the future for any close scrutiny.

For James Connolly, as an Irish Socialist, the problem was not one that could be evaded. In Ireland, the agrarian struggle continued the old instinctive use of attacks on property, including now cattle-maiming. It also threw up, in 1880, that Irish contribution to world politics, the boycott, a form of non-violent coercion that as practised in its native land, against the obnoxious individual, may be supposed to have borrowed from the Catholic practice of excommunication (though it had an English analogy in 'sending to Coventry'). The official Irish political movement was playing the Parliamentary game, but with an Irish difference, inventing the tactics of obstruction in order to strangle Westminster with its own red tape. But the extremist wing, Sinn Fein, made force so much the touchstone of patriotism that (as Connolly protested in an article in 1899) Ireland was unique in having a 'physical force party' agreed on nothing except the rightfulness of violence, erecting into a principle what revolutionaries everywhere else looked on merely as a weapon. Socialists neither extolled nor repudiated force in itself, he declared, but would stick to peaceful methods so long as the other side did so.[58] Like Ernest Jones before him, Connolly was not altogether meeting the practical dilemma. That a ruling class will at some stage abandon lawful procedures is certain; at that stage it will already be prepared for action, while its antagonists will not be, unless they have got ready in advance.

Paradoxically, the nearest to a mass political rising in Ireland was the Ulster rebellion of 1914, not against Britain but against separation from Britain. The alacrity with which British Toryism supported it was a revelation of how at bottom a ruling class always thinks of law and order as meant for its subjects, not for itself. The affair took place against the unsettling background of a warlike Europe long committed to the colonial rivalries and arms race about to explode in the Great War. In that period a mystique of force was not confined to Sinn Feiners. A year after Connolly wrote his article, a group of English Liberals deplored the spectacle 'of force and aggression becoming not only too often employed as means towards good or tolerable ends, but actually worshipped and glorified as ends in themselves.'[59] Strident imperialist propaganda was accompanied during the Boer War years (1899–1902) by a reappearance of Tory mobs, breaking up anti-war meetings. They included a good many students, whose patriotic zeal was loudly applauded by the Press. Pro-Boer speakers sometimes came close to the fate of the anti-war MP lynched at the close of Galsworthy's play *The Mob*.[60] From this time on there was also the rivalry with Germany, setting Volunteers polishing their buttons with fresh enthusiasm.

In those years, with labour militancy reviving once more, there were further experiments at nipping it in the bud by short, sharp treatment. Liberals were in office after 1906, and, as often happens with Liberals everywhere, were anxious to prove that they could keep order; especially the fire-eating young Winston Churchill at the Home Office, who brought artillery into Sidney Street to deal with a few anarchists, and during a railway strike 'despatched the military hither and thither as though Armageddon was upon us'.[61] Now and then, down to 1911 at Liverpool and in Wales at Llanelli, strikers were fired on. This approach was then dropped, as likely to do more harm than good, but many lesser degrees of brutality were complained of. Doubtless some of the rough handling of strikers and demonstrators was due to bellicose local police chiefs or their men, but it fitted into a definite enough programme. On the workers' side, similar tactics might be made use of on the spur of the moment. An Anglican clergyman who stumped the country as an anti-Socialist open-air speaker found that he usually got a fair hearing. But once in Attercliffe, that Faubourg St Antoine of Sheffield, 'a gang of hooligans tried to run the lorry from which I was speaking down a steep hill . . . . At Leeds an anarchist tried to stab me in the back, and at Norwich, which is the roughest place I know of, I was knocked off the platform.'[62]

Systematic defiance of law and order came not from Labour, whose leadership was increasingly committed to Parliamentarism, but from the 'Women's Social and Political Union', founded by Mrs Pankhurst, a barrister's widow, in 1903. Women – like the peoples of the Celtic fringe – represented a partially distinct race, indifferent to rules and conventions they have had no part in framing; and, being most of the time restricted to a narrow family circle, natural antinomians when outside it. Many working-class women were used to being knocked about by their husbands, and to be knocked about by a policeman came to much the same thing. Male rather than conservative prejudice hardened the government's heart against the Suffragettes, whose own politics were unpredictable: Mrs Pankhurst was later a Tory, one of her daughters an ardent Socialist. It is a pity that since women got votes they have tailed behind man-made organizations, as the enfranchised workers for long tailed behind the Liberal party.

During the Great War, when men of other armies mutinied or deserted or went home, British troops, like the Germans and Turkish, went on to the bitter end with extraordinary stolidity. Still, the vibrations of the four-year cannonade were enough to shake the willing suspension of disbelief in its rulers even of the British people. Unsettlement might have been more far-reaching but for events in Ireland, not only terrible but to most Englishmen incomprehensible, and ending in a bloody civil war. Elsewhere the mood of revolt was strongest on the 'Red Clyde'. Here in 1919, the centenary of Peterloo, it was authority that took the law into its own hands, as so often before. In the 'battle of George Square' at Glasgow, a big meeting of strikers was attacked and broken up by the police.[63] This was on 31 January; on 10 April the move, appropriately intensified, was repeated at Amritsar, when a large concourse of Indian nationalists was fired on and several hundreds killed, on the same principle of getting in the first blow and frightening the public by a severe example. In Britain resentment found an outlet in the 'Hands off Russia' campaign, which cautious Labour leaders were willing to sponsor as a substitute for struggle on issues nearer home.[64] In the summer of 1920 when the founding conference of the Communist party was held, a fresh occasion arose for thinking out the basic question of ends and means, but it was, as before, left hanging in the air, most delegates probably content with the guiding-line offered by one of them: 'that the aim of the Communist party was the minimum not the maximum of violence'.[65]

Again in 1926 the General Strike revealed an astonishing capacity for orderly action and initiative, but anything that might have come of it was lost for want of any national leadership worth the name. Subsequently the spread of fascism abroad, the disappearance of one constitutional régime after another, gave Parliamentarism in Britain a new lease of life, even with the 'National Government' in charge of it. Fascist brutalism, moreover, deterred the left wing from anything that might seem to resemble it, except in a strictly defensive spirit as in the East-End resistance to Mosley's Blackshirts. Even students adhered to strict political discipline; they thought in terms of 'mobilizing the broad masses', and direct action was no part of their vocabulary. Like nineteenth-century radicalism, Communism identified itself with armed action abroad, and found its battlefield in Spain. At home, the most authentically British development of the 1930s was the hunger-march, a form of class confrontation still within the boundaries of moral force. It was not altogether unlike the march of the Manchester 'Blanketeers' in 1817. It had an affinity with Gandhi's new tactics of civil disobedience in India. On the whole, after the storm aroused by the Amritsar massacre, the British government – unlike the French or Dutch – was not trying to shoot its way out of its colonial troubles, and Gandhi's non-violence was designed to encounter an opponent of this elastic, compromise-seeking type. Now, as before, a comparatively battle-free Empire helped to limit strife at home.

Since the Second World War, with its further transforming effects, loss of Empire has helped to make for a more natural attitude, liberation from the old muscle-bound posture of imperial dignity. Political effervescence of less orthodox types has once again been more obvious in the Celtic marches than in the phlegmatic Anglo-Saxony. On Christmas Day in 1951 the Stone of Scone was purloined from Westminster Abbey by four Scottish students, and later some letter-boxes were blown up because of their cypher 'Elizabeth II'. This was too nostalgically romantic to bloom for long; but Welsh nationalists more recently have graduated towards schemes for blowing up bigger things than letter-boxes. Of most significance in the past few years has been the student movement. Direct action – often in the shape of war – has always had more attraction for youth than for age, but it is only in universities that youth comes to form a separate estate, and one readier than a labour movement to acquire a cosmopolitan outlook and responsiveness. The guerrilla tactics that have come naturally to it have resembled in their unconventionality those of the Suffragettes.

There have been symptoms of an infection spreading to older groups as well. Early in 1971 a 'Resistance Movement' to prevent obliteration of villages by a third London airport was heard of, and the Rector of Dunton promised his blessing to anyone taking up arms to defend his home – as we have all been taught from childhood that we ought to do. There is today an impatience with old-fashioned procedures which, even to the extent of their genuineness, are exceedingly rounda-bout, with no such straightforward means of expression as some countries possess in the referendum. Democracy of this kind comes to feel, like the interminable Chancery suit in *Bleak House*, 'a slow, expensive, British, constitutional kind of thing.'[66] In our sprawling amalgam of capitalism and bureaucracy and State Socialism, Parliament begins to seem hardly better as a 'conflict-resolver' than in Tudor days. Faith in old ways of achieving progress, whether on Liberal or on Marxist terms, by slow, patient sapping and mining, gives way to a search for short cuts, a desire for action here and now, aimed at small immediate goals instead of complete transformation of a system grown so vast and complex that to transform it all seems hardly possible. Thus the inevitability of gradualness presents itself in a new guise, no longer tied to rigid observance of a Parliamentary rule-book or time-table. If our ancient régime ever does come to an end, it may be through pressure of opinion stiffened by the cumulative effective of numerous small nibblings and scratchings. Before this happens, recourse by the other side to direct action, official or unofficial, must be expected in the future as in the past.

NOTES

1. Welsh and Irish, whose political terminology is of English forma-tion, seem to have no equivalents of their own. German and Swedish also use the English words. In French, Spanish, Portu-guese, Italian, Russian, Chinese and Japanese they have found a literal translation. More popular in America before 1914 was the Anarchist phrase 'the propaganda of the deed', akin to that of the Spanish Anarchists' *propaganda por los hechos*. I am indebted for this information to colleagues in the History and Language Depart-ments of Edinburgh University.

2. J. Morley, *On Compromise*, Thinker's Library edn (London, 1933), pp. 61–2.

3. J. C. Dickinson, *The Great Charter* (London, 1955), p. 10.

4. R. Hilton, review article in the *New Statesman* (28 August 1970).

5. H. M. Lyle, *The Rebellion of Jack Cade, 1450* (London, 1950), pp. 19, 21.

6. Ibid., p. 22.

7. M. E. James, 'Obedience and Dissent in Henrician England: the Lincolnshire Rebellion 1536', *Past and Present* (1970), no. 48, p. 7.

8. *Sermons by Hugh Latimer*, Everyman edn (London, 1906), p. 26.
9. S. T. Bindoff, *Ket's Rebellion 1549* (London, 1949), pp. 16, 19.
10. *Julius Caesar*, Act 2, Sc. 1.
11. *The Age of Louis XIV*, Everyman edn (London, 1926), chap. 4. Cf. Balzac, *Le Lys dans la vallée* (1835): 'Les Anglais offrent ainsi comme une image de leur île, où la loi régit tout, où tout est uniforme dans chaque sphère, où l'exercice des vertus semble être le jeu nécessaire de rouages qui marchent à heure fixe.' Nelson edn (Paris, 1939), p. 252.
12. See *The Life of the Reverend Dr John Barwick, DD*, by his brother Peter (trans. from Latin, 1724): there is a specimen cypher on pp. 408–9. Cf. M. Ashley, *John Wildman, Plotter and Postmaster* (1947).
13. *Barnaby Rudge*, chap. 52.
14. Something like this struck some foreign observers of riots in Calcutta in 1970.
15. See D. Marshall, *Eighteenth-Century England* (London, 1962), pp. 477–80.
16. E. P. Thompson, *The Making of the English Working Class* (London, 1963), p. 602.
17. Cf. T. J. Johnston, *The History of the Working Classes in Scotland* (Glasgow), p. 195: 'for years afterwards no stranger's life was safe, even gaugers being stripped naked and hunted from the district'.
18. 'Mark Rutherford', *The Revolution in Tanner's Lane* (1893), chap. 1.
19. See C. Hill, 'The Norman Yoke', in J. Saville (ed.), *Democracy and the Labour Movement* (1954).
20. See Thompson, op. cit., pp. 557–8, 578, etc.
21. Johnston, op. cit., p. 305.
22. *Mary Barton* (1848), chap. 15.
23. Thompson, op. cit., p. 486; cf. p. 553: 'Luddism was *a quasi-insurrectionary movement . . . .*'
24. *Sybil, or the Two Nations* (1845), bk. 4, chap. 4.
25. Thompson, op. cit., p. 530.
26. Ibid., p. 522.
27. See two recent studies: J. Marlow, *The Peterloo Massacre* (London, 1969), which is very critical of the authorities' conduct; and R. Walmsley, *Peterloo: the Case Reopened* (Manchester 1969), which is very sympathetic towards it.
28. E. J. Hobsbawm and G. Rudé, *Captain Swing* (London, 1969), p. 262; cf. p. 263: 'From no other protest movement of the kind – from neither Luddites nor Chartists, nor trade unionists – was such a bitter price exacted.'

29. See *The Life of George Crabbe, by his Son* (1834), chaps. 3, 10.
30. 2 March 1831; see G. O. Trevelyan, *Life and Letters of Lord Macaulay* (1876), chap. 4. Macaulay's next sentence was: 'Save the multitude, endangered by its own ungovernable passions.'
31. P. Hollis, *The Pauper Press: A Study in Working-Class Radicalism of the 1830s* (London, 1970), p. 41.
32. M. Beer, *A History of British Socialism* (London, 1929), vol. 2, pp. 73-4.
33. I. Prothero, 'Chartism in London', *Past and Present* (1969), no. 44, p. 81.
34. Y. V. Kovalev (ed.), *Anthology of Chartist Literature* (Moscow, 1956), p. 147. The poem belongs to 1847.
35. See J. Saville, *Ernest Jones, Chartist* (1952), p. 22. Cf. his words after his arrest in 1848: 'In your agitation maintain peace, law and order, respect life and property, but do not – oh! do not be political cowards.' (Kovalev, op. cit., p. 360). He wrote an account of the peasant revolt of 1381, which he saw, too pessimistically, as ending in mere failure and ruin, as a result of the rebels growing reckless and drunken (ibid. pp. 347 ff.); he may have feared that the same fate would befall an armed rising of workers.
36. Charles Kingsley, *Alton Locke* (1850), chap. 28.
37. *The Life of George Crabbe* (1834), chap. 9.
38. George Eliot, *Felix Holt, the Radical* (1866), chap. 11.
39. Ibid., chaps. 31, 33. Cf. Dickens, *The Pickwick Papers* (1837), chap. 13; A. Trollope, *Can You Forgive Her?* (1864–5), chap. 44; *The Revolution in Tanner's Lane*, chap. 25.
40. *The Memoirs of Private Waterfield*, ed. A. Swinson and D. Scott (London, 1968), show that soldiers could be on friendly terms with ordinary folk in Yorkshire – where Waterfield's regiment had been sent to quell riots – in 1843 (see pp. 15–16).
41. Thompson, op. cit., p. 560.
42. J. G. Lockhart, *The Life of Sir Walter Scott* (1838), chap. 46.
43. Hobsbawm and Rudé, op. cit., p. 255.
44. Marlow, op. cit., pp. 97-8.
45. Hollis, op. cit., p. 253. Cf. *Sybil*, bk. 6, chap. 3:
    'If the Capitalists will give up their redcoats,
    I would be a moral force man tomorrow.'
    'And the new police', said Mick. 'A pretty go, when a fellow in a blue coat fetches you the devil's own con on your head, and you get moral force for a plaster.'
46. *Mayhew's London* (selections from H. Mayhew, *London Labour and the London Poor*, 1851, ed. P. Quennell, n.d.), pp. 52–3.
47. A. Jenkin, *The Nations of Britain since the Industrial Revolution*, Our History Series no. 54 (London, 1970), pp. 6–7.

48. Cf. Beer, op. cit., vol. 2, p. 93: 'The simple, emotional, and enthusiastic nature of the Welsh working men . . . expects sensational deeds in any popular agitation.'

49. Sir R. Coupland, *Welsh and Scottish Nationalism: A Study* (1954), pp. 180–3.

50. P. Quennell (ed.), *The Journal of Thomas Moore 1818–41* (1964) p. 85.

51. In February 1848; see C. Woodham-Smith, *The Great Hunger. Ireland 1845–9* (London, 1962), p. 342.

52. *Cheap Clothes and Nasty*, by 'Parson Lot'.

53. Tennyson, *In Memoriam* (1850), cxxvi.

54. *Letter to the Marquess of Lansdowne, KG, on the Late Revolution in France*, 3rd edn (1848), p. 165.

55. *Barricade* dates from 1588 in Paris; *sabotage* from about 1870. See C. T. Onions, *The Oxford Dictionary of English Etymology*.

56. See D. Torr, *Tom Mann and his Times* (1956), chap. 15.

57. See for example *Signs of Change* (1888), p. 116.

58. 'Physical Force in Irish Politics', in J. Connolly, *Socialism and Nationalism* (Dublin, 1948), pp. 53–5.

59. F. W. Hirst, et. al., *Liberalism and the Empire* (1900), p. vi.

60. Produced in March 1914; the play deals with mob hysteria of the Boer War type, though Galsworthy invents an imaginary colonial war as background.

61. A. G. Gardiner, *The Pillars of Society*, 1916 edn, p. 154.

62. A. Goldring, *Some Reminiscences of an Unclerical Cleric* (1926), pp. 144–6. When he spoke in Hyde Park, he says rather self-importantly, 'every bully and swell mobsman in London seemed to have been engaged by the Socialists to break up the meeting'.

63. See W. Gallacher, *Revolt on the Clyde* (1936), chap. 10: 'Police made a savage and totally unexpected assault on the rear of the meeting, smashing right and left with their batons, utterly regardless of whom or what they hit'.

64. This point is discussed by Mrs T. Brotherstone in a study of the period now in progress.

65. Cited in J. Klugmann, *History of the Communist Party of Great Britain*, vol. 1 (London, 1968), p. 39.

66. Dickens, *Bleak House* (1853), chap. 2. In a BBC talk on 28 May 1972, E. J. Hobsbawn argued interestingly the case against terroristic tactics as futile.

II The Threshold of Violence

ROBERT BENEWICK

Direct action has become increasingly confused with political violence. There is a tendency prevalent today, to associate with violence any attempt to bring collective pressure upon the State or upon specific institutions within the State by means outside the formally constituted channels and procedures. The many forms of politically inspired direct action – mass demonstrations, civil disobedience, civil disruption, mob action, guerrilla warfare, sabotage, terrorism, insurrection (which hardly exhausts the list) – are treated as synonymous. At the same time, as if to reinforce this identification, direct action on the part of the State is excluded.[1] Conflict, the essence of politics, is translated as the politics of confrontation, as much by official rhetoric as by activist ideology, thereby conjuring up misleading images frequently associated with violence and force. The student sit-in, for example – no matter how orderly – has come to be viewed in this light. The distinction between political action that becomes violent and that which is organized to promote violence has been blurred.

The consequences for society of equating direct action with political violence are many, and since the State by definition possesses a monopoly of the legal use of force they have implications for democratic politics.[2] The equation ignores the fact that violence is endemic to all societies[3] and paradoxically may encourage officially-sanctioned violence as a counter to violence. Direct action suggests to conservatives control by the police and to liberals control of the police. The police, however, are only one party to conflict and along with other belligerents a manifestation of a symptom rather than a cause. By asserting that direct action is extra-constitutional, which seems descriptively neutral and innocent, the legitimacy of both the objectives and methods of the activists is undermined. Participation in what is conventionally regarded as a traditional political activity is also inhibited. Those in authority, whether a government or perhaps a university, assume arbitrary powers of discretion to decide which groups and which demands are acceptable, and on what and whose terms.

In other words, the equation is symptomatic of an approach to politics which focuses on means so that the nature of the resolution of conflict is effected in such a way that fundamental issues are avoided. Hence, the 1936 Public Order Act was not aimed at Fascism. Although it contributed to the curtailing of Fascist exploitation of the economic and social conditions of East London, it did not ameliorate those conditions. What needs emphasizing at this juncture, however, is that the consideration of direct action is not just a matter of calculating the frustrations of x number of groups or minorities against what may be interpreted as the general good or public will. Legitimate demands and valuable proposals may be obscured by the manner in which they are presented or have to be presented. It is not only a problem of balancing civil liberties with the stability and security of the State. What is at stake are the values and ends for which the State is deemed to exist and whether they are being furthered or diminished. As once seen by Henry David Thoreau, 'They are the lovers of law and order who observe the law when the government breaks it.'[4] Nor is it exclusively a matter of choosing between the tolerant and the intolerant, the tolerable and the intolerable. Violence can wear many disguises so that at the very minimum the job is to resist providing further masks so that a beginning can be made in identifying and evaluating it.

The purpose of this chapter is to make a modest contribution in this direction through establishing a perspective on contemporary direct action by providing an example of political violence from the recent past. In doing so, an attempt will be made to describe a threshold of violence in the English polity.[5] This threshold, whether explicit or implicit in law, is essentially an abstraction and not necessarily static for it will be conditional upon circumstances. In so far as it can be identified for political activity in England, it is the point beyond which a stable, democratically-styled, albeit imperfect, order is unable or unwilling to countenance from within organized, collective and sustained abuse, disruption or threats to the State or any part thereof, even if civil liberties have to be violated. The accent is on the nature of the threat, the methods employed and the violence being sustained over a period of time. Short of a revolutionary situation, the problem is the highly delicate balance between liberty and order; whereas order is necessary for liberty, order as well as disorder can erode it.

The example chosen is that of the Fascist and anti-Fascist violence in England in the 1930s. Although this has been examined in detail elsewhere, the present exercise is fortified by the Cabinet Minutes and the Home Office and police records that are now available for the period.[6] By demonstrating the tolerance, perhaps the over-indulgence, that existed until the limits of decency were deemed to have been exceeded, it becomes possible to describe a threshold. The relevance for today is the apparent lowering of the threshold of violence to encompass forms of direct action that would be excluded by conventional and traditional criteria for political violence. Its significance lies in the nature of the government response to both exceeding and lowering the threshold. When the existing threshold of violence is perceived to have been exceeded, are the powers of the State adequate to control the situation? The question posed rests on the assumption of a set of liberties permissible in a democratic society – permissible in terms of its furtherance as well as its maintenance. When the threshold is lowered, is the State over-compensated by an increase in power at the expense of civil liberties? Here the assumption rests on an abuse of power.

II

Before describing the specific nature of collective and systematic violence as practised by the Fascist movement in England, there are a number of considerations that have a direct bearing on direct action today. The British Union of Fascists was founded by Sir Oswald Mosley in 1932 after he had exhausted the conventional political channels in an attempt to have his economic proposals adopted. It was a period of economic crisis that was to prove more severe elsewhere than in Great Britain. The decade has been shrouded in a great deal of romantic myth and political legend. The reality is more remarkable, given the seriousness of the issues and the disruption and responses experienced in other industrial countries. What made these years remarkable was not the extent of the militancy or the intensity of commitment but the relative quietude and decorum of political activity and discourse.

Similarly, what was important about the BUF was not its presence but that its presence was marginal to the mainstream of English politics. The explanation is largely to be found in the course of political development which along with industrialization was highly advanced, in sharp contrast to Germany and Italy. A political culture was established, deeply implanting the values, beliefs and practices of democracy. This did not mean that Parliamentary institutions were not subjected to criticism, but there was little evidence of massive disaffection from the political system. The conditions and tradition upon which to base revolutionary or counter-revolutionary appeals and movements were absent.[7] Equally important, the political élites did not feel threatened. The economy persisted, the political institutions survived unaltered, and the ruling groups remained entrenched. In short, there were no dramatic changes in the power relationships.

The ultimate objective of the BUF was the takeover and transformation of the State. This did not necessarily entail an insurrection in terms of an armed assault upon the political system. The accession to power and the subsequent creation of a Fascist State could be achieved under the cloak of constitutionality, as was the case in Nazi Germany. Yet as A. J. P. Taylor has written in reference to Sir Oswald Mosley, 'If he could not persuade, he would impose his ideas by force. Fascism meant this and could mean nothing else.'[8] What is clear is that the BUF could not be characterized as a pressure group or as a direct action group. It did not achieve Parliamentary representation nor more effectively did it possess a recognized and formalized relationship with Whitehall. In this sense direct action could not be viewed as either supplementary tactics or a last resort. It is obvious to all that when members of the National Farmers' Union demonstrate, they are not employing Fascist methods. The distinction should also be plain between the Fascists and the direct action groups who do not have formal and effective access to the decision-making process, and whose resources are mainly militancy and numbers available for mobilization. Unlike the Campaign for Nuclear Disarmament, the Stop The Seventy Tour Committee or the London Squatters campaign, the Fascists were not fundamentally concerned with issues that could be resolved within existing institutions or with those that could be remedied by reforms of the institutions.[9] Rather, the BUF sought the radical restructuring of the entire system, embracing a political, social and cultural revolution. The end result would be a dictatorship. It also follows that the Fascists are to be distinguished from those minorities who have turned to direct action to achieve increased recognition, status and participation among other and more concretely conceived objectives.

Standing apart and opposed to the political system, the BUF was prepared to promote and provoke collective violence. Mosley endeavoured to dispel accusations that they would take power by force. His position paralleled that of the Italian Fascists. The Blackshirts posed as the defenders of the State and its liberties against a loosely-defined Communist threat. An economic crisis was seen as inevitable, and it would be necessary to meet force with force. This was the doctrine as set forth originally in *The Greater Britain* and omitted from the later editions.[10] And along with the inevitability of a crisis was the inevitability of Fascism 'by one road or another'.[11] Whatever else, Mosley was a determined politician who fashioned a serious programme so that his Fascism must be taken at face value.

The BUF was also organized to display violence. The Fascist trappings first borrowed from Italy and then from Germany and the paramilitary style and behaviour of Mosley's 'instrument of steel' are a matter of historical record.[12] Whether inspiring or pathetic, appropriate or incongruous, the uniforms, the banners, the salutes, the posturings and the attempts to achieve disciplined, precisioned, military-styled formations were provocative of violence. This provocation, the movement's self-ascribed defence of law and order at its meeting at Olympia in 1934 and its anti-Semitic campaign challenged public tolerance and government prudence to a point that can be described as a threshold of violence.

It is apparent then that violence was not incidental to Fascism, regardless of its particular national manifestation. This is to be distinguished from the organized disruption that was promoted by the Stop The Seventy Tour Committee and which became violent.[13] The provocation of the latter is of a different nature. So are the terrorist activities of the Angry Brigade, although no less excusable than Fascist violence. There is another implication for contemporary direct action in that commentators, particularly Liberals of the generation whose political upbringing was in the 1930s, seek to identify some radical and student groups with pre-Second World War Fascist movements.[14] Among the parallels they cite are propensities towards irrationalism, romanticism, élitism and a desire for action rather than discussion – Mussolini's and Mosley's anti-democratic preferences for 'work shops rather than talk shops'.

This approach, which stresses the similarities and excludes the differences which are decisive, is as misleading as the claims of those radicals who describe Western liberal democracies as Fascistic because of their all too apparent imperfections and repressions. Or even more to the point is the violent rhetoric of the outraged deputy dean who felt that the Nazis would have envied the tactics of his students.[15] Both sides offer a disservice, for inexact and intemperate language provides a smokescreen for those forces in society anxious to curtail civil liberties. The advocates of law and order are thus able to adopt the mantle of rational discourse. It is also indicative of the lowering of the threshold of violence. Consequently, the terms of the debate change the nature of the spectrum of civil liberties from one of preservation and extension to one of restrictions.

What Fascism was about is correspondingly obscured. The European Fascist movements shared a combination of characteristics: nationalism, militarism, militant anti-Communism and the rejection of democratic values and practices.[16] It was the peculiar combination of these characteristics that distinguished Fascism from other authoritarian movements of the right and the left. Its most unique feature, however, was the idealization of violence as a value and a means.[17] These characteristics were present in BUF ideology and practice, taking into account that the Blackshirts never came close to achieving a Fascist-styled dictatorship. Mosley stressed the national development of Fascism within an international movement. Yet it was not simply a matter of ideological identification, for Fascism provided him with the model by which he expected to capture and exercise power.

Finally, although the State was the BUF's ultimate objective, the ensuing conflict was between two minorities – Fascist and anti-Fascist. Moreover, whatever the long-term aims of some of Mosley's opponents, anti-Fascism, symbolic and real, was the basis of their immediate struggle. This differed from a situation where the survival of the State was in jeopardy and where the belligerents were able to enlist mass followings. There is also only the slightest resemblance with the conflict currently taking place in Northern Ireland. The political cultures are quite distinct: the relationship of the belligerents to the political and economic systems differ; and only occasionally was there violence on the present scale. Moreover, the BUF's intensive anti-Semitic campaign in East London, however serious, failed to arouse traditional hostilities to the level of a community rupture, resulting in what Robert Baxter describes for Northern Ireland as tribal warfare.[18] The Blackshirts were essentially intruders in East London rather than an indigenous force rooted in the traditional and cultural antagonisms of the area.

The tasks of the State in the Fascist/anti-Fascist conflict were two-fold. The first was that of a referee between two movements on the periphery of the political system and in varying degrees opposed to it.[19] The second task was to afford protection and insure the safety of a minority section of the population – the Jewish community. The Jews, unlike the coloured immigrants today, played a more passive role, for their rights had been formally secured. Anti-Semitism and racialism added a further dimension to political violence in that persons as well as property were subjected to direct and intentional abuse. In the execution of its tasks, the internal guard of the State, the police, became a party to the conflict. They remained, however, belligerents in the traditional sense for as previously noted the legitimacy and credibility of the political system was not at stake and the violence done to persons and property, although deplorable in a civilized society, was containable. The police were not seen as an object for conversion, nor as the symbol of a repressive or ineffective State. The overt issues in regard to the police were the manner of their intervention and whether equal protection and treatment was provided for both belligerents and the Jewish minority. The problem as viewed by the government was the maintenance of public order and for the opposition parties the price that would have to be paid in terms of civil liberties and the extension of police powers. That the conflict was resolvable within the boundaries of conventional politics helps to account for the success of the Public Order Act where similar legislation had proved ineffective in Germany.[20]

III

The BUF was, at first, content to propagate a serious policy, to employ provocative language and to rely on the novelty of its paramilitary image in order to establish a political identity. Its pose was defensive. The self-proclaimed defenders of law and order, Fascists, did not seek out their opponents. It soon was apparent with the mounting disorder that they did not have to bother. Among the interested, however, few were fooled. The Home Secretary, concerned rather than alarmed, placed the responsibility on the Blackshirts, despite their public protestations.[21]

Fascist meetings followed a set pattern. The Leader would arrive later than the scheduled time to permit his followers to warm-up with Fascist songs, including some favourites from Italy and Germany. Entering the hall to the cheers of 'Hail Mosley' and to a wave of out-stretched arms, the idol of British Fascism accompanied by a guard of honour would proceed to the platform, which was draped in Fascist flags and Union Jacks. Mosley would stand alone in the focus of the spotlights while his uniformed stewards would be stationed around the perimeters of the hall and at the ends of each row of seats. In a powerful speech of some length, he would skilfully oscillate between dissecting the intricacies of the economic crisis and provocative tirades against the conspirators whom he held responsible. Without losing his stride Mosley would allow attention to be diverted from himself to the Blackshirts, who would converge wherever disorder was likely to occur.

It was violence rather than spectacle or oratory that dominated the rally at Olympia in June 1934, where British Fascism received a setback that may never have been achieved by legislation or police action. Whatever their motives, the Fascists' tactics proved a colossal blunder. Olympia was the largest meeting that the BUF had organized and was an opportunity to increase prestige and publicity. It was also an occasion for the anti-Fascists to mobilize their forces. The Communist party, in particular, had elaborate plans to make their presence felt, and the Blackshirts were prepared to receive them. In retrospect it was a quali-fied anti-Fascist triumph for the escalation in violence stirred public reaction. Many of the movement's backers, sympathizers and well-wishers deserted the cause or returned to the realm of conventional politics.

The moment seemed ripe for legislation, if not to increase the powers of the police, at least to curb the trappings of Fascism for the threshold of violence had been exceeded. The Cabinet records are not conclusive on the failure to legislate. The Parliamentary time-table seems to have been the main obstacle – yet this raises the question of priorities. It is also possible to infer a regard for civil liberties and a concern for the consequences of their curtailment rather than a sympathy or a tolerance for movements of the extreme right, as some contemporary critics suggested. In any case, an enduring lesson was that breaking the threshold extracts a heavy toll so that the government's reluctance proved an accurate assessment of the Fascist threat at home and of public values, in that Olympia was a turning-point in Mosley's fortunes.

The question of public order legislation had been raised previously at Cabinet level when the national hunger marches had been considered and in reference to the Fascists immediately prior to Olympia. The public outcry following that meeting inspired detailed treatment. What was particularly noteworthy about the discussions was the manner in which the Home Secretary, Sir John Gilmour, resisted the request from the police for sweeping powers, and the way in which his Cabinet colleagues tempered his own modifications. Due regard was shown for what Parliament would accept, and what the public would bear. For example, the police pressed for the regulation of processions and outdoor meetings as well as indoor ones and for a ban on paramilitary organizations. The Chief Constables consulted were practically unanimous that they should have the power to regulate the route of processions and ban those that were intimidating or likely to cause a breach of the peace. The Home Secretary felt that these proposals would be unacceptable to Parliament and countered with a drastically diluted version. He agreed that the police should be given the power to control processions, but proposed that they should only be allowed to prohibit those meetings and processions which interfered with the transaction of business by public authorities or resulted in clashes with rival meetings. Gilmour also recommended that the possession of an offensive weapon be made an offence.[22] The banning of meetings and processions was 'strongly criticized' in the Cabinet, mainly on the grounds that they were usually the only means available to the poor and that too much power would be placed in the hands of the police.[23]

As for paramilitary organizations, a study had been undertaken of foreign legislation. The Home Secretary wanted to go beyond those countries that had solely banned the wearing of political uniforms, and he was supported in this view by deputations from the Parliamentary Labour Party and the TUC. The police favoured legislation along the lines of a recent Swedish Act. Gilmour was dubious, presumably because that Act stressed declared purpose as well as behaviour and suggested that the burden of guilt should be shared equally between leaders and followers. He emphasized that any legislation of this nature must be based on 'as precise a definition of overt acts as possible' and offered his own formulation.[24] The Home Secretary was counselled that any legislation must be based on established principles of the British Constitution.[25] This was in accord with Gilmour's position before Olympia, when he argued that the legislation of other countries placed more power in the hands of the government than would be acceptable in Britain short of a national emergency.[26]

The leaders of the opposition parties were consulted. The extension of police powers to enter meetings was generally welcomed. The Labour party favoured the prohibition of paramilitary organizations, but the opposition Liberals were split over its practicability. Gilmour reported that the attitude was that it was for the government to decide whether or not to go ahead.[27] Here the matter rested.

It was some months before the BUF's anti-Semitic campaign gained precedence over the movement's programme for radical economic and political change. Meetings and demonstrations continued throughout Britain and were for the most part free from disorder. The battleground had switched to the environs where anti-Fascists clashed with Fascists but more often with the police. One incident is worth recalling for it reveals the difficulties involved for a new pressure group in gaining official recognition – although particularly, if not uniquely, complicated by its area of representational interest – as well as the defensive attitudes of the police.[28]

While Mosley was addressing a BUF rally in the Albert Hall in March 1936, an anti-Fascist demonstration in Thurloe Square nearby was broken up by the police with some violence. Demands for a public inquiry were refused by the Home Secretary, so the National Council for Civil Liberties initiated their own in expectation that further pressure on the government might induce an inquiry. This too was resisted. (The NCCL was founded in 1934 and had achieved some success in amending the Incitement to Disaffection Bill.) As for the Thurloe Square inquiry, it represented one in a series of complaints against the police emanating from a number of quarters. It also suggested a lowering of the threshold of violence in what the police were willing to tolerate. The police reaction to the NCCL report was that six months had elapsed and public interest had waned. More important, the police viewed the organization as one whose primary purpose was to criticize and attack the police and recommended prudence in granting an inquiry as it would afford status and encourage 'troublesome activities'.[29] Their attitude towards the NCCL did not change during this period. Allegations following a Fascist meeting in 1937 were dismissed by the police, who described the Council as a body exploiting disorder, principally caused by their own supporters, to attack the police.[30] While on another occasion during the same year, reference was made to 'their close subterranean connections' *vis-à-vis* its Secretary and the Communist party and that its *modus operandi* was to vilify the police.[31]

The BUF's anti-Semitic campaign created a climate of violence in East London. Street-corner meetings were the centre-piece of their activities and in sum were more serious than the periodic mass demonstration, for they incited an atmosphere of tension, intimidation and provocation. When it is considered that the residents of East London were subjected to a campaign of constant harassment, approaching a reign of terror, in conditions of economic deprivation, it is remarkable that they were so pacific in their behaviour. For Mosley to write, 'What occurred in East London was much exaggerated . . .' is a travesty of the facts.[32]

Pressure was brought to bear upon the Home Office by the House of Commons by various deputations and through police records to step-up surveillance and for increased diligence. A number of measures were put into force.[33] For example, instructions were issued that at outdoor meetings two policemen were to be posted within hearing distance of the speakers, and if they became abusive the police were to err on the side of action rather than inaction.[34] Yet almost a year later, the Commissioner of the Metropolitan Police complained about the lack of vigilance[35] and even with the passage of the Public Order Act prosecution remained difficult.[36]

By the autumn of 1936 the anti-Semitic campaign had reached maximum intensity and the government was forced to act as a consequence of the Fascist/anti-Fascist battle that never took place on 4 October. The proposed BUF march through East London was diverted at the last moment, but the clashes between the anti-Fascists and the police which had begun earlier in the day continued. The threshold of violence had been threatened and exceeded. The Commissioner of the Metropolitan Police stated in his *Annual Report* that there was 'little doubt that serious rioting and bloodshed would have occurred had the march been allowed to take place'.[37] It was also apparent that future Fascist marches of the same magnitude could lead to further serious threats to public order.

The events of 4 October proved to be a catalyst, public pressure mounted, and the government almost immediately began to consider legislation. The Home Secretary, Sir John Simon, in placing the matter before the Cabinet, argued that what was needed was not emergency regulations but the strengthening of the existing law. He was opposed to granting additional powers to a Home Secretary on the grounds that his jurisdiction was restricted to the Metropolitan police, that it would meet strong opposition and, most significantly, that a future government of 'strong party complexion might use them in a partisan fashion'. He advocated that prospective legislation go beyond a uniforms' ban and include the regulation of processions lest the government be accused of singling out the Fascists to the advantage of their opponents. Moreover Fascism, in whatever dress, was now provocative. This was the result of events on the Continent, the 'hysterical fear' that anti-Semitism may gain a grip on England and the improvement in the techniques for attracting and concentrating large numbers of people.[38] The Cabinet in accepting the need for legislation adopted the position that by making it clear that the government would not tolerate attacks on minorities or disruption to public order they would gain the approval of public opinion. In anticipation of criticisms that further restrictions on civil liberties were being imposed, it was agreed that restrictions were necessary because of the abuse of liberties from some sections of the public.[39]

The Bill that was actually introduced into Parliament was far more comprehensive, prohibiting paramilitary organizations and ranging over the wide field of public order. It is not the purpose of this chapter to discuss its application or assess its contribution to the demise of British Fascism beyond its relevance to the themes already developed. It certainly would be rash to make extravagant claims for its success. The BUF was defrocked and its processions through East London were subsequently banned. Yet the main sources of trouble, the street-corner meetings and the daily harassments, continued. Indeed, the number of meetings did not diminish[40] and on the Home Secretary's own admittance Fascism in whatever dress was by then provocative. In areas of Jewish population, anti-Semitism remained an exploitable and explosive issue, and reference has already been made to the difficulties of bringing prosecutions.

What is important to recognize is that the BUF was further discredited, violence as a political style remained unacceptable, and anti-Semitism failed to gain legitimacy in national politics. The manner in which this was achieved had implications for the methods of direct action, because the police were prepared to lower the threshold of violence further and encroach on civil liberties. In particular, the Commissioner of the Metropolitan Police requested legislation to ban processions 'once and for all'. The occasion was a BUF march through South London one year after the climax of the East London campaign and nine months after the enactment of the Public Order Act. On this march, 2,500 police were employed to accompany 3,000 Fascists, and 113 arrests were made. Among the arguments used by Sir Philip Game in his submission were that processions were an inconvenience, a drain on police resources, a method confined to extreme political movements with relatively little support, and although they may have been necessary when the vote was restricted, this was no longer the case.[41]

IV

A number of issues are raised by the way of summary and conclusions. It was suggested at the outset that there is an apparent lowering of the threshold of violence today. There is a tendency to confuse different forms of direct action with political violence. The distinctions between actors and between their activities have been obscured. The problems of rhetoric and labels has hindered proper evaluation. The difference between action that becomes violent and that which is organized to promote violence is often too narrowly interpreted. The law is seen to have been broken when no actual offence has been committed. In so far as this is occurring, it is a way in which political élites can cope with the increased demands and pressures made upon them through the various means of direct action. It is indicative of a growing insecurity among the political élites as they respond to events abroad, confront the actions of militants at home, and are presented with the claims of groups that ordinarily function through the recognized and accepted channels. It is also indicative of a growing institutional rigidity. The lowering of the threshold provides a government with discretion to bestow approval or disapproval, and to sort out the demands that it is willing or unwilling to process. It shifts attention from substantive issues to the means of their presentation. And it grants the State further licence to counter violence, perhaps with violence.

Some of the longer-term consequences have also been spelt out or are implied in the above. Legitimate claims and valuable proposals may be lost to society. The government may assume further powers of arbitrary discretion. The fear of investing the State with further powers – either by extending prerogatives or curtailing checks – diminishes. As for civil liberties, the spectrum changes from one of extension and preservation to one of restriction.

The changes in the role of the State also have implications for the threshold of violence. Historically, the State has acted to protect the rights of private property and the vested interests of élite groups. With the rise of industrialization and the growth of democratic politics, it became concerned with furthering the rights of the majority as well as the maintenance of public order. The State has also acted on occasion to insure the rights of deprived and distressed minorities. This was a motivation behind the passage of the 1936 Public Order Act and is enshrined, if only in principle, in the race relations legislation of the 1960s. The question that remains is whether the powers vested in the State, originally intended to further and protect the interests of majorities as well as minorities, might not in different circumstances be used against those majorities and minorities. A Home Secretary in the 1930s expressed similar fears, and a Commissioner of Police was eager to deprive the public of a fundamental liberty. Neither respect for the public nor public opinion represent eternal safeguards. Firm action on the part of a government will normally receive public approval, for such steps would be in accord with a political culture that values strong government and leadership. To maintain the balance between liberty and order, the assumption that the politics of protest is legitimate and valuable must constantly be affirmed.

History does not repeat itself in the same way, but it does arm us with knowledge. The violence that accompanied political and social change was held to be largely tamed in Britain by the 1930s. The conduct of the General Strike of 1926 bears impressive testimony to this. Yet in the 1930s there was an attempt to introduce violence as a style of politics, and it reached serious proportions, at least for the Jewish community. It is fair to argue that violence is not a value in the political culture although it has not been eliminated from British politics and society. The resort to political violence has been minimized, and the violence today, excepting Northern Ireland, has been minimal. There are no conclusive guarantees, however. And the danger may well be of a different order. The lowering of a threshold established in the context of paramilitary violence so that it applies to other forms of direct action suggests the possibility of over-reaction on the part of the State. What is all too apparent is a willingness in some quarters to enhance the powers of the police, when the problem is really one of controlling the police. Moreover, direct action, let alone violence, creates a climate favourable to the police. At the same time, those who advocate violent methods seem to forget that violence can be used to resist change. How a government responds, ideology aside, depends on its confidence and perspective – both of which have been distorted in recent years.

As yet the stage has not been reached where the political élites supported by overwhelming opinion are ready or willing to repress civil liberties and rights for the sake of law and order. There is, however, another dimension, by no means new or novel, that requires consideration and a personal judgement: that is, the objectives of groups that turn to direct action. This dimension is too often ignored or repressed by politicians determined to defend their powers and prerogatives, by social scientists attempting to maintain their 'neutrality', and by the public misled and ill-informed by the media. Despite possible consequences for the future and taking into account that the conditions which led many to join a Fascist movement were not rectified, the government acted prudently and properly. The Fascists would have destroyed democracy and civility. There are groups today that would further both, although their actions sometimes deny them. Those of us who share these goals are placed in the unenviable position of persuading the activists to evaluate methods and the government to consider goals as well as methods. Beyond this, rational discourse and rational action (for it is often not enough just to be heard) require their own militancy to expose those who would lower the threshold of violence in order to preserve their privileges which give rise to direct action in the first place.

NOTES

1. That the State also engages in this form of political activity is a point made most forcibly in the preceding chapter by V. G. Kiernan, 'Patterns of Protest in English History'.
2. The right to bear arms enshrined in the American Constitution challenges this classical approach.
3. See the important book by E. V. Walter, *Terror and Resistance* (New York, 1969).
4. 'Slavery in Massachusetts', *Walden and the Other Writings of Henry David Thoreau* (New York, 1937, 1950), p. 669.
5. Gavin Drewry suggests a similar notion, 'threshold of tolerance', in his chapter 'Political Parties and Members of Parliament'.
6. Robert Benewick, *Political Violence and Public Order* (London, 1969); 2nd revised edn: *The Fascist Movement in Britain* (London, 1972).
7. The presence or absence of an English revolutionary tradition is in dispute especially within the New Left. Compare E. P. Thomson, *The Making of the English Working Class* (London, 1963) and Perry Anderson, 'Origins of the Present Crisis' in Perry Anderson and Robin Blackburn (eds.) *Towards Socialism* (London, 1965).
8. The *Observer* (20 October 1968).
9. The BUF did act more conventionally on occasion in order to further its ultimate objective, as in its publicity campaign against British involvement in a European war.
10. Compare the 1932 edition, pp. 150–1 with the 1934 edition, p. 181. See also his libel action against the Daily News Ltd, *The Times* (Law Reports) (6 November 1934).
11. Oswald Mosley, *Fascism in Britain* (1933), p. 8.
12. Mosley in his autobiography has chosen to emphasize its military rather than its Fascist inspiration, but the two cannot be separated. *My Life* (London, 1968), p. 303; see also Robert Skidelsky, 'The Problem of Mosley', *Encounter* (September 1969), pp. 77–85 and the interview with Alexander Mosley, *The Guardian* (1 July 1971).
13. See the chapter by Peter Hain, 'Direct Action and the Springbok Tours', and his book *Don't Play with Apartheid* (London, 1971).
14. For an excellent critique of this attitude, see Philip Green, 'Can it Happen Here?', *The New York Times Magazine* (20 September 1970).
15. *The Times* (7 May 1971).
16. See S. J. Woolf (ed.), *European Fascism* (London, 1969).
17. See Henry Picker (ed.), *Hitler's Table Talk* (Bonn, 1951), p. 227 where he spoke of war as 'the most powerful and classic expression

of life' and p. 661 where world domination was seen as resulting in perpetual war rather than peace.

18. See the chapter by Robert Baxter, 'The Second Ulster Crisis'.

19. The difficulties in viewing the State as an impartial referee are discussed in the chapter by Robert Mast, 'Law and Order in Comparative Perspective'.

20. This point is curiously devalued or misunderstood in an otherwise perceptive critique by Peter Sedgwick, 'The Problem of Fascism', *International Socialism* (February/March 1970), pp. 31–4.

21. 23 May 1934, CAB 24/249 C.P. 144 (Public Records Office); 2 July 1934, CAB 24/250 C.P. 189 Appendix (Public Records Office).

22. 11 July 1934, CAB 24/250 C.P. 189 (Public Records Office).

23. 18 July 1934, CAB 23/79 29 (34) 2 (Public Records Office).

24. 11 July 1934, CAB 24/250 C.P. 189 (Public Records Office).

25. 18 July 1934, CAB 23/79 29(34) 2 (Public Records Office).

26. 23 May 1934, CAB 24/249 C.P. 144 (Public Records Office).

27. 31 July 1934, CAB 23/79 31(34) 7 (Public Records Office).

28. See the chapter by Tony Smythe, 'The Role of the National Council for Civil Liberties.

29. Mepol. 2/3089 (Public Records Office).

30. Mepol. 2/3104 (Public Records Office).

31. Mepol. 2/3112 (Home Office 502735/265, 25 June 1937) (Public Records Office).

32. Mosley, op. cit., p. 213.

33. 16 July 1936, Mepol. 2/3043 (Public Records Office).

34. 3 August 1936, Mepol. 2/3043 (Public Records Office).

35. 29 June 1937, Commissioner's Office, *Memorandum to Officers in Charge of Districts* (Public Records Office).

36. Mepol. 2/3109 (Public Records Office).

37. *Report of the Commissioner of Police for the Year 1936*, p. 26.

38. 12 October 1936, CAB 24/264 C.P. 261 (Public Records Office).

39. 14 October 1936, CAB 23/85 57 (36) 2 (Public Records Office).

40. Summer 1936 to November 1938, Mepol. 2/3043 (Public Records Office); December 1938 to November 1939, Mepol. 2/3127 (Public Records Office).

41. 5 October 1937, CAB 24/271 C.P. 230 (Public Records Office).

III Liberal Rationality and Political Violence*

BHIKHU PAREKH

It is commonly argued that in a liberal democracy which allows its citizens ample opportunities for peaceful change, a citizen can never be justified in using violence. My intention in this chapter is to question this view and to show not only that violence can have a place in the liberal democracy but also that in some cases it is provoked and made necessary by the rhetoric and practices of the liberal democracy itself.

To avoid the possible criticism that the beliefs I ascribe to a liberal were never fully held by any of the great thinkers of the past whom the academic consensus regards as liberals, it should be said that I am not concerned here with any particular theorist and his ideas, much less with a school of political theorists and their ideas, but rather with the theoretical assumptions underlying the practice of societies we have come to call liberal democracies. This is so because I am primarily interested in those beliefs and ideas that inspire and influence our actual political practice; and while it is true that many historical thinkers have contributed to the evolution of these beliefs, none of them can properly be called the 'father' of liberal democracy. Indeed there is much in the writings of Hobbes, Locke, Bentham, Acton, J. S. Mill and de Tocqueville, regarded by different commentators as the liberal thinkers *par excellence*, which we today would regard as unworthy of acceptance by a liberal democratic society. When I therefore talk of liberalism in this chapter, I refer to nothing more pretentious than a loosely-knit body of beliefs held by most members of a liberal democratic society. And if a critic contends that some of the views I ascribe to liberals are held only by a dwindling minority of them, I would be content to maintain that they still constitute one powerful trend in liberal thinking. In brief, then, this chapter is an essay not in the history of ideas but in philosophical sociology.

I

Liberalism and democracy are not necessarily compatible: while one emphasizes the resolution of disagreement by debate where ideally

---

* I would like to thank those who have commented on this chapter, particularly Professor A. R. Desai and Miss Usha Mehta.

everyone is convinced and won over, the other resolves it by vote where some are silenced. However, the two have been married for the last few decades to yield a society we call a liberal democracy. Based on the *liberal* belief that men are rational in the sense that their views and behaviour are based on, and can therefore be changed by, rational argument, the liberal democracy enshrines free and public debate right into the heart of the political process, in the hope that men will argue with each other and reach a common agreement. Based on the *democratic* belief that men are legally and politically equal, it reposes the ultimate political authority in the hands of the people who, not being able to meet regularly to conduct their common affairs, assign it to their periodically elected representatives. A liberal democracy thus provides free elections where governments are created or destroyed; a free Press that facilitates the emergence of public opinion; a Parliament where different opinions are represented and debated openly and publicly; and an official opposition that keeps a watch on the activities of the government and whose criticism of it has a cutting edge because of its willingness and ability to provide an alternative government.

In such a society where political decisions are reached after a full and public debate in which everyone who had something to say had a full opportunity to do so, argues the liberal democrat, it is never likely that an opinion will go unrepresented or a grievance unredressed. It may be the case that a decision is taken by the government or by the community that an individual citizen may strongly disapprove of. But it is always open to him to continue to persuade or pressure them as long as he wishes. If in the end he finds that he is unable to win them over, he must accept this as a necessary price every citizen has to pay. If everyone always insisted, says the liberal, that his views alone were right, and refused to carry out a decision with which he disagreed, the life of the State would be paralysed. Once a citizen has done his best to persuade others, he must accept the outcome of the debate and abide by it. At no point can he be justified in disobeying the law or in using violence. With all its imperfections, the liberal democratic system, it is argued, is better than any other; and deserves the fullest allegiance and loyalty of its members.

Now clearly the theory of political obligation implied by the liberal democratic theory is substantially correct. If an individual has a full and equally effective share in the conduct of political affairs, and if his good is considered equally important in determining the objectives of government policies (that is, if his society gives him full and equal recognition both as a subject and as an object of social policy), he has the fullest obligation to obey its laws, and he cannot be justified in disobeying a law or in resorting to violence to change a law or a policy he considers unjust. He may, of course, disapprove of a law, but no

C

individual can be a member of a State on his own terms. What is more, other members of the State are his equals, and therefore for him to insist that his views alone should prevail is to insist that they should accept him as a dictator, as a more privileged person than they. And this is unfair.

While the theory of liberal democracy is thus right to rule out violence, its embargo on violence would be justified *in practice* only if its practice matched its theoretical idealization. The basic thesis of this chapter is that it does not. For analytical convenience let us separate ballot and discussion, the two main pillars of liberal democracy, and consider them in turn.

The democratic theory captures the essence of the system of ballot when it looks upon it as a substitute for bullet. The ballot has all the crudity and rigidity of the bullet. Like the bullet, its power depends on its numerical strength: the more heads I can count in my favour, the more I win, just as the more heads a general can break, the greater are his chances of subduing his enemy. It is, of course, true that morally there is a significant difference between breaking and counting heads. But the difference can be easily exaggerated. Imagine a community in which a matter is put to vote every time a disagreement arises, and in which the majority automatically votes one way. The minority, which is never allowed to speak and is systematically outvoted, is as good as politically disenfranchized. What makes its plight really unbearable is the democratic mythology that justifies its virtual disenfranchizement in the name of democracy, and extracts from it, in return, a commitment never to use force against the democratic society. If the members of the minority were living under a tyranny, they would at least have been released from the obligation not to use violence; and the overt violence of the tyrant might have at least dramatized their misery. Thus the ballot could easily become a means of political oppression, that is not necessarily more humane for being democratic.

Again, the ballot, understood as an electoral pressure, is available only to a majority; a minority, like a poorly-equipped army, lacks political weight and strength. No doubt, the majority and the minority are fluid groups with shifting membership; but this is not so when they are clearly divided on racial, religious or ethnic grounds. And here a minority is completely at the mercy of the majority. Further, electoral pressure is exerted at the end of a long period, while the crucial question may be one of opposing a particular policy or piece of legislation that might be considered grossly unjust or iniquitous. The electoral pressure, or the threat of it, is of little avail here. Again, there are issues on which it may not be possible to exert electoral pressure at all, as when all the available political parties take a common stand on them. Take, for example, the temporary denial by the British government of the civil and political rights of the Asians in Kenya. Until recently both the major parties in Britain took more or less the same stand on this question, and therefore a citizen who felt differently had no political channels available whereby to express an effective opposition to the government policy. It is true that a determined minority can mobilize public opinion and influence the major political parties; but this requires a super-human effort in a society whose members are mainly devoted, and are encouraged to remain devoted, to the pursuit of their private activities and are not involved in the political life as a matter of course.

What makes the ballot acceptable, then, is the fact that it is located in, that it is a part of, a wider process of persuasion and discussion in which it is possible for a citizen to persuade others, including the government, to his point of view. That is to say, the ballot has a moral justification only when it comes at the end of a long process of serious, genuine and open-minded discussion in which every opinion has had a full opportunity to challenge and influence all others. The case of the liberal-democratic theory against the use of violence thus rests ulti-mately on its ability to provide a genuine, free and open-minded discussion in which the participants undertake to follow what emerges from the discussion as the most reasonable course of action. Judged by this standard, which the liberal-democratic theory itself has set up, its practice turns out to be unsatisfactory.

One of the dominant inspirations of the liberal society is the view that man is essentially a desiring being, a being who is unceasingly engaged in the gratification of his constantly multiplying desires. Historically speaking, it is this principle that has determined the ethos of the liberal society. The basic orientation of the liberal society is to produce as much as possible and as efficiently as possible, and thereby both to raise the level of consumption of its members and to reduce the amount of energy they expend in the productive process. This has meant that the social economy is directed towards the creation of the units of production that are large, mechanized and insulated from outside interference. As the large and efficient corporations that the liberal society has created are geared to unlimited production and therefore survive on unlimited consumption, they have no choice but to plant and titillate new desires; and a climate is created where unless one keeps pace with the objects constantly pumped into the already satiated market, one feels that one is not really living, that one is becoming as old-fashioned and obsolete as last year's car. As long as wages are rising reasonably faster than prices, the consumer feels that he has no real reason to complain or to 'waste' his time taking an active interest in the affairs of his society or of the world at large. And with the loss of interest in how society ought to live or how ideally oneself ought to live, there is almost a complete atrophying of the social, moral and political dimension of life.[1]

It is not only that the individual – a shadowy and ultimately inconsequential figure in a society where corporations alone have power and reality – counts for little, but also that he is incapable of challenging corporations and changing anything except with the help of another corporation. And then it is this new corporation that swallows him, so that he ends up by exchanging one mode of incorporation or absorption for another, one bureaucracy for another, one type of manipulation for another. Indeed, the State itself is a large corporation governed by a huge bureaucracy that allows its citizens little creative and effective role. In such a highly pressurized society, politics is a battle, a contest, in which two or more political armies are locked. The aim is to win the contest; to get into power and remain in power. This means that each party must speak with one voice, must establish a clear chain of command, and must fashion itself into an efficient instrument of action. No doubt, as members of a liberal society they must be free to speak their mind; but their discussion has to be regulated so that it does not give their party the appearance of a 'divided mind', of a party that cannot make up its mind, of a party whose members wear different ideological masks.

The result is that dissent is seen as 'rocking the boat', as opening the way to enemy influence, as an irrelevancy that impedes people from 'getting on with the job'. The critic who points to a minor grievance is listened to, provided his criticisms are punctuated by a fulsome praise of the institution he is criticizing. But if he probes its very basis and proposes a different way of restructuring it, he is immediately suspect as, at best, a well-meaning but naïve idealist, and, at worst, as is often the case, its enemy. While dissent is tolerated and is indeed regarded as the distinguishing characteristic of the liberal society, it is welcome only if it is not radical and 'too' critical. Instead of seeing, therefore, that the critic might love the institution just as much as, and even more than, its staunchest defender, and instead of being grateful to him for taking the trouble of thinking about the well-being of the institution and proposing ways of promoting it, the authorities in every institution have come to see him as a cross to be borne, as a nuisance to be tolerated in order to salvage the liberal conscience. It is a remarkable paradox of the liberal democracy, which, historically speaking, began as a political system resting on discussion and reason and which conceptually defines itself as a government by persuasion and critical reason, that it has reached a point where the free and powerful citizen, so cherished by the classical liberals, has little hope of persuading the government or his fellow-citizens, and where the very continuance of the society requires such a hardening of intellectual and political positions that discussion and dissent are the first casualties. When the liberal belief in persuasion is frustrated by the very social and political structure that it has spawned, the liberal rhetoric of critical rationality wears very thin indeed.

The liberal theory of persuasion postulates that different opinions have an equal ability to compete in the market-place of ideas. But this is a condition that is not satisfied by the liberal democratic society, though it must be said in fairness that beyond a certain point it cannot be satisfied by *any* society. In an inegalitarian society it is only to be expected that different groups would not have equal access to sources of information or to media of communication, nor would they be able to marshal talented people to represent their views. Therefore their opinions are bound to vary greatly in quality, content and persuasive power. But even if they were guaranteed full formal and material equality, they would still remain unequal. Since a social structure is not an abstract but a specific and determinate type of organization, and embodies a particular conception of life, it inevitably encourages certain types of opinion and discourages others. Once an opinion or a practice gains currency, it has on its side the weight of inertia, social respectability, and, what one might call, the credibility of existence. It has already become a part of people's life and therefore they are more disposed to retain than to change it. As it is accepted by the majority of the community, it is considered a respectable and responsible opinion to hold, while other competing opinions and practices still remain confined to a tiny dissident minority, and therefore belief in them tends to be associated with naïveté, irresponsibility and immaturity. What is more, if the very fact that an opinion or a practice has taken roots in the life of the community means that it has a certain vitality, a potency, a power to resist the corroding pressure of criticism, it also means that a challenge to it amounts to a challenge to the entire structure of beliefs and practices of which it is an integral part.

Thus the opinions and practices that are widely accepted inevitably enjoy an overwhelming psychological and moral superiority over those still contending for allegiance. Equal competition of opinions therefore is a myth. This means, further, that no legal or moral principle can be completely impartial between two opinions and practices. As law aims to maintain order, its main concern *qua* law is and must be to avoid provoking disorder by upsetting established expectations, and therefore it cannot but be partial to the *status quo*. The only occasion when it would feel compelled to alter the *status quo* is when it realizes that the disorder threatened by the critics is likely to outweigh that threatened by its upholders. Which is to say, incidentally, that the very nature of the law often calls for violence as its principle of motion. Morally, too, an action is justified when, among other things, it causes minimal suffering and disturbance, and this means ultimately that an already established practice has a built-in moral advantage over one that is proposed. The latter has to be much better than its rival in order to be its equal. In practice, therefore, every moral principle is necessarily far more sympathetic to the continuance than to the alteration of the *status quo*, and if other things are equal, it would generally deliver a conservative recommendation. Thus if law and morality by their very nature are partisan and partial towards what already exists, and if social and economic inequality imposes serious limits on dissident opinions and practices, the liberal theory of persuasion needs radical revision.

The liberal theory of persuasion is also frustrated by the liberal psychological, moral and political theory. The liberal theory of rational discussion presupposes, rightly, that the participants in a debate are willing to argue and to be persuaded by each other, and in general to pursue what issues from the debate as the most reasonable course of action. But then the liberals take the view that man is basically a selfish creature who is concerned to maximize his own interest, so that he is prepared to listen and, indeed, can be expected to listen to others' arguments only as long as they do not affect his interest, at any rate, as long as they do not require him to make serious sacrifices of his own interest. Thus the process of discussion is circumscribed and limited right from the start. Persuasion, after all, is an activity that occupies the intermediate realm between what can be demonstrated or proved and what is a simple matter of taste. When an argument can be proved or demonstrated, as in the natural sciences and mathematics, one does not need to persuade another. One simply silences him by a series of logically right steps or by an undeniable piece of evidence. And when something is a matter of taste, for example that you like vanilla ice-cream and I like raspberry, or that you like a red tie and I like a blue one, no persuasion is possible because my preference is not based on inter-personally recognizable reasons of whose force I could try to persuade you. Persuasion, therefore, necessarily presupposes that I must be able to depend on you to consider my arguments seriously, that I must be able to *trust* you to try your best to see their force. It is precisely this condition that is denied by the insistence that every man must pursue his own interest, since how can I trust you to consider my arguments and interests impartially when I know that you view everything only from the standpoint of your own interest?

The liberal democrat can respond to this tension between his theory of rationality and his theory of self-interest in one of two ways. Either he can sacrifice the limiting condition of self-interest and argue that men must ignore the considerations of self-interest when they debate about the best way to promote the common good, or he can jettison the rhetoric of rational discussion and see society primarily as an interplay of interests in which the more powerful interests always win. It is generally the second alternative that the liberal has taken; that is to say, he has generally opted for bargaining instead of debate, for competition instead of co-operation, for horse-trading instead of creative reconciliation; in short, he has opted for the introduction of the methods of the marketplace into the deliberative assembly. Now when decisions are reached after bargaining and horse-trading, they inevitably favour those whose bargaining position is stronger, with the result that those who cannot bargain 'from the position of strength' would constantly be tempted to use the only weapon they have – to come out into the streets and compel the government to take notice of their grievances. Or, if the government chooses to clamp down on them in the name of law and order, they may have no alternative but to go underground and resort to terrorism. In either case, their recourse to unconstitutional methods would seem fully justified since, where politics is a matter of bargaining, they, like their more privileged fellow-citizens, are constantly encouraged and, indeed, required to look after their own interest, and cannot have an obligation to refrain from violence if they see in it the best way to promote their interest.

Even if the liberal theory of rationality was extricated from the psychological theory of self-interest and the political theory of bargain, it would still remain inadequate. As it is predicated on the assumption that the members of a community are all interested in pursuing their own private activities, it believes that the best, the most rational way of organizing it is one where the law carves out for its members clearly demarcated private spaces to which each of them remains confined to 'mind his own business'. A rational man in the liberal view is one who keeps his distance from others, who obeys the law, who is cautious and calculative, who minds his own business, who recognizes the equal right of others to their privacy, and who receives or covets nothing that does not accrue to him from the agreed process of bargaining. Rationality, in short, is defined in terms of the ability to observe rules. Rational behaviour is rule-following behaviour and, conversely, irrational behaviour is unruly behaviour, that is, it is not based on rules.

In this conception of reason, a neat and sharp contrast is drawn between reason and passion or emotion. (For the present purpose I am using the two terms interchangeably.) It is argued that passion is the enemy of reason, that it weakens reason, darkens it, clouds it, misleads it. Anyone who shows passion is regarded as a person in whom reason does not yet rule, and who is therefore not fit enough to rule others or to play the game of politics. Indeed, he is a man not yet fit enough to live in the civil society, a man not yet civilized. The liberal is deeply afraid of passion and feels profoundly uneasy in its presence. In a system of insulated egos inhabiting neatly demarcated social spaces and related to each other only externally by agreed rules, emotion introduces elements of mutual involvement, informality, intensity, and dilution of social rigidity with which the liberal does not know how to cope. This contrast between reason and emotion leads the liberal into one of two directions. Either he sees life as a constant battle to subdue emotion, until life becomes a thoroughly de-emotionalized rational artifact, or he neatly separates reason and passion, assigning them to the public and the private sphere of life respectively. In either case, the liberal game of politics is played according to rules, the violation of which is considered a sign of undeveloped political rationality. Therefore, those who refuse to abide by rules, or those who feel and speak passionately about political issues, or those who refuse to compromise and bargain and decline to be deflected from their stand, are considered to be men in whom passions have accumulated to an uncontrollable degree. As good and rational men, the liberals, of course, wish that things could be otherwise. But they feel that they must regretfully accept the fact that many of their fellow-men unfortunately are not yet fully rational; and that, therefore, while resigning themselves to the fact that some overheated human kettles do need to let off steam from time to time, they, the liberals, must prepare themselves for defending the existing social order either by severely punishing disorderly behaviour or by ritualizing it and providing for its periodic release.

Irrespective of whether we prefer the strong-arm attitude of the conservative or the paternalistic and tolerant indulgence of the liberal, we are not taking passions and emotions seriously and are putting them outside the realm of politics. The liberal fails to realize that passions are not necessarily irrational. For example, a passionate hatred of injustice, or anger at an opponent's hypocrisy, or wrath at his chicanery, or rage at being treated like a child are all not only rational but are indeed the only proper responses to the situation in question. Because the liberal lacks a proper theory of the role of reason and passion or emotion in political life, his is a highly emasculated conception of public life in which the skills that have come to matter most are those of soft political salesmanship, seductive and smooth public relations, and a hard and manipulative bargain within the agreed framework of rules. A single conception of public debate comes to dominate public life, and those taking a different view of political rationality and therefore of public debate find that the scales of public life are already weighted against them.

One consequence of this narrow conception of reason is that it gives rise to an ideologically biased contrast between moderation and extremism. The liberal is right to reject extremism as irrational, but he is wrong to define it so widely as to include everyone who is not a cautious moderate. An extremist, properly speaking, can be defined as a person who insists on realizing an ideal, irrespective of its cost. Some particular evil strikes him as so grotesque, and it absorbs his moral and political imagination so much that he feels it must be removed at all costs, and as quickly as possible. He is a one-eyed man who has set his heart on realizing one single ideal, either in a general or in a specific context. And since either he does not recognize the moral claim of other values, or he attaches very little weight to them, they do not enter into his moral universe, and their loss does not appear to him as a moral cost against which to assess the morality of his contemplated course of action. Thus an extreme egalitarian pushes for equality irrespective of how it affects values like liberty, order and the integrity of the family. Either he does not accept them as values, or he puts them so low in his moral scale that he does not see the moral need to *balance* equality against them or to *moderate* its claims with theirs. For him, time has collapsed into the immediate now, and morality has slumped into the achievement of a single end. As all morality for him resides in the end, means are regarded as amoral, and the choice between them is considered a purely technical matter of finding out how effectively to realize the end. Means are considered as nothing but instruments or 'mere means', and have no moral component that could regulate or moderate the pursuit of the end. Since an extremist does not care what means he chooses as long as he achieves his end, the delicate moral weighing up of the different ways of realizing an end has no meaning for him.

A moderate, on the other hand, is a person who recognizes a number of values, and therefore constantly moderates the claims of one with those of others. He pursues a course of action whose moral cost – and there is no moral act that does not sacrifice some moral value – in terms of the values damaged or sacrificed is minimal. He is naturally cautious lest he should unduly disturb people's settled patterns of life or provoke them into a rebellion. But he knows that order is *only* one value, and he would, therefore, be prepared to disregard it if he felt that there were over-riding claims of other values, like equality or justice or freedom. As he values order he would be willing to try peaceful methods; but as he also values justice, he would have to weigh up their respective claims. And he may then decide that, on balance, the claims of justice are greater and that some degree of disorder is therefore morally justified. Thus a moderate is not *necessarily* opposed to violence, nor does he make a fetish of caution. Indeed, if he did, he would be an extremist and not a moderate.

Given this distinction between a moderate and an extremist, the limitations of the liberal view become obvious. The liberal fails to realize that one can be an extremist in one's moderation just as a moderate may have to become an extremist in order to wean away a society from the path of extremism, or in order simply to make the voice of moderation heard. A conservative who would not remedy a grave evil or who would consistently let slip unique opportunities for improving society, on the ground that he cannot be absolutely certain that his measure would not produce any consequence that he had not anticipated, is clearly an extremist in his caution. Extremism is not the monopoly of the dare-devil revolutionary.

Because of his naïve moderation – extremism distinction, the liberal is unable to account for the concept of radicalism, and his tendency is to identify it with extremism. Surely, this is a mistake. Marx, for example, set up goals that were radical, even Utopian, and yet he was prepared to pursue them in a way that did not make their realization excessively costly. He advocated peaceful struggle and agitation, and urged violence only as a method of delivering a society about to be born. He was thus a radical and yet not an extremist. Again, a radical who believes that modern technology opens up clear and realizable possibilities of a new society and agitates to achieve this is not an extremist, but a moderate. A radical can moderate one value with others and use extreme methods only when they are absolutely necessary. In the ultimate analysis, then, the difference between a radical and a moderate is not that one is an extremist and the other is not, or that one is reckless and the other is cautious, but rather that the moderate is far more partial to order and the established practices than the radical, and is inclined to tolerate evils which the radical thinks ought to be rectified and can be rectified without much social upheaval. In defining moderation very narrowly and extremism very widely, the liberal constructs an extremely simple political spectrum that makes it impossible for him to understand the preoccupations and the sensitivities of the radical. What is worse, coming to realize that the liberal is able to communicate with him only if he, the radical, takes an extremist position and thereby fits into his categories, he is constrained to *play* at being an extremist, and, under certain conditions, even to *become* an extremist. Further, having been cast in the image of an extremist, the radical reciprocates by casting the moderate in the image of a conservative or even a reactionary. The result inevitably is not just a political or an ideological polarization but also a moral and an emotional one, with the inevitable breakdown of any sensible dialogue.

II

Because the liberal does not understand why radicals and others feel passionately about certain issues, he generally fails to comprehend their use of violence, and oscillates between extreme determinism and equally extreme volitionalism, between regarding violence as an effect of social forces and regarding it as an act without social antecedents and context. When violence occurs in a liberal democratic society, the conservative tends to see it as an unruly behaviour on the part of the 'misguided' and 'incorrigible' masses, while the radical's immediate reaction is to see it as a justified and proper reaction to the 'tyranny' of the unjust and oppressive social system. The liberal differs from both. Given his theory of rationality, he cannot accept violence as a rational way of redressing grievances. His tendency, therefore, is to look for the *causes* of violence, for those frustrations and grievances that *spark* it off, for those *forces* that create a state of *emotional* tension which seeks *release* on the *slightest provocation*. What is striking in these expressions is that violence is seen as a product of underlying causes and therefore as an act for which its users cannot really be held responsible. Indeed, it is seen as a disease that has to be diagnosed and cured, as a tantrum whose origins, inscrutable to its victims, are to be traced by others. While this approach has the merit of allowing the liberals to express their sympathy for the objectives of violence but their disapproval of its method, and while it salvages their theory of rationality in the face of hostile evidence by enabling them to argue that rational men never resort to violence, and that when they do, it cannot be their conscious choice, it is open to several objections, as we shall presently consider.

As we remarked earlier, there is also the volitionalist streak in the liberal. The liberal approach to violence is what one might call a first-look approach. In determining the responsibility for the use of violence, the liberal asks who started it, who threw the *first* stone, and assumes that whoever threw the first stone was the person really responsible for the trouble. Thus the liberal account of a violent incident generally begins with the expression, 'the trouble started when . . .'. As it is the frustrated victim who generally throws the first stone, all troubles are fathered on him. Thus it is the worker and not the economic system, the poor and not the unjust social order, the native and not the colonial system, that are blamed for violence. Now apart from its extreme superficiality, what is striking about this approach is its ideological analysis of the concept of cause. To equate the first throw with the cause is to arrest the long chain of social causation arbitrarily and conveniently at a point where the blame can be shifted from the system to its victims. Indeed, it is to suggest that the first throw created violence *ex nihilo nihil*. While the liberal analysis of violence has swung between these two extremes of determinism and volitionalism, its concern for justice inclining it towards the former and its concern for order towards the latter, it is the determinist approach that has generally been the more dominant, and, in any case, is far more disturbing.

While the determinist approach is *humane* in the sense that its shows concern for the grievances of those using violence, paradoxically it is also *dehumanizing*. By treating them as unwitting and helpless play-things of external causes, it takes away from them the distinctively human capacity to choose and to accept responsibility for the consequences of their actions. In treating them as men whose actions cannot be seen through their own eyes and in terms of the meaning and significance they themselves attach to them, it refuses to accept them as men capable of undertaking meaningful actions at all. Their actions are *interpreted for* them, and meanings and significance *attributed to* them. Further, as their actions are caused by environmental factors, the basic task is to remove these causes, and obviously the unfortunate victims can hardly be expected to identify and deal with them. The way is cleared for the liberal élitism and paternalism.[2] In classifying human beings into two groups (namely those whose actions can be understood in terms of their intentions and those whose behaviour can only be understood in terms of underlying causes that have to be traced for them by others, those whose behaviour is self-explanatory and those whose behaviour is puzzling and needs explanation), liberalism – and the liberal social science – creates an ideologically-based inequality that is all the more obnoxious and dangerous for being paraded in the name of 'science' and 'rationality'.

The trouble with this approach is that it tends to perpetuate, and even intensify, violence. While some adults might welcome the protective presence of a guardian, others are bound to resent it. And even those who welcome it initially often come to resent it once they grow in confidence and self-respect. Liberals then come to be despised as do-gooders, as men who would run others' lives for them, as men ultimately interested in perpetuating others' dependence on them, as men who would not join them as equals in their fight for justice but who would rather use their privileged position in the system to intercede on their behalf with their friends in power.[3] The angered liberal, shocked by this ingratitude, withdraws his support, or pours venom on the 'illiterate' and 'uncivilized' hooligans, and turns illiberal.

But there is a further, theoretically far more interesting, difficulty with the liberal approach to violence. Unlike the Conservatives who locate rationality in, and indeed define it in terms of, the traditional practices of the community and who therefore regard the historical community alone as fully rational, and unlike the Communists who locate rationality in the process of history, liberals regard it as the unique property of the individual. For them, it is only the individual who can be fully rational, who can collect relevant evidence, weigh it up impartially, dispassionately formulate ends, and devise plans to realize them. The collective or group behaviour in their view necessarily represents the lowest common denominator of rationality. It is capable of having even this minimal degree of rationality only if the behaviour of the collectivity is governed by clearly laid down rules and procedures. As we saw earlier, the liberal conception of rationality is defined in terms of the ability to follow rules. This leads the liberal to divide collective behaviour into that which is institutionalized and that which is not. The former refers to the behaviour of established institutions, of groups that are structured and incorporated into the society and are therefore capable of behaving according to rules. The latter refers to the behaviour of the crowd, of those like the unemployed, the immigrants and the adolescents who are outside the social system and who, being unincorporated and unstructured, are believed incapable of rationality. While the liberal is prepared to credit institutions with some degree of rationality, he cannot see crowd behaviour as anything other than irrational.

Clearly the contrast between individual and group rationality, and the further contrast between institutional rationality and crowd irrationality, are too neat to be tenable. It is simply not true that individual rationality can be dissociated from group rationality. Indeed, individual rationality is largely intelligible only as an aspect of social rationality. When an individual takes a decision in the privacy of his study or the solitude of his inner and autonomous private space, the boundary of his choice is already sketched out for him by the actual alternatives available in his society, and generally the only question for him is which of them he should adopt. What is called calm deliberation and impartial assessment of facts conjures up a rather naïve picture of a sovereign moral individual planning a bold and creative initiative in a dumb and pliable environment, and ignores the fact that the social environment imposes such powerful internal and external constraints on the individual that his deliberation and choice are often no more than a resigned and predictably predetermined response. The dominant ethos of society so conditions the individual consciousness that it is often rendered incapable of imagining that an alternative to the way society and its institutions are run is practicable or even possible. In such a situation the idea of a rational assessment of alternatives sounds hollow. Indeed, rationality, as liberals have defined it, not only becomes impossible but turns into its opposite. To take an example, when the inexorable logic of the bourgeois-industrial society creates industrial giants whose continued existence requires constantly expanding overseas markets and an expansionist foreign policy, it becomes irrational to oppose such a policy, since that would only result in a large-scale unemployment in the country. What would generally be regarded as immoral thus becomes the moral thing to do! To put the point differently, in an irrational society an individual's or a government's rationality may ultimately

77

turn out to be irrational, just as what is called irrational behaviour may be the only rational response to an irrational social situation. In short, almost analogous to the classical question whether man can be good in a bad society, there is the question whether a man can act rationally in an irrational society. The answer in each case is that for the most part he cannot. In considering rationality only from the individual's point of view, the liberal is seriously incapacitated from comprehending the contortions individual rationality suffers under irrational social constraints.

The other contrast between institutional rationality and crowd irrationality also cannot be accepted in its general form. It implies that rule-governed behaviour is necessarily rational and normal. A liberal democrat, no doubt, admits that an institution cannot be as rational as an individual, but he insists that since we need institutions, since institutions can be rational only up to a certain degree, and since their behaviour can be maximally rational only when it is rule-governed, we ensure the highest possible degree of institutional rationality when we set up rules and procedures. The liberal democrat has a clear bias in favour of 'normal channels'. In this procedural and positivist view of rationality, if a decision has been taken after a 'calm' discussion and according to established rules, and if it does not question or deviate from the facts about people's wants, desires and the established social arrangement, it is rational, irrespective of whether those apparently normal men are really capable of discussing issues objectively and critically, whether their calmness is not the result of a closed mind, and whether the so-called facts are not artificial, or rather, contingent necessities created and reinforced by vested interests. It is a sobering thought that slaves have been bought and sold, minorities exterminated, and the Vietnamese butchered by discussions reached through normal channels.

Nor, conversely, is crowd behaviour necessarily irrational either in its objectives or in its use of violence. It may be directed at achieving justice or at fighting a mad and suicidal policy. And violence may be the only way of making an impact. It may then be the expression of the most rational emotion. It is, of course, true that some may engage in riots, because of their carnival atmosphere or because of their contagious influence. But this is no less true of the 'normal' method of social control in which some may join because it gives a protective façade to their sadistic urges, or because it is fun to be on the side that wins or beats people up. Riots, again, are not necessarily formless or senseless, nor are they without a rationale and a rationality. Violence is generally a language through which feelings of desperation are conveyed, and therefore it has a meaning, a sense, and cannot be sense-less. To treat it as sense-less is to deprive the political language of a useful dialect. And when riots are the only way a sluggish authority can be stirred into action, they are clearly rational and certainly more so than those normal and traditional practices that have lost their rationale and only hinder the satisfaction of worthwhile demands. Riots and other forms of violence have a *rationale* when they serve a useful purpose in politics – the purpose of reminding the rulers that their interests are not necessarily identical with those of the entire society, and they have a *rationality* when although those engaged in them are not able to articulate their objectives, they are nevertheless seeking objectives that are fairly specific and defensible.

Because the liberal fails to understand violence, he fails to cope with it either at the theoretical or the practical level. Having taken a highly rationalistic view of reason, the liberal finds violence a freak, mad, marginal and pathological phenomenon in whose presence he feels extremely uneasy and with which he does not know how to deal. As a rationalist, he condemns the method of violence, and yet he is aware of the injustice that provoked the violence in the first instance. The way he resolves his dilemma is clearly illustrated by the way most universities have handled student sit-ins. In case after case,[4] the liberal university vice-chancellors and especially the liberal staff have argued that *both* the university and the students were *equally* to blame, and that they should both make small concessions symbolic of their continuing goodwill and agree to bury the bygones. In almost every case, the real issue was left undecided. When everybody is blamed and deemed guilty – the staff, the students, the administrators, wider society, the government – responsibility is diffused and no one can be blamed. The obvious result is that the liberal approach promotes neither the respect for the law nor the cause of justice, and as we shall presently see, it sows seeds of further violence in the future. At the theoretical level, the liberal position is in a mess and does not rest on any clear principle. If the 'disorder' was the result of a grave injustice and if this was the only way the injustice could have been 'dramatized', disorder should be welcomed and injustice immediately rectified. If, on the other hand, there was no grievance underlying it, the law should take its toll.

In burying the bygones and in refusing to take a clear stand, what the liberal does is to deprive the act of violence (or of sit-in) of its concentrated impact. As the basic issues are not discussed, the act is trivialized and its meaning is destroyed. And in fudging the issue by introducing endless and dubious qualifications in a spirit of misconceived objectivity, the liberal divests the debate of a focus, of a nucleus. A unique deed is dissolved into an 'interesting incident'; the moral energy and moral attention of the community that should have been concentrated on the substantive issue are diffused over a large range of procedural and trivial concerns. The result is that an event is wasted, an opportunity is lost, and each party, not yet shown if it is wrong and how, feels cheated of its prize and waits for the next occasion when it can strike more forcibly to get what it wants. Unwilling to exercise authority lest he should appear authoritarian, unwilling to use force lest he should appear illiberal, and equally reluctant to face the issue squarely lest he should have to restructure the institution radically, the schizophrenic liberal, torn between conflicting sympathies, is content to defuse controversies and thereby unwittingly invites further violence.

III

How then should we conceive violence? And how should we respond to it? As it is not possible here to consider these in any depth, we can only sketch tentatively the broad outlines of an alternative approach.

We can agree minimally that the political society exists in order that its members can live a good life in an ordered manner. The maintenance of order requires that the right to use force should be concentrated in the hands of the State, and citizens should be forbidden to use force except in clearly outlined situations. The State, however, is not a chance crowd of men who happen to live together, but a historical and cohesive community of men who share a common way of life and a common identity, and whose lives criss-cross and overlap in so many ways that they have developed a sense of concern for one another. Ultimately, it is nothing short of an institutionalization of sympathy in space and time. It therefore aims to create conditions in which its members can live a good life. What these conditions are, if and how best they can be secured by law, and what type of order is the most desirable, are questions on which its members, being capable of independent thought, hold different views. On occasions they feel passionately about certain issues and feel so outraged and revolted by the actions of their government or of their fellow-citizens that they think they must take a stand and fight – with force if necessary. Whether they use violence to attract attention to their grievances, or to secure political visibility, or to communicate a sense of desperation and urgency, or to pressurize the government into deciding an issue in a certain definite direction, it is their conscious and deliberate choice. Even the most spontaneous and unpremeditated acts of violence involve an ineliminable element of choice, since no matter how unbearable their miseries, men are never mere puppets in the hands of their environment.

As a deliberate act of responsible beings who know what they are doing, violence deserves two responses. It clearly violates the law, and must therefore be disapproved and punished. At the same time, it is an act that is clearly aimed at attaining certain objectives, and therefore other members of the community are obliged to enter into a dialogue with those using violence to determine how desirable their objectives are and how best they can be achieved. The two responses are integrally related. Offenders can be punished only because they are regarded as responsible beings, as men who are capable of forming intentions and accepting responsibility for their actions; but then if they are regarded as responsible beings, none of their actions can be dismissed as 'irresponsible' or 'irrational'. That is to say, the authority can punish them *only* on condition that it is prepared to listen to them, to enter into a dialogue with them, and to join them in co-operatively exploring the nature and ways of meeting their demands. Conversely, the offenders are obliged to accept the punishment if they are to be justified in asking the government to enter into a dialogue with them, since in asking the government to do so, they are asking it to treat them as responsible citizens, and this implies that they are willing to accept the authority of its laws. In a sentence, violence can be punished only on condition that its objectives are taken seriously. Except in the case of a slave, all obligations are reciprocal; if the government does not fulfil its duties the citizen cannot be asked to fulfil his, and vice versa.

There is a further point. As the use of violence generally[5] involves violating a law, it has to be disapproved. But it may have been intended to dramatize the iniquity of a law or of a policy, or to wean the community away from insanity. Its objectives, then, are clearly laudable, and its use deserves to be approved and commended. That is to say, though the *initial* judgement on violence has to be one of disapproval, the *ultimate* judgement might be different. To put the point schematically, political judgement on the use of violence is made in two stages. At the first stage, one asks if a person has really violated a law, and one determines his guilt or innocence. At the second stage, one asks why he, a responsible being, chose to violate the law, and one asks what his objectives were – if they were laudable and whether violence was the only way to achieve them. If his action was intended to draw the community's attention to an unjust law, or to an iniquitous political decision, or to a mad foreign policy, or to a bureaucratic perversion of a legitimate demand, it was clearly intended to enrich and improve the community, and was thus guided by the highest considerations of political duty. Indeed, it is the fault of the community that one of its loyal members had felt compelled to risk his life, liberty and reputation to wean it away from an unjust and irrational policy.

The question whether violence was the only way to achieve these objectives is very difficult to answer. In a liberal democracy, various methods of peaceful pressure are available to a citizen, which he should first exhaust before resorting to violence. However, 'exhausting all the peaceful means' is a slippery concept, since in a sense no means is ever exhausted. Like the Vietnam peace negotiations in Paris, one can always turn up at a negotiation-table week after week and year after year, just as one can keep demonstrating in front of the Pentagon all one's life in the hope that one day people will see the value of peace. The concept of 'exhausting all the peaceful means', therefore, has to be defined somewhat narrowly to mean trying peaceful methods *as long as* they evoke a well-intentioned and serious response from the government. When, for example, negotiations are reduced to repetitive soliloquies or to a public relations exercise, they are likely to be found futile. One also needs to ask if the peaceful methods that may require years to yield results are, on balance, morally better than the continuance of an evil for such a long time. After a careful moral calculation, one might conclude that, on balance, the moral price is not worth paying and that one ought to try other means to remedy an evil rather than wait until the possibilities of peaceful persuasion are exhausted. Negro slavery most certainly eventually would have been abolished in America, but would it have been morally and politically rational to let it continue for another hundred years simply because one felt one ought to 'exhaust' all peaceful means? One might even conclude that by always insisting on exhausting all the peaceful means one might so wear out the patience of the community that the peaceful means might come to be discredited, and that it is therefore in the interest of peaceful methods themselves that one should not make ideological fetish of them.

Legally speaking, then, political violence, like any other type of violence, has to be disapproved, but politically it may be judged to be desirable. Of the two, the political point of view is higher. Law exists to serve the purposes of the political society and derives its significance from its ability to realize them. It therefore loses its rationale, and even its rationality, and therefore its power to oblige, when obeying it is likely to destroy or weaken the basis or frustrate the purposes of the political society. Indeed, as we observed earlier, underlying every law is a preference for a particular form of political order, and therefore it has ultimately to be judged in terms of the desirability of that political order. This means that while the legal point of view determines the legal guilt or innocence of the agent, the political point of view determines whether there are considerations that *attenuate* his guilt and even *exonerate* him. Thus, if the objectives of a person using violence were laudable and if he had done his best to attain them peacefully, his legal guilt is over-ridden by higher political considerations. If, on the other hand, his objectives were laudable but he had acted precipitately and without regard to the constitutional methods available to him, his guilt is at best attenuated. In either case, the theoretically important point is that his legal guilt is not *cancelled* or *negated*, because then he would have to be considered innocent, which is clearly not the case. He has violated a law and therefore from the legal point of view he remains guilty. What the political point of view has done is to *over-ride* or *supersede* or *diminish* his guilt.

If what has been said so far is correct, it follows that we must draw a clear distinction between criminal and political violence. While the former springs from anti-social motives and involves using society for one's private ends, the latter arises from the desire to change the community and involves risking one's life for the sake of what one takes to be the community's well-being. As they are different, they are clearly subject to different criteria of evaluation, and therefore it is odd that acts of political violence, which are essentially political and not merely legal acts, should be adjudicated by judges whose training and background and professional tradition equip them to judge all acts only from a narrow legal point of view. Of course, despite the liberal belief, judges never, as indeed they cannot ever, do this in practice, since neither the law nor the evidence is ever entirely unambiguous; it has to be interpreted and evaluated, thus opening the door to the intervention of political preferences, as the Chicago trial in America and the trial of Cambridge students in England so dramatically showed. By definition, a political act raises political issues and can be judged properly only in political terms. Take, for example, a group of people who feel most strongly that their government's policy with respect to another country is muddled, immoral, arrogant and unable to promote their real interests. They try to argue with the government but it refuses, or misleads them by giving false information, or lies to them or deceives them in a number of ways, all too familiar. In sheer desperation, the people concerned engage in acts of violence, say, burning a minister's car and a few public vehicles. The government rounds them up and prosecutes them. The judge, concerned simply to enforce the law, asks if the men in question have violated a law; and as they clearly have, he puts them behind bars. When the political protesters start explaining why they violated the law and what they were really after, the judge rejoins that he is not interested in political questions and that his role is simply to enforce the law. What appears to the former as the crux of the matter, as its very essence, is dismissed by the judge as utterly irrelevant to his judgement of it. These men protest against the judge's behaviour and verdict on the ground that while the judge was right to conclude that they had violated the law, he was wrong not to see that their act of violation was only one aspect of their total act; indeed, that it was only incidental and instrumental to what they were really trying to do, namely to arouse the community to awareness of a gross moral evil. Their act, in their view, was essentially *political*, and that is how it ought to have been judged. To judge the act solely or even primarily on the basis of its undoubted, but incidental, illegality seems to them tantamount to judging the total act on the basis of only a part of it; indeed, it seems to them that the judge was judging not the *same* but *another* related act.

We are thus confronted with a serious philosophical problem. It seems wrong to judge an essentially political act solely on legal grounds. And yet the radical alternative – that the judges should take account of the political issues involved in a case – is clearly unsatisfactory. Judges may be Fascists, and this the radical clearly would not like. What is more, political issues are highly complicated and judges cannot pretend to any expertise in solving them. Besides, while the radical alternative is right to suggest that law and politics cannot be separated in the way the liberal theory of separation of powers assumes, it is wrong to go to the opposite extreme of fusing the two. This would take away from the law the ability to realize the objectives of certainty, predictability and reasonable impartiality that it exists to secure. In any case, the fusion of the political and the judicial function is unnecessary, because in almost every community the political process retains ultimate control over the judicial process. In all criminal cases, it is the government that is the prosecutor and therefore it is free to decide whether or not to prosecute a person. Again, it is the government that has the ultimate right to alter the judicial sentence by means of a pardon and other such prerogatives. Thus both what goes into the judicial process and what ultimately comes out of it are subject, rightly, to overall political supervision. Any greater degree of control would only end up by corrupting *both* the judicial and the political process. It is natural that when one is dissatisfied with one set of people, namely politicians, one should wish to turn to others, namely judges. But this would not do.

Professor Dworkin[6] has suggested that one way out of the dilemma outlined earlier would be for the government not to prosecute protesters when they are guided by high political motives, when the community itself is gravely divided on the issue in question, and when the action of the government does not enjoy the unqualified support of the legislature. The argument could be extended further to imply that the judges themselves should take a more charitable view of the protesters in this type of situation. Professor Joseph Sax[7] has suggested that there is much to be said for a trial by jury in such obviously political cases. As he shows so distinctly, the history of the jury system and the great eighteenth-century debate about its powers shows clearly how its powers were increased precisely in order to deal with this type of political situation. Professor Sax's argument could be carried even further, and we could argue that while it does not make sense to cast jurors in the role of political experts, or in that of a mini-legislature sitting in judgement on the government's policy, they could certainly be expected to take a broader view of the acts of the protesters and to ask themselves if the general community, of which they are a reliable barometer, is genuinely split on the issue, and what view the community as a whole is likely to take of the acts of the protesters. As the law lays down the maximum penalty for the act, the jurors cannot err on the side of political vengeance.

Ultimately, however, the question of violence is not a judicial but a political question, and it is only at the political level that it can be tackled. Thus whether the government will decide to prosecute criminals or not, or what attitude the jurors will take towards the political violence of their fellow-citizens, depends on the general attitude towards political violence prevalent in the community. And here, as outlined earlier, it is essential that we should learn to see violence as a political and not a pathological phenomenon. It is not unknown for posterity to honour as great benefactors those men who were punished as criminals by their contemporaries. Besides, we do condone, and indeed, honour, the violence of those who have used it in the interest of the community as, for example, in a civil or an international war, or in an act of espionage, or in thwarting a robbery. The fact that political acts generally reveal their significance only after years and decades, and the fact that the historical judgement, which is based on the full knowledge of all the consequences of an act, is the only wholly satisfactory judgement on it, ought to incline us to take a larger historical view of our contemporaries and their actions. To put the point differently, our approach to violence needs to be politicized, and our approach to politics historicized. Only then would our evaluation of political violence have satisfied the two most basic criteria of political judgement – that the act performed and the act judged should be the same, and that the act should not be judged on the basis of the impulsive reaction it provokes but on the fullest possible knowledge of its actual consequences and historical potentialities.

NOTES

1. For a fuller discussion of how liberal morality is essentially civil morality and lacks both a political and an internal subjective dimension, see my Introduction in Bhikhu Parekh (ed.), *Dissent and Disorder* (World University Service of Canada, 1971).

2. 'There is something impertinent in the assumptions they [the liberals] make about me', James Baldwin in 'Liberalism and the Negro: A Roundtable Discussion', *Commentary* (March 1964), p. 37.

3. Gunnar Myrdal cynically remarks, 'I think the most encouraging thing which has happened in America in recent years is the rebellion of the Negro group, because that rebellion will help the liberals to get into power and do the job that has to be done', *Commentary*, op. cit., p. 42.

4. See, for example, Louis and Mary Lusky, 'Columbia 1968: The Wound Unhealed', *Political Science Quarterly* (June 1969).

5. In almost every society there are occasions when violence is permitted by the government as, for example, on a student rag day, and when it is required by it, as, for example, in a war. But these cases of ritualized violence are not relevant for our present purpose.

6. 'On Not Prosecuting Civil Disobedience', *New York Review of Books* (6 June 1968).

7. 'Conscience and Anarchy', *Yale Review* (June 1968).

IV Three Languages of Change: Democracy, Technocracy and Direct Action

ELIZABETH VALLANCE

My main concern here is to compare and contrast the language of representative democracy – its framework and assumptions – with the language of direct action. Even at a superficial level, the two are clearly different. The radical protester, for example, is often at pains to dissociate himself from the connotations of the orthodox political language by referring to the same empirical elements by a quite different terminology. Thus convicted murderers (within the democratic framework) become 'political prisoners', affluence transforms into 'alienation', or low labour costs become 'starvation wages'. These different denotations, I would claim, are based on a contrasting framework of assumptions and perspectives. Those involved are, in fact, playing different games. But playing different games, having different frameworks, need not in practice mean total incompatibility. To illustrate this, I shall look briefly at the framework and language of technocracy, which unlike that of direct action seems to have been easily, not to say eagerly, assimilated by that of representative democracy. Throughout the chapter, in referring to 'direct action' and 'representative democracy' (or 'orthodox politics'), I have in mind something like an ideal type of these activities, the main elements of which will, I hope, become clear as I continue. I am, of course, aware that some forms of what might be thought of as direct action are quite compatible with representative democracy as presented, but it is my contention that such activities have been assimilated into the representative system by accepting its frame of reference (value structure, ranking of priorities, etc.). To this extent, within my scheme, they are better understood as part of the structure of representative democracy rather than of direct action.

Wittgenstein's notion of a 'language-game' is useful in this context in a number of ways. It emphasizes the diffuse social bases of language and it underlines the importance of the acceptance of the rules of the language-game by those involved in it. Ideas are given clear meaning in language, only so long as these rules are accepted, and, although to challenge them is not impossible, it has no meaning within the framework of the game. (You can 'checkmate' the Queen, but you can't call this game chess.) Changes in the rules can only be brought about with the full recognition and approval of the body controlling the procedure of the game (in the language-game context – society). Seen in these terms, when two groups talk about the same external circumstances in quite dissimilar terms, they are using two language-games – two sets of rules and assumptions.

Language is an important point of contact with the world; it is also an important means of communication between people. But language does not only describe the world, nor is it simply something we use to express ourselves. The world we describe is not a 'thing'; a single unequivocal whole which itself sets the limits of the language which we use to try and make sense of it. Rather language itself is important in shaping our impressions by limiting the possibilities of our world, so making it more manageable and familiar. Every society has its conventions, its values, its world-pictures, and these are enshrined in its language-games. ('To imagine a language,' says Wittgenstein, 'is to imagine a form of life.'[1])

Words do not 'mean', rather they are used to convey meaning, and what is conveyed depends as much on the hearer as on the speaker. Conveying 'accurate' meaning then depends largely on the hearer and speaker having a common 'form of life' – shared assumptions and values, shared conceptual frameworks. Thus, the commonly-accepted background of assumptions and values within a community will give meaning to the basic abstract vocabulary of its politics – a vocabulary that would otherwise be ambivalent, and literally meaningless.

It is not very difficult to get outside the confines of any particular language-game on a purely conceptual level. All one has to do, in Wittgenstein's terms, is imagine another 'form of life' which gives rise to another language-game. (We can make sense of the form of life, and hence understand the language-game of the Pueblo Indians, even when we do not share it.) But to conceptualize, to understand externally the form of life, the assumptions and framework of another culture is not the same as accepting it internally, for ourselves. In politics, where the aim is not merely to understand or to conceptualize, but to persuade, it is difficult to step outside the conventional framework of a particular system. The connotations of a particular political language-game are set by an audience committed to these connotations. To go outside of these is to invite misunderstanding and the charge of irrelevance. This is so because political terms are so often not realistic descriptions of a situation which can be challenged simply by pointing to discrepancies between 'description' and 'reality' but symbols, evocative of the social attitudes of the community involved. On this level, any criticism of the accepted community norms – such as those implicit in direct action – are bound to be resisted. Loyalty and intensity of belief are strengthened by the very language in which political issues are discussed, and often some of the possibilities of a situation will go unrecognized, simply because the framework of the language-game does not allow them to develop.

The boundaries of meaning in political language are to a great extent set by the accepted value pattern and political symbols of the particular society in which the language-game is played. And again, the connotations of the terms of political discourse are not themselves simply formed by an individual or group imposing their 'meaning' on those terms. Political discourse is, if not an autonomous development, at least a development affected more by social norms and patterns than by individual decisions as to meaning. Marshall McLuhan seems to be making this point when he says, 'A language is, on the one hand, little affected by the use individuals make of it; but, on the other hand, it almost entirely patterns the character of what is thought, felt or said by those using it.'[2]

This much can, I think, be said about the social texture of language in general and clearly has special significance for such a verbal and symbolic activity as politics. But what of the structure and style of political language itself in so-called democratic societies? Political language shares the preconceptions and the symbolic uses imposed by the social framework, but it has, over and above these, its own particular norms and objectives enshrined in its language-game. A key example is the acceptance of compromise, and of the weighing of positions and interests, as a *sine qua non* of political action. If politics is about the allocation of values, competing claims for such values will have to be mediated and conciliated. If interests were not diverse, or if 'values' were not scarce, there would be no need for the compromise which is the characteristic feature of this level of political activity. Political language here is characterized by its wide perspective and its assumptions of the political role as the identification and pursuance of the most suitable policy, in over-all terms, in the situation. Even so-called 'ideological' politics, where compromising the ideology would seem to be impossible, can often be seen in this framework. The ideology – the principles – come to be considered as only one facet among many of the over-all situation. Their status as 'principle' (and hence uncompromisable) is devalued, so that they become simply a factor to be given some weight in the final decision, but not the exclusive privilege of determining what is done. This is not, of course, to say that decisions are not very often justified and explained in terms of political principle. Policies are often presented in terms either of the general value symbols of the community (such and such a policy is 'humane' or 'democratic') or, less frequently perhaps, in terms of the published principles of the government ('. . . as stated in our election manifesto . . .'). But here, justifying a policy in terms of a principle is not at all the same thing as pursuing a policy because of a principle. This is a point where, as I'll later want to say, direct actionists and orthodox political actors diverge considerably. They are involved in different language-games, and confusion arises when either or both assume that similar words (denotations) mean similar frameworks and hence connotations.

I think that some such referential framework as I've outlined here is assumed in most Western-style democracies. Politics proceeds on the assumption of many constraints on the situation, and the political art is taken to be determination of what policy can feasibly be pursued in this situation. Associated with this is also the need to limit the number of alternatives, and to convey, in a manner gauged to win support, the decisions of the political sphere. Since one of the myths associated with democratic politics is that the government 'puts into practice' the will of the electorate on specific issues, the government must appear to consider public opinion (and will consider to a greater or lesser extent that it does this, for it too is subject to the conceptual framework of democracy). But public opinion left to itself may become public opinions of such diversity and number as to be quite unmanageable from the politician's point of view and extremely emotionally disturbing from the public's point of view – disturbing because part of the psychological force of democratic politics is the feeling that participation is significant and that the government is clearly influenced by the will of the people. Having a huge number of differing viewpoints, however, blurs the lines on which the government is seen to be taking its decision. The majority will cannot be seen to be implemented, or even given significant consideration, when there is no clear majority position. And so another part of the political role, mirrored in orthodox political language, is that it is the place of the political sphere to identify the political problems – to limit the legitimate political alternatives – in any particular situation. This simplification means that politicians themselves can define the problem on which the electorate is then supposed to make its opinions known. Simultaneously, the electorate is made to feel secure in the knowledge that the issues with which it is concerned are 'the real political issues.' Often, this kind of identification of the issues results in the defusing of these as politically contentious. The problem is presented, that is, as an administrative or technical one, rather than as one involving a real choice of alternatives. (Not whether we go into the Common Market, but whether we take three or six years to become fully integrated; not whether we have a third London airport, but where it is to be sited.) I shall return to this aspect later.

If this outline characterizes to some extent the political language-game, it is now possible to see the extent to which, and the ways in which, other language-games impinge upon, relate to, modify or are assimilated by the political. I propose to look at two of these – very briefly at the technocratic framework, and in more detail at that of direct action. I think that the way in which the technocratic framework has been absorbed by and assimilated to the political shows up some of the reasons why that of direct action has not. (After all, technocracy is a relatively new development which has yet been rapidly accepted by the political realm; direct action in democracies, on the other hand, has quite a long history during which governments could surely have accommodated it if they had been able to.) Both technocracy and direct action seem to have strong claims to be heard in a political context, in that both seem to suggest certain priorities in political decision-making. But, I shall argue that technocratic language is both necessary to and usable by the orthodox political participant in a way that the framework of direct action is clearly not. And the former is assimilable to orthodox politics partly because of the 'ambivalence' of its language which, though perhaps technically precise (that is precise in its own context), can be used in a number of ways by the political sphere.

If political language is concerned with expressing what can be done given the limitations and constraints of a situation, technocratic language is set in terms of what must be done given a certain rational frame of reference. To this extent the two seem incompatible. The impulse of the politician is to recognize and choose between shades of grey, of the technocrat to put a case in terms of black and white. And the present political concern with experts at every level (as evidenced in Britain by, for example, the Fulton Report, the emphasis on specialist committees in suggestions for Commons' Reform, and even the recent creation of an 'interdisciplinary advisory committee' to the Cabinet) is, I think, only partly a matter of conscious policy. It is much more a matter of diffuse social pressure and of the realization of the 'halo effect' which surrounds an administration clearly committed to the rationality of the expert, as opposed to what is, probably mistakenly, seen as the only alternative – amateurish intuition.

So it is fair to say that technocratic language would probably have found its way into politics whether the politicians had wanted it to or not. As it is, it has been positively welcomed into the political embrace. This has been possible partly because politics still insists on its own autonomy and supremacy: the economist, sociologist and physicist are seen as presenting partial views of the situation on which it is still the place of the politician finally to decide. His is the overall view which must surely (it is solemnly agreed) take into account the various expert opinions. In practice, of course, it is often very difficult for the political actor to repudiate the findings of an expert inquiry. If he does, he is laying himself open to criticism for reverting to intuitive (that is, in this case, pre-rational) modes of thought. This was, for example, exactly the kind of criticism which met President Nixon's refusal to endorse the findings of the Committee on the Social Effects of Pornography and Obscenity (which consisted almost entirely of experts).

I have already mentioned as characteristic of the political framework, the specification or definition of the issues, which often involves their reduction to the uncontentious level. It seems clear that the technocratic framework has been absorbed so easily into the political not only because the political can finally claim autonomy, can claim simply to be using the various partial frameworks of the various expert positions in coming to an overall political decision, but perhaps mainly because, given the present esteem in which the technocrat tends to be held in Western societies, it is a valuable political weapon to be able to quote his findings. In other words, technocratic findings are used less often in actually making political decisions than in justifying them. In this way, controversial issues of public policy may be removed from the language-game of political debate and put into that of uncontentious, apolitical, technocratic 'fact'. And, since no non-expert, and certainly not the political, really knows what the specialist language and technical detail mean, or are worth, what is utilized is not the actual finding of the expert, but merely his prestige in contemporary society as the new philosopher King. (I am aware that this analysis is not normally applied to the relationship between politics and technocracy, but it seems to me often to fit the facts of present political experience better than that analysis which points out the dangers of technocratic takeover. But the danger for democratic practice seems to be more in the realm of the politicians' symbolic use of technocratic findings.)

Even in the case of Nixon mentioned above, where one would seem to have an example of a politician confounded by the experts and forced to take up a position against them, I think one can see experts being skilfully and politically used. The President rejected the Committee's report because he wanted to impress on his silent majority that he was not carried away by the supposed findings of liberal, intellectual specialists, and that the moral and aesthetic values of white, Anglo-Saxon, middle-class America would not be further eroded by his endorsement. He was, in fact, using the experts to appeal to the people against the experts.

In whatever ways it is used, technocratic language is useful to and extends political language. Compromise is still necessary (even as between differing expert opinions) and the over-all political perspective is seen as being enhanced by more precise information in particular areas. If the technocrat is simply kept in his place, the technocratic framework can only be useful to the political in its tasks, for example, of framing the public's political concerns, and having decisions, however arrived at, accepted with the minimum of dissent by the electorate.

The same cannot be said, however, for the language and assumptions of direct action. Direct action I take in its widest sense to be any challenge to the competence of the political arm which results in private individuals taking the initiative by directly opposing the political line on a certain policy or policies by acting against them. As I have said, it might intuitively be thought that the assumptions of politics and technocracy were incompatible; it might equally be assumed that the underlying assumptions of orthodox politics and direct action might be assimilable. After all, both are concerned with the political task of ordering priorities and changing the existing situation in some significant respect. Whereas, however, political language could quickly take account of the technocratic framework (and indeed capitalize on it), the same is certainly not true of the framework of direct action. This is, I think, an outcome of the assumptions which lie behind the language-game of the latter, and which challenge many of the assumptions of the orthodox democratic political language-game.

If politics speaks the language of what can be done (given constraints and a wide perspective), and technocracy the language of what must be done, because rational, direct action speaks the language of what must be done, because right. Clearly there is some initial incompatibility between the first and the last of these. In abstract terms, if something is right, it is incontestable and uncompromisable, and it must be followed. If something is wrong, it must be totally opposed. There is no satisfaction in having principle partially instated. Either we disarm unilaterally, or we do not; either a cricket tour is cancelled, or it is not. To this extent, the language of direct action poses an initial problem for the orthodox political framework. Because the latter is accustomed to the language of conciliation and compromise – the language of bargaining – this is almost the basis of its whole viewpoint. Many interests will have to be given a say, and the game ceases to work if anyone breaks the rules by insisting that his hand is the only one which can be played. So at this level, the two languages are running on parallel lines, neither accepting the pre-conditions of the other, and both perhaps slightly perplexed by what appears to be the naïveté or corruption of the other.

The orthodox politician here can be hamstrung by the conception of politics as fundamentally a negotiating activity, if these people, the protesters, are seen within this framework as articulating interests (albeit in a very unconventional way). They are then seen as easily dealt with by the usual methods, that is, by seeing how far their interest if considered politically relevant, can be accommodated when other pressures and perspectives are taken into account. But this whole approach forces direct action into the mould of the conventional interest group, which has itself become a part of the political system and shares the language and presuppositions of that system. Most successful interest groups accept the framework of negotiation; their success seems to depend on working within the political mentality of the market-place. They do not oppose the system itself; they accept the rules of the game; they know that they must often ask for four to get two, and so compromise is as much a part of their language (although perhaps not as explicitly) as that of government.

But, on the other hand, behind direct action must be the assumption that the system itself is faulty. If it were not so, if democracy were, as its symbols and myths proclaim, responsible to public opinion and reactive to social evils, the need for direct action itself would disappear. The very existence of this form of expression carries an implicit criticism of the existing political framework. And so, the political system is not accepted by this group; for them, compromise is not a norm (you do not compromise principle); when they ask for four, they mean four, not two; they are not willing to let the politicians decide the relative merits of their case among others; they act without asking for permission.

What direct action does, then, is to sin against the rules of the conventional political language-game in a number of ways. Because of this, the orthodox reaction can only be either to try and force the phenomenon into its own framework – see it, that is, as conventional interest articulation – or to deny it any sort of intelligibility at all. This latter reaction means that the activist is seen as being in a state of nature as it were, in relation to the rest of the community (represented by the political realm), and can accordingly be disciplined by the community. His demands, at any rate, are not to be taken seriously by the community, or if they are, they are taken over, presented and directed in a manner chosen by the politicians.

This latter notion, of the political lead in the choice of issues, leads to another basic incompatibility between conventional politics and direct action. They have very different perspectives on the selection and presentation of issues. I've said that part of the job of the democratic politician is seen as being to present the political problems and priorities to the general public. The choice of which issues are the 'important' ones at any particular time is an outcome of political decision. There is no particular reason why law and order should be the dominant political concern of a certain period, any more than say housing, or education. All could be presented as equally pressing. But the politicians perhaps feel capable of making a better case, showing more laudable concern and winning more support on the one than on the others. And so, for a time certain issues drop into limbo, while others are developed and debated with fervour.

This is not simply a matter of corrupt manipulation of the public, which is often the implication of the radicals' emphasis on the contrast between moral political activism and immoral political manipulation, the contrast between putting the issues straight and distorting and defusing them. For within the language-game of politics, the presentation of issues is an important job of the politician. The selection of which concerns are to be taken up now, in what order of priority, and often the specification in quite definite terms of what the problems 'really' are, these are all seen as quite legitimate and necessary activities within the system. This is not, then, some highly organized conspiracy consciously attempting to deprive the people of their right of choice; it is simply the quite practical response to the requirement of support mobilization, and the best way to get most people marching together is to make sure that they are all marching to the same tune.

Similarly, the attempt so often to defuse the political issues, and to present them as simply non-contentious administrative or technical problems, overcomes the chaos which would result if everybody really did have an opinion and expected it to be directly taken into account.

These presuppositions are just that – presuppositions. The orthodox framework which has developed is only one possible framework, but it is of course, so all-pervasive in Western-style democracies that it becomes for most people the only intelligible point of view. It is seen as 'how things are', and the language and symbols in which the system is examined and explained lend credence to this belief, because that language itself sets so many of the limits of examination and explanation. It is not, in fact, thought of as a point of view at all. One is reminded of the lady who, when asked by the pollster about her political allegiance, replied irritably, 'Young man, I'm not interested in politics: I am a Conservative.' Conceptual frameworks, points of view, are often only identifiable from the outside: from the inside one's conceptual framework is one's world.

Seen against this background then, direct action is, when not totally unintelligible to the orthodox position, a direct reversal of much that makes up that position. For direct action, compromise makes politics a dubious enterprise; and the pre-packing of political issues is clearly unacceptable. For here, the whole aim of direct action is to choose the issues, to ignite instead of defuse, to question the priorities, to refuse to be content with a choice on issues which are themselves seen as inherently irrelevant (or at least of secondary importance), or as presented in such a way as to make them so. Professor Galbraith makes a similar point on economic choice when he talks about the naïveté of assuming market control as a consumer protection.[3] The idea is that the consumer is sovereign, and what is produced and consumed can only be a manifestation of the wants of consumers. But what they want, as Galbraith points out, is quite obviously decided not by their free choice, unimpeded by external factors. The market itself is determined to a large extent by the manufacturers who have geared their production and marketing accordingly. It is the producer who is sovereign, and Galbraith stresses the manipulation of wants by means of the projection of images and the appeal of symbols. Consumer choice, he points out, can only be exercised among the alternatives which producers choose to make available. The public, one might say, did not suddenly wake up one morning desiring above all things, stripes in their tooth-paste: they were rather brought to realize the immense advantages – social, cosmetic, aesthetic and even dental – of this desirable commodity. Their choice is then limited to whether they buy it or not, and strong social pressures make it likely that they will. The parallel with politics is, I think, quite clear. Within the orthodox sphere, the marketing of pre-packaged choices is very important, and clearly seems necessary if the consensus element of democratic politics is to be maintained. Again, this cannot be fully explained in terms of some spectacular conspiracy theory, but in terms of the framework and priorities of conventional political practice. The challenge of direct action is on the level of the language-game itself: exercising consumer choice (with all its inherent limitations) is not enough. Far more important from the point of view of this challenge is to go back a step and actually determine the choices themselves.

Goals and ends in politics are often utilized as symbols of society's image of itself, of where it is going, eventually, because it is that kind of society. They are much less often actually realistic programmes of action. They are used, that is, to show that what is being done should be acceptable to a public sensitive to the evocative notions of a 'freer', more 'humane', 'more equal', etc. kind of society. And oppositions equally use the same accepted goals to suggest that surely we are not (and we all know that we are not) the kind of society which allows schoolchildren to go without their milk and school meals, so that we can have sixpence off income-tax. The goals themselves are comfortingly equivocal, so that they can be used to make such appeals in almost any political circumstances; and, so that they satisfy a great many perhaps incompatible outlooks of public and government. Thus, conflict is reduced by each seeing its own viewpoint as admirably expressed in the suggested goals.

And so, political issues are marketed and political policies decided on by the politicians. They cannot, of course, just decide on anything; total arbitrariness is limited, if not constitutionally, at least to some extent by the established values of the society. For although these values themselves are hardly explicitly definable, they have at least developed conventional connotations and relations to certain empirical situations, which make them clearly unsuitable justifications for certain policies. Still, many possible policies could be shown to be compatible with these values, and could, therefore, be justified in terms of them. So that the politicians have pretty wide discretion on issue and policy choice at any particular time.

Direct action, however, insists not only on deciding its own issues and priorities, but on the notion that such priority decisions, once made by the people, should then be put into practice by government. Goals are not then merely symbolic (although they may be that too). They articulate real aims which should be filled out by concrete policy action. This reverses a significant, if often unacknowledged, part of the conventional framework, and confuses the orthodox practitioner. And he may not know why he is confused, because he is not consciously manipulating public concern; he feels that he does share the direct actionists' notion of democratic participation; but he works within a framework where democratic participation has to be controlled and exploited as part of the pragmatic response of the practical politician to the problem of 'getting things done'.

Perhaps the most disconcerting aspect of direct action for the politician is its refusal to talk. A case is not presented, it is acted on. There may have been talk at some point, not bargaining talk, but demands put and either shelved or refused. But, by the time direct action is reached, the time of parleying is passed. Talk, on the other hand, is the whole basis of politics – to persuade, to inform, to order. When a group does talk with the political sphere, it must be within the bargaining framework. Some direct action may, I think, be seen as an attempt to get in a better bargaining position. The Palestinian hijackings were direct action, but they did not end with either the actions themselves or with immediate political agreement to demands. Rather, the hijackers became conventionally political when they began to trade on the basis of their position, when they agreed to compromise, to a share in the political cake. At this point, they were accepting the political language-game, whereas their original action repudiated it. But still, they have to some extent defeated the system in forcing a government to accept their definition of the priorities, to take account of their claim in their terms, and not in its own. They have dictated the importance of the issue, and have not given government the chance to decide to relegate their claims.

But it is uncertain whether any group of direct actionists, having got to this stage, will be able to maintain their original position of strength. They seem to have achieved a compelling position *vis à vis* government, for the moment. But, in stepping back into the conventional political bargaining framework, they have *ipso facto*, at the least lost some of their mystique. Government can now deal with them in its own terms: they seem no longer such an unknown factor. Rather they are seen as advancing claims which the political arm has simply conventionally to take into account. And the impulse of government is always to capitalize on the fact that it now feels itself to be back in command. It will, therefore, try to take the initiative from the radicals and itself control the developments originally begun by direct action. President Johnson's War on Poverty, for example, is a case of an administration's attempt to institutionalize, and so control, the direct action in the ghettos. The war, as Peter Buckman says, 'was created, inspired and executed by the affluent governing élite which, reluctant to relinquish any part of the decision-making, ran the programme, despite promises to the contrary, in a manner described by those for whom it was intended, as "welfare colonialism".'[4] Buckman's description throughout suggests a huge conspiracy theory; and the situation may, as he suggests, be lamentable; it is also quite understandable. Not, I think in terms of the conspiracy notion, but in terms of the orthodox political framework. A government cannot allow itself to appear out of its depth for long and still maintain democratic support. To take over the intiative is the best way of making sure that you keep within your depth. The important thing is not just coping, but being seen to be coping. Direct action itself challenges this impression, and it is, therefore, necessary to rebut the challenge, by first bringing the issues themselves back under control.

And the fact that existing governments can generally fairly easily restore what they see as the normal balance in this sort of way is, I think, indicative of another distinction in perspective between direct action and orthodox politics. Direct action challenges, among other things, the competence of political institutions. But these institutions form part of the psychological comfort which people derive from the political game as normally played. Abstractions like justice and equality and democratic participation are seen as residing in them. Direct action, in challenging the competence of these institutions, also calls into question the complacent confidence in them. And it intends to do so. But when people are no longer reassured by those symbols of justice or democratic procedure, their consequent uncertainty, and the irritation which grows out of this uncertainty is directed not against the questioned institutions, but against the questioners who have destroyed the comfort by showing, as it is easy to do, that the symbol is not a reflection of reality. Criticism of a purely rational (albeit constructive) nature, may well be mistrusted, and may even be labelled 'destructive', because whatever is suggested as an alternative to the old usage cannot by its very nature immediately replace the comfortable familiarity and hence the confidence in the old. Its 'destructiveness' is not in suggesting no alternative, but in suggesting that a purely rational alternative will fill the gap left when the accepted procedure is superseded. Emotionally, psychologically and symbolically, this is not so.

This is not, of course, to say that most radicals are naïve enough to think of political symbols as having direct existential import. They are quite conscious of them as symbols; and part of their aim is to change priorities and so replace old with new symbolic content; to make, for example, political participation and involvement something much more direct. This assumes, of course, that people really want this involvement and 'direct control' of their destinies as a kind of Kantian assertoric imperative. This need not be so. What people get from democracy may be more in the way of psychological comfort than of material comfort, and this may be how they prefer it. Seen in this context, insistence on what they consider to be too much participation may be as upsetting as too little. And it's surely mainly for this reason that, challenged by direct action, existing governments generally find it so easy to reassert control in a conventional way. People want their democratic symbols of choice and participation, but they just as certainly want those of firm and competent government. It is possible, of course, to take a Marxist line on this, and say that, come the Revolution (whether actual or symbolic), people hitherto bound by false consciousness will become conscious and necessarily choose real involvement as opposed to the spurious form that they now accept. But so long as the radicals are, as Buckman approvingly says, 'armed with ideals (but not an ideology), strong on rhetoric and weak – deliberately so – on concrete proposals',[5] the language-game which they challenge will remain much stronger and more persuasive than their own.

NOTES

1. Ludwig Wittgenstein, *Philosophical Investigations* (Oxford, 1969), chap. 7, s. 19.
2. Marshall McLuhan, *Myth and Mass Media* (Stoke Ferry, 1959).
3. J. K. Galbraith, *The New Industrial State* (London, 1967).
4. P. Buckman, *The Limits of Protest* (London, 1970), chap. 3.
5. Ibid., p. 50.

V The Study of Violence

ROBIN JENKINS

Introduction

'The trouble started when . . .' Every time that a newspaper article deals with violence, it almost invariably begins with these words and with the perspective implied by them. The article then proceeds to explain that the trouble started when an individual or a group threw some stones, started fighting with the police, or fired a gun. It continues with an elaborate description of what happened after that and how the authorities restored 'law and order'.[1] Perhaps this treatment of violence is only to be expected when one considers that the journalist burdened with the task of reporting it has not made a special study of the issues involved, and in any case is not professionally interested in understanding them. The journalist's job is to get news, and violent behaviour makes good copy.

It is the task of the social scientist, on the other hand, to interpret and explain society, yet when he turns his attention to the subject of violence, he generally takes the same perspective as the journalist. Ted Gurr, who has recently written a large book[2] which 'proposes some general answers to three basic questions about our occasional disposition to disrupt violently the order we otherwise work so hard to maintain',[3] defines violence as 'all collective attacks within a political community against the political régime, its actors . . . or its policies'.[4] There are at least half a dozen key assumptions implicit in this definition – assumptions that many of those who share his dominant perspective might well argue against. I want to concentrate on the dominant assumption, which is that when one studies violence, one studies *behaviour*.

The journalist never pretends to report much more than people's actions, but to explain behaviour and to explain human society are quite distinct problems: to confuse one with the other, as does Gurr and as do the majority of social scientists writing on violence, has scientific, political and policy implications that cannot be ignored. I shall explore them one by one.

Scientific Implications

It is assumed by most social scientists studying violence that violent behaviour is the proper focus of their study. The essential characteristic of this approach is that violence is reduced to violent behaviour. Violence only exists when violent behaviour is present, that is, when the behaviour and attitudes of the actors are violent. The behavioural definition of sociological concepts is fairly general, and one finds, for instance, a similar set of definitions around the concept of conflict.[5] Given a behavioural definition of conflict, there is, for instance, no conflict in a factory unless the management has locked the workers out or the workers have withdrawn their labour. Without manifest conflict behaviour, there is no conflict. A behavioural definition of conflict or violence necessarily results in an anti-historical and utterly empiricist approach to the problem. Within such an approach, class conflict, for instance, only exists when there are barricades in the streets and various missiles flying over the top of them in both directions. It is not necessary to document the weaknesses of empiricism here, but it is salutory to mention the culs-de-sac that this approach brought about in the natural sciences. Where would biology be if we still categorized animals according to their habitat (sea, land or air) rather than according to their internal structure (mammal, reptile, fish, etc.)? Where would we be if chemists still classified chemicals in terms of their shape and colour instead of in terms of their molecular structure? External appearances in the natural sciences are largely irrelevant, and, if studied, are misleading. It has been argued recently that the same applies to the social sciences. If it is not scientifically fruitful to define the concept of violence in terms of violent behaviour – and I think the work of Gurr, Coser and others has demonstrated quite adequately that such definitions are vacuous at best – then what is the alternative?

It is necessary to introduce the concept of structural violence at this stage. Perhaps it is better to return for a moment to the wider concept of conflict. A structural definition of conflict is independent of behaviour and attitudes – in fact it is independent of actors altogether. Conflict behaviour and conflict attitudes might well be present in a situation of structural conflict but they are merely *symptoms* of conflict. This point can be illustrated by taking the most obvious example – class conflict. According to the behavioural definition, there is class conflict if there are strikes, etc. According to the structural definition, there is class conflict wherever there is a capitalist mode of production in which the rational interests of the workers who sell their labour are necessarily in conflict with the rational interests of the capitalist who buys that same labour. The conflict is located in the structure of the capitalist mode of production, and it has nothing to do with the attitudes, beliefs or behaviour of either the workers or the capitalists.

Likewise with violence, it is possible to talk about structural violence or violent structures. If, for the sake of argument, we define violence as physical damage to, or deprivation of biological needs from others,[6] then a simple bivariate analysis of life expectancy against social class will show that in capitalist societies, structural violence is administered to the working class in sufficient quantity to result in earlier death than other groups. The concept of structural violence is, of course, implicit in the Marxist theory of Revolution, which, stated crudely, says that as the degree of structural violence or exploitation increases, so also does the tendency towards class consciousness. Whether this theory is true or false is difficult to say, because the problem of measuring the economic surplus (which is the only way of measuring the degree of exploitation) has never been satisfactorily solved.[7]

The question now is which of the two definitions of violence is the most *scientifically* fruitful? In order to formulate an answer, it is first of all necessary to make a distinction between the production of knowledge and the social uses of knowledge, or, in other words, between social science and social technology.[8]

Social science produces knowledge about objectively existing social structures: its theories are principally determinist and cannot be stated in terms of acting subjects or purposive action; its criterion of relevance is scientific and this is generally expressed in terms of 'explanatory power'. Social technology, on the other hand, uses knowledge about objectively existing social structures for the solution of practical (necessarily political) problems; its theories are interventionist and have to be formulated in terms of acting subjects, their values and goal orientations; its criterion of relevance is practical.

I am in no way suggesting that these definitions of social science and social technology are complete and, indeed, there is a lot of work to be done on the problems involved in these definitions. I am only arguing that it is important and necessary to distinguish between the production of knowledge and its social uses.[9]

If these definitions are applied to the discussion on violence, it is clear that structural violence is a scientific concept, whilst behavioural violence is a technological concept. This is important because a technological theory is, in fact, a strategy for action and therefore presupposes an actor. Whilst a scientific theory generalizes, a technological theory is necessarily relevant for a particular actor in a particular situation.[10] This has extremely important theoretical consequences. The identification of the researcher with an agent 'in fact means that he puts himself in the place of the agent and looks at things from his perspective. This agent is at the same time part of the object studied. Thus in a social technological theory, there is necessarily an identification of the researcher with his object. He is at the same time both subject and object of the research'.[11]

The implication is clear; if the researcher is working with a behavioural definition of violence and therefore a technological theory of violence, he is necessarily looking at the problem from the point of view of a particular actor. The crucial question is – which actor?

Political Implications

It is instructive to return for a moment to the quotation from Gurr and to continue it:

> What are the psychological and social sources of the potential for collective violence? What determines the extent to which that potential is focused on the political system? And what societal conditions affect the magnitude and form, and hence the consequences of violence?[12]

In his preface, Gurr argues that 'this book is as likely to be read by rebels as by rulers, and suggests as many courses of action for one as for the other.'[13] He assumes the position of the politically neutral, objective, social scientist but unfortunately he cannot have his cake and eat it because he operates with a behavioural definition of violence. His work is therefore in the field of technological theory and presupposes an actor. No applied social researcher can claim to be neutral unless he completes several studies of the same problem from the different points of view of the various actors concerned.

If violence is seen as certain types of behaviour and attitudes, then violence is 'caused' by those who first show the symptoms of violent behaviour or attitudes. Returning to the newspaper reports of the violence in Notting Hill on 9 August 1970, one can see that the black militants were the first to engage in violent *behaviour*, and it was therefore this group that 'caused' the trouble. In searching for the roots of the violent behaviour, this approach inevitably lists a number of subjective factors which are frequently psychological. Often it is assumed that the subjective perceptions of the actors that first engaged in violence are unrealistic or false, and this in turn leads to a vast amount of theorizing about 'the problem of communication' and 'noise' and 'the need to improve communication', etc.

The point, however, is that the behavioural definition of violence, which attributes the cause of violence to those who first showed signs of violent behaviour, inevitably ends up by blaming the underdog in the situation, because it is he who 'starts it'. Thus in Algeria it was the native peasants who started it, not the French; thus at Ford's at Dagenham, it was workers who started it, not the management; thus at the University of Essex, it was the students who started it, not the Vice-Chancellor or his Senate. Having determined which actors started the violent behaviour, this approach is then able to suggest ways of dealing with the situation, so that the violent *behaviour* is not repeated.[14] This is moving into the realm of policy implications, but it is instructive to look at how the violent behaviour was dealt with in Algeria, Dagenham and Colchester. In Algeria, the peasants were given nominal political independence whilst the French bourgeoisie continued to own and run the Algerian economy for their own profit; in Dagenham, the management co-opted the workers through a series of productivity agreements that were designed by 'management consultants' to blur the central issues; in Colchester, the Senate co-opted students as minorities on to committees that had no power.

In other words, co-opt some of the leaders from below and make them into instruments of the élite (thereby confusing the issue amongst those left down below), teach the élite to be good manipulators and clever in-fighters, introduce agreements that make it look as though something is being shared, and the issues that were originally the focus of the violent behaviour – which in general are issues concerning lack of power – will be forgotten for a few months or a few years.

This perspective is so much part and parcel of modern sociology, almost all of which takes a behavioural approach, concentrating on the analysis of behaviour, attitudes, values and beliefs, that one can almost say that it is all social technology and little to do with social science at all. The question is – whose technology? The critique of American sociology by Nicolaus is instructive:

> . . . the eyes of sociologists, with few but honourable exceptions, have been turned downwards, and their palms upwards. Eyes down to study the activities of the lower classes, of the subject population – those activities which created problems for the smooth exercise of governmental hegemony. Since the class of rulers in this society identifies itself as the society itself – therefore the problems of the ruling class get defined as social problems . . . . The things that are sociologically 'interesting' are the things that are interesting to those who stand at the top of a mountain and feel the tremors of an earthquake.[15]

For a number of accumulative reasons, then, the behavioural study of violence, like the behavioural study of any other aspect of social reality, ends up asking technical and strategic questions that are relevant only to the problems of maintaining power for élites. It is useless for sociologists like Gurr and Coser and Bienen and others to write prefaces to their books[16] proclaiming a political neutrality that is necessarily denied by the very perspective they have chosen as their starting point.

What of the political implications of the structural approach to violence? It needs emphasizing at the outset that a scientific theory can not be formulated in terms of actors, their wishes or beliefs. This statement requires substantiation and justifies a brief digression. In the natural sciences, it is accepted that active principles have no place in scientific explanation. At one time, the fact that a stone fell downwards and not upwards was explained in terms of an active principle, contained within the stone, which made it 'want to' fall downwards. Physics made a great leap forward when this type of explanation was rejected in favour of a structural principle or force acting on the stone from outside – gravity. The old explanation, in terms of active principles, can now be seen for what it is – not a scientific explanation but a technological principle which tells you what to do if you want a stone to fall downwards, and what not to do if you want it to move upwards.[17] This diversion might seem both trivial and irrelevant, but the basic issue that is at stake – concerning the distinction between the production of knowledge and its social uses, between science and technology – is tremendously important if we are ever to build a social science that is both scientific and useful.

A structural theory of violence looks for structural sources of violence. In this sense it does not involve actors. If it is found that certain sectors of a population tend to die earlier, and that the same sectors contribute more than their fair share of the prison population, it seems to me to be important to ask some questions about the structural determinants of these phenomena and their relevance to the total system. If the conclusion of such an investigation is that the social system has certain structural elements – like exploitation – that are both inherent in the system and necessarily result in violence being done to certain sectors of the population, that conclusion has political implications. A scientific, structural understanding of violence might lead some social scientists to the rational conclusion that they must now study the technology of revolution because violence is endemic to the system they have studied and can only be ended by changing the structure of the system. If a scientific analysis of violence can come to the conclusion that the only way of ending this violence is to overthrow the system, there will clearly be many social pressures which discourage or prevent scientific research on the subject, and this is, of course, the case. This becomes clear when one considers again the example from medieval physics. When physicists first proposed structural theories and rejected explanations in terms of active principles, they were persecuted by the Church; the Church had a vested interest in certain explanations of physical reality. That battle was won by science and apart from a few obscurantist episodes, like Lysenko's peas in Stalin's Russia, the natural sciences have won the right to ask *any* question about *any* aspect of physical reality. The same can not be said for the social sciences. The ruling élites of most of the societies that presently exist have a vested interest in certain explanations of social reality, and it is not possible to ask any scientific question you like about the social systems that we live in. It is hardly surprising, then, that when a social scientist does ask scientific questions about such 'dangerous' subjects as conflict and violence, his work is labelled as 'subversive ideology'. Since social science in our society at this time plays a passive and compliant role towards the ruling élite, we end up in the odd position where scientific explanations are rejected because they are 'political' or 'revolutionary', whereas technological theories, which generally look at the society from the perspective of the élite, are accepted as 'value-neutral', etc. when in fact they have nothing to do with scientific explanation at all. It is socially acceptable to do research on the technology of minimizing violent behaviour, but it is not acceptable to do research on the structural causes of violence, because the élite does not want to understand or explain society; it only wants to control society.

Policy Implications

Inevitably, I have encroached on this section whilst discussing the scientific and political implications of the behavioural approach to violence. Those who study violence as behaviour and attitudes are theorizing at the level of social technology; they are interested in strategies of handling situations, in solutions to practical problems. However, their work is not informed by a scientific study of violence so their solutions are necessarily phrased at the level of manipulating and influencing attitudes and manifest behaviour.[18] They might thereby put out the fire but they will not tackle its causes and they will not prevent other fires. The validity of the structural theories of violence[19] is somehow admitted by the fact that they are strenuously rejected with reasons that vary with the situation. Fundamentally, the behavioural approach to violence comes down to the policy advice that you must influence the attitudes and behaviour of those who have been acting violently. Sometimes this is a job for the psychiatrist, sometimes it is for the social-psychologist, but always it is defined as a problem of socialization into the *status quo*. This approach is much wider than just studies of violence and is reflected in the currently popular argument that criminals should not be punished but brainwashed into the acceptance of social norms on private property.

To summarize: almost all studies of violence tackle the subject from the behavioural perspective, which concentrates on the attitudes, beliefs and actions of individuals and groups. I have argued that this is not a scientific perspective but a technological one, that scientifically, this perspective and all the work that is characterized by it is thoroughly inadequate. In addition, the behavioural approach results in a perspective and a way of defining the problem that is necessarily conservative, oriented to the maintenance of the *status quo* and unable to even conceptualize the possibility or necessity of structural change.

Some have argued that 'sociology is not now and never has been any kind of objective seeking out of social truth or reality'.[20] It is not accidental that symposia on violence are organized at a time when those at the bottom of our society are increasingly engaging in violent behaviour against both property and symbols of State power like the police. It is a sign of the moral turpitude and political servility of the sociological profession that it now sees fit to engage in studies of violent *behaviour*, concentrating therefore on the study of the actions of those at the bottom of our society – the black immigrants, the unemployed and the drop-outs.

At present it is still possible for sociologists to hold symposia on violent behaviour, but if they continue to look at their society through the eyes of their élites and devote their professional abilities to such problems as the 'minimization of violent behaviour', they will themselves be seen (rightly) as a symbol of State power and oppression, and will become (rightly) the object of physical violence themselves.

NOTES

1. See, for instance, *every* morning paper for 10 August 1970, and the way they reported the fight between the police and black militants in Notting Hill the previous day.
2. Ted Gurr, *Why Men Rebel* (Princeton, New Jersey, 1970).
3. Ibid., pp. 7–8.
4. Ibid., pp. 3–4.
5. See H. Schmid, 'Peace Research as a Technology for Pacification', *Studies in Progress* (Copenhagen, 1970), no. 5.
6. See the definition put forward by Galtung in *Journal of Peace Research* (1969), no. 3.
7. See P. Sweezy, *The Theory of Capitalist Development* (London, 1956), for an elaboration of the problem.
8. See Schmid, op. cit.
9. For justification of this view and further elaboration, see Schmid, ibid. and N. Poulantzas, 'Political Ideology and Scientific Research', in Dencik (ed.), *Scientific Research and Politics* (Lund, 1969). See also L. Althusser, *For Marx* (London, 1969).
10. See Schmid, op. cit., p. 50.
11. Ibid., p. 51.
12. Gurr, op. cit., p. 8.
13. Ibid., p. x.
14. See Schmid, op. cit., pp. 8–25 for an analysis of the policy implications drawn out of a typical piece of industrial sociology.

15. Speech given by M. Nicolaus at the Annual Convention of the American Sociological Association, 1968: 'The ASA Convention', *Catalyst* (Spring 1969).
16. Gurr, op. cit.; L. Coser, *Continuities in the Analysis of Social Conflict* (London, 1967); H. Bienen, *Violence and Social Change* (Chicago, 1969).
17. These ideas are expanded in N. Poulantzas, op. cit.
18. For examples of this approach, see H. Graham and T. Gurr, *Violence in America – Historical and Comparative Perspectives* (London, 1969), especially chaps. 17, 18, 19, 21, 22 and the conclusion.
19. For instance, F. Fanon, *The Wretched of the Earth* (London, 1967). See also A. G. Frank, *Latin America: Underdevelopment or Revolution* (London, 1970), especially chaps. 8 and 9.
20. Nicolaus, op. cit.

VI Law and Order in Comparative Perspective

ROBERT MAST

This chapter is about an area of human affairs that is increasingly capturing the attention of people in high and low places throughout the world – law and order. It is at once a political slogan, a social process, an ideology and a device for repression. 'Law and order', as a concept, has numerous dimensions which must be considered in order to understand fully why a fervour, even hysteria, for law and order has literally swept across the world. Among these dimensions are the concepts of freedom, justice, democracy and equality, as they are counterposed in the political, economic and social contexts, as well as the separate concepts of law and order.

This chapter takes the point of view that social change is occurring so rapidly in the present era that established political systems and philosophies are being deeply challenged by counterforces and counter-ideologies. The response to such challenges varies with individual political and social conditions, but generally there is an initial effort to accommodate the challengers; falling short of that, there is repression. The systems are called many things: the *status quo*, the old guard, the capitalist (or Communist) order, the owners and controllers, etc. In sum, they represent the dominant patterns of material control and social philosophy which have been inherited from the past. The imposition of new or untried political-social orders comes hard and is fought by established systems. 'Law and order' is the slogan that summarizes the effort by establishments to maintain themselves in the face of threatening forces. In general, these threatening forces are progressive, since they draw upon social-political philosophy that stresses the equality of man, in a universal sense, and the articulation of such equality in concrete materialistic and political ways. The progressive forces, it is suggested, also emphasize certain life-style ideologies that come from the philosophical traditions of European intellectual thought that stresses individual freedom and liberty; but it is here contended that such traditions are counterposed against the dominant value of equality, and thus a major modification to the early European philosophers is being made, principally along Marxist lines. New ideologues have arisen in the post-Second World War era who are trying to articulate these philosophical-social dimensions into concrete political action programmes. To a great extent, they are representatives of the Third World or groups which have become self-consciously political in recent years. They have very different identities but share existential and logical orientations to the world in which they live. Their manifest concerns are with the equal distribution of wealth, democratization of decision-making, freedom of individual expression, and a tolerant acceptance of new life-styles. They are increasingly synthesizing the main streams of both Eastern and Western philosophy into a dynamic, progressive whole which, in one fell swoop, speaks to the main problems that have always faced man and seeks Utopian solutions to such problems.

The principal proponents of ideological synthesis and Utopian solution are those individuals and groups who are alienated from the present world: racial, religious, cultural and ethnic minorities, as well as minorities whose prime consciousness comes from identity based on economic inequality, age and sex. These are vanguard analytical groups that are taking their individual experience and generalizing it to man; and they are suggesting solutions or actually living their solutions in experimental ways so as to discover themselves and to educate others to new life possibilities. This whole process is rapidly becoming an international one. From one point of view, the result has been chaos; but from another, progress. Those who believe that chaos reigns tend to be proponents of law and order, and it is found that such people are the defenders of dominant national values, morals, honour and order. They are the self-proclaimed national protectors and increasingly fight against 'the enemy within' who, they believe, wishes to destroy a way of life. The recent 'law and order' experience in the United States has many qualitative parallels in other countries since the philosophical issues are similar. The specific historical and structural conditions, of course, greatly differ from other nations, but an analysis of the American experience can shed light on other situations; thus, the major discussion will be focused there. The conceptual dimensions of the 'law and order' issue will be considered in some detail, with concrete illustrations provided, where possible, for amplification.

Underlying Dimensions of the 'Law and Order' Issue

Though space limits their full development, there are several philosophical and social dimensions that must be considered in order to understand the complexities of the 'law and order' issue. The concepts of equality, freedom, justice and democracy will be briefly treated and an attempt made to relate these concepts to the present topic. The four concepts will be treated separately for purposes of analysis, although in concrete terms they are separate parts of a package which, it will be seen later, is intimately related to fundamental issues brought quickly to light in radically changing societies; but the issues are always latently present in any society.

Democracy

This concept implies a political decision-making apparatus which is responsive to the majority will of the people, ranging from the town hall or tribal council to the representative parliaments of the industrialized Western nations. The principle of democracy is supported by progressive forces everywhere, but its practice is quite another issue. From one perspective, a truly democratic system is possible only in small decision-making systems such as small towns, tribes, or neighbourhoods where face-to-face communication is possible for all people. In complex societies, it is highly questionable whether an elected representative can ever capture the people's will, or whether it can be interpreted at all. The opinion poll is one shoddy device that is increasingly used by politicians, but its validity defects are well known: in short, the poll merely scratches the surface of opinion, which is formed, not by the articulation of the needs of the people, but by clever opinion-makers who reflect establishment ideology or policy. Thus, the will of the people is generally not served in so-called democracies, and this is especially so for those with low power due to status based on minority identity.

Beyond this, an equally fundamental problem concerns the extent to which majority opinion represents the *right* opinion. This was discussed by James Reston of the *New York Times*:

> The principle of 'majority decision' is unarguable and unavoidable if the nation's business is to go on. But this is quite different from the notion that 'majority opinion' is the right opinion. Walter Lippmann, the columnist, noted this fundamental distinction between opinions and decisions more than forty years ago.[1]

Reston then quotes Lippmann:

> The rule of 51 per cent is a convenience. It is for certain matters a satisfactory political device. It is for others the lesser of two evils, and for still others it is acceptable because we do not know any less troublesome method of obtaining a political decision. But it may easily become an absurd tyranny if we regard it worshipfully, as though it were more than a political device. . . . Nobody can seriously maintain that the greatest number must have the greatest wisdom or the greatest virtue. . . .[2]

As Lippmann says, there can easily be a tyranny of the majority, when that majority is mesmerized by ideas that have been manipulated by clever opinion-makers who serve their own selected self-interests. Probably the best recent example of this was Richard Nixon's appeal to the 'silent majority'. This appeal to that proto-typical God-fearing, flag-waving, responsible, average American (ostensibly represented by a Dayton, Ohio, machinist's wife) was undoubtedly calculated to win the Congressional elections; but, according to one American left-wing weekly, it had more ominous implications:

> Nixon is a reactionary whose policies depend on a reactionary or at least docile and fearful electorate. By attempting to lull the anti-war sentiment of the American people with his pseudo-peace proposals, frighten the masses with over-emphasis on terror bombings, revive anti-Communist psychosis and bring back the Cold War, the administration appears to be setting the stage for a new wave of reaction.[3]

A mere review of both the 1968 American elections, in which Nixon, Humphrey and Wallace all played upon the 'law and order' theme, and the 1970 elections in which that theme was even more of a focus, suggests that a 'wave of reaction' is indeed the order of the day. Under conditions of tension produced by demands for stopping the Vietnam war, providing for the liberation of ethnics, women, homosexuals and youth, creating the basic necessities for those in poverty, reducing the alienating effect of modern living conditions, and cleaning-up the environment, the American public is in a state of massive confusion. Conservative politicians are capitalizing on this confusion and, rather than seeking constructive and progressive dialogue on the basic issues (and thus putting classic democracy into practice), they are exploiting it in ruthless ways, making a travesty of the 'will of the people'. Indeed, ruthless opinion-makers are making opinion on the basis of what is politically expedient, not on the basis of what is right or wrong in terms of fundamental human needs. In very concrete ways, out-worn myths are perpetuated in the 'national interest' by appeals to the 'law and order' slogan. The people do not know what opinion to have, so they take on the line which is most immediately available to them *via* mass communication media, most of which are dominated by those who directly represent the various power élites.

It is to be noted that people's democracy is of increasing concern to many, and attention is being directed to it in many places. Perhaps one good illustration comes from the community organization efforts that resulted from the federal poverty programme in which neighbourhood councils were formed to provide 'maximum feasible participation' on the part of deprived blacks and poor. The pure democracy process that was set in motion was counter-productive from the point of view of the opinion-makers since the people began to articulate quite fundamental questions and offer radical solutions. This was not anticipated by Washington or by the state and municipal governments. In effect, people's democracy went too far; it began to threaten the foundations upon which racism, exploitation and poverty are based. People's democracy sought truth and made a special effort to sort out right from wrong. The standards used in this process were universalistic and basic rather than particularistic and superficial. There is an object lesson in this experience: democracy is a progressive concept which is given lip-service by all – right or left – but its structure and meaning must be analysed in the light of the real conditions of power. It cannot be seen merely as a sterile statistical phenomenon (51 per cent making a majority). That is a regressive approach, because the statistical majority can quite easily be captured and mystified by the rhetoric and slogans of those presently in power. The only meaningful approach to the concept of democracy must involve the analysis of the moral content of rhetoric and slogans. Thus, we must inquire into the issues of freedom, justice and equality.

Freedom

This concept is fundamental to the 'law and order' issue, but it is a most complex thing because it has as many meanings as there are people to express them. It has been discussed from the time of the early Greeks up to the present, and there are still contradictions and ambiguities connected with the concept because the conditions of freedom are relative to the realities of political life and the ideologies accompanying such realities. All sane people desire to be free: slaves revolt; spouses seek emotional outlets outside marriage; national liberation movements flourish; 'freedom riders' were one vanguard of the US black liberation movement; women seek freedom from male oppression; youth seeks freedom from hypocritical authority. The desire for freedom is natural and has been articulated historically from Aristotle, through Locke Voltaire, Hume, Montesquieu, through Franklin Roosevelt's Four Freedoms (speech, worship, want, fear), through political expressions such as the *Magna Carta*, the US Bill of Rights, the League of Nations and the United Nations to the present national liberation and freedom movements which exist in practically all societies.

Some tend to compartmentalize freedom into two major divisions: moral and political. The former bears upon the rights of man while the latter deals with the necessity for some control of natural, selfish impulses in the interests of the common good. This is not an unwieldy distinction for analytical purposes, but it is vital to consider both as two parts of a total process. Political freedom is a structural (democratic) expression of moral prescriptions. Thus, if true democracy reigns, with truly moral underpinnings, a progressive condition prevails. But this is clearly not the way things are or ever have been, because the specific definitions of freedom vary with the possession and capability of exercising power. To take freedom to its over-logical conclusion, it includes the freedom to oppress, exploit and subvert others. This is the absurdity of the efforts of organizations like the American Civil Liberties Union which protects the rights of any individual or organization to 'do its thing', regardless of the moral content of such action. Thus, the ACLU will, at the same time, defend the legal rights of the Ku-Klux-Klan, anti-war protesters, the John Birch Society, and black activists. The ACLU effort is a worthy, liberal cause, but it limits itself, as do other liberal organisations like the Anti-Defamation League, to a formalistic, stylistic defence of freedom, and gives too little attention to the specific moral content of the pressing social problems that are the basis for protest, dissent and disruption. Indeed, it pursues the Lockean tradition which laid the foundation for the famous statement in the US Declaration of Independence that all men 'are endowed by their Creator with certain inalienable rights; that among these are life, liberty and the pursuit of happiness'. These rights are important, but in the abstract are contentless and amoral. How, it might be asked, are such rights to be guaranteed? Through what precise distribution of power and goods? Liberals beg these fundamental questions and tend to view freedom as an ideal end point. They also cannot countenance the seeming contradiction that results from some quite real philosophical agreements between New Left anarchists and arch-conservatives like Barry Goldwater (the 1964 Presidential candidate). Their agreement is on the issue of freedom and little else. Both support the notion of freedom for extremely different reasons. So we cannot analyse the 'law and order' issue from this perspective alone, because it leads to sterility. Perhaps another conceptual dimension might shed further light, or perhaps lead to additional confusion.

Justice

This is one of the favourite concepts of those with a liberal persuasion as well as of those with either radical or conservative tendencies. As with freedom, it comes from the European liberal tradition, but it is beset with some of the same problems. The concept has been defined by Russell Kirk as 'the principle and process by which each man is assured of the things that belong to him'. The concept of justice is given full treatment in the Fifth Amendment to the US Constitution: 'No person shall . . . be deprived of life, liberty, or property, without due process of law'. Most cases dealing with individual freedom are handled under this constitutional provision.

But what does it really mean for a person to be assured the things that belong to him and to be guaranteed these things by due process of law? The most immediate and conspicuous answer is that things that belong to a person and are protected by law are the things that *exist* both in the sense of personal property and in social power. Simply spoken, if nothing belongs to someone, or belongs unequally, then this kind of justice assures that the person will *continue* to have nothing. If a person has something, then justice will guarantee that such ownership will be perpetuated and the *status quo* will be retained. It is a cliché though a profound one, that this is the rich man's justice or the white man's justice; the rich man's or white man's due process of law. Why are the British prisons full of debtors to the point of suffocation and why are the American prisons full of blacks (a full 40 per cent)? Why do the American Black Panthers claim that all black prisoners are political prisoners? In both cases, justice is being exercised on the basis of prevailing material and political ownership. The police and court systems are under the direct control of élites whose political and economic power is exercised by elaborate legal structures which serve élite interests considerably more than non-élite interests.

If classical justice is to be done, fundamental moral issues must be examined; the content of justice must be examined; the interests that are served must be reviewed. This can only be accomplished by a consideration of the concept of equality.

Equality

This concept is fundamental to the 'law and order' issue, and is also begged or dismissed most often. The implications of its meaning are of profound importance and obviously offer the most basic reason for dissent as well as for defence. Equality suggests sameness, uniformity, even match, no advantage. Reality is not like that, though theologians and philosophers have constantly said it should be. Equality is a condition in which no person takes undue advantage of another; in which social rules apply to all people alike. This Utopian state is unreachable, but it is so rarely aspired to; and perhaps the aspiration, the effort, is all that is possible.

A favourite slogan, and indeed an ideology that was believed by many, in the civil rights period of US race relations was 'equality of opportunity'. This slogan (and social goal) was incorporated in the federal, state and municipal laws that purported to redress the grievances of black people by assuring equal opportunity to achieve the good things of life. This turned out to be both a farce and a dupe for black people, because it was based on assumptions that were logically contradictory; that never could be put into practice because of the class structure of society and institutionalized racism. Equality, as such, is possible with radical structural change; with a redistribution of power and resources. But equality of *opportunity* for black people or poor people is impossible in a system of private property, juxtaposed with paternalistic and racist ideology. The opportunity structures simply do not exist in a society characterized by scarcity of morality, to say nothing of material resources. But equality of opportunity was a myth that filtered through many levels of society. It temporarily mesmerized the black community; it made the white liberals placid, and they clucked their tongues with righteous satisfaction at the progress being made in race relations. This all characterized the US situation in the 1950s and early 1960s, but such a placid response was exploded in the late 1960s with urban riots.

Then the Kerner Commission came out with the *Report of the National Advisory Commission on Civil Disorders* after the following pontification by President Johnson when he addressed the nation on 27 July 1967:

> The only genuine, long-range solution for what has happened lies in an attack – mounted at every level – upon the conditions that breed despair and violence. All of us know what those conditions are: ignorance, discrimination, slums, poverty, disease, not enough jobs. We should attack these conditions – not because we are frightened by conflict, but because we are fired by conscience. We should attack them because there is simply no other way to achieve a decent and orderly society in America.

By implication, at least, his mandate dealt with the fundamental issue of equality, but it is quite clear also that his rhetoric was intended as a sop to those who showed sincere concern for inequality and for those of whom, contrary to what he said, he was genuinely afraid, namely, black militants. What was the result of his famous Commission that thrilled the white liberal with its conclusions? One of the best summaries was provided by Andrew Kopkind:

> All in all, the Report has become a basic document in the platform of American liberals for social reform, a catalogue of problems and a programme of solutions. But by and large, those who were cheered by the Report's solemn platitudes or impressed by its torrent of statistics missed its essential political functions and its crucial social consequences. It presented – and legitimized – a specific view of the riots and a particular understanding of America that now constitutes the standard approach to the treatment of social ills . . . . The very acceptance – and acceptability – of the Report is a clue to its emptiness. It threatens no real, commanding interests. It demands, by implication or explication, no real shifts in the way power and wealth are apportioned among classes; it assumes that the political and social élites now in control will (and should) remain in their positions. By

avoiding an approach to the riots as events of political insurrection, or as part of a world-wide response to an overbearing US empire, the Report makes sure that social therapy will be applied only to surface effects, not systematic faults.[4]

Kopkind's criticism of the Kerner Report has clear implications also for the critical issue of poverty in the USA which is one of the sharpest contradictions in a supposed affluent society. With the 'rediscovery' of poverty by 1960s-style muckrakers like Michael Harrington, it was found, for example, that the upper 20 per cent of the American income population receives nearly 50 per cent of the national income, while the lowest 20 per cent receives only about 5 per cent of the national income. The work force as a whole takes home about 90 dollars per week, while certain élite worker groups, such as construction workers in New York City, take home about 300 dollars per week. These are alienating contradictions which must be understood and analysed as being of direct causal importance to the development of a social-political condition which spawns protest, which in turn spawns 'law and order' reactions.

Equality, of course, has many dimensions. It is quite simple to recognize the economic dimension. It is less simple to understand equality in terms of racial, sexual, age, life-style or ideological criteria, but do this we must because these are critical components of America's current freedom movements to which 'law and order' advocates are reacting.[5] The relative absence of equality may be viewed as the foundation of protest. To be relatively unequal is to be relatively unfree to make democratic decisions and/or to have the power to implement such decisions. With some few exceptions, all societies exhibit conditions of inequality for some groups. Today, the consciousness of inequality on the part of such groups is rapidly rising; indeed, such consciousness is sweeping the world. The United States exhibits a most complex array of self-conscious groups fighting a system for larger amounts of power. Though that system grudgingly gives up small bits of power here and there, and though a philosophical and legal order purportedly provides for the equality of all, the empirical facts are quite the contrary. Demands for equality produce hostile responses, polarization and a 'law and order' mentality. This is an irrational contradictory mentality when analysed in terms of the sociology of 'law and order' and the philosophical bases underlying it. Let us now turn our attention to that area.

Law

Most of the Western liberal democracies have laws or executive orders that purport to protect the rights of minorities, to guarantee equality of opportunity for all citizens or to redress grievances of citizens against whom there is discrimination. The civil rights laws in Britain and the USA are examples in the area of race relations. Other social legislation in both countries attempts to regulate gross economic discrepancies. Laws and policies from the New Deal, Fair Deal and poverty programme in the USA and the modified British Socialist schemes are examples. These efforts may be seen as 'good law', representing enlightened, egalitarian social goals. Though clearly inadequate to create equality, they may be seen as steps in the right direction. Later it will be demonstrated that, at least in the USA, the effect of such 'liberal' legislation was to set in motion a process that was not anticipated by the legislators and which produced a movement towards repressive law to reduce the velocity of social change.

Law may be seen to have at least two major dimensions: progressive – that which attempts to set moral standards, influence behaviour or reorganize some political or economic aspect of society – and regressive – that which serves the interests of ruling classes, maintains a *status quo* and negatively sanctions dissent. Civil rights law would be a relatively conservative example of progressive law. Such law in Western societies which regulates the economy and polity as well as law intended to stifle protest are examples of regressive law. Law of the latter type is quite a normal matter and to some extent is viewed correctly as an order-maintaining device necessary to the stability of societies. Civil rights law, especially in the USA, was seen by many as having a norm setting function which would restructure the relations between the races by regulating discriminatory behaviour and ultimately having an educational function in the reduction of prejudice. These assumptions are quite similar in the British civil rights experience.

In the 1950s, law sociologists in the USA, captured by liberal assumptions, had great faith in the efficacy of civil rights law to have a major impact on race relations. Most of their assumptions were at the level of attitudes, but some believed, perhaps for the wrong reasons, that the actual structure of race relations would be greatly influenced. Sociology textbooks usually incorporated material that reflected the great number of civil rights laws being written at the federal, state and municipal levels. For example:

> The dogma that law is impotent to change intergroup relations has been sharply challenged by contemporary social science. Yet not so long ago we found it easier to accept a Sumnerian view of things . . .[6]

Of course, this was referring to William Graham Sumner's famous views that 'acts of legislation come out of the mores' and 'legislation to be strong must be consistent with the mores'.[7] In the 1950s and early

1960s social science was captured by a set of myths promulgated by race relations practitioners which purported that behaviour could be strongly influenced and new norms set by 'creative' civil rights law. Many thought that Sumner had finally been disproven. Typical of such an optimistic view is the following by Will Maslow:

> Law is a many-splendoured thing of infinite resource. In Roscoe Pound's phrase, it can make habits instead of waiting for them to grow. It is the best weapon we have to achieve the goal that Alexander Pakelis once described as 'full equality in a free society'.[8]

Maslow's optimistic view, along with most, was based on the assumption that discrimination by the dominant majority would be controlled through the moral and police force of the State. His reference to Pound is undoubtedly based on Pound's writings on the social control function of law. Long ago Pound noted that the primary function of the State is social control, exercised by law which is the systematic and orderly application of force by appointed agents.[9] Such social control was assumed to be directed against those who discriminate – their overt behaviour would be sanctioned and, if necessary, punished. This would open a door to minority group integration into the mainstream of American life. Nothing was said of the manner in which the minority group would push open the door, what it wanted once it began to enter, and whether it even wanted to go in. In actual fact, some American blacks did go through. For them – the black bourgeoisie – the positive function of legal sanction seemed to be operating: some barriers to employment, voting, housing, education and access to public accommodation were lowered. But the vast majority of blacks remained effectively outside the system. However, for them another thing happened as a spin-off from civil rights law: they experienced a revolution of rising expectations from the content and promises of civil rights law; they began to consider seriously the idea of 'full equality in a free society'. Either through the catalytic efforts of white liberals or through their own self-help efforts (Southern Freedom Riders, lunch-counter sit-ins, Poor People's Campaign, etc.), they began to test the real intent of civil rights law. They found that much of it was rhetorical and gratuitous; it set public policy, but it was completely devoid of radical mechanisms that would influence the political and economic structures that were responsible for the class and racist nature of society.

A similar thing occurred in the area of poverty. One would assume that the 1960s showed that American norms regarding poverty had reached such a point that the society was prepared to launch a massive attack. This was partially true if one considers the anti-poverty legal machinery and social organization emerging from the Kennedy and Johnson administrations that was designed to eliminate poverty. Poor people began to organize at the neighbourhood level to lift themselves up by their bootstraps, and this was both sponsored and blessed by the government and liberals at all levels. Another revolution of rising expectations occurred in poverty areas all over the USA and another bitter disappointment went with it. Poor people found that anti-poverty social goals were basically liberal rhetoric with no real mechanisms to alter the economic foundations of a class order.

Accompanying the failure of and dissatisfaction with both the civil rights and anti-poverty programmes was the American involvement in South-East Asia. This involvement also was established by law in the form of legal norms inculcated in the American public and articulated in such pronouncements as the Senate's Gulf of Tonkin Resolution which gave President Johnson a free hand to conduct the war. In the face of racism and poverty as well as the profound immorality of the war, a massive wave of dissent eventually swept the country. It involved all sectors of society, with the greatest involvement coming from the middle classes. The contradictions of the situation strongly influenced and politicized many, especially youth and minority and poor groups.

Order

In the face of the reduction of emphasis on eliminating racism and poverty, the obvious reluctance of élites to allow meaningful criticism of existing policy, the recognition of the blatant fact that the *status quo* was not about to shift through any 'legal' efforts on the part of deprived people, the stage was set for the facing of truth, soul-searching and strategy-finding on the part of those committed to egalitarian structural change. They decided that establishment law (that mandated equality without mechanisms for structural change) was sterile and gratuitous law – a sop to the deprived groups and the white liberals. Existing machinery could not redress grievances and advance social change in any satisfactory way – the machinery had to be changed: new decision-making devices had to be created; outmoded institutions had to be destroyed. A revolutionary militancy began, part of which was located in radical organization and part in the form of the alienated drop-out. Individuals organized on the basis of their prime social identity – black, Puerto Rican, Mexican American, Indian, youth, poor and, later, women. Abstractly, they caused a fearful challenge to the establishment; concretely, they produced social disruptions and civil disobedience and thus a threat to order.

Sociologically, order is a state of affairs in which *established* institutions are working 'normally'; that is, a state in which the rules of the current game are being obeyed, the shots being called by those in power; there is domestic tranquillity because of obedience to existing law. A state of order is incongruous with a condition of change, since the latter creates disorder by definition. Social scientists who apply theories of order in their work are interested in such fields as social control and deviant behaviour. They inquire into the question of how 'deviance' is controlled by ruling authorities. There are implicit, and frequently explicit, assumptions in their work that deviance (defined in many ways) should be controlled for the stability of societies. Stability, rather than equality and freedom, is more important. This kind of analyst works hand in glove with, and is strongly supported by, ruling authorities, since it is the essence of ruling authority that the business of a society cannot go on without order and stability through ruling law.

But the contradiction of the need for order and the need for equality, freedom and justice fell hard on the USA in the latter part of the 1960s. Order, indeed, was breaking down through the actions of those who were challenging the system. The Lemberg Center for the Study of Violence indicates that in the period 1967 through 1969 1,625 racial disorders occurred.[10] Add to this the numerous anti-war, poverty and group liberation confrontations, increasingly manifested in civil disobedience, bombings, picketings and property destruction, and it is evident that establishment order was in jeopardy. How is this condition to be assessed? This chapter takes the position that structural change in any meaningful perspective can only occur through the struggle of deprived and disenchanted people. It is unfortunate, but true, that such change is not tolerated by ruling élites, and their response is to revert to the social control function of the State through its police power. This may be 'responsible' government, but it is not necessarily progressive government.

How do others see the breakdown of order? It all depends on the political perspective of the observer. The reactionary perspective is best summed up by George Wallace:

> If you walk out of this hotel tonight and someone knocks you on the head, he'll be out of jail before you're out of the hospital, and on Monday morning they'll try the policeman instead of the criminal. . . . That's right, we gonna have a police state for folks who burn the cities down. They aren't gonna burn any more cities.[11]

The conservative-liberal perspective is articulated by Sidney Hook, who discussed the necessity for people to obey the civil rights laws which he thought were far in advance of the actual situation in the USA.

> Our present task is to bring home and reinforce popular consciousness of the fact that those who violate their provisions [civil rights laws] are violating the highest law of the land, and that their actions are outside the law. Therefore, our goal must *now* be to build up and

strengthen a mood of respect for the law, for civil obedience to laws, even by those who deem them unwise or who opposed them in the past. Our hope is that those who abide by the law may learn not only to tolerate them but, in time, as their fruits develop, to accept them.[12]

Hook's approach is at least twenty years old. It was tried and tested and found unworkable, but still represents a favourite conservative-liberal point of view. Operating essentially within the order framework, the left-liberal position is one of confusion and frustration. Representing this tendency, I.F. Stone says:

Men are moral beings, and to take from the terrorists their moral justification is the only way to strike at the heart of the terror spreading round the globe. A society operates by habit and consent, and if these begin to break down, it is helpless. Police are effective only if they confront occasional and peripheral disorder. If even a sizeable minority declines to obey the rules, the task of law and order becomes insuperable.[13]

From reactionary to left-liberal, the emphasis is on violence, disorder, terror; not equality, freedom, justice. And the mass media do their part to stress some quasi-social science jargon and half-truths. *The Saturday Evening Post* once spoke of a kind of 'saturation point' for tension. After it is reached, who knows what might happen:

It is hard to believe that even the most altruistic and broadminded white man can avoid, in this day, the suspicion that every black man wishes him ill; or that even the most rational of negroes can avoid harbouring the same suspicion of every white man. The nervous system can take only so much tension, only so much fear and anxiety, and then it cries out for peace at any price. Law and order, we call this . . .[14]

Time magazine also spoke of tension:

Millions of Americans in 1970 are gripped by an anxiety that is not caused by war, inflation or recession – important as these issues are. Across the US the universal fear of violent crime and vicious strangers – armed robbers, packs of muggers, addict burglars ready to trade a life for heroin – is a constant companion of the populace. It is the cold fear of dying at random in a brief spasm of senseless violence . . . for a few pennies, for nothing.[15]

Oh, if the turmoil in the USA could only be analysed with such a simple approach! Clever politicians, conservative demagogues and *status quo* managers do several grievous things to the American population: first, they raise the social tension with jargon and half-truths;

secondly, they appeal to regressive and divisive ideology; and thirdly, they stampede the population into a belief that the devil tramps the street outside, ready to pounce on unsuspecting victims. They seldom try to differentiate crimes against person and property from political disorder; both these are interpreted as a breakdown in social harmony, and often the cause is suggested as being some devil-type Communist or anarchist. When crime statistics are objectively presented, it is found that the 'crime wave' is something of a myth. Fred Graham exploded this myth in an excellent article by noting that ex-Attorney-General Ramsay Clark used to say that the average individual's chance of being a victim of a crime of violence is once in 400 years, and that if one wished to improve the odds he could avoid his relatives and associates because they are statistically the most likely to do him harm. Graham also pointed out that the alarmist FBI plays crime-numbers' games that dramatically display a nation whose crime rate is rising in alarming proportions. He suggests that rather than publicize the fact that some unfortunate individual is murdered every forty-eight minutes, the FBI could have told the country that the average citizen's chances of becoming a murder victim on any given day are about one in two million.[16] But more immoral than distorting the known crime increase, is the unwillingness or inability of élites and their representatives to acknowledge the distinctions between crime, in a capitalist context, and civil disorder, in a political context. Of course, it is quite impossible for them to face these distinctions because they thus will be attacking themselves. Rather, the distortions, dishonesty and immorality become more insidious by popular appeals to base hatreds and gross confusion through 'law and order' rhetoric.

Law 'n Order

The two concepts of law and order, separately capable of theoretical analysis when applied to concrete situations, become, when combined into one concept, a slogan and strategy for repression. 'Law 'n order' is a term of the common person as well as of the person in high places. It is a desirable goal for right-wingers and an undesirable condition for left-wingers. It is a slogan used to manipulate the electorate and frighten the fearful by those seeking repression of dissent. A state of law and order, in itself, is desirable under conditions of egalitarianism. That is, sane women and men desire an ordered existence under moral, equitable law, which provides equality and free expression. This is not the condition which exists in the world today.

'Law 'n order' is a social condition in which fear of change or loss of privilege promotes social hysteria. It is a condition in which demagogues exaggerate, manipulate and mystify those who are precariously or ambiguously placed in society. And the targets frequently used by such demagogues are those individuals and groups who seek moral, egalitarian solutions to social problems. They are the scapegoats. America thought, for example, that the McCarthy witch-hunting and red-baiting days were gone forever, but Vietnam produced another flag to rally round. Back in 1965 when Vietnam was beginning to escalate into a war of major proportions, the Communist scare began again to be applied: the devil, conspiracy theory was raised again. Senator Frank Lausche of Ohio, speaking to the US Senate, told of the result of his investigation into anti-Vietnam demonstrations:

> These are the product of Communist leadership. Countless innocent, uninformed youth of the country are participating in them, not knowing that they are following the flag of the Reds and bowing to the voices of the Communists dictating how they shall create disorder and bring the United States into disrespect.[17]

Admittedly, such demagogues have found it rough going in the 1960s with these tactics: the American people may have become tired of it all. But they have responded to the cry of 'crime in the streets', even though it is objectively less serious than the FBI wishes to make it; and they have also responded negatively to the demands for life-style changes primarily on the part of youth. Perhaps the cultural revolution among youth is the most frightening thing for the older generation, and it has been greatly played up by the demagogues. The cultural revolution is intimately connected with politics, as seen by the authorities, by the so-called 'silent majority' and by those making the revolution. The authorities are organizing to repress 'the enemy within' through co-ordinated police action at all levels, computerized intelligence and the infiltration of 'subversive' organizations. They are operating on the assumption that a small minority of people desire to destroy the American system and are using various subersive tactics to that end. And the American people have been led to believe that this is the case, if we can rely on a Harris Poll in the summer of 1968 which showed 81 per cent of the respondents believing that law and order had broken down.

Clearly, many of those seeking change in American institutions do think that a new system must emerge, and that old and outworn institutions must be destroyed. Some seek rapid destruction through bombings and assassinations. Others create political action organizations. Others opt out of the system. As a result, those in charge of the present system use law to stop this rapid change process. The recent federal conspiracy law is one of the latest results of this thrust. The 1970 election campaign was a disturbing expression of the politics of repression. 'Law 'n order' goes marching on.

However, the politics of repression is not a static process. It is a negative response to change, but it has positive implications. The problems facing a society are brought to full light, looked at closely, deliberated and debated. Repression of dissent goes only so far. Then adjustments are made, reforms are entertained, demands are met – and the system, which was being so closely guarded by its protectors, changes into a new form. Perhaps political and social polarization is a necessary requirement in this process. Perhaps some forms of violence are also required. Societies do not change gracefully, but they *do* change. In that process the moral issues that have always faced the world are once again reviewed, and another small progressive step is taken.

NOTES

1. James Reston, as quoted in *The Times* (8 October 1970), p. 8.
2. James Reston, ibid.
3. *The Guardian* (17 October 1970), p. 9.
4. Andrew Kopkind, *Hard Times* (Washington DC, 15–22 September 1969), no. 44, p. 1.
5. See Robert H. Mast, 'The New Freedom Movements in the United States', *Race Today* (September 1970), pp. 303–5.
6. George E. Simpson and J. Milton Yinger, 'The Sociology of Race and Ethnic Relations', in Robert Merton and Leonard Cottrell, Jr (eds), *Sociology Today* (New York, 1959), p. 390.
7. William Graham Sumner, *Folkways* (New York, 1959), p. 55.
8. Will Maslow, 'The Uses of Law in the Struggle for Equality' (paper presented to the Reassessment Conference of the National Community Relations Advisory Council held at Atlantic City, December 1954), p. 18.
9. Roscoe Pound, *Social Control Through Law* (New Haven, Conn., 1942), p. 25.
10. From an untitled report by the Lemberg Center for the Study of Violence, Brandeis University, Waltham, Massachusetts, dated 18 May 1970. The Center notes that its data come from newspaper clippings and thus 'the frequency of confrontation and other incidents is most likely greater than that which is reported in the Press, and therefore the data presented represent a base minimum only'.
11. Fred J. Cook, 'There's Always a Crime Wave: How Bad is This One', *New York Times Magazine Supplement*, p. 39. Cook was quoting a typical passage by Wallace in his 1968 campaign speeches.
12. Sidney Hook, 'Social Protest and Civil Obedience', *Humanist* (Autumn 1967).
13. *I. F. Stone's Bi-Weekly* (21 September 1970), p. 2.

14. 'Law and Order', *Saturday Evening Post* (1968), p. 25.
15. 'What the Police Can – and Cannot – Do', *Time* (13 July 1970), p. 44.
16. Fred P. Graham, 'A Contemporary History of American Crime', in Hugh Davis Graham and Ted Robert Gurr (eds), *The History of Violence in America* (New York, 1969), p. 501.
17. Robert Crater, 'Senator Hits "Peaceniks" in Draft Bill', The *Pittsburgh Press* (19 October 1965).

PART TWO

Contemporary Studies

A RECOGNITION, REFORM AND REACTION

VII The Second Ulster Crisis

ROBERT BAXTER

History is very important in Ireland. Slogans, such as 'Remember 1690', and the commemoration of past events, be it the 'Glorious Revolution' or the Easter Rising, have an honoured place in local life. How far back you go depends on who you are. The Catholics will refer to 1916, the Protestants to 1690, and increasingly the English will think wistfully of 1169, when they first came to Ireland, and now wish they had not. In recent history three elements are worthy of note. The first is the sectarian tradition. This is not concerned solely with religion but runs into all aspects of social life. Social cohesion into the two Protestant and Catholic communities is very strong, but cohesion within the two communities is in some respects weak. Hitherto, the Protestants have been rather good at maintaining a high degree of political unity, though after the crisis began in 1968 they started to fragment. In religion, however, they have long been broken up into often minuscule sects, all of which have an enthusiastic, if diminutive following, the most recent addition being Paisley's 'Free Presbyterian Church'. Such sects flourish in the fertile soil of Ulster long after they have withered away in stony England. The Catholics, due more to outside influences than to their own inclinations, have maintained a monolithic religious unity, but in politics have rarely been able to work together for long, so that even when they are under considerable pressure, besides being divided into the two older Nationalist and Republican parties, they were represented in Stormont by six Social Democrats, four Nationalists, one independent MP (who was elected as a Nationalist), one Republican Labour MP, and to some extent also by the one Labour MP. There were thirteen non-Unionist MPs in Stormont and the largest group consisted of the six loosely associated Social Democrats. To a large extent, the causes of this fragmentation are obvious. Ireland is small, and Northern Ireland is tiny. There are only one and a half million people in the province, and in such a small community it is hardly surprising that personalities should acquire considerable importance. Protestant political cohesion has arisen out of the need for unity to maintain control of the government, while Catholic political fragmentation is the result of frustration and the knowledge that the fruits of office are permanently denied to them. An interesting point is the exclusive attitudes of the political organizations. Until recently, the Unionists had managed to avoid the worst rigours and at least claimed to represent all Protestants. However, with the smaller groups, including the Unionist off-shoots, there is a narrowness often associated with religious sectarianism. In some organizations – for example, the Protestant Unionists – it is quite apparent, but the atmosphere pervades even the centre groupings and one is often tempted to believe in the need to be exclusively non-sectarian to be in the Labour party (as well as militantly moderate to join the Alliance party).

A second point that stands out in recent Irish history is the tradition of violent resistance to government authority. In the years before the First World War, the Unionist leaders resorted to treason and armed rebellion in order to defy the attempts of the British government to impose home rule, and when the British government gave way before the Unionist blackmail, the southern Catholics resorted to armed rebellion in order to take by force what they could not get by argument. The atmosphere of 1912 – the year of the Unionists' treason – was revived in 1969. The extreme Unionists again resisted the demands of the British government that they should reform, and the Protestant working class rioted in the streets. They obviously felt that they could defy London and get away with it. They had done it once before, and they saw no reason why they should not do it again. Hence the need for British troops to shoot down Protestant rioters in October 1969. The chief legacy of the 1912 crisis has been the weak position of the civil authority. The Ulster Protestants will accept the authority of the government as long as they see that it is exclusively *their* government, but they will be prepared to defy it if it no longer appears to be the champion of their own interests. They have been encouraged in this attitude by virtually all Unionist politicians since Lord Randolph Churchill played his 'Orange card' in 1886, not only by extremists such as William Craig, the former Minister of Home Affairs, but even by Lord Craigavon, who was Prime Minister of Northern Ireland from 1921 until 1940. He was the man who uttered the now famous description of Stormont as 'a Protestant Parliament for a Protestant People', among many other sectarian pronouncements, and ensured the identification of the Northern Ireland government with the Protestant community. In 1969 all this began to vanish. Stormont carried out reforms which for decades had been resisted on the grounds that they would be the prelude to a Catholic takeover. London again seemed to be on the side of the Catholics, and the Protestant loyalty to the regime started to crumble.

On a different level is the final point to note about recent history in

Ulster – the long period of relative tranquillity and prosperity it has enjoyed since 1945. During the post-war period the standard of living had steadily risen and civil disturbance had subsided. Economic and social issues had begun to preoccupy people as the trade union movement grew in strength and sectarianism receded. Had the government carried out reforms over a period of years through the 1960s, so removing the most obvious grievances, it is possible that violence might have been avoided. The government did not reform, and until October 1968 showed no intention of reforming, leaving the grievances to fester. When the protests which arose quite rapidly during the summer of 1968 suddenly erupted into violence, the tranquillity was shattered and everyone was taken by surprise. Until then it had looked as though Ulster might undergo a peaceful process of modernization, but the resistance of the government of O'Neill to any real change ensured that it would now be a violent process.

Against this background, one can look at society in Northern Ireland and see a number of fundamental problems. In many respects the most important problem is anthropological. Two tribes were thrown together into one State; the larger runs the State and fears that any concessions to the smaller will lead to its own destruction – so it refuses concessions. Faced with complete alienation from the political structure, the minority tribe either sulks in its reserves or increasingly erupts into violent protest. The protest, however, is not about particular abuses but about the system itself, and no amount of local government boundary changes, and one man, one vote reforms will get round this problem. The tribes are two communities which have a great deal of social autonomy. Segregation is not complete but it is extensive, and neither community wants to desegregate, for both fear being exposed to the other. Religion is, in this situation, just the badge of the community – a man's religion decides what his values and attitudes will be, cutting across class lines. This is developed in cultural attributes – the desire to develop the Gaelic language and honour Irish (as opposed to British) traditions among the Catholics, and the insistence among the Protestants on copying English traditions, including teaching English history. The similarity between the situation in Ireland and colonial experience in Africa and Asia has been pointed out,[1] and the parallels of the Tamils in Ceylon under Bandaranaike, the Turks in Cyprus under Makarios, and the Baganda in Uganda under Obote suggested. As Dr Roger Scott has observed: 'whereas modern societies tend to deplore the raising of primordial loyalties to the level of political supremacy, new States often use them as a basis for the demarcation of political units and the distribution of resources.'[2] In comparing Ulster with States such as Ceylon, Cyprus and Uganda, Scott placed it in the category of those new States which, in Geertz's terminology, 'are abnormally susceptible to serious disaffection based on primordial attachments'.[3] He related the notion of primordial attachment to the

> tendency for individuals to identify themselves with groups based on ties such as race, language, tribe or (in this case) religion, which are largely immutable and independent of any commitment to the civil authority of the State. At the time of the formation of Ulster, it was the fear on the part of the Ulster Protestants that they would lose their sense of cultural identity and come to be dominated by the Catholicism that they had abhorred and resisted for centuries, which ultimately persuaded the British government to create a divided Ireland. Since then, it is the Catholic minority within Ulster who have been motivated by precisely the same fear.[4]

The struggle on the part of both communities to maintain their cultural traditions leads to the impossibility of integrating society in Northern Ireland, and those Ulster 'moderates' who talk of 'bringing the two communities together' (a favourite 'moderate' phrase) are completely missing the central problem. The two communities do not want to be brought together, and indeed would, and do, violently resist any effort directed to this end, for they see in all such moves an attempt to undermine their cultural traditions, and comments such as those by former Prime Minister O'Neill about treating the Catholics decently in order to make them become just like good Protestants only serve to confirm the fears of the minority and heighten Catholic suspicion of Protestant good intentions. The Catholics do not want a policy of cultural assimilation any more than the Protestants do in a united Ireland, yet the Protestants, far from seeing the similarity of the two communities' attitudes, regard Catholic defence of their culture as an act of treason against the Northern State and a sure sign that the Catholics reject its legitimacy. The problem is not to find ways of 'bringing the two communities together', for we have seen that whenever they get together they end up by killing each other. The need now is to find a way of assuaging the Catholics' suspicions about Protestant cultural imperialism inside Ulster, and the Protestants' fears about Catholic cultural imperialism over Ireland as a whole. Only after both communities feel that their values and traditions are secure can the problem of integration be approached. A premature approach ends, as we now know, in bloodshed. It is for this reason that such segregated institutions as the schools occupy an important position in Ulster. The Catholics, through the Church schools, and the Protestants through the State schools (which are institutions of Protestant culture) maintain their communal culture, and both resist attempts at desegregation. It is fashionable to believe that the greatest resistance to integration in education comes from the Catholic Church, yet it should be remembered that an attempt by the Northern Ireland government to integrate the schools in the 1920s floundered on the opposition of the Protestant Orange Order.

Parallels have also been drawn between Northern Ireland and societies in the developed world with similar types of problems. An obvious one is that of the Southern States of America where the struggle between the white and black communities seems to be carried out in the same sort of terms, with the combatants worried about similar concerns. Those in Northern Ireland who organized the protest movements of 1968 and 1969 were quick to seize upon the analogy. They saw themselves pressing for similar political and social rights as the leaders of the American minority, and borrowed the songs, methods and slogans of the United States, as well as the title 'Civil Rights'. The Protestants' reaction in Ulster, under the leadership of Paisley, mirrored the backlash of poor whites in the Southern states. Both seem to be the rearguard action of insecure people in a highly traditional society that has suddenly become mobile. The poor whites and the Protestant working class are both dispossessed groups who have little economic cause for satisfaction with the old régime, yet both are reacting viciously to any attempts to change it, and the Civil Rights leaders in both countries insist that they want to help the dispossessed of both communities, and not just act as spokesmen of the minority community. Yet both the poor whites and the poor Protestants have to cling to the last shreds of self-respect that they possess. They have always been taught that no matter how badly off they might be, they are better off than the minority group, and they are not now prepared to abandon their little bit of status and lower themselves (in their own eyes) by making common cause with their supposed inferiors against the leaders of their own community. Hence the complete absence of significant working-class Protestant support for the Civil Rights movement, and the strong rally to Paisley, who seemed to be the only person prepared to defend them against the encroachments of the protesting minority.

The similarities between the Catholics and the blacks are not quite as simple. It seems fair to suggest that the large majority of American blacks still want integration, and are fighting to merge the black and white communities in America.[5] This is not the case in Ulster. For a short while it looked as though the Catholics might be abandoning their desire to preserve their own community and were, in seeking full and equal political rights, opting for integration with the Protestant community. The defeat in the 1969 Northern Ireland general election of some Nationalist MPs, including McAteer, their leader, by Social Democrat oriented Civil Rights leaders, Hume and Cooper, suggested a new departure in Catholic political action. Ever since the creation of the Northern State in 1921, the Catholics had wavered between two forms of opposition to the existence of the State. The Nationalists, after initial uncertainty, opted for 'constitutional' opposition – they took their seats in Parliament, ran local authorities, and accepted membership of government bodies. The Republicans steadfastly refused to participate in governing Northern Ireland. They would not take their seats as MPs and were often prepared to support the violence of the Irish Republican Army with which they were associated. The Nationalists are deeply conservative and thoroughly deserve the epithet of 'green Tories'. They have been closely associated with the Catholic Church and have never been concerned with social and economic issues. The Republicans, traditionally more radical, have in recent times embraced Socialism, and the political differences between the two groups led to an ideologically immobile political system. The Nationalists were with the Unionists on the far right, the Republicans refused to join in any political debate, and Labour was too weak to have much impact.

The Civil Rights movement, in bringing about the collapse of the Nationalists, has helped the Catholics to move leftward. Hume and Cooper, former members of the Labour party, supported progressive social and economic policies and tended to see allies in the British Labour party rather than in Fianna Fail, the governing party in Dublin and ally of McAteer. Immediately after the 1969 election it seemed possible that Hume and Cooper would lead the Catholics into a Social Democrat party, which might even embrace the Labour and Republican Labour parties, and work within the State, not to overthrow it but to make it operate in their own interests. Discussion of the border and concern over reunification gave way to debates on housing and unemployment. Mr McAteer, who was later to give public support to the Dublin Cabinet ministers accused of complicity in gun-running, was for the moment at least, irrelevant. Perhaps something might have come of this political change had it not been for the riots of the summer and autumn of 1969. The spring hopes were choked to death by the tear-gas, and in the Protestant-Catholic dialogue, the old script-writers were back. The Catholics might have turned to the Civil Rights leaders in a burst of enthusiasm for integration but their interest waned under the impact of police truncheons, and the role of Hume and Cooper as effective anti-Unionists became more important. The Civil Rights movement had caused more trouble for the Unionists in six months than the Nationalists had in fifty years, so Hume was accepted as a new leader and the man who had unseated McAteer in the Northern Ireland election of 1969 was supporting him in the British election of 1970. The circle was complete. McAteer had been irrelevant the previous year, but his renewed prominence in 1970 was not because he had changed, but because, fundamentally, the Catholics had not changed. They might toy for a while with new attitudes towards Stormont, but now that they were under pressure, they were quick to return to the old policy which McAteer represented. His candidature in 1970 was based on two simple policies – Catholic unity and the reunification of Ireland. Hume accepted it and supported him. Only Cooper and Wilton, significantly the only two prominent Protestant Civil Rights leaders in Derry, were suspicious. Cooper gave lukewarm support and damned Hume with faint praise, while Wilton offered outright, though ineffectual, opposition. In Derry at least, Catholic unity triumphed over Civil Rights.

Even Miss Devlin fared little better. Perhaps more clearly than Hume, she owes her position in Mid-Ulster to her abilities as an anti-Unionist and, in Catholic eyes, an anti-Protestant. She has fought as a Socialist and has been critical of the Catholic Church (though anti-clericalism is not a new force in Irish politics as the history of Parnell shows). Nevertheless, her strength lies in her effectiveness as an anti-Unionist. She has been as unsuccessful as Hume in winning a Protestant following, though she has been successful in maintaining Catholic support which returns hed to Parliament as a Catholic MP, and picturesque though she may be, she is not as relevant as Hume to the politics of Ulster. Hume established a claim to the leadership of the Catholic community. He had behind him supporters and an organization that were his own and not somebody else's. Miss Devlin is still dependent on the traditional Catholic organization in Mid-Ulster, and her supporters are, as she admits, not Socialists; they are people who like her personality but think little of her policies. Like McAteer, her basic policy in the 1970 election was Catholic unity. The reassertion of their communal tradition has underlined the difference between the Catholics and the majority of the American blacks. The Catholics are striving for recognition and the right to be Catholics with their own culture. They do not want to integrate.

Another analogy which is occasionally suggested for Ulster is Germany during the rise of the Nazi party. There is some initial attraction in this idea too. Although Paisley's most evident supporters are working class, he has a fair amount of lower-middle-class support – people who have a stake in the existing system and who are worried about the material consequences of Catholic demands and the resultant disorder. The cry of 'law and order' has an appeal to them, and they see Paisley as the only strong man on the scene. The phrase, 'I don't agree with everything he says, but . . .', is not uncommon and there are a number of putative Von Papens in the Unionist party who would be prepared to put Paisley in power, thinking they could control him in their own interests. Paisley himself preaches a peculiar brand of populist Socialism, mixed with prejudice and a religious drive to restore moral values and reassert local pride. Perhaps conscious of the link, one of his clerical supporters contested North Islington in the 1970 general election as a National Front candidate.

A number of writers have drawn attention to the association between extreme religious and political beliefs – Lipset observed that 'rigid fundamentalism and dogmatism are linked to the same underlying characteristics, attitudes, and predispositions which find another outlet in allegiance to extremist political movements'.[6] Paisley has long been associated with extreme religious leaders in the United States, where the links between fundamentalism and support for extreme right-wing politics is readily apparent. Many of the poor whites are devoted adherents of evangelical sects, and church attendance is noticeably high in both the southern states of America and Northern Ireland. The exclusive attitudes preached by fundamentalist religion overflow into the political sphere where political opponents are not regarded as being mistaken, but as being wicked – the man who believes that only members of his church can be saved and see the Kingdom of Heaven is quite likely to believe that only members of his party are honest citizens, and that opponents want to destroy the State.

> Belief in the literalness and purity of Biblical teachings makes fundamentalists resistant to social and cultural change; they are affronted by moral relativism, increasingly lenient sexual mores, the decline of parental authority, and other aspects of the secular modern world . . . they see the world as strictly divided into the saved and the damned, the forces of good and the forces of evil . . . the main danger to the faithful is from the corrosion of faith by insidious doctrines.[7]

This was written about America, but it is highly relevant to Northern Ireland, for it points to the type of society that exists there. Resistance to social liberalization is fierce. Not only are reforms such as the abortion, sexual offences, and divorce laws of Britain not introduced, but periodic efforts are made to reinforce censorship of films, and one of the first acts of the Northern Ireland Parliament when it was created was to strengthen sabbatarianism by closing public houses on Sundays. The importance of these activities, or lack of activity, is in the sort of society that they represent. It is still rather puritan, neo-Victorian in its outlook and, particularly in its sabbatarianism, is repugnant to Catholics.

The Catholics for their part give rise to similar theologically based objections on the Protestant side. Protestant politicians often justify their hostility towards Catholicism in general and the Irish Republic in particular by referring to Catholic social policy and its political implications. They have a point. The Catholic Church has a poor record as far as civil liberties are concerned. The Church's support for Franco's régime in Spain, its early hostility to the French Republic, its open interference in Italian politics, and the frequent association of dictatorial régimes with Catholic countries, as in Latin America, are all cited by Ulster politicians as justification for their anti-Catholic attitudes. Even nearer to home, they denounce the special position of the Church entrenched in the constitution of the Irish Republic, the literary censorship, the ban on divorce and contraception, and the backward, Church-dominated, education system. To a large extent, this is all hypocrisy. Only when compared with some Catholic countries does Ulster appear as a haven of liberalism. The very Unionist politicians who denounce the Irish Republic's literary censorship try to impose a complete ban on X-films in Belfast, and Northern Ireland's education system lags a long way behind Britain's. Nonetheless, the point is made. There are objectionable aspects of the Catholic Church's record, and they make good propaganda. And in sharp contrast to Southern Ireland, the North's constitution does at least guarantee the ecclesiastical impartiality of the law.

All these aspects of society in Northern Ireland raise a number of important questions about the State itself – questions which have been asked by political theorists who usually raised them in connection with countries where, as events have shown, they were not relevant. The most obvious is the worry of John Stuart Mill and de Tocqueville about the tyranny of the majority. This has in general been proved to have been a groundless fear about the development of the political system in England, but Mill was right about the way democracy has developed as far as Northern Ireland is concerned. Perhaps the problem is that Ulster is too democratic, the grass-roots have too much power, and the political leaders have too little ability to control their rank and file. The struggle first of O'Neill and then of Chichester-Clark to carry policies through Stormont in the face of grass-roots opposition revealed the weakness of the leadership's control over the Unionist party. It is relatively easy for a popular upheaval to upset the leadership in a way that would be impossible in the British Labour or Conservative parties. Members of Parliament have no privileged position when seeking re-election, but often have to struggle to retain their party's nomination – there is no National Executive Committee to protect them, no Central Office powers to refuse endorsement to a locally-chosen candidate the leadership might dislike. Consequently MPs have to be responsive to popular attitudes. They cannot afford the luxury of Edmund Burke's freedom of action, and those who have high ideals about representing the community soon discover the harsh reality that they are no more than their local party's delegate. All this is very democratic; it gives the people a considerable amount of influence in politics, but the people are not particularly liberal, at least not in Ulster, and they show little concern for the rights of their defeated opponents. This was one of the immediate causes of the Civil Rights demonstrations in 1968. The Protestant refusal to treat Catholic social needs justly, particularly in the field of housing, eventually aroused violent opposition. But, like the Bourbons, the Protestants have learnt nothing. Local resistance to egalitarian reforms, such as a points system for house allocations, is fierce, and local government is to be reconstructed, not because of popular demand but because politicians, especially in London, far removed from public pressure believe that change is necessary.

Popular resistance to reform had a considerable effect on the credibility of the Northern Ireland government which during the course of the disturbances moved from the position, under O'Neill, of a government that did not intend to give anything away but tried to persuade the Catholics that it did, to the position, under Chichester-Clark, where it was prepared to concede considerable reforms as a result of London's intervention, but tried to pretend to the Protestants that it was not giving anything away. The initial crisis, following the rioting in Londonderry in 1968, led to O'Neill's 'Five-Point Programme' of December 1968, which promised an ombudsman for Northern Ireland. This was the only unequivocal concession, for the other four points in some cases took away with one hand what was given with the other: Londonderry town council was suspended, but instead of being re-formed it was replaced by a commission whose chairman was a Unionist city councillor from Belfast; houses were to be allocated on a points system, but each local authority was left to draw up its own system, and quite a few refused to do so. In other cases the reforms offered were no more than hopes: although the company vote in local elections was abolished, no commitment at all was made to concede 'one man, one vote'; and similarly the only reform of the Special Powers Act that was promised – the repeal of those provisions which conflicted with Britain's international obligations – would come only 'as soon as the Northern Ireland government considers this can be done without undue hazard'. The government refused any concessions on the two cardinal demands of the Civil Rights Association. The franchise and the Special Powers Act were to remain unreformed. Despite an effort by the government to persuade the Catholics that their grievances were being dealt with, the Catholics remained unconvinced.

After becoming Prime Minister in May 1969, Chichester-Clark tried the same tactic as O'Neill, but with slightly greater subtlety. His government conceded reform – one man, one vote was agreed to, and the structure of local government was to be reformed – but at the same time, it reserved the power to itself by proposing to take away from local authorities most of their important functions. This time, the Catholics were more sympathetic, and though there was still a great deal of suspicion, there was a greater belief in the intention of the new government to carry out reforms. The outbreak of fresh and far more serious rioting in the summer of 1969, however, produced a new crisis with a new grievance – or rather, the revival of an old one. The Catholics were now concerned about the police and the B-Specials. They had, of course, been concerned about them before, but the use of B-Specials during the summer riots added a new urgency to this problem. The summer crisis culminated in two rounds of reforms, which were either announced by, or provoked by, Callaghan. In August, the Hunt Committee was appointed to investigate the police force, two senior civil servants were sent from London to Belfast, and London started hinting that the B-Specials would be disbanded. This was hotly denied in Belfast, where the Unionist government was under strong pressure from its right wing. The Unionist hard-liners broke the party truce which followed O'Neill's fall, by attacking the proposals to reform local government. Now they turned their attention to the defence of the B-Specials. Just as O'Neill had tried to convince the Catholics that he was redressing their grievances, even though he was not prepared to offer any reforms, Chichester-Clark had to carry through the reforms while pretending to the Protestants that nothing was being changed. Neither was successful.

Chichester-Clark's position became even more difficult after Callaghan's second visit early in October 1969, when the recommendations of the Hunt Committee were accepted. The two most controversial were the proposals that the police should be disarmed and that the B-Specials should be replaced by the Ulster Defence Regiment under the command of the British Army (and hence London) and the Royal Ulster Constabulary Reserve, an unarmed civilian force under local control. This in effect meant the disbanding of the B-Specials. The Unionist government was further embarrassed by Callaghan's decision to create a central housing authority and to scrap the Unionists' scheme for reshaping local authorities. The loss of control over housing was a heavy blow to local patronage, for it removed much of the local councillor's influence in obtaining houses for his supporters (such an occurrence had provoked the demonstration at the Caledon housing estate at the start of the Civil Rights Campaign in July 1968), and it abolished a way in which local councils could help maintain the balance of power by strategically siting Protestant and Catholic estates. Faulkner, as Minister of Development, had been responsible for drawing-up the scheme for local government reforms which was a fairly respectable piece of gerrymandering designed not only to preserve as much power as possible for the Unionists while giving a few authorities over to Catholic control, but also in all probability to protect the Unionists' position when Northern Ireland Parliamentary boundaries were revised by the commission that had been set up the previous year with instructions to respect local authority areas. The government's efforts to carry out these new reforms and pretend to the Protestants that it was not conceding anything important became even more frantic as the demand was taken up by Craig and Paisley that the police should be re-armed and the B-Specials saved. Protestant hostility eventually produced Belfast's worst rioting later in October when mobs on the Shankill Road clashed with the police and army, killing one of the policemen they wanted to re-arm.

The resistance of the Protestants to making concessions to Catholics arises directly from the view most people have of Ulster's politics as a 'zero sum' equation. Catholic gains can, in the eyes of the Protestants, only be at Protestant expense, and vice-versa. To a large extent, this is a true assessment. The Protestants have so deeply entrenched themselves and monopolized the State that they have to surrender their privileges if the Catholics are to advance, so Protestant resistance to change is hardly surprising. This goes back to the reason for the Protestant monopoly – the attitude of the two communities to the State – and here the question of legitimacy arises. When the British government sought a solution to the Irish problem, the Protestants made it quite clear that they would resist violently the authority of an all-Ireland government in Dublin and deny its legitimacy. The alternative then was to give the Protestants their own State in the north. This would include some Catholics, who would deny the legitimacy of the northern State, but their resistance would not be quite so violent, so this was the preferred solution. The northern State was set up and the Catholics did deny its legitimacy. Their representatives refused to help to run it and they set themselves the task of overthrowing it. What little power they had, they used to obstruct the Stormont government – the Catholic-controlled county councils of Fermanagh and Tyrone refused to recognize the authority of the Belfast government, so the Unionists did the only thing they could do in the circumstances; they gerrymandered the county electoral divisions to ensure a loyal majority. Thus the gerrymander of local government came about. From the point of view of the Protestants, there was no use in letting the Catholics run any local authorities because they would only use their power to cause a breakdown in the system. The attitude of the Catholics served only to confirm the Protestant belief that they wanted to destroy the State, and from the very beginning opposition to the government became synonymous with opposition to the State itself. There could be no patriotism outside the Unionist party, and to oppose the government was disloyal. So the State became closely identified with the Unionist party – the

State was its State, the police its police, the laws its laws. The other side of the coin meant that the State was not the Catholics' State, its police not their police, its laws not their laws. Indeed not only was the State not their State, even worse, it was their enemy's State, and as such its legitimacy could not possibly be recognized. There were periodic attempts to oppose it with violence, but it was clear that the Catholics could never hope to overthrow it. The most they could hope for was to be left in peace to live in their own community. This they were not allowed to do. They were harassed and persecuted at first, until this gave way to the disability of being excluded from economic and political power.

The improvement in economic and social conditions following the Second World War led to an easing of tension, and the Catholic community began to reassert itself and gain confidence. The Civil Rights movement represented an attempt to remove the discriminatory disabilities under which it suffered. To some extent, the violence of the Ulster crisis might have helped it to do this. Some laws were changed, but above all, the British government was forced to lay the ghost of 1912 and prove that it would no longer be intimidated by the violent defiance of its authority by the Protestants. At least the Catholics gained confidence in the determination of London to ensure justice, though the defeat of the Labour government in 1970 was received with despondency. The support given to Callaghan by Hogg before the election, and the public image of Maudling helped to reassure the Catholics that the Conservative party had come a long way since 1912, though they were not entirely convinced, and there is still a long way to go before the Protestants will have abandoned the position, essentially irreconcilable with the authority of the State, expressed by the former Unionist Prime Minister Lord Craigavon, who declared 'I have always said I am an Orangeman first and a member of this Parliament afterwards.'

NOTES

1. Roger D. Scott, 'Ulster in Perspective: The Relevance of Non-European Experience', *Australian Outlook*, vol. 23 (December 1969), no. 3, pp. 246–57.
2. Ibid., p. 250.
3. C. Geertz, 'The Integrative Revolution: Primordial Sentiments and Civil Politics in New States', in C. Geertz (ed.), *Old Societies: The Quest for Modernity in Asia and Africa* (London, 1963), p. 109.
4. Scott, loc. cit.
5. Obviously not all American blacks want integration. Some of the more militant want separation, advocate the use of violence, and

see the State machinery and the police as the servants of the ruling community. In this there is a similarity with the Ulster Catholics.

6. S. M. Lipset, *Political Man* (London, 1960), p. 108.
7. R. E. Wolfinger, B. K. Wolfinger, K. Prewitt and S. Rosenhack, 'America's Radical Right: Politics and Ideology', in D. Apter (ed.), *Ideology and Discontent* (London, 1964), pp. 282–3.

VIII Race Relations in British Politics

HANNAN ROSE

Whatever the difficulties of defining 'race' and 'race relations' for the purposes of academic research, it is accepted politically that Britain has a race relations problem. The key fact in any assessment of events during the period 1960–70 and in attempts to project possible future developments is that the 'problem' is considered as being caused by the immigration into this country of Commonwealth citizens (but not of aliens). It is, therefore, the process of arrival and entry of coloured people that has been the focus of political concern, rather than their position once they have arrived and entered – their 'integration' into the community.

A first question, therefore, is why this has been the case, and why problems of integration have taken second place. The factors which could determine the future pattern of the politics of race relations in Britain might be expected to emerge from the answers.

The Pattern of the 1960s

During the 1950s, attempts were made to bring governmental attention to the problems associated with the concentration of immigrants, especially from the West Indies, in particular areas. These attempts were directed towards securing assistance for local authorities and other bodies concerned with housing, welfare and employment as much as to resolving the problems by curtailing immigration. The firm answer of the government was that any special measures, either to help immigrants or to regulate their entry as members of the Commonwealth to the mother country, would be discriminatory and undesirable.

In effect, the orthodox position of the authorities represented the general orientation of anti-racialist opinion, which felt secure in the belief that major politicians agreed with the consensus of liberal views. After the 'race riots' of 1958, there was increased concern about the position in Britain. This was allayed by the handing out of a few exemplary prison sentences and the conviction that the incidents were isolated and did not represent the true situation. It was inconceivable that any government could betray policies that were at the heart of the creation of the Commonwealth and were the most important of the values upheld by Britain. There was still no agreement on the need for special policies to tackle problems associated with immigration.

Thus, when the Conservative government suddenly announced the decision to introduce immigration control, the liberals were caught on the wrong foot. The initiative had been seized by those who defined the problem as one of the immigration of coloured people into this country, and this break in the previous consensus set the pattern for the political consideration of race relations throughout the 1960s.

In a sense, this is a lament for opportunity lost. If an attempt had been made in the 1950s to promote a conception of an integrated society, with the understanding that problems of housing, employment, welfare, etc. associated with the arrival and settlement of immigrants were not *caused* by the immigrants, it would have been more difficult for the advocates of control to define the issue on their own terms. The problem was defined as immigration, and the solution seen as its restriction, so that in the 1960s the two major parties played a numbers-game. Neither wished to be outbid in its promises to the electorate of the numbers of potential immigrants who would be excluded by its policies.

The immigration control lobby had a number of advantages in this situation, particularly the fact that numbers can easily be communicated to the public whilst abstract views of the values of a multi-racial society are more amorphous. Similarly, in public debate, warnings of imminent disasters have more effect than promises of distant pleasures. It is factors such as these which must be considered when explaining the political success of the advocates of restriction. They were, and continue to be, able to represent themselves as speaking for a wide section of public opinion, articulating common fears of continued 'alien' immigration.

Indeed, this view of the process whereby immigration control was introduced has virtually become the accepted version of events, but its accuracy must be doubted. It is more likely that the advocates of control led public opinion, which was largely unaware of the existence of a problem, and turned immigration into a public issue. This hypothesis casts doubt upon the assertion that conventional pressure group mechanisms were responsible for the change in policy from liberal non-intervention to the commitment to control. It is doubtful how real the pressure groups (such as the Birmingham Immigration Control Committee) were. It can be argued that many similar pressure groups with at least the same degree of support are a constant feature of the political scene without having any success at all, let alone the degree of success enjoyed by the advocates of immigration control in the 1960s.

This perspective poses problems for theories about the nature of democratic representation. The criteria on which the Conservative government apparently based its acceptance of the restrictionist argument were that this was a policy on which they could appeal to the electorate, that its implementation would cost little, or that the restrictionists were friendly or potentially friendly to the Conservative party. Against this, the opponents of restriction had little or nothing to offer: they had no clear policy at all; if they produced a policy based on an analysis of the situation in terms of housing, education, welfare, etc, it would involve considerable expenditure, and alternative courses of action would win no support at all.

It would, therefore, appear that the Conservative government responded to the inflation, if not the outright creation, of a demand, and processed this claim upon the system as if it were legitimate and coherent. Once this had been done, the 1964 Labour government found it impossible to maintain the illegitimacy of the demand for immigration control. The liberals, who had reacted to the introduction of control with horror, could not restore the *status quo ante*, but found themselves having to respond to the situation in the terms which had already been defined: the problem was inevitably seen, by politicians and public alike, as one of immigration.

Here we must consider the factors which prevented the liberals from exerting more effective pressure. There were the factors on which the Conservative government based its adoption of the policy of control: these still affected the political balance. The liberals were still not agreed on what policy to adopt: whether Britain should aim for the assimilation of immigrants, cultural pluralism or structural pluralism. Consequently, they could not begin to consider the strategy which would be required to produce the desired result. For a number of reasons, commitments to further expenditure were not welcome. Finally, the Labour party appeared in more danger of losing voters who were thought to be anxious for further limitation of immigration, than of losing the support of liberals and intellectuals who opposed it.

This interpretation of the factors involved in the success and failure of pressure on the British political system appears to be substantiated by the first minor success of the liberal lobby, the 1965 Race Relations Act. This merely implied commitment to equality for all, regardless of race. Its cost was minimal, and it could be presented to the electorate as an expression of political values unrelated to the issues which centred on demands for further immigration control. Subsequent events have consolidated this pattern: the White Paper on Immigration and the 1968 Commonwealth Immigrants Act gave major concessions to the restrictionists, whilst the liberals achieved only minor success with the Race Relations Act of 1968.

Perhaps the most significant factor of all is that the discussion so far has made no reference to the potential political action of the immigrants themselves. For most, if not all, of this period, the minority group has been composed of migrants. As such they have not been oriented towards taking an active interest in British politics: their immediate concerns have been their economic position, housing and other immediate needs. They have not been in a position to formulate claims on the system or take action to further such claims. Their interests are still oriented to the society from which they came, and considerable connections with that society are kept up in the form of payments for dependants, correspondence with relatives and friends, the arrival in Britain of further migrants from their area and, of course, periodic visits to their homeland. Above all, the immigrants' perception of their position in this country has not motivated them towards participation in British politics.

It is essential that this is clearly understood, for as these perceptions and attitudes change, there will be important consequences for the way in which race relations can be treated by the political system. Originally, many immigrants saw themselves as temporary residents in this country, here to earn and save some capital which would enable them to return home. But as families are brought over, and children are educated here, the commitment to this country becomes permanent. The insecurity arising from the feeling that racial prejudice in Britain is increasing only delays this process slightly.

This is of great importance. Whilst the immigrant himself, attracted by the better economic prospects, is prepared to accept an imperfect position in British society, he does expect that his children, either born or educated here, will enjoy the benefits of full participation. The children themselves do not consider themselves to be immigrants: all they know of their parents' society is learnt at second hand. The fact that their parents were immigrants does not make them willing to accept 'second-class' citizenship in the only society they know.

The politics of the immigrant groups, then, has been minimally concerned with British politics during the 1960s. Leaders and politicians in the immigrant groups have been involved in activities which are defined within the political activity of Britain – lobbying against immigration restrictions, pressing for legislation against discrimination, joining or attacking community relations councils and so forth. However, their activity has been directed as much, if not more, towards considerations within their own community organizations and groupings, rather than towards representing the whole minority group in its relations with British society. There have been a few attempts to create organizations which would participate in politics on behalf of all immigrant groups, but they have not found conditions appropriate to their intentions.

Looking Into the 1970s

As immigrants come to regard themselves and their children as members of British society, they will begin to make demands on society and try to use the political process to pursue their claims. If the liberal philosophy of the 1950s, which proclaimed the irrelevance of colour, had been maintained, then coloured immigrants would have been expected to participate in politics as individuals. Since the host society and its dominant culture defined them as a minority of coloured Britons, this is how they are likely to see themselves. This poses considerable problems for the political system.

Consciousness of race is becoming an important factor throughout the world, and so, in this country, claims are likely to be articulated in terms of the interests of the coloured minority. Yet this will be considered to be illegitimate, since Britain has no tradition of dealing with political behaviour which explicitly recognizes the importance of ethnic and group affiliations. The dilemma is sharpened by the actions of the 1960s, which, in defining the immigration of coloured Commonwealth citizens as a problem, has run counter to the tradition that colour is irrelevant. The real problem for Britain will be to decide whether collective group action, based on identification as a coloured minority, will be acceptable. Much will depend on whether the coloured minority, conscious of its identity and wishing to participate in the affairs of society, will find the political system responsive to the articulation of its demands.

In a sense, the quiescent period of the 1960s has been a very bad experience for British politics. In effect, the political parties in the 1960s were able to appeal to public opinion, directing policy against the coloured minority group without having to fear a direct response from it. No preparation was made for the group's entry into full participation in the political process, nor any definition of the way in which such participation should be structured. The politics of race relations has been an issue between white Britons about a coloured minority group, with that group virtually powerless to affect the outcome. The extent of this powerlessness is perhaps best indicated by the fact that the only response to threats of a further immigration control Bill in 1968 was a demonstration when the battle had already been lost. There was no reaction against the political system, because the group did not see itself as a full and continuous participant in that system: powerlessness when the group wishes to be included in the process of British politics might have very different results.

The first reaction would be protest through activities such as demonstrations. This is a characteristic reaction of groups which are denied, or see themselves as being denied, an effective voice in decision-making.

The form of protest is more likely to be influenced by the prevailing climate in Britain as established by the activity of other groups excluded from the political mainstream, rather than by any pattern adapted from experience in their previous societies. In the first place, the coloured minority group would be in a position where the behaviour pattern of the majority would strictly circumscribe the possible forms of activity: the protest would be aimed at forcing the majority to recognize the legitimacy of the minority's demands with inclusion and participation in the dominant white structure as the primary object. Further, there is no one pattern of political activity on which the group could draw. They come from a variety of backgrounds in societies very different from Britain, but they largely share the belief that the institutions of Parliamentary, representative democracy on the Westminster model is valid and inherently reasonable.

There is no reason to believe that violence plays any part in the political systems from which the leaders of the group will draw their experience, and in the internal politics of the communities during the 1960s, there has been no evidence of the existence of a style of behaviour that involved violence. Activities are thus more likely to be determined by the form of protest activity used by other groups – petitions, lobbying, marches, sit-ins, non-violent direct action or whatever – and this will depend on wider considerations than the state of race relations. Broadly, it would appear that the way in which protest is formulated depends on how responsive the political mechanism is perceived to be, and the extent of policy change necessary for the group's demands to be met.

If this is the case, the danger of extreme or violent forms of direct action and protest would arise only if the traditional political process proved to be totally unresponsive to the demands of the coloured British minority group, and if the political system itself came to be seen as illegitimate. In such situations, small groups could take to violence, and the behaviour of a wider section of minority group members would represent a direct challenge to the political system (as rioting in Ulster and elsewhere is an obviously political activity). It seems, therefore, that any attempt to deny the reality and legitimacy of the coloured minority group in society and politics is likely to initiate an unhappy pattern of events. If the group is denied access to the political system and to social participation, it will be forced to resort to protest activities. If this is rejected it will lead to the group's refusal to recognize the validity of the political process, a situation which will be perceived as justifying the original assertion. The behaviour of the minority group will be considered to constitute 'the problem' – and this might be thought to be no more than the logical conclusion of a policy which deemed the immigrants to be 'the problem' in the 1960s.

From this perspective, the real task for Britain is to establish the basis upon which future participation of the coloured British in social and political processes will be acceptable. The major responsibility lies with the dominant white community, but the decision cannot be made without taking full account of the feelings of the coloured groups. As a result of developments since 1960 in this country, and, in a wider perspective, the general pattern of race relations on a world scale, the liberal solution of the 1950s (in which colour of skin is irrelevant) no longer seems possible. In some way, therefore, the social and political participation of a group based on colour (or a number of coloured groups differentiated by cultural, religious and linguistic traditions) will have to be accepted as legitimate in a form of pluralist society. Such a development would include in the society a large number of people who would otherwise find themselves in the position where only direct action would offer a means of articulating the political and social demands they might wish to make.

Conclusion

Race relations as a political issue in Britain has been primarily concerned with the immigration to this country of coloured Commonwealth citizens. This orientation has resulted from the response of the political system to pressure for such limitations. Whether this pressure existed before the first step was taken to limit immigration or not, agitation against immigration has subsequently become legitimate and politically acceptable. Reaction to this pressure has been belated and ineffectual, because the liberals who would have resisted this tendency have been in a weak political position. Their only success has been the limited legislation against racial discrimination.

Up to the present, the immigrant groups have not been oriented towards participation in British politics. As they cease to consider themselves immigrants and become citizens, with the expectation that their children will enjoy full participation in society, they will increasingly form a group making claims on, and acting within, the political system. A transition to some form of plural structure in politics and social affairs could be achieved once the justice of the claims is accepted. If this does not happen, there could be resort to more disruptive forms of direct action.

IX Black Consciousness

ALEXANDER KIRBY

Mark Bonham Carter was not far from the point when he described British Black Power leaders as 'Hungarian admirals': the numerical strength of the groups they represent is certainly low, though just how low is uncertain – 'those who tell don't know, and those who know don't tell'. But to conclude from this that they are simply paper tigers would be wrong; as Colin McGlashan wrote,

> There are no Black Power leaders in Britain with any following worth twopence, and there never have been. But that does not mean that the words of black spokesmen, however strident, are unrepresentative and should be ignored. Like anyone who aspires to leadership of a group, men like Jeff Crawford, Michael Abdul Malik . . . or Roy Sawh understand and articulate with great accuracy the feelings and frustrations of black Britons; they do not create them.[1]

Arguably, the very title 'Black Power' is dangerously misleading even in the USA from which it sprang: if Stokely Carmichael hadn't produced it, it would, with its twin evocations of negritude and virility, have done credit to the backroom boys of the CIA as a label calculated to alarm and alienate Middle America. It is even less accurate in its British usage, particularly as it is almost unfailingly applied by Press and public to some imagined monolith, a nightmare incubus preparing to gnaw the vitals of the body politic. Black Power's facts are at once more prosaic and more hopeful than its legend.

There is no single Black Power movement in Britain, but rather a bewildering *mélange* of varied groups, some well-established, some small in size and short in life. Far more fragmented than rumour paints them, they are also far less wedded to a belief in violence as a necessary means, though most are radical enough to compare the violence of poverty and repression with the violence which is a reaction to them. Nor are they all the black élitists they are made out to be: many will work with committed whites and few will go on from 'black is beautiful' to claim that white is intrinsically anything else. What unites them all is not necessarily either their methods or their goal, but their genesis: they are black groups seeking to develop a black life-style which answers their particular needs of time and place and soul. In their diversity, their willingness to exhaust 'every means necessary' before considering the use of violence so often credited to them (I have yet to meet one black leader who talked without prompting of violence, or seemed even to think it worth mentioning to me) and their attempts to equip the black psyche to meet the white on equal, not superior, terms, they are ill-served by the Black Power tag. Black Consciousness is more accurate, though less satisfying:

> If SNCC had said Negro Power or Coloured Power, white folks would've continued sleeping easy every night. But *Black Power!* Black! That word *Black*. And the visions came of alligator-infested swamps arched by primordial trees with moss dripping from the limbs, and out of the depth of the swamp, the mire oozing from his skin, came the black monster, and fathers told their daughters to be in by nine instead of nine-thirty.[2]

Black Power (the popular title is the simpler, and will be used here) is a response to the black man's history and his present. So for a white man fully to understand or judge it is an exercise in the impossible. Yet Black Power is constantly judged by the white majority in Britain; the judgements made depend, obviously, on the criteria and assumptions used. This attempt to describe Black Power draws on two sets of assumptions, or beliefs: those external to the black community (the present attitude and behaviour of white society) and those which are internal (the history which has brought black people here and made them what they are).

It is the 'internal' assumptions that are, for a white, totally a matter of belief and not at all of experience. But unless we are deaf and blind, we cannot any longer doubt that the fact of being black has for so long been a source of oppression, humiliation and inhumanity that blackness today has as its concomitants confusion and anguish. When these are joined by self-awareness they will issue in a search for individual identity in terms of the group. But all such attempts to get under the skin, to picture the black experience, must fail. The imaginative gap is too wide, and the nearer and more urgent task is to persuade ourselves and others that it exists and must be reckoned with. Black suffers by generations and centuries of white exploitation – physical, mental, spiritual: take it or leave it.

The nuts and bolts of the black condition in Britain today are well enough documented though no less hotly denied by a society which cannot face life without scapegoats. Immigration laws and practices whose aim is to exclude black people, a Race Relations Act which barks the right notes but has teeth to bite no one; a much vaunted race relations industry which is starved into irrelevance; local authority indifference and malpractice; an educational system inadequate to white needs, let alone black; smugly ethnocentric mass media; an assumption by society that blacks are divinely ordained to come last in the queue for jobs, housing, or anything else in short supply: all combine to keep black people firmly in place as the new helotry, here on sufferance, and to remind them how happy we should be if they weren't here at all. The white poor, who have most to gain from making common cause with black demands, are allowed – or encouraged – to see themselves as competitors for the favours of the capitalist welfare state. If there weren't any blacks, we should indeed have to invent them, unless we could face the prospect of working to end class injustice.

But this is a largely uni-causal view of race in Britain, and one that can be only a single element in any evaluation of a phenomenon which traces its roots back to the experience of slavery. No single analysis or categorization can do justice to Black Power, if only because the concept attracts a variety of individuals who see in it widely differing potentialities, and because it is a highly dynamic and volatile force, shaped by the larger society at least as much as it contributes to society's moulding and markedly responsive to international changes and developments. But, at the risk of arbitrarily imposing an alien set of values (bound to be incomplete) on groups which demand a totality of commitment and experience, not of externalized judgement, I think it is even now possible to discern three distinct aspects of Black Power. The three differ in their goals; but it is important to accept that they do not represent watertight concepts, in that each individual may express all three in succession or hold them all in some uneasy and probably unknowing combination. Nor is it always possible to describe distinct Black Power groupings in terms of one or other of the three, as all are likely to play a part, large or small, in the consciousness of a particular group. For want of better terms I describe the three aspects below as cultural, integrationist and revolutionary.

Cultural Black Power? I have suggested that black people in Britain are conditioned by two sets of circumstances, the historical and the geographical, the past and the present, internal and external, black and white. Cultural Black Power is a response to the first of each of these pairs: it is an affirmation that, despite generations of dispossession, there is a black inheritance; that black men need no longer struggle towards the sunlit uplands of white values, because black is beautiful. Cultural Black Power – black nationalism – for the first time in centuries gives the black man a chance to find his own identity in a black frame of reference. Thus it is an end in itself, not a means. Thus, too, it is the most basic and most potent form of Black Power, as it is the blackest, and it must to some degree underlie all other Black Power formulations. Its outward expressions can range from Afro hairstyles and dress through African and Third World history classes to a refusal to countenance any association with Whitey and his works. But whatever form the expression takes, the inward reality that it connotes is potentially creative and liberating. Blacks have existed in the West solely as derivatives, dependants, capable of assimilation into 'civilized' society only on that society's terms, and only when as individuals they showed themselves willing to disown their community. Now there is in embryo a community in which they can find meaning. It is remarkable how often those responsible whites who clamour loudest for 'integration' (innocent perhaps of an understanding of its implications) are quickest to condemn Black Power as retrograde, separatist, 'black racism'. But it is simply Aristotelean to argue that you don't make equals through treating unequals equally: anyone who is prepared to see a multi-racial society as an exercise in pluralism should welcome that emerging black consciousness which alone will equip blacks to meet whites with an equal psychological security, with their own identity. The growth of black nationalism is profoundly important for the avoidance of racial conflict and for the ending of racial injustice.

If integrationist Black Power seems a contradiction in terms, then it is the terms that are at fault. What is not debatable is that there exists in Britain a group of black people who see their future as inextricably involved with white society and its fortunes, and who believe that only black solidarity will enable them to gain the place they are entitled to. Reformers rather than revolutionaries, pragmatists more than ideologues, they see Black Power as a tool to help them to achieve racial and social justice. The adherents of integrationist Black Power are often middle-class professionals who have learnt the lesson of the ethnic voters of New York, of the fruits of Jewish solidarity in Britain. Yet they are by no means self-seekers: many of them stand to gain less from the spread of black consciousness than fellow blacks further down the ladder, but see in its spread the best hope of averting the polarization that must follow unremitting inequality in employment, housing and education. Black Power under this aspect can be expected to stimulate interesting reactions from white society. Where will the political parties stand if blacks convince themselves that political power is best achieved separately? At the moment, the politicians who actively seek black support and involvement between elections can be counted on a few fingers. Interestingly, most of them (for example, Andrew Faulds, Sydney Bidwell, Joan Lestor) seemed to fare better at the last general election than did their colleagues who, through idleness, political cowardice or any other factor, ignored their black constituents except in the run-up to polling day. What will be the reaction of trade unions which find themselves marching beside all-black unions – a state of affairs that is probably not far off in parts of the West Midlands, for example. The effect on commerce, too, of black economic separatism could be considerable; if black people can make themselves as self-reliant a community as the British Cypriots, they will be exercising very real Black Power, to the cost of White Power. Those who are working for economic and political Black Power, in fact, see their role as the creation of another interest group to challenge the many which already constitute the checks and balances of White Power. They are acting from motives of self-preservation and self-advancement, not of domination or doctrinaire separatism. If they achieve the strength and unity they seek, they will constitute an important part of any pluralist strategy.

Revolutionary Black Power, too, sees the creation of black consciousness primarily as a means: its end is the overthrow of capitalism and neo-imperialism. For this group, Britain is only one of several theatres; the revolution will come first perhaps in Africa or the Caribbean, later in the USA and Britain. Yet they are not simply classical Marxists-Leninists, despite their diagnosis of racism as a symptom and a tool of capitalism; they claim to be able to make a unique contribution to the revolution by virtue of having inherited the black experience. Many plan to return to the West Indies to hasten the revolution there, or to join the freedom fighters in South Africa. The particular contribution they are making to British political thinking is to call into question the underlying assumption of the integrationist/pluralist approach: what kind of society is it that we are grudgingly offering black people a share in? They will answer that Western society is so sick, with its materialism, its parochialism and its straightforward inhumanity, that they want no part of it – an answer not radically different from the white liberals' claim that the black community in Britain acts as a trace element in society, showing up the weaknesses and injustices that have oppressed the British poor for generations. Black Power revolutionaries possess a breadth of vision that enables them to see the speciousness of arguments for arming South Africa, the timorous fallacies of Western 'aid' to the Third World, as the inevitable accompaniments of the white supremacy syndrome which stunts their lives here – a connection by no means always made by white liberals. Of all Black Power groups, the revolutionaries have the furthest aim, the longest reach. Not surprisingly they are the group most likely to ally themselves with white radicals, ranging from Young Socialists through Third World groups to community relations councils. The reason for such alliances is soundly tactical – that these days radicals cannot afford to be too choosy in finding mutual support when confronted by colossal apathy and virulent opposition. But the black revolutionaries manage to transcend the forced opportunism of their tactics with the saving humanism of their concept of revolution. Thus Herman Edwards wrote:

> The black man today is giving [the white man] a warning and that is that *we shall overcome* while he is caught up in the psychological fixedness of white supremacy. We shall move with love and purity for the betterment of humanity, where all peoples of the world will live in peace and harmony without the criminal action of white or black supremacy.[3]

The strategy of the Black Panthers in the USA has been (though police infiltration and shoot-outs have sharply and dramatically curtailed its activities) to provoke the sort of confrontation with white America which can be solved in only two ways: by massive repression, or by accepting the Panthers' demands for justice. They have acted thus in the belief that even the silent majority will see and accede to the righteousness of their demands rather than acquiesce in the degree of violence and injustice which will be the alternative. A similar strategy of confrontation, not for its own sake but to bring a sick society to its senses, motivates many British Black Power revolutionaries, though they would admit that the granting of their demands would amount to revolution rather than reform.

Attempts to describe the range and activities of Black Power groups founder, partly on the impossibility of categorization, partly on the difficulty of obtaining accurate and up-to-date information, partly on the very fissiparous nature of the multitude of existing groups. Thus the old Universal Coloured Peoples' Association split into the Black Power party and the Free University of Black Studies, the Black Unity and Freedom party, and the Black Panthers. And one of the most imaginative and, at times, promising of groups, Michael Abdul Malik's Adjustment Action Society, with its complex of potential supermarket, mosque, living-quarters, etc., collapsed into a state of disarray from which it probably will not recover. Undoubtedly some groups have an excess of leaders over followers and add to the observer's confusion by an existence that is scarcely more than nominal. So the fact that the three groups described in slightly greater detail below are not typical should not blind the reader to the fact that no group is typical: *all* Black Power groups differ so much in relative incidentals (leadership styles, for instance) that there is no choice between an arbitrary selection for description and a biography of every existing group (running probably into several thousands). But I believe that each of the three I have selected does illustrate at least one of the aspects discussed above.

The Black Panthers have a borrowed name, but not yet much of the battle-hardened quality of their American counterparts. Their strongest branch is in Brixton, with others in Acton (which mustered a turnout

of over 300 for a Black Power film show), Stoke Newington, Birmingham, Manchester, and possibly elsewhere. Their activities have two
foci: the development of an awareness of black history and identity
through African history classes and a youth club, and publicizing
allegations of racially discriminatory local practices, especially in so far
as these concern the police. They have a hard-core organizing group of
perhaps a dozen in Brixton: what their total strength is no one will say,
quite possibly because no one knows, as black kids will drift in and out
of informal membership in a way which defies enumeration. The
Panthers are, in their activities, primarily a cultural and nationalist
Black Power group, though they are almost certainly also revolutionary
in their long-term aims so far as they have thought these out. Almost
all their members are young, and most are alienated, often through
unemployment: Black Power as a strategy for integration has little
appeal for them.

The one group of West Indians in South London presents a marked
contrast. It has been active in one ward where blacks predominate, in
the certainty that it is possible to mobilize them to the point where
they can decide a local election. In 1970 it cut its teeth in the GLC
elections; the next year it put up several candidates at the borough
elections in May. It is also on the point of launching a black co-
operative, designed to concentrate economic power and self-help
within the black community. The co-operative will exist initially
by selling shares, with the possibility later of acquiring a shop, offering
loans, etc. The group's members see their place and their future very
definitely in Britain. That being so, they want to participate from a
position of strength.

In stark contrast to both black nationalism and economic, 'integrationist' black consciousness is the highly developed political consciousness of the Black Unity and Freedom party. For them, blackness
connotes a unique historical and geographical contribution which they
can make to the class struggle – historical, because black men have for
centuries formed the sub-proletariat of the imperialist world, and
geographical, because neo-imperialism still calls the tune to which
their countries of origin have to dance, and colonialists *manqués* still control the societies to which they have migrated. For them Black Power is
a means towards – an aspect of – a larger confrontation: 'It is not a
political slogan, not an ideology, for it has neither political thought
nor an economic base. The slogan has outgrown itself.' The BUFP sees
itself as the sole heir of the old Universal Coloured Peoples' Association,
and sees its work in successive phases: it concentrates now on the
unorganized working class, to which it tries to match its idiom, with a
view in time to attracting the support of the organized lumpen-
proletariat. Will it co-operate with whites ? 'Yes, but we're concentrating

at the moment on the black workers simply because we can't organize everyone.' Again, they'll work with the Irish National Liberation Solidarity Front: 'the Irish are the niggers of Europe', and with the Palestinians, and other minorities with revolutionary colonial bases. The BUFP works with what it sees as its primary constituency in terms it thinks will be intelligible to it. So it will demonstrate against what it sees as police brutality, conscious that this is an idiom immediately understood by alienated, disorganized and mainly young black people. But it casts its net wider: at its weekly open meetings, it attracts as many as seventy people, by no means all of them party members, who are anxious to know more of what it intends at local level. Active in South-East London, it has branches also in Moss Side (Manchester) and Stoke Newington. Its work programme includes the formation of tenants' associations (in this respect, in New Cross, it is achieving a remarkable degree of co-operation with a largely white-run neighbourhood council), work with educationally sub-normal black kids – though it thinks there is need for work with all ESN children, it is concentrating on black ones because of their alleged and well-substantiated over-representation in ESN schools, and is planning a summer school for them in co-operation with the neighbourhood council – and playgroups both for pre-school and for older children. This programme of reaching out to the black community, it believes, will enable it to take the first steps along the road of educating black people politically, of enabling them to see their predicament in a class, not a race, context. But the discipline it demands of its own members makes few concessions to political naïveté; they shall:

1) study Marxist-Leninist-Mao Tse-Tung thought in a creative way;
2) work in the interest of the black masses;
3) unite with the majority of black people and oppose careerists, double-dealers and conspirators;
4) regularly consult with the masses;
5) make criticism and self-criticism.

Among the party rules appear the following injunctions:

Do not take a needle or a piece of thread from the masses.
No party member must have drugs or weed in his possession.
No party member must be drunk on duty.
When arrested, party members must give only their name and address, and will sign nothing.
Elementary legal rules must be known and understood by all.
Each member must submit a weekly report of his daily work.

157

Political classes are compulsory for all members. These must be held
at least once per week in each branch.
Only office staff are to be in offices. All others are to sell propaganda
and to do other political work out in the community.
Every member must read politics for at least one hour per day.
All branches must submit in writing a weekly political report.

The party's short-term programme calls *inter alia* for 'an immediate
end to police brutality'; 'an immediate end to the harassment of black
people . . . by racist immigration officers'; 'an immediate repeal of the
so-called Race Relations Act, since it is a tool to be used against black
people'; the repayment to black people returning to their homelands
of 'all monies paid into the various national insurance, pension and
superannuation funds'; for full employment, for the release of all black
people held in racist prisons since they have not had a fair trial, for trial
by black juries and judges, for an end to 'racist education . . . in all
schools where there are black children, there must be black people on
the governing boards', and for 'decent housing . . . . If white racist
landlords will not let to black people and since the councils are very
little better, we demand that a proportion of housing loans must be
set aside for black people by the councils, so that black people can buy
their own homes in areas and among people with whom they can relate'.

Pipe dreams? Too theoretical by half? I saw the Black Unity and
Freedom party in action, picketing a magistrates' court where a number
of its members were appearing on charges – which it considered
trumped-up – of obstructing and assaulting the police and of using
obscene language. Thanks to good organization and willingness to
co-operate with whatever allies were available (in this case the neighbourhood council), they were able to accompany their picketing with
leaflets produced in less than twelve hours from the time of the original
incident. It is by tactics such as these, if by any, that they will convince
the black masses that they have some practical, undoctrinaire insights
to contribute; and it is only after they have established their own
credibility with black people that they may have the remotest hope of
having any impact on the organized white working class. Unlike several
other Black Power groupings, they seem to have identified the first rung
on the ladder they will have to climb if they want to realize their goal
of making a peculiarly black Marxist-Leninist contribution to the
international revolution. And they appear to have a realistic view of
the distance which stretches between activating black consciousness
('the crazies always want action, spontaneity is their *raison d'être*, but
there's more to it than that') and the revolution they're aiming for. By
tackling society at its weakest, least organized points, its contradictions,
they hope to close the gap.

Those who seek to draw a parallel between black consciousness in Britain and the American experience should be prepared heavily to qualify it. True, the USA has its black nationalists, its black culture groups: men like Ron Karenga, LeRoi Jones, and, until his departure to join Kwame Nkrumah in Guinea, Stokely Carmichael. There are, too, the better known black revolutionaries: the Panthers, the Black Stonerangers of Chicago, and others, who are thorough-going Marxist-Leninists. In addition, there are the black separatists identified with Elijah Muhammad – their aim is the creation of an all-black State in the southern states of America. Black capitalism – economic black consciousness – is less of an organized force than it may prove to be in Britain. But more important for any comparison than the internal structuring of the black groups themselves is the context in which they are set, and here the differences between America and Britain – so far – are more striking than the similarities. Of particular significance are two factors, comparable to those which determine the growth of self-awareness in the black community in Britain: the historical-geographical and the attitudinal. Black men have been present in significant numbers for far longer in the USA than they have here. Temporally and spatially they are black Americans with a stake nowhere except in the society of which they are part; even those who are now able to be called black Britons can still think of their parents' societies of origin as providing them in some sense with an alternative base. Thus they are, psychologically at least, equipped to call the bluff of the repatriation lobby. The racial attitudes of white American society are a part of that society's ethos, in which conformity and success play a greater part even than they do in British patterns of thought and feeling. So a group which is identifiable with poverty, with a sense of difference, is more likely to arouse antagonism there than here, even without the trauma of the recollection of slavery and emancipation. This in turn, with all that it implies of increased conflict, has affected the quality of leadership and the degree of commitment of the led. Simply because the racial climate in Britain is chilly and threatening rather than in a vicious state of war, it is still possible for black people to live lives not vastly different on the surface from their white peers. One Black Power worker expressed it thus: 'The white man in Britain is far subtler than in the States. The British have had much more experience of controlling people – they're better at being hypocritical, if you like.' Perhaps the next five or ten years will enable us to unlearn our hypocrisy and achieve a transatlantic openness in our racialism.

Given all the rationalizing and the evaluation of Black Power, seeing the sense it makes in the context of White Power, what does it mean for most black men in Britain? Answer: very little. It enjoys the active support of a very small minority indeed, and the understanding and adherence of not many more. It is predominantly a West Indian phenomenon, and it is noteworthy that at least two Black Power leaders of Asian descent come themselves from the West Indies. The reason for the failure so far of Black Power to win many Asian adherents is probably to be found in the highly developed social cohesion of the Asian community: why seek for political or economic solidarity under a black label when it's already available to you with a Sikh or a Hindu ticket? (It is worth remarking that one of the least well-organized Asian groups in Britain – the East Pakistanis of Spitalfields and Aldgate in London – have begun to show signs of self-defensive solidarity, such as the formation of vigilante groups, more often associated with the straight Black Power ticket). West Indians have not shown anything like the same degree of organization: where they have formed groups and associations, these have been mainly social and recreational or economic (credit clubs), organized often on an island basis. But this pattern is beginning to break down with the growth to adulthood of their black British children. This generation tends to define its peer groups either as its white compatriots of similar interests (compare the racial gap-bridging abilities of reggae and pot) or as its black fellow-victims – particularly of unemployment. 'Black Power is a young scene', said one girl. 'The first generation are so glad to be here they'll take anything. But not us.' Increasingly, ideas of Black Power will attract a growing following of young West Indians: what they make of it will depend very much on what white society makes of them. Once again, self-fulfilling prophecy may determine events, for if society is constantly fed the stereotype of violent, destructive Black Power it will blind itself to the concept's potential and force its adherents into fulfilment of Middle Britain's worst fears. And potentially the reverse is true; if it is allowed to develop in its own way, Black Power can give the black community a sense of identity it has not had, a degree of morale with which it may come to terms with society. What those terms are is not yet clear; but the liberals who are quickest to see the immigrant presence here as a trace element in British society should, hopefully, be quickest to recognize that Black Power can broaden this role into an evaluation of society's aims and values, not just its mechanics. What Black Power will be depends on the calibre of the leaders it is allowed to produce and on the degree of imagination white society is able to show towards it: what it is now is impossible to say, except that it is quintessentially black. It is the beginning of a working-out by the black man of his own destiny: it is his assertion of his own adulthood, his rejection of the role of child-like adjunct to civilization, by turns amiable, useful and threatening. If white men can accept the validity of blackness in its own right, they too will ultimately benefit. For, ultimately, 'Black is beautiful' is a celebration of humanity.

NOTES

1. *The Observer* (16 August 1970).
2. Julius Lester, *Look out Whitey, Black Power's Gon' Get Your Mama* (London, 1970).
3. *Venture* (January 1971).

X From Civil Disobedience to Confrontation

PETER CADOGAN

In 1956–58, the resurgence of civil disobedience in Britain brought to an end twenty years of political acquiescence, and marked the beginning of a new era of political engagement which ten years later was to develop into confrontation. The break with the past was so sharp that it is difficult now to recapture the aura of fatalism which so thoroughly pervaded the air before the decisive events of 1956.

From 1945 to 1956 politics was identified with the Parliamentary and party systems and involved people only in relation to these institutions. Either things were done through the permitted channels or they were not done at all. Year after year, differentiated only by variations of political colouring, the same rituals were automatically performed: meetings, conferences, resolutions, elections, power-struggles, and well-behaved demonstrations in Hyde Park and Trafalgar Square. They became quite peripheral to political realities, and for thousands of active people they were shattered when those realities were brought home with dramatic force by Suez and Hungary.

In October 1956 England was on the brink of rediscovering civil disobedience. Massive demonstrations against the Suez adventure ignored Parliament and challenged the authority of the government. Eden's defeat came just in time. In the same week, in Budapest, Russian tanks destroyed the myth of Moscow's Communist internationalism. It was never to revive; and with it, in England, went the Communist party's hegemony of the left. The way was clear for something new.

Civil disobedience meant different things to different people, but its essence, common to all, was the rediscovery of personal responsibility in action. It was occasioned by a new awareness that Britain was engaged in the deeply offensive business of arming itself with the weapons of mass destruction. By acting with devastating disregard of all moral considerations – to say nothing of 'purely' political responsibility – the State had forfeited the obedience of the individual. Personal disobedience became a categorical imperative.

The Break with the Past

The meaning of 1961, when civil disobedience reached its height, can be fully grasped only in relation to the larger political situation in the midst of which it had developed. That situation was in its essential respects a consistent and clearly traceable extension of the politics of the Second World War. Oddly enough, many people are still unaware that the war had any politics. Yet most of our present troubles stem from the years 1939–1945 and the countless 'arrangements' then made that were to shape the nature of the post-war world.

The war was fought in a spirit of national solidarity unprecedented in this country. Motives were undoubtedly mixed. They ranged from anti-Nazi idealism through self-defence to traditional conformity, but the result was astonishing in its universal character. In the terms of national mythology, we had a 'good war'. We went it alone for a while and held out; we performed miracles of invention and organization; we discovered some kind of spiritual and social unity – without, how-ever, suffering either the trauma of enemy occupation or the appalling casualties we had known in the First World War. Moreover, with our Russian, American and other allies we were victorious.

The consequences for post-war politics were disastrous: there was no call to question the system. The misgovernment of Britain, graced with the impeccable vindication of victory, acquired a new lease of life. Great concern was expressed about the details. During the war, an impassioned debate had swept the country about our war aims, and in countless barrack-rooms and mess-decks the groundwork was done for the Labour victory of 1945 – but the debate was confined to the social services and the domestic record of the parties before the war. It resulted in nothing more sweeping than the Beveridge Report and the Butler Education Act. No controversy erupted over foreign policy, or 'defence', or the power of the Treasury in post-war England. Western Europe lay in ruins; and Britain, without a Monnet, rejected the Continental opportunity of the century in favour of the insular Eden tradition at the Foreign Office. Without provoking a single reaction of any consequence, we turned to the Americans and abdicated in Europe.

The silence which accompanied this momentous move seems, now, extraordinary. Not only were no pertinent questions asked but appar-ently no questions even presented themselves. When the young people poured out of the armed forces and into the universities and colleges of 1945–6, the most radical political message in the land was that of the then powerful Communist party. This was 'Implement *Let Us Face the Future*' – the 1945 election programme of the Labour party. The Communist party swept the board in elections to any number of critically important trade union committees and eventually dominated the Student Labour Federation so effectively that Transport House had to set up NALSO (National Association of Labour Student Organizations) in order to keep the Labour party in the student picture at all. Other radical voices – pacifist, anarchist and Trotskyist – were tiny, inconsequential, sectarian and unheard. The Bevanites, round *Tribune*, never developed any capacity for political organization outside the paper and its Parliamentary group. 'Victory for Socialism' proved abortive.

In 1948 the Czechoslovakian *coup d'état* and the Berlin airlift testified that the Cold War, begun in 1917 and only interrupted since 1941, was again renewing its grip. Stalin provided endless targets for John Foster Dulles and Ernest Bevin. Completely self-defeated as regards the independence of its foreign and defence policy, the British Labour government slowly ran out of steam. It expired of its own powerlessness in 1951.

The Soviet Union had no Bomb. Its cities were shattered and its farms in ruins. Stalin had to play for time – hence the conformist role of all the Communist parties in the West and the insurrectional role of their opposite numbers in the Orient. In 1948, Communist insurrections were attempted in Malaya, Burma, Indonesia and the Philippines at the behest of the 1947 'Zhdanov line'. Greece, tragically, was caught in the middle. In 1950, as part of the technique of temporizing, the Communist parties of the world set up, at Soviet instigation, the World Council of Peace round the Stockholm Peace Appeal against nuclear weapons. Peace promptly became a dirty word. (The attacks that were levelled with such indiscriminate vigour against the Stockholm Peace Appeal took no account, of course, of the unsparing effort put into it by countless individuals who were wholly genuine in their intentions. What could one do? As there was no other campaigning peace movement, one either went in with the Communists or did nothing.)

The British Labour party denounced the Stockholm Peace Appeal without providing any alternative. In 1950 Monnet came to Britain to sell the idea of the Common Market (as yet unborn) and was frozen out by civil servants and politicians alike. Churchill, we now know, privately admitted to being out of his depth as a peace-time Prime Minister from 1951 to 1955 and in his Europeanism was up against his only possible successor, Sir Anthony Eden, and the whole of the Foreign Office. He hung on to office and Britain drifted meaninglessly in the wake of the USA.

Such British initiatives as there were only made matters worse.

Thus, of his activities at the Geneva Conference of 1954, Eden wrote: 'I decided to persevere at our next meeting with my plan for what I called a "protective pad" . . . . It would be best if Communism could be held at arm's length, clear of Cambodia and Laos and halted as far north as possible in Vietnam.'[1] On 24 June 1954, Churchill and Eden flew to Washington. They saw John Foster Dulles who 'seemed ready to countenance the partition of Vietnam'.[2] Just as in 1945 British troops had occupied Vietnam, halved it, and handed back the southern half to the French, so with ironic appropriateness the notorious partition which exists today was devised in the British Foreign Office. Unspeakable disasters, now familiar, were later to follow. At the time, nobody in Britain was interested. The intricacies of foreign policy merited only the attention of the elect.

In 1956 a crisis abruptly dispelled the apathy and compelled a response: British troops landed in Egypt to take the Suez Canal. The recoil was unmistakable, but it did not come before Donald Soper and some co-signatories (Stuart Morris, Sybil Morrison, John P. Fletcher, Hugh Brock, Alex Wood, Reginald Reynolds) wrote in a leaflet:

> The government, by its adventure in the Suez region, is leading the nation to ruin and disaster. The government policy has forfeited the goodwill of the United Nations and the Commonwealth.
> Nothing short of Civil Disobedience is now true patriotism. Therefore I plead with my fellow countrymen to refuse to take part either in fighting or the provision of transport and ammunition for this dreadful blunder.

1956–1958

An immediate consequence of Suez and Hungary was the New Left. At Oxford it formed round Stuart Hall and the editorial board of *Universities and Left Review*, and elsewhere among disenchanted ex-Communists round E. P. Thompson and John Saville and their *New Reasoner*. The two journals were later fused as *New Left Review*. Thousands of students throughout the country rallied to the new unspecifics of 'commitment'. *Tribune* rallied Bevanism for the last time.

The Labour party, in opposition as it had been since 1951, found itself in the midst of a struggle being waged for not less than the very soul of the party. However, the terms of the argument always remained essentially Parliamentary; the new leaders of the New Left, most of them emergent professional sociologists, operated entirely within the system and in due course they faced the inevitable problems that arise from the lack of solid independent organization. For all that, the New Left was free of both Transport House and King Street, and it was genuinely *moving*. After so many static years it brought a feeling of liberation. It had mystique.

At the same time, something else was afoot in England and the signs could be read in a number of different directions. John Osborne and Colin Wilson were its immediate prophets. Joan Littlewood's Theatre Workshop was in the middle of its seminal first decade. Folk music suddenly (or so it seemed) ceased to be esoteric. Sociologists 'discovered' the theory of alienation in the humanism of the younger Marx. Bertrand Russell, through the Pugwash conferences of scientists, worried the custodians of nuclear secrecy. A sense of the tragedy of southern Africa, mediated by Michael Scott and Trevor Huddleston, reached small but significant numbers of people in this country. Sartre, Brecht and Pasternak registered. Among the teenagers came the first indications of the youth revolution that was to acquire dominating importance in the 1960s. In 1956 the rock 'n roll craze hit Britain, Teddy Boys were suddenly everywhere, and coffee bars proliferated.

But what was the focal point? Where was the centre in all this? What was to make it coalesce in some way that would be meaningful politically?

The Catalyst

The answer was the Bomb. The cause of nuclear disarmament was tailormade for the English situation. The politically disenchanted and the young needed a myth, a cause round which 'to unite and fight'. It had to be remote, essentially intangible, yet with enough substance to merit defensible moral indignation. The Bomb had everything. There had been two threats of nuclear war since 1945, the first in Korea and the second, at the time of Dien Bien Phu, in Vietnam. True, the success of the first Russian sputnik had changed the situation: the balance of terror had arrived. As Dean Acheson remarked to his Cambridge audience in October 1958: 'When nuclear power equates, conventional power decides.' Nevertheless, atmospheric tests were proceeding, and confirmation that a *balance* of terror existed awaited the Cuban crisis of 1962. It was enough to go on.

The tests themselves were in fact a more than adequate incitement. No jeremiads were needed to exaggerate the simple facts that the Americans and the Russians were loading the atmosphere with fall-out, British tests had begun, and French and Chinese tests were in prospect. Measurement of the fall-out revealed good cause for disturbance. Milk was beginning to be suspect – or was thought to be suspect; the distinction had marginal relevance.

Thus the danger was domestic, and it was at exactly this moment that the enemy was located at home in the Atomic Weapons Research

Establishment at Aldermaston and in the installation of Thor rocket bases in and around East Anglia in 1957-8. The first Aldermaston March took place in 1958. It was conceived by the Direct Action Committee (comprising mainly young members of the Peace Pledge Union) and taken up by CND (founded at the beginning of 1958).

Right from the beginning, the nuclear disarmament movement had these two very different wings: the first committed to non-violent direct action (a synonym for civil disobedience) and the second committed ultimately to Labour party politics. Thus Michael Randle and Pat Arrowsmith worked in uneasy alliance with Canon Collins and Peggy Duff. Direct Action was not a breakaway from CND. It preceded it and was independently organized; for years subsequently it provided CND with endless 'copy', since on nearly every occasion when civil disobedience took place the Press gave the credit to 'CND' despite Canon Collins's disavowals.

It was over the Thor rocket bases that significant civil disobedience began first at Mepal near Ely and then at North Pickenham near Swaffham in Norfolk. In 1957-8 East Anglia was the scene of some bizarre developments. The Thor bases were built under the conditions of the greatest secrecy. Countless people down to typists and telephonists were given to understand that under the Official Secrets Act they would be subject to dire penalties if they breathed a word to anybody about what was going on. But the construction of massive concrete bunkers on derelict airfields is not the kind of activity that can be concealed, and members of the Ely Labour party soon told their friends in the Cambridge Labour party that a base was being built at Mepal, six miles from Ely. (Cambridge later became the centre of one of the first and strongest CND groups, based quite unambiguously on the left of the local Labour party.) The Local Trades Council was then put in the picture and a Joint Committee of the Labour party and Trades Council was set up to organize action at Mepal. The present writer was the organizing secretary of that Joint Committee.

It was decided to hold what would have been a perfectly conventional march from Ely to the base, with a meeting at the site – had it not been for the Official Secrets Act. Officially, the bases did not exist. The Ministry of Defence rang the organizers to say that the demonstration must be called off. The Secretary of the Cambridge Labour party took alarm, resigned and disappeared from the political scene. The Joint Committee met to consider the situation and unanimously decided to proceed as planned. No one was more insistent about this than Robert Davies, later MP for Cambridge and one of the prime movers of the action.

The march was a success. Some 300 people took part, including the late Arthur Skeffington, Anthony Greenwood, John Horner and the three prospective Labour party candidates for Cambridge, Huntingdon and the Isle of Ely. The marchers called at the house of Sir Harry Legge-Bourke (MP for Ely) on the way and some were invited into his living-room where he solemnly declared to them that there was no such thing as the rocket base on his own doorstep! He was invited to come to see for himself, but declined. The meeting on the base and the publicity given to the action as a whole quite destroyed the security curtain and exposed the rockets to the ridicule which, even on military grounds, was all they were worth. They were liquid-fuelled and had to be raised to the erect position before their tanks could be filled. They took some forty-five minutes to fire – and this a year after the success of the first sputnik. Their installation had barely been completed when the decision was taken to dismantle them.

But the important publicity came in December 1958, when a peaceful protest, organized by the Direct Action Committee, took place at the Thor base at North Pickenham. Forty-five of those who walked on to the site to obstruct the operation of the massive concrete mixer were arrested – Pat Arrowsmith and Michael Scott among them. Nationally and internationally, the publicity was extensive.

The story from then on has been told in detail by Christopher Driver in his book *The Disarmers*[3]; how the DAC was superseded in 1960 by the Committee of 100; how civil disobedience moved from remote military sites to the centre of London and other cities; how the scale mounted from a few scores of demonstrators to many thousands until, in September 1961, 1,314 people were arrested in Trafalgar Square for attending a prohibited demonstration.

The issues here, however, concern the character and quality of civil disobedience: why it did not develop past a certain point, and why, at that point, did it begin to give way to 'confrontation'?

The Nature of Civil Disobedience, 1958–1963

The pioneers in the DAC were pacifists, who, under the influence of the Gandhi tradition, had developed a campaign-tactic distinct from those of the Quakers and the Peace Pledge Union. Their symbolic direct action had the power to command attention. Arrests were news. Individuals who put themselves at risk impelled others to take notice. The transition from the DAC to the Committee of 100 in 1960–1 constituted a shift from symbolism to what either was, or was intended to be, mass action on a scale that would worry the government. The need for this was held to arise from the situation itself. At that time, Bertrand Russell thought that nuclear war was likely within twelve months unless drastic action was taken to stop it. His point was taken. Events were later to prove him wrong, but in 1961 there was every justification for profound anxiety as one crisis followed another with alarming rapidity: the Bay of Pigs invasion, the building of the Berlin Wall, the Russians' biggest-ever nuclear weapon-tests in the atmosphere, a major financial crisis, the Congo *débâcle*, and the deaths of Lumumba and Hammarskjold.

Socialists and anarchists poured into the ranks of direct action to join the pacifists. A great and eventually unresolved debate began between those who saw non-violent direct action as a principle and those who saw it as a tactic. To Russell, it was a tactic, a device to secure necessary instant publicity and support in a dire emergency. Nevertheless, the general policy of the DAC prevailed on demonstrations. The briefing for demonstration after demonstration had a similar character.

1) Try to get to the objective.
2) If you are stopped by the police, sit down.
3) When told by the police to move, refuse to do so. (The individual has to make up his own mind over this, bearing in mind the possible penalties and his own personal circumstances.)
4) When being removed by the police, offer no resistance, go limp and insist on being carried away.

The atmosphere was quiet and controlled. There was no shouting, no running, very little hostility to the police and a general conviction that the self-evident rightness of the case for unilateral nuclear disarmament would rally such support that the day would be won. The first nine months of 1961 seemed to provide good grounds for so thinking. But then the crises passed, and it became apparent that nuclear war was not imminent. In December 1961, a series of demonstrations inspired by the DAC school in the Committee were poor in conception and worse in execution. Nearly all the VIP support fell away.

The great rethink began. It moved in two new directions simultaneously, away from both pacifist symbolism and emergency mass mobilization.

The school of the first direction asked: If non-violence is our means, and means are ends in embryo, what is the nature of our ends? What do we mean by the non-violent society, and what can we start to do now that will take us towards it? The outcome was the notion of the 'public assembly' based on that of ancient Athens; the idea of the 'parallel society' evolving not side-by-side but over and against present society; the concept of the volunteer in government instead of the representative; decentralization, industrial democracy, the redundancy of Parliament, internationalism; and a new way of internal organization for the movement itself based on conveners of small groups linked by telephone, the free association of regional groups in a national committee, the replacement of annual conferences by quarterly meetings, and the virtual abolition of voting in committee in favour of something that approximated to the Quaker unanimity principle. Some of the results were rewarding. Early in 1962, all traffic was halted round Parliament Square for a public assembly to pin-point Westminster's guilt by default; in the spring there followed the first 'free' demonstration in Moscow's Red Square since the early 1920s; the first moves were made to found a Factory for Peace in Scotland; public conscience began to be awakened to the needs of the homeless in hostels; direct attempts were made to carry the debate to men serving in the armed forces; thirteen regional committees and a national committee replaced the old original committee; there was a new magazine, *Resistance*, and a series of 'way ahead' conferences to develop discussion and action.

The second school was quite different. It was not interested in non-violence except as a necessary but temporary tactical concession to the movement's own weakness. Its supporters produced, early in 1962, a bald statement of their objection to self-sacrificial sit-downs. Called *Beyond Counting Arses*, it was a tough document devised by the Trotskyist 'Solidarity' wing of the Committee. This too got results: a pamphlet written in Russian, in the name of the London Committee of 100, was given out at factory gates in Moscow, where it commanded at least as much attention as the simultaneous demonstration in Red Square. It was with similar effect that the sensational *Spies for Peace* document exploded in the context of the Aldermaston march of 1963.

The Conflict

Civil disobedience in the years 1958–62 was as successful as it was respectable. There followed a year of fierce debate, turmoil and action, and then in the summer of 1963 the collapse of 'the mass movement' as such. The hard core carried on until 1968, by which time the idea of civil disobedience had become common property.

The movement was 'respectable' in its regard for the sanctity of property as well as of people. There was, for example, an interminable debate over the ethics of using wire-cutters to get through barbed wire: was this non-violent? There was another debate over the lengths to which non-cooperation should be taken. Given that one should be carried to the police bus, should one insist on being carried from the bus to the police cell and from there to the court room? Should one pay fines or insist on going to prison? Should one accept binding-over or, again, go to prison? On all these questions, it was possible in theory to take a 'pure' position, but common sense and personal circumstances made it unacceptable or impossible for most people in practice. A few, like Pat Arrowsmith, did reject all compromise, but it was impossible for others to identify with her because they had examinations to pass, jobs to keep, mortgage payments to make and marriage partners' and children's wishes and interests to be taken into consideration. A movement with an absolutist basis could not grow. At the same time, the movement was rootless. Despite the number of young people involved, the youth revolution lay three or four years ahead. There was support from the universities but only from small groups. It had no other territorial, industrial or professional basis. An attempt to build an Industrial Committee failed. The movement never evolved an agreed philosophy that would have enabled it to transcend the differences built into its original electicism.

Had grave international crises continued as 1961 suggested they might, then there would have been a different story to tell. But they did not. The peace movement found itself in the fatal position of 'looking for issues' round which to maintain a movement on a scale matched to crises. In the event, there were two such issues – the first was the Cuban crisis of the autumn of 1962 and the second was the Greek royal visit of the summer of 1963. The result was instant revival followed by instant decline.

There was a moment in the Cuban demonstration which was fleetingly but unmistakably prophetic of future confrontation. There had been a massive demonstration in Whitehall. The whole street had been blocked, then the demonstration, still large but somewhat reduced, made for the American Embassy (and later for the Russian and Cuban Embassies) to the slogan, 'East and West – Hands off Cuba'. Many hundreds of demonstrators were sweeping up Regent Street, occupying the whole width of the road (another characteristic of confrontation), when a single police bus disgorged its twenty-five policemen. They immediately formed a line across the road to stop and hold the march. According to the usual briefing, the demonstration should then have stopped – one did not push policemen, as to do so would be violent. But this time there was no hesitation. The demonstrators outnumbered the police by at least ten to one, probably far more, and they went straight through the cordon. There was no violence, only a firm push. The police could do nothing and turned to walk with the demonstration.

In all previous demonstrations, 'the enemy' had had a certain abstract character – the action had been against nuclear weapons that were not being used or against tests whose effects were largely conjectural. But this time the enemy was real. That Saturday the Russian ships were approaching Cuba and the American ultimatum had been given. High explosives were literally in motion in time and space. *The war threat had reached the point of actual confrontation and the response to it was of a like kind.* But the Russian ships turned back.

As in the Suez crisis, a development of awareness and organization that had insurrectional implications was still-born.

The situation was in principle similar in 1963 when the King and Queen of the Hellenes made their State visit to London. To Bertrand Russell and to the International Sub-Committee of the Committee of 100 (from which he had by then parted company), there was no doubt that the visit was undertaken as a political boost to the far right in Greece and that if it was successful, the cause of peace and freedom would suffer. It had to be appreciated that the Greek monarchy was not of the constitutional order. The *coup* that eventually took place in 1967 was foreseen years earlier. The event differed from the expectation only in that it centred on the Colonels and not upon the King – a difference of no great political substance.

Russell had resigned from the Committee of 100 in the autumn of 1962, after a difference over the Public Assembly that took place at the Air Ministry in September, but he and his secretariat came together with the Committee for the last time in the *ad hoc* 'Save Greece Now Committee' set up to organize the Greek demonstration. It was done mostly from the committee's office in Goodwin Street. Peter Moule was then the National Secretary. The explicit aim – to wreck the State visit in order to foil its political purpose in Greece – was achieved. A series of demonstrations confronted not only Queen Frederika but also Queen Elizabeth. It was impossible to expect the insular English to understand that these were actions related to the internal situation in Greece, and the peace movement took a hammering for the Committee of 100's pains. Peter Moule, Terry Chandler and George Clark (the last quite fortuitously) went to gaol. Again, as in the case of Cuba, the objective was immediate and particular, and this time the last remnants of the DAC tradition of action went by the board. There were scrum-downs against police cordons. The Communist party, committed to the Parliamentary game, covertly, and for the first and last time, took part in a Committee action. What had been the peace movement was moving left and into confrontation.

Vietnam

It was after these new experiences had probed the frontiers of a new kind of action that confrontation as a consciously conceived form began to emerge in the context of the war in Vietnam.

As from the summer of 1963, and after the Greek demonstrations, the old movement nosedived. The Test Ban Treaty removed much of the old incentive, but the decisive factor was the approaching general election. The left-wingers in the peace movement flocked back into Labour party action and to the colours of Harold Wilson.

Every MP nominated for the Council of CND in 1963 now refused to accept nomination. Shortly afterwards, even Canon Collins pulled out. The Cuban crisis of 1962 had ended the politics of massive retaliation, and the future belonged to wars of counter-insurgency. The big escalation in Vietnam was still to come. 1964, with its general election, was a highly domestic year apart from the crisis in Cyprus, and to meet that the Committee of 100 set up another project, the Peace in Cyprus Committee, to bring Greeks and Turks together in London.

The Vietnam war had been twice escalated; the first time by President Kennedy in 1961 when the SEATO disguise was abandoned and American military involvement became overt, and the second time when the bombing of the North began in 1965.

For years Russell had been almost a lone voice attacking the American involvement in Indo-China. In close association with him, a new group, the VSC (Vietnam Solidarity Campaign), launched its activity round the slogan, 'Victory for the NLF'. For two years it campaigned but did not grow significantly. There were various reasons for this. The VSC was also engaged in promoting the War Crimes Tribunal and Ralph Schoenman's activity and influence were heavily involved with that. At the same time, and immediately after the 1965 Aldermaston march, Lord Brockway, the late Sydney Silverman, the late Konni Zilliacus and others with the backing of CND had started the BCPV (the British Council for Peace in Vietnam), and this body, centred in Westminster and meeting always in committee rooms of the House of Commons would no more countenance confrontation than it would civil disobedience. So long as the BCPV embodied people's hopes, it inhibited their action by confining it to merely propagandist activities in association with the Parliamentary Labour party. What was left of the Committee of 100 turned its attention to the American bases at Lakenheath, Mildenhall and elsewhere, and to the problem of British involvement in the war, the training base for South Vietnam run by the British Army in Johore, the 600 British troops building military airfields in Thailand, the availability of Hong Kong for American supply and communications purposes, the past role of Sir Robert Thompson in Saigon, and British political support for US policy. But it was too complex an approach. The VSC message had charisma, or at least acquired it in 1967 with the help of Tariq Ali, but this was, interestingly enough, after the VSC and Russell had parted company.

To its simple message, the VSC added a simple target – the American Embassy in Grosvenor Square. Finally, it took full advantage of the *ad hoc* principle pioneered by the Committee of 100 between 1962 and 1964, and set out to promote the creation, not of VSC groups, but of *ad hoc* committees for the next demonstration in universities and colleges up and down the country. At this very moment, the great bonus of the 1960s fell right into their lap. Quite suddenly, out of the blue, the youth revolution materialized. It is not possible to understand how confrontation happened without seeing the youth revolution for what it was. A couple of million men had been demobilized in 1945–6. A year later began the bulge of babies that was soon to play havoc with the schools. In 1964, a vast new generation arrived on the 18-year-old scene. The Beatles and Mary Quant were its prophets, and the summer of 1965 was the season of flower-power and the heyday of the hippies. After two years in universities and colleges, the political eruption took place in the autumn of 1967. It was on a VSC demonstration that started from Trafalgar Square and went to the American Embassy. Suddenly it was different. The new people, the young, had turned out. Vietnam demonstrations suddenly had mystique. Their organizers could hardly go wrong.

The confrontation briefing, which clearly emphasized the *size of the demonstration*, went as follows: the march should occupy the whole of the road; no one should allow himself to be arrested and if he was it was the business of others to rescue him by suitable action using the force of numbers; the object was to get into the Square (and in so doing to defeat the power of the State that had vetoed the entry); everyone should link arms for physical strength when embattled in order not to be divided by the police charges and for the fortification of morale; police cordons should be broken by sheer physical pressure, that is by pushing (there was actually very little violence in the sense of fighting). The new approach worked. Tens of thousands galvanized themselves into action. For the first time, the movement found an established territorial-professional basis – universities, colleges and schools.

The great anti-climax came with the third and biggest of the confrontation exercises – that of October 1968. The nine-month long preparations and the person of Tariq Ali had been given an enormous build-up by the Press. In the event, the demonstration was in fact a non-event, a tame exercise that expired in Hyde Park with a conventional meeting and no 'confrontation' at all. Within days the whole movement fell to pieces. Why?

Diagnosis of Defeat

Like civil disobedience before it, confrontation had no political theory, no developmental character, no roots in reality. It gave passing substance to a marriage of young idealism and the cause of Vietnam. It was a fashion, a peg to hang rebellion on, a hope, a fantasy.

The leaders, of course, did have a political theory of sorts –the neo-Marxist notions of the International Marxist Group and other sects – but this meant very little to the thousands on the march.

Each demonstration was geared to itself and to the next demonstration. It was a closed world and, being closed, had to be repetitious. After two assaults on Grosvenor Square, the leadership looked elsewhere for a target and failed to find it.

Either confrontation must make for the ultimate challenge of successful insurrection or it must be content with being an essentially religio-political exercise, that is a complex of incantations and rituals concerned with the elevation of the elect for their own sake, the complementary 'mortification of the flesh', and the security and prosperity of the church, party or sect. These characteristic elements of religious sectarianism down the centuries exactly exemplify the nature of confrontations' leftist leadership in 1967–8. Politically and historically, it began with Ernest Jones, the Chartist, and ended with Tariq Ali.

It was plain from the way that Pat Jordan, the main organizer, talked at the pre-demonstration meetings that he did not look beyond the next demonstration, did not want to look beyond it, and strongly discouraged anyone else from doing so. The demonstration was an end in itself. This can only mean that the organizers did not want to succeed and consciously or unconsciously prepared the way for their own defeat. The thing was much too big for them. The death-wish is built into primitive confrontation. In order to cope with the future, its leaders have to cut their following and objectives down to a size they can manage. They wrestle, also, with the insoluble problem of charisma. A religio-political movement has to have a charismatic leader in whose passionate personality and eloquence are subsumed the related passions of the thousands who follow the leader. This is no basis for that egalitarian mobilization of independent ability on a significant scale without which no serious challenge to anything can be sustained.

After Confrontation – What?

The hard negative lesson learnt from the combined experiences of civil disobedience and confrontation is that the State is not going to be defeated by action on the streets alone. This is not necessarily to discount action on the streets where it is combined with other things. But it is that combination – however constituted – that will be crucial.

Nothing has been said here about the American experience of confrontation. That, however, is where one needs to look in conclusion, for in the USA there is some new writing on the wall. It began with draft refusal, it continued with desertion and then with individual acts and small collective acts of mutiny, and, as the John Pilger *World in Action* film has shown, with 'Quiet Mutiny' throughout the whole US front line in Vietnam. The 'grunts', the 18-year-old front line troops who have to do all the actual fighting, had decided against the war. The object of the exercise, as far as they were concerned, was *not* to make contact with the enemy. Sent out on patrol, they sat down as soon as they were out of sight of their own base, wait, and then returned to report 'no contact' with the enemy. An over-enthusiastic or officious officer was liable to receive an American bullet in his back. The President began to call the troops home, not because he wanted to change his policy in Vietnam, but because unless he did so his own troops would have changed it for him. This, after all, was a familiar situation in the First World War. We have forgotten about it because it was not repeated in the Second World War. In 1917–18 half the French army mutinied, and most of the Russian army did the same, as did the German navy at Kiel.

Mutiny is insurrectional action from within. If and when it is linked with positive political inspiration (as it was when the Petrograd Garrison changed sides in October 1917) the result is revolution. One must not read too much into what happened in the front line in Vietnam – but read one must. Back in the USA is the other side of the American revolution – Black Power in the cities. Add to these things, the campus revolt and the problems of inflation insoluble within the military-industrial system and the explosive potentials are manifestly critical. Eventually something will break.

In England the situation may seem tame by comparison, but beneath the surface there are signs not unlike those in the USA. It may well be that historians writing of 1970 will record not the general election but a letter to *The Times*[4] from Lt.-Col. J. H. B. Acland, Commanding Officer, Second Battalion Scots Guards. In this unprecedented testimony, a senior serving officer attacked and denounced his superiors in much the same way as the 'grunts' in Vietnam attacked the 'lifers', the enlisted professional soldiers in safe jobs behind the lines. Acland wrote: 'The country cannot be getting value for its money when the number of soldiers available to fight decreases, whilst there is no reduction among the civil servants *and staff officers who push the paper around the Headquarters*' (author's italics). In the same letter Colonel Acland publicly acknowledged 'appalling turbulence in the infantry'. He broke the most sacred written and unwritten rules of the army and *no one dared to touch him*. The system is a house of cards and senses it. If everyone sits tight, says nothing and does nothing, it will continue to stand: *après nous le déluge* – so runs the Establishment's rule of thumb.

A situation similar to that of the military exists in the Civil Service. Mr William McCall, the General Secretary of the Institute of Professional Civil Servants, wrote in his monthly journal *State Service:* 'The fact remains that unless there is manifestly fair treatment of the service there is a likelihood of a major collapse of morale.'[5] The

Department of Inland Revenue, on whose operations, after all, the government is absolutely dependent, is in a very difficult situation because of substantial desertion (let us use the right word) by its highly skilled staff. Senior tax officials have a thankless task of the greatest difficulty and complexity to perform as government after government uses fiscal policy as an economic regulator. Eventually, the sheer personal strain becomes too much, and they quit for better jobs with better pay in the City. Politics is above all the business of soldiers and civil servants; and the professional machine, by its own admission, is running down.

Conclusion

Answers are conspicuously missing. After a century of ideologies we are rightly suspicious of ideas. Yet without ideas there is no hope. If we are to act together effectively, we need to understand what is happening to us and to agree about what to do. We need an inspired non-charismatic classless realism that is good enough to move two or three million thoughtful people. It is a cause without a name.

NOTES

1. Anthony Eden, *Full Circle* (London, 1960), p. 123.
2. Ibid., p. 131.
3. C. Driver, *The Disarmers: A Study in Protest* (London, 1964).
4. *The Times* (15 August 1970).
5. Quoted in *The Times* (11 August 1970).

XI Remember your Humanity and Forget the Rest

GEORGE CLARK

Introduction

Behind the direct action which disrupted the opening ceremony of Westway and the struggle to establish social rights for the dispossessed and excluded minorities living in the Golborne Ward of North Kensington lies a seething discontent. This discontent will remain until some fundamental decencies are established, and will certainly not disappear until the citizens of the area are in control of their own affairs. This is what the action is all about in North Kensington, and it is likely that other areas in London and in cities throughout Britain will be the scene of similar action in the future.

In order to discuss the reasons why certain people take direct action, let me explain my own involvement with different forms of action over the past ten years. It began in Notting Hill in 1958 when, through the *Universities and Left Review*, we attempted to organize a tenants' association following the race riots in the area. Then, as the nuclear peril grew to crisis proportions, my commitment to action outside the Parliamentary system was confirmed with the formation of the Campaign for Nuclear Disarmament and the marches from Aldermaston to London. This seemed to be the only way to break the official silence which surrounded the whole question of nuclear arms, and it succeeded. But it was not enough, and by 1961 my position had changed radically. Initially, my involvement and action with CND was a form of simple protest, but three years later I was a convinced nuclear pacifist. After helping to form the Committee of 100, I thought through the question and became deeply attached to the philosophy of non-violence.

The nuclear disarmament movement unquestionably changed the nature of British politics, and made a significant impact on the lives and thinking of those who became involved in the movement. All the old verities about the relationships of war and politics, and about violence and power seemed to be irrelevant. As I reflected on the questions this proposition raised, I became increasingly convinced that war itself, in all of its forms, is the basic social system, within which other modes of social organization conflict and conspire. In trying to find a way of changing this system, there seemed to me to be a critical interdependence between the need to change the structures and, at the same time, the need to change personal behaviour. Non-violence became for me a way of life, a new adventure, a source of power based upon love and truth, and a lever for social change.

Gradually I moved away from CND and began to experiment with ways in which this lever might be applied. After forming an outfit called Caravan Workshops, a journey around Britain and a visit to America led me to the conclusion that the best way was to start work at the local level, in areas of deprivation, where the discontents and inequalities are sharpest. I chose to go back to Notting Hill where for the past seven years or so I have been engaged in community organizing which involves a high degree of innovation and experimentation.

My various stages of progress are explained in this chapter. Clearly it is a personal account and it leaves out forms of direct action such as industrial strikes and the like which, for the purpose of comparison, would have been helpful to the reader in assessing one form of action against another. I have been persuaded to write this piece because of the paucity of material on the subject of direct action, and if these notes go some way to filling this gap then they will serve a useful purpose.

Prelude to Action

To understand how a popular and radical extra-Parliamentary movement emerged around the issue of nuclear disarmament, we must dip into the politics of the decade which preceded it. The 1950s saw the appearance of modern affluence. It was, at the time, a highly confusing phenomenon, and few people knew quite what it meant or how it should be interpreted. Post-war affluence disturbed every apple-cart for it suggested that society was undergoing fundamental changes and yet, in its basic structure, it was clearly not changing at all.

There were significant changes in the occupational structure of society, but the old working class was not disappearing. New patterns of personal and social aspirations and expectations were emerging, but Britain was not becoming more middle-class. Class was not abolished but was merely renamed 'social stratification' as relations between the classes were modified by the rise to the top of the pyramid of the new meritocrats and technocrats. The advent of the Labour party to power in the immediate post-war years did not see the overthrowing nor the abdication of the old ruling class. Tamely incorporated by Labour, they learned to share their place in the sun with the new political élite.

The majority of people, still divorced from the political processes, were caught up with the routine of daily life and were busy chasing the myth of affluence. The ordinary citizen might not understand why he had enough money in his pocket to purchase a refrigerator, washing machine, and television set. It was sufficient that he was released from the controls of a war economy and that the spectre of pre-war unemployment and dole queues was evaporating in a general air of well-being and full employment.

The political élite neither made nor manufactured affluence, and they were as deluded by it as was the man-in-the-street. However, they did respond to it and tried to capture it. A public so acquiescent was a godsend, and with adroit stage management of the economy they rode it for all it was worth. The crest of the wave of post-war affluence was capped with one of the most immoral slogans ever coined: 'I'm all right Jack'.

The politics of the 1950s had become entrapped within a received system in which decisions of importance were confined to the élite at the top of the pyramid and the all-important issues of the day, such as the uses of the new technology and the manufacture of nuclear weapons, were kept out of public debate. The failure to raise these questions in public was to prove almost fatal, and the ultimate disaster of a nuclear holocaust was only narrowly averted in 1962 during the Cuban missile crisis. But it was because of official silence on this vital question in the late 1950s that a protest movement grew up, which was to match the size of the Chartist movement. The forces which brought it into being were nuclear violence and the threat of nuclear extermination to all mankind. The new technology was not merely manufacturing washing machines and television sets: in silence and away from the gaze of public debate, the technical development of the implements of violence had reached a point where no political goal could match their destructive potential. It was to break this silence that thousands of respectable middle-class people joined the young Aldermaston generation. Such was the urgency of the situation that they felt it more important to vote with their feet than place any more reliance on the ballot-box. When Aneurin Bevan, at the annual conference (1956) of the Labour party, said in a heady debate about the use of nuclear weapons: 'You cannot send a British Foreign Minister into the Conference Chamber naked', it seemed that the Parliamentary route for change was no longer possible. The emphasis by both the Labour party and the Conservative government on political and economic continuity and government by consensus was inappropriate to the needs of the times. Loyalty to the system finally snapped when Duncan Sandys announced in the Defence White Paper issued by the government in February 1957 that in future British defence policies would be based upon the independent nuclear deterrent and later in the same year, that Britain would test her first H-Bomb in the Christmas Islands. The announcement sparked off an open rebellion which was to consist of direct action at the nuclear air bases, marching (that old traditional form of protest) in numbers that had not been seen in this country for almost a century, and civil disobedience by thousands who preferred to risk imprisonment rather than allow the government to continue with its nuclear policies. That rebellion was called the Campaign for Nuclear Disarmament and the Committee of 100, and it lasted for almost six years.

The movement which emerged was overwhelmingly young. It was a generation that had been born in the shadow of the Bomb dropped on Hiroshima and all their young lives had been overcast with the pall of nuclear dust as new weapons were tested. Nursed and suckled at the breast of the welfare state, they knew nothing of the grim pre-war years of dole queues and unemployment. Captivated by the idealism of banning the Bomb, in one unilateralist gesture they threw themselves into the new form of direct politics with an enthusiasm which was to change the nature of political action in this country and to inspire the formation of similar movements all over the world.

Involvement and Commitment

My own involvement was not sudden. The invasion of Suez by Britain – when we had pledged to the United Nations that we would not act unilaterally on any military venture – appalled me. I attended a huge rally organized by the Labour party and was encouraged by the slogan of the rally – *Law Not War* – for it seemed to speak very much to our feelings. But whilst the campaign was mounting, the Russians invaded Hungary and by the end of 1956 it seemed impossible to reconcile the events of Hungary and Suez with the statements and behaviour of politicians at home. There seemed little that could be done. But during 1957 the issues became much clearer, particularly when the debates on nuclear weapons and their use took place. My response was to turn away from the Labour party because it was not possible to square their commitment to nuclear policies and their opposition to the military adventurism of the Tory government.

Nuclear weapons were turning me into a pacifist, and increasingly I came to feel that the only way to avoid the ultimate horror of universal suicide was to seek the alternative of non-violence, both in personal relationships and in the conduct of affairs between nations. The marches from Aldermaston to London, lasting as they did for over four days, provided ample time for discussion and for thinking through problems which the political parties seemed both unwilling to, and incapable of, resolving. Direct action was a release – and hopefully an example. After three marches, each of which grew more and more successful, it seemed inadequate. We might win the Labour party conference, and indeed by 1960 we did, but Hugh Gaitskell demonstrated most convincingly that the power of the party was not with the conference. Those of us who were caught up with the politics of the nuclear disarmament movement were divided. There were those who believed that the only way was to keep marching and in between times to argue and persuade the doubters of the need for a solution in Parliament. On the other hand, there were those, and I was among them, who remained unconvinced. One of the main reasons was that even if the Labour party agreed to renounce the use of nuclear weapons, their determination to remain firmly within the NATO alliance meant that we would never be completely free of nuclear politics, and it seemed to follow from this that the threat to man's existence would therefore remain.

At this point in 1961, Bertrand Russell and Michael Scott issued their now famous call for mass civil disobedience. Once more, action was more attractive than debate. I was one of a group who wrote the first draft of a message which Bertrand Russell finally gave under the title 'Act or Perish', which brought into being the Committee of 100. The problems of civil disobedience worried me a great deal as it seemed wrong to take action for ourselves and to take the law into our hands, no matter how great the justification. Gandhi provided the answer: his advice to the movement for Indian independence on the question of civil disobedience had been that only a deep respect for the law and the Constitution could ever justify breaking the law. For Gandhi, there was a critical interdependence between the need to change the political structures and changes in personal behaviour, and I thought that this was right. The pollution of the atmosphere with nuclear dust, which was endangering the health and even the lives of human beings not yet born, was wicked by any definition of that word. The threat to use the weapons by the nuclear powers was the final obscenity. Such a government could not command respect. Only by breaking its laws could it be possible to convey to those who governed the depth of revulsion, only by accepting the consequences of breaking the law would it be possible to persuade them how seriously we felt. I became committed to non-violent resistance, including disobedience, to a government which was set on a wholly immoral course.

During the years of marching I had acquired some experience in organizing, and with the new Committee I agreed to act as Chief Marshal for the demonstrations we proposed to mount. We had come a long way from those early days in 1958 when at a rally which launched the Campaign for Nuclear Disarmament, Canon Collins, the Chairman, said: 'We are seeking a short, sharp campaign to bring the politicians to their senses.' He had in mind a campaign which would last for eighteen months to two years. Now, three years later, we were embarked on a course which at the outset would have been unthinkable. Curiously enough, many of the arguments which were used against the Committee of 100 were much the same as those used against the Campaign for Nuclear Disarmament. In 1958 it was considered 'undemocratic' to try and use pressure to change the policy of the country by marching. Political commentators all advised CND to use the political machinery. By 1960 the Aldermaston march had become a national institution, and marching at Easter was more fashionable than the traditional Easter Parades.

Some of us who became committed to civil disobedience had no desire to become a national institution and were quite determined not to be incorporated by a system which was capable of manufacturing nuclear weapons. My earlier ignorance of the nature of the political dilemma which nuclear weapons posed was now cleared up. War itself is the basic social system, within which other modes of social organization conflict or conspire. In 1958 the march began as a protest against the conspiracy of silence on the issue of nuclear weapons and against the testing of these weapons. By 1961 my own position had changed radically. When I joined with Russell and other members of the Committee of 100, I was fully committed to a struggle which would not end until the system itself had changed.

Prison and the End of the Road from Aldermaston

The depth of commitment I had managed to attain was to sustain me for the three years which followed, during which time I spent some months in prison. The first demonstration we organized went off without a hitch, and I felt that we should build on this success. More than 5,000 people took part and there was not a single arrest despite the fact that we besieged the Ministry of Defence for three hours and occupied the pavements surrounding the building. But my colleagues had different ideas. The only success that would satisfy them was the creation of a situation in which the whole machinery of government was brought to a halt and all the gaols were filled with anti-nuclear demonstrators. They felt we must push on quickly and planned for demonstrations to be held every three months. Both the next two demonstrations seemed to indicate they were right. In April 1961 another 5,000 people took part in the second demonstration, and 800 people were arrested and fined. After this, activity reached a frenzy. Early in September, a week before the third major demonstration was to take place, the government arrested fifty members of the Committee, including Bertrand Russell and his wife.

They arrested us under an old medieval law enacted in 1366, and sent us to prison for periods of one and two months, depending upon how they viewed our importance to the Committee, because we refused to be bound over to keep the peace. When asked by the Bow Street magistrate whether I would undertake not to demonstrate, I remember saying that it was I who required the government to keep the peace – and received two months for my trouble. Following our imprisonment, the government invoked the 1936 Public Order Act and forbade the Committee to use Trafalgar Square. Demonstrators risked prison sentences of up to six months, yet more than 12,000 people took part in a demonstration that lasted more than eight hours and during which more than 1,300 people were arrested. It looked as though I was wrong and my colleagues right.

However, at this critical point in the development of the movement, the government began to take a more sensible line in dealing with us, and the Committee over-reached itself. Faced with large numbers of demonstrators, the authorities imposed fines on the greater majority and began systematically to impose increasingly long sentences of imprisonment on the organizers. Within another three months of the September demonstration, the Committee were in the field again, this time outside the main air bases. The authorities chose to make an example of the six main organizers, and by making use of the somewhat dubious Official Secrets Act they sentenced them to twelve months' imprisonment.

I was in prison at the time and although heartened by the determination of so many people to continue the struggle, it saddened me to see the Committee walk so easily into a trap. The search for sensations in order to keep in the public eye, and the aim of bringing the whole war machine to a standstill by filling the gaols was romantic and pure adventurism. Such a movement requires time to build up its strength and leadership, time to learn the disciplines of unfamiliar tactics. But above all, time is required to build up courage and sustain members of the movement when things are going badly.

The Committee never recovered from the savage sentences imposed on the six members who went to prison for twelve months over the Wethersfield demonstration, but it must be admitted that there were other factors involved in its decline. In June 1962, an agreement was reached between America, Russia and Britain which brought about a partial Test Ban Treaty, under which all three powers agreed not to test weapons in the atmosphere. This satisfied many of those who supported the Campaign for Nuclear Disarmament and the Committee of 100, but it did not satisfy people like myself.

Taking Action for Ourselves

I reached the conclusion that it would be necessary to move away from 'national demonstrations' and search for a basis of a movement which was prepared to go beyond moral gestures and symbolic actions. It had become clear that mere criticism and pressure on the authorities and on public opinion was not enough, and that our protest was becoming sterile. So in the summer of 1962 I organized a journey around Britain which was to last for five months and to take us over a distance of more than 5,000 miles. The object was to carry the message of Aldermaston to every village-green, form CND groups where none existed, and strengthen those already in existence. We called the outfit Caravan Workshops.

In the course of the journey, we discovered how little real democracy there was in the towns and villages and how much reliance there was on central authority in London. People with party political loyalties were very reluctant to break away from these loyalties even when they knew that their party was wrong. It was also apparent that disillusionment with CND and the Committee of 100 was also setting in, and that local secretaries were ceasing to organize.

During 1963 our conceptions about ourselves began to change, and the group which we called Caravan Workshops moved steadily away from CND. This change came about during the course of organizing four projects which we devised to test some of the assumptions that were made about the Campaign and our own new thinking.

We presented ourselves to the rest of the CND movement as a group concerned primarily with furthering the quality of our work and effectiveness in campaigning. We recognized that this would involve us with problems concerning the relationship between people and government. But we also recognized that only a great deal of study and intellectual work would enable us to establish the connections between the problems of achieving disarmament and the issues of social change in a non-violent and disarmed society. Once again I was head on against the problem of changes in structure and changes in behaviour.

The way ahead was not at all clear. Even the prospect of a change of government in 1964 brought no relief. On the contrary I recall thinking at the time how irrelevant it was – even to the point of not voting. How different it had been in 1956, when not only was I caught up in the business of the election but also organized the stewarding arrangements for public meetings in three London constituencies, one of them being North Kensington. So I took a year off, and was fortunate to find hospitality on a farm belonging to a friend. Ploughing fields, 'spudding' thistles, planting trees, seemed a seventh heaven after the seven hectic years of campaigning, and slowly my thoughts turned to more conventional employment.

But, of course, it could not be. I was too committed to changing the policies of the government, whether Labour or Conservative. I had always maintained that this could only be done by keeping steadfastly to the single and most urgent issue of nuclear disarmament. Now this view was changing. Social change requires a more total experience, and I began to realize that the kernel of the matter rested in the problem of powerlessness. I was given the opportunity of visiting America, and I chose to go there to look into questions of technology and social change. I also hoped that I might see something of the American Civil Rights movement.

The lower end of the East side in New York seemed to be the epitome of an old print of the slums of British cities in the nineteenth century. The humiliation which the poor suffered and their powerlessness to survive the brash aggressive drives of unbridled private enterprise and rugged individualism were quite unbelievable. The numerous 'winos' lying on street pavements totally disregarded by every passer-by, the soup kitchens in chapels which served hymns and prayers as a prerequisite for the soup, the ghetto at Harlem – all these shocked the senses and outraged every sensibility. I moved on from New York to other major cities, and in each there were the ghettos of the poor and the black. I learnt at first hand about the bad housing, the overcrowding, the high infant mortality and disease rates, which are an abominable disgrace in any civilized society and utterly immoral in the midst of an affluent society.

In the midst of the despair, which is caused by the effects of life in the ghettos of poverty and outright discrimination, there was reason to hope. Civil Rights activists were encouraging the ghetto dwellers to organize themselves, and were achieving success. To overcome powerlessness, those most affected were being persuaded that by taking action for themselves change could be achieved. I came back to Britain determined, and hopeful, that I had found a way through some of the difficulties which I was experiencing before going to America.

Fasting for Vietnam

It was not possible to make an immediate start. The war in Vietnam was being escalated by the Americans, and Prime Minister Wilson appeared to be supporting them. On my return, I went straight from the airplane to a teach-in at Central Hall. All the usual array of radicals were speaking fine words, none was agreeing with the others, and no positive course of action that made sense to me was being proposed. The teach-in was rather like seeing a parade of ghosts from the past, and I was in no mood to be haunted.

A number of ministers in the new Labour government had marched with me from Aldermarston to London. It seemed just possible that they would respond to a message of love rather than be bullied into submission by great pressure. So I thought it best to undertake a public fast, and chose Parliament Square as the venue. The fast lasted for twelve days and made some impact. But I see now that it was also arrogant to suppose that in a country where we are unused to talking to each other in this way it is sufficient to fast for twelve days. The fast as a method of communication with an obstinate authority should not be used so lightly. Probably it should only be undertaken as a last resort when all other attempts to reach the minds of those whose policy you would like to see changed have failed. Since it is a last resort, the preparation for it must be careful and as public as the fast itself. One last thought on this, although I am not at all certain as to whether it is correct, if a fast is undertaken on an issue as serious as the war in Vietnam then it should be carried through to the death. Nobody can doubt any longer after they have read the evidence of Lieutenant Calley about the reasons for the massacre at My Lai that this war is a monstrous crime against humanity, for which we are all responsible and accountable.

Community Action in Notting Hill

The effects of a life of poverty take their toll. One of the greatest difficulties facing people in this situation is that of relating policy and legislation to actual events. Those who are poor do not usually approve of the way decisions are made, and feel that the rules are unfair, loaded against them, and that the law itself is in some fundamental sense fraudulent because it is the backbone of a system which seems so clearly to benefit those with power at the expense of those who do not have it. It does not matter much whether this is true or not; that it is so keenly felt means that nothing will be done unless it can be demonstrated that these rules can be changed and some benefits can be gained by those who are excluded.

The successes and the failures of the projects which have been mounted in Notting Hill since I started community organizing there in 1966 are significant not only because of the importance of the explicit objective to provide people living in the area with organizational and tactical weapons to act on their own behalf. They are important also because of the implications which successful community organizing have for the way in which decision-making is institutionalized in the nation.

I have already referred to the nature of modern technology, and this needs to be set alongside the trend towards decision-making by distant bureaucratic professionals and hidden politicians. What emerges after five years' work in Notting Hill is the hope that through the efforts of militant community organization in which local people are taking action for themselves it will be possible for a new framework of local decision-making to be created and for this to have real power. The success in getting a popularly elected neighbourhood council in the Golborne Ward is an example.

Direct action in community politics is quite different in quality from the kind which needed to be taken by CND and the Committee of 100. What we have attempted in order to achieve an effective and responsible intervention has been the organic combination of three elements: objective study (the Notting Hill Housing Survey in 1967 and the Golborne Community Plan in 1970), pilot work in order to demonstrate possible solutions and improvements (for example the Notting Hill Housing Service) and thirdly, when normal methods and quiet activity are insufficient to alter an intolerable situation, democratic and non-violent pressure on the responsible authority to stimulate its awareness and to evoke hope and active participation in the local people (the organization of the Social Rights Committee is perhaps the best example to give for this third element).

It is still too early to say what the success in Notting Hill is going to mean or how it will come about. What can be said is that the borough council has been stimulated into a new awareness about the problems of North Kensington: they have made some very large concessions during the past three years and look as though they are going to make many more. On the ground, there is a community spirit and a sense of being in charge of their own affairs that many commentators would have said was impossible five years ago. Both of these are pre-conditions for any fundamental change and it would be rash to make any prophecies about the future.

The election of a neighbourhood council will certainly see a sharpening of the issues and demands which the local community is likely to make. The usual *scenario* painted by social workers when appealing for resources is one which depicts the handicaps and disabilities. Often as not, at least part of the blame for the conditions will be placed on the residents. Local people see it differently. Take these three statements (excerpts) from the election addresses of three of the successful candidates in the election for a neighbourhood council:

Some of the conditions people are expected to live under are scandalous and would never be dreamed of by people in better circles. To my mind the Borough Council, up to now, has shown too much apathy to an area that has been called one of the worst slums in the United Kingdom. I would endeavour to do all in my power to see that the situation is changed for the better.

Housing is horrible, sanitation is a scandal, education is a farce, old age is a crime, and to be young is to know torture. We can put an end to this sad state of affairs if we join heart and hands and fight for a decent existence.

This neighbourhood council could be a good thing for us and will give us all a chance to have our own way in how the area is rebuilt.

These are the voices of people who have gained sufficient confidence to say plainly what is wrong, and express their determination to set matters to right.

Conclusion

It took almost five years to reach the point where the community work which was started in 1966 began to show dividends. In one very real sense, the election of the Golborne neighbourhood council was the greatest prize of them all. Local residents in one of the most deprived communities in all London situated in the Royal Borough of Kensington and Chelsea – the third richest borough in London – have shown their determination to take control over their own lives.

The election was a curious affair. Organized by an independent committee of middle-class community workers and clergy, it lacked the almost essential ingredient of conflict about issues which makes an election attractive. The successful candidates are extraordinarily representative in age and ethnic groups. These are the people who will shape a programme of social and physical reconstruction for the area: 100 acres intensely overcrowded in houses which have lacked reasonable economic investment and with a population that has been denied or excluded from (for one reason or another) the normal benefits of this society. How these twenty-six councillors – who have at this moment no statutory powers – gather power to act on behalf of their neighbours will greatly influence the possibilities for genuine democratic participation and control throughout Britain. It may well prove as significant for the future of deprived communities as was the establishment of trade unions for the nineteenth-century labouring classes.

The role of the community work which laid the foundations for this possibility has been that of catalyst, enabler and facilitator. Action over the past six years has been of the order that will awaken a new awareness in the hearts and minds of the local authority, and evoke hope that change can be achieved by the efforts of the local people. This is the very essence of the non-violent philosophy, seeking sources of new power to overcome powerlessness. It requires only that those who undertake this role should be prepared to live with, laugh with, cry with, and if necessary die with, the community that is being served. There is nothing to lose and everything to gain which, after the material and physical reconstruction, is a sense of dignity and first class citizenship. In the process of reconstruction, new values can be found which will hopefully re-invigorate the moral and social fabric of the society after which meaningful social change can begin to take place. The process is evolutionary rather than revolutionary, in the sense that the word is usually used. But the change that takes place can be more revolutionary than the overthrow of government by violent means.

One of the paradoxes of the times in which we live is that the more dubious and uncertain an instrument violence has become as an agent of change in international relations because of the nature of nuclear weapons, the more it has gained in reputation and appeal among radicals seeking social and political change. 'Power grows out of the barrel of a gun' is a slogan much in vogue and very often used by those who most fervently believe that the State is an instrument of violence wielded on behalf of the ruling class. Power may well be achieved in this way, but it is reasonable to ask what has been gained.

Engels defined violence as the accelerator of economic development, and stressed in his analysis that the process remains determined by the conditions which preceded the violent action. This is an aspect of the ends and means argument which is little discussed. I have introduced it into these conclusions in order to establish the all important connection between the direct action of the activist who responded to the appeal of Bertrand Russell at the time when the nuclear peril was greatest and the community worker who takes direct action on behalf of a community in order that local people shall find hope and courage to take action for themselves. What they both have in common is an assertion of our essential humanity. Large issues surround the most simple forms of direct action. Both before and after the action, there is a need for theory about the quality of the change which is intended – but it is not a prerequisite of the action. The action can be the learning process, and for those who are trying to build a new world for themselves it is essential.

Modern technological societies appear to have an inbuilt mechanism within the system whereby – to put the matter crudely – the rich grow richer and the poor grow poorer. Progress within the society is no longer conditioned by anything other than a technical calculus of efficiency. The search for truth about our existence and the search for a just and equal society are no longer personal nor easily amenable to experiment. They are abstract, mathematical and economic. The world that is now being created by technical means is an artificial world and very different from the natural world out of which grew our Parliamentary institutions based on a rather woolly liberal humanist philosophy. It is a technology which can produce abundance on a scale which could produce a new Garden of Eden for man, yet at the same time it is this same technology which can produce the forces of self-destruction of man. The central question of our time is how we can take control and build for ourselves a new paradise. One explanation for the attraction of violence among radicals today is the frustration they feel at the inaccessibility to the means of control.

My experience is that they are not there to be found. We must deliberately and consciously choose another way and create for ourselves new sources of power. Governments and rulers may send out their edicts, but this does not mean that we must obey – especially if those edicts turn us all into criminal lunatics bent on our own self-destruction. In such a situation, we must remember our humanity and forget the rest, and there is no better place to make a start than at the bottom of our society where hardship, discontent and inequality are most keenly felt and most sharply defined.

NOTE

Since writing this chapter George Clark has founded the Committee for City Poverty which is likely once more to involve him in national politics. His work in North Kensington realised a major goal when the Greater London Council agreed to embark upon a partnership with the Golborne Neighbourhood Council in replanning and re-building the Swinbrook area of Golborne for the residents living in the area in May 1972. Thus the attempt to bring in those who are powerless and usually excluded from the decision making processes has been successful and provides a model for what can be achieved in other parts of the country.

XII Direct Action and the Springbok Tours

PETER HAIN

Direct action played a crucial role in the campaign against the Springbok tours to Britain of 1969–70. If any one factor could be singled out in the overwhelming success of this campaign against the white South African tourists, it would be these direct action tactics which formed the basis of the campaign strategy.

For the background to the development of direct action in this campaign and for an understanding of its importance, we must look first to the build-up in opposition to apartheid in sport. This began soon after the Second World War, when racial discrimination and segregation within South African sport began to be challenged for the first time by non-white sportsmen. In the early 1950s, the non-white sports bodies inside South Africa began to press for recognition and representation in South African sports teams. They approached and lobbied white sports bodies. They approached and lobbied international sports bodies. For over ten years they presented the reasoned case against white domination of the country's sport. But, at almost every point, they were met with a stubborn refusal both to remove racialism from sport and to recognize their rights as sportsmen.

And as the campaign for non-racial sport inside South Africa gathered momentum, its leaders were first intimidated and later suppressed, as the security police attempted to crush their activities. Officials of the sports organizations prominent in the campaign were driven into submission by intimidation, imprisoned, banned or forced to leave the country. But still the international sports organizations refused to acknowledge the case for non-racial sport and to recognize that non-white sportsmen had just as much claim to international representation.

The emphasis of the campaign then switched to outside South Africa. And after the years of conventional lobbying, petitioning and letter-writing that had met with no response, a new strategy was called for. The campaign for non-racial sport now sought to isolate white South Africa from international sport. And as the 1960s drew to a close, pressure mounted by the campaign forced the world sports organizations, one after the other, to cut links with the all-white South African bodies.

Some sports remained defiant in their appeasement of apartheid in sport. Prominent amongst these were cricket and rugby. No amount of patience, no amount of lobbying, no amount of reasoned argument, it seemed, could persuade these sports officials to recognize and advance the cause of non-racialism in sport. It was their narrow intransigence that produced the militancy which was to form the basis of the successful British campaign against the Springbok rugby and cricket tours.

It was out of this atmosphere that the campaign to stop the 1970 cricket tour grew. Frustrated by the attitude of the cricket authorities, and determined to strike an effective blow against apartheid, the Stop The Seventy Tour Committee formed in August 1969, and decided to build the campaign on the foundation of direct action tactics aimed at physically stopping the matches; this decision was taken partly, also, because of the fresh impact it would make publicity-wise. But at this early stage, there was no clear campaign perspective on direct action: the organizers simply wanted to stop the tours, and sit-down tactics seemed the most appropriate. In addition, through the open public threat of direct action, it was hoped that the tour would be cancelled.

By the time the STST Committee was launched at a Press conference in September 1969, its initiators had begun to realize the significance of the Springbok rugby tour, due to take place that winter; prior to this, attention had centred on cricket, largely because of the controversy in 1968 over Basil D'Oliveira, the Coloured South African cricketer who played for England. But now the campaign focused on the rugby tour. It began to gather momentum from a position of almost no coherent overall organization, and by the time the tourists arrived at the end of October it had reached a position of amazing depth of support and commitment. The strongest single contributory factor in this startling growth in campaign strength was the re-arranging by the rugby authorities of the first match, against Oxford University. The match was switched, principally because of the threat of disruption, sparking off public interest in the campaign.

Direct action now assumed a life of its own. The *threat* of sit-down demonstrations which would cause the abandonment of the matches, and so of the tour, could not be ignored: it captured the attention of the general public and was extremely newsworthy. From this time on, the Press coverage – which achieved massive proportions throughout the campaign – never let up. In addition, the direct action tactics captured the imagination of many potential demonstrators who saw the opportunity to influence directly the issue of protest by involving themselves in action which would be immediately effective. On the other side,

G

the sports authorities were recognizing that they were being put in a position where they had little alternative but to react and, leading on from this, to change their stance on sports apartheid.

Almost overnight, a mass movement sprang up against the rugby tour which, in turn, became a strong lever against the cricket tour. There were demonstrations at every one of the twenty-four tour matches; two matches had to be switched from their original venues because the authorities felt that the grounds were indefensible; while the match in Northern Ireland was abandoned because of the explosive situation in the province coupled with the build-up in opposition to the game.

A countrywide campaign developed, growing in strength as the tour went on. Intense pressure was exerted on the authorities by the force of the demonstrations in the first month; by the time of the successful disruption of the sixth match, at Twickenham, which was stopped for some ten minutes as demonstrators poured on to the pitch, the whole tour was in severe jeopardy. The matches were only able to go on protected by the massive police resources. In addition, public order was being strained. The mob violence at the fourth match at Swansea caused a public outcry, and there was grave concern amongst the authorities. At this match, the police discarded all pretence at impartiality and gave the nod to rugby 'stewards' whose declared intention was to attack the demonstrators. In the ugly scenes that followed, many non-violent demonstrators were indiscriminately assaulted. The wounds of Swansea hung over the rest of the tour. It was clear that any recurrence of the provocative role of the police and their open collaboration with rugby stewards who, unlike the vast body of supporters of the game, could quite candidly be described as 'thugs', would force the Home Secretary to intervene. As it was, he called a conference of Chief Constables to discuss the situation.

From the simple, and perhaps initially inarticulated, threat of direct action tactics, a major political controversy was fast developing, embracing not only the issue of racialism in sport, but also the whole question of public order.

But the tour continued, stumbling through right to the end. After the first month of the three-month itinerary, the grounds were enveloped by a network of security. Then the barbed wire went up around the perimeter of some tour venues – until, finally, the grounds began to assume the appearance of armed camps. Match disruptions, centring around the invasion and sit-down tactics, became more difficult. And, with just over half the tour completed, the campaign organizers decided to extend activities outside the specific area of the matches themselves. Direct action protests were staged at the Springboks' hotels and at the start of their coach journeys. On the morning of the international match at Twickenham on 20 December, an attempt was made to drive the team's coach away. It was only partially successful. But the point was made, and soon afterwards the Springbok manager threatened to take his team home unless security could be increased.

Throughout the tour, the pressure on the authorities hardly let up. The fact that the campaign had a rigid time-table of targets set out for it was an advantage, as this injected a sense of urgency into the organization and meant that there was little time for interest to flag or morale to drop: activity had to be virtually continuous. In many ways, the principal strength of the campaign strategy was psychological. An example of this was the almost hysterical reaction to the simultaneous painting of slogans on fourteen county cricket grounds one night in January; this altered the whole atmosphere of the campaign as it strikingly demonstrated both the countrywide strength of the movement and the potential of action at the grounds. The *threat* of direct action was often more imposing than the reality of militant protests. The unpredictability of the campaign tactics made life difficult for the authorities. On the one hand, they were never sure where the demonstrators would strike next, and, on the other, they were constantly uncertain what form the protests would take. This also made for a harrowing experience for the players who were under a state of semi-siege, real or imagined, throughout the tour.

When the tourists finally left for South Africa at the beginning of February, even though the rugby tour had not been stopped, it was obvious that the cricketers would find themselves in an impossible situation. The game itself had been somewhat peripheral to the tour, while the strength of the movement had been strikingly demonstrated.

Campaign attention now focused on its original target of the cricket tour, due to start at the beginning of May. From the foundations laid during the rugby campaign, public opposition was mobilized on a massive scale. And, behind the scenes, campaign organization was consolidated. The build-up towards the dramatic climax in late May had begun.

Shortly after the end of the rugby tour, the cricket tour was cut from twenty-eight matches to twelve, because the cricket authorities felt that they would only be able to defend the smaller number which were to be played at seven tour centres. The starting date, moreover, was put back a month, to the beginning of June.

By this time, an extra dimension had been introduced into the tour arena. Armed with their new 'law and order' campaign, inherited from America, the Conservative party seemed determined to exploit the tour for electioneering purposes. Since the Labour government had always opposed the tour, and was obviously desperately hoping that it would be called off, it was clear that the campaign would become the focus for a party-political skirmish.

Also becoming significant was the growing concern and interest in Black Africa. The wide publicity achieved by the campaign throughout Africa was partly responsible for this. But more important was the fact that pressure on the tour became an avenue for exposing the whole British position on Southern Africa and on race in general. Unconsciously, the tour became the focus for something of a showdown-between the black Commonwealth and Britain. In consequence, the whole issue developed into a major international row. This row centred principally around the Commonwealth Games, which were to take place in Edinburgh in July 1970. As the cricket tour drew nearer, the rumours of an African boycott of the Games, unless the tour was cancelled, crystallized into a positive threat and, ultimately, into a direct public statement of intent from nearly all the African and Asian countries in the Commonwealth. The black Commonwealth was forcing Britain to make a choice: between the white cricket tour and the multi-racial Games. This was not simply a matter of racialism in sport – it went much further than that. Black Africa, India and Pakistan wanted to know on which side of the racial fence Britain stood.

In the meantime, the issue had developed from a public controversy in Britain to a political storm. From a small, student-based committee, the anti-tour campaign had become a mass movement. The issue was being exhaustively debated throughout the country – on television and radio, in the Press, in the home, the school and the public meeting. This mass debate produced a situation where the STST Committee took something of a back seat in the fresh initiatives being taken at a public level. Trade unions were coming out against the tour. Public figures were speaking out on the whole issue. The Church was taking a stand. Even Parliament debated the tour. This happened almost spontaneously: there was no centrally organized drive in the STST movement to capture the support of these areas of public opinion. STST set an example and others followed. And it was this great depth of support for the anti-tour campaign that made possible its ultimate success, because it gave the campaign a legitimacy and a certain public respectability. But, in the final analysis, it was the threat of direct action which was the most important factor both in the cancellation and in the mobilization of public opinion.

The militancy of the campaign was primarily responsible for its wide publicity. Not all of this, admittedly, was good publicity for the campaign, but all of it contributed to the massive impact. It was this militancy, also, which forced moderate opinion to take a firm and active stand against the tour. The Fair Cricket Campaign, formed at the beginning of May 1970 under the chairmanship of David Sheppard, the Bishop of Woolwich, is the most striking example. Many in the FCC, although holding strong feelings on the issue, would not normally have involved themselves in protest politics; but they felt it necessary to provide a lead so that the moderate view did not go by default.

This apparently unlikely alliance between militants and moderates was made possible partly because of the undogmatic nature of the STST movement. Although committed to direct action, campaign organizers nevertheless refused to be rigid in their approach either to methods of action or to working with others with whom they had tactical differences. Thus the whole movement against the tour was essentially based upon a coalition of forces – differing in tactics and approach, but firmly committed to the same objective: the stopping of the tour. Campaign unity was also helped by the specific aim of the movement, which allowed little scope for the negative, theoretical wranglings which surround many protest movements. But to understand the nature of the STST movement, it should be appreciated that it was based almost entirely on local initiative and organization. The National Committee did not direct the movement, it co-ordinated activities. Local action groups and regional co-ordinating committees were autonomous in both organization and tactics, and were responsible for arranging local demonstrations. This loose structure enabled a variety of viewpoints to come together in common action. Had it not been for the structure of the movement, it is doubtful whether the mass commitment would have sprung from the essentially militant base and leadership. It is interesting to note in parentheses, however, that the more dogmatic and self-styled revolutionary left groups refused initially to give their backing to STST, because it 'was concerned with a side-issue not central to the struggle against Capitalism'. But when the bandwagon started rolling they were quick to jump on it.

The depth of this mass commitment and the strong feeling against the tour is hard to explain without looking at the atmosphere in which the campaign emerged. This emergence and the subsequent success rested in part on a series of fortuitous accidents. But, more important, the STST movement gave expression to the growing discontent with conventional politics amongst radicals who felt that Parliamentary politics had been totally devalued as an agent for fundamental social change by the Wilson Labour government. STST, with its irreverent by-passing of the conventional political structure, became a symbol for the aspirations of young radicals in particular. It also gave expression to the feeling of frustration, amongst many people holding progressive views, at the fact that racialism and Powellite agitation was going effectively unchallenged in Britain by established politicians. The Springbok tours became a means of expressing, not merely their abhorrence of apartheid, but also their disillusionment at the way the debate on race in Britain had degenerated.

As the campaign drew on, race relations in Britain became an increasingly serious factor in the cricket tour issue. There was a strong feeling of resentment at the insult to the black community in Britain posed by a touring team selected on racial lines from a racialist system. Many people began to appreciate that lofty and moral pronouncements against racialism had to be backed up by positive action. The contradiction between improving racial harmony at home and effectively appeasing racialism abroad, was also exposed. There was fear of a racial confrontation, and the authorities were seriously concerned.

By the beginning of May, with the tour only a month away, an enormous pressure group was exerting itself on the cricket authorities. An additional factor was soon to be introduced; rumour was rife that the Prime Minister would call a general election in June. The possible clash of the election with a potentially explosive series of demonstrations, gave rise to fresh speculation that the tour might have to be called off. This was strengthened by the confirmation that the African and Asian countries would definitely boycott the Commonwealth Games. The tour issue had now become a political headache at the highest level. Much was at stake. There was the deep-rooted opposition to the tour. There was Britain's position in the Commonwealth. There was the danger to race relations throughout the country. There were the consequences for the political situation, with concern over the possible effect on the position of the Labour government. And, hanging over all this, there was the threat to social order posed by the direct action tactics.

In the first two weeks of May, it appeared that the cricket authorities were wavering. A flock of high-level delegations descended on Lords throughout this period. At the same time, there was a positive swing against the tour. Where before it could be argued that tour opponents were in a minority, it was now clear that opposition to the tour was immense. By this stage, the only public body of any standing which supported it was the Monday Club, backed implicitly by the Conservative party. The Conservatives had systematically exploited the tour issue, but now even Tory leaders were holding their fire; they, apparently, did not relish the prospect of an election fought in the unpredictable and volatile atmosphere that would surround the tour.

Then, the Cricket Council, the governing body, announced that it was holding an emergency meeting on 19 May to consider its position. And, on 18 May, the Prime Minister announced the general election, to be held exactly a month later. It was widely thought that this meant that the tour was off. So confident was Fleet Street that some evening newspapers even went to the extent of confirming the cancellation several hours before the announcement of the Cricket Council's decision.

But the Council, true to form, decided that the tour would go ahead as planned. They also decided, again with predictable inconsistency, that there would be no further 'Test Tours' with South Africa until 'cricket is played, and teams selected, on a multi-racial basis in South Africa'. In its entirety, the decision pleased no one – even tour supporters were annoyed at the concession over future tours. Yet still the drama was not over. The next day, in a mixed atmosphere of incredulity and anger at the Council's decision, the Home Secretary, James Callaghan, announced that he had asked the Cricket Council to meet him to discuss their decision. A meeting took place on 21 May, and afterwards it was announced that Mr Callaghan had asked the Council to cancel the tour, for reasons of 'broad public policy'. The following afternoon, the Cricket Council met once again and shortly afterwards stated that it had acceded to the government's request and cancelled the tour – 'with great regret'. The Seventy Tour had been stopped.

The stopping of the tour marked the climax to one of the most successful protest movements in recent times. The campaign, which had emerged in the summer of 1969 and exploded into action at the end of October, had achieved its objective. Spearheading the campaign, the STST movement had grown from an idea in the minds of a few people in August 1969, to an active force which brought out over 50,000 people in demonstrations against the rugby tour, and finally was the catalyst which led to the cancellation. The great strength of the movement and the public opinion aroused led first to a national controversy in Britain, followed by something of a political crisis coupled with an international controversy. And the cancellation was the culmination of pressures due to these forces.

For a closer understanding of the movement which caused this political upheaval, one must also appreciate the organizational difficulties facing STST. One of these was the fact that the direct action strategy adopted depends for its success, particularly in public terms, on a strong element of novelty and unpredictability. This, of course, with the heavy security, often meant that there was a conflict between effectively organizing surprise protests and alerting the Press in time. Another drawback to the campaign strategy was that, while public debate on the issue was exhaustive and brought the realities of apartheid and apartheid sport home to people, discussion on the tactics of demonstrating degenerated completely. The distinction between non-violent direct action and violence became, in the public's mind, at best blurred and at worst non-existent. Even the Bishop of Woolwich followed the general Press hysteria over direct action and implied that sit-down disruptions were acts of violence. It was only towards the end of the campaign that the discussion began to reach a rational level.

It was often said that STST's militancy alienated potential supporters and increased support both for the tour and for white South Africa. Yet this accusation never stood up to the facts. By the end of the campaign, opposition to apartheid was at its highest in Britain since the outcry over the Sharpeville shootings of 1960; while the true nature of South Africa's sports system was exposed and support for the policy of isolating white South Africa increased. Indeed, one of the major successes of the campaign was to make apartheid a national issue in Britain, and in this sense it was of vital importance, regardless of its ultimate success in stopping the tour.

Justification of the direct action strategy may be approached in two ways. The first is by comparing it with other forms of direct action that occur continually in modern society and are on the increase. Some of these are institutionalized: industrial strikes, for example, have been an accepted form of organized action – yet they cause far more general social disruption than interfering with a cricket or rugby match. At a different level, a pertinent parallel can be drawn with mothers and their children disrupting traffic in protest against the absence of a zebra-crossing at traffic danger spots: far from being frowned upon, this is often actively encouraged by the mass media and commands much public sympathy and support. Likewise, how many of the solid country gentlemen whose wrath was vented on the anti-Springbok demonstrators, raised a word of criticism at farmers driving their tractors through country towns, disrupting traffic and causing chaos in shopping centres to draw attention to their grievances ? The fact remains that various forms of direct action are socially acceptable. The second approach is the more positive one. This is that direct action tactics were the only effective means of challenging racialism in sport and its importation into Britain. As the history of the campaign for non-racial sport shows, other tactics had failed. And when the need to take a positive stand against racialism is balanced against the right to watch a cricket match, there ought to be no doubt where we should stand.

The consequences of the tour cancellation and the enormous impact of the campaign have yet to be fully appreciated. It was finally responsible for putting white South Africa on the path into total sports isolation, by the use of, and threat of, direct action in the sports which had seemed safe from outside pressure. As a result of the campaign and of the other major strides against apartheid in sport made in 1970, the white sports system in South Africa was thrown into confusion, with calls from sports officials for national summit meetings with the government, and with unprecedented calls from white sportsmen for a less racial sports policy. The sports issue has also been an important factor in opening up the cracks that are beginning to appear in the apartheid system. It focused world attention on apartheid, and was also a great morale booster for both black South Africans and the white radicals remaining in the country.

In Britain, Press coverage was massive and continuous. The full impact was increased by the fact that the campaign reports appeared on both the news and sports pages. The sporting world and sporting public had to emerge from its vacuum to be confronted with a moral issue which posed many questions, not merely on racialism, but also on the whole role of sport in society.

The political importance of the campaign is almost self-evident in the fact that the government had to intervene directly. Not many protest movements have forced a British government into this position. For all the criticism of the intervention, which came mainly from the right, the fact remains that the circumstances at the time left the government with little alternative but to step in. In so doing, it set a precedent of sorts and raised cries of infringements of private rights – although the significance of its intervention in establishing a precedent has been blown up out of all proportion, especially when one considers the growing influence and control of the apparatus of the modern State. But the cricket tour had to be balanced against a possible racial split in the Commonwealth, a deterioration of race relations in Britain, the sacrificing of the Commonwealth Games and the fact that it was, politically and socially, a 'hot' issue.

The campaign and the government's role obviously raise important questions about the autonomy of private bodies. For example, those most vociferous in their condemnation of the STST movement and the government did not ever discuss the fact that bodies such as the MCC and the Rugby Football Union are not democratically accountable or answerable to anyone except, to some extent, their own membership. As far as the narrow question of sports organization is concerned, one may argue that this is a satisfactory position; but when questions of much wider social importance arise out of the activities of these bodies, then the whole issue becomes more complex.

It can hardly be denied that the campaign, and in particular its militant strategy, helped the general back-lash on 'permissiveness' that is prevalent in British society today. But its influence in this back-lash, and on the 'law and order' issue, was more one of strengthening already entrenched positions than contributing positively to any social move to the right. Much play was made, particularly by white South Africans, that the campaign had helped to put the Conservatives back in power. But, although STST was to some extent an election issue (with questions being raised at the election meetings of some Liberal and Labour candidates), this has not been supported by any serious political commentator. Where the campaign could well have had some effect is through the race issue which was certainly a factor in the election results. One undeniable result of the campaign was to expose some ugly signs of racialist feeling in British society, and STST came under criticism from those who felt that this was harming the cause of racial harmony in Britain. But their position is a very unreal one, because racialism can only be fought out in the open. More important to the future of race relations, I believe, is the fact that many people took a positive and committed stand on the issue.

Looking to the future, the success of the campaign against the Springbok tours may have an important bearing on the development of protest politics and, more specifically, on the campaign against apartheid and racialism. STST showed that a militant movement could command mass support; that direct action tactics could be highly effective while still keeping the active sympathy of a broad spectrum of public opinion.

It would be wrong to generalize too freely from the campaign, as the circumstances were very special. Equally, it would be short-sighted to underestimate its importance. For this was not just another protest movement. It aroused enormous interest. It captured the imagination of many. It gave expression to the deep feeling of opposition to racialism within British society: the courage, commitment and enthusiasm of campaign supporters was testimony enough to this. But above all, perhaps, it achieved its objective. And it is in this striking achievement, rare indeed in protest politics, that a pointer to the future lies. We may be in the process of a dramatic switch in the strategy of protest movements campaigning on both the great moral issues of the day and also the less dramatic issues in the local community – a switch away from big, symbolic demonstrations parading through London's West End towards direct action on specific, and to some extent narrow and winnable, issues. If this switch occurs, protest politics could become, not merely an irritant to the authorities, but a positive threat. One of the biggest, and most troubling, questions that remains is whether we can discipline ourselves to maintain such a militant and effective momentum while at the same time remaining firmly committed to a non-violent strategy.

XIII Universities and Violence

BRIAN MACARTHUR

Starting a chapter on the subject of universities and violence, one struggles to resolve countless perplexities and contradictions. As a university correspondent with four newspapers since 1962, and after two years of active involvement in the National Union of Students from 1960–2, it is obvious both that the canvas has changed since 1960 and that the student generation since 1967, or the articulate, cutting edge of it, *is* different from the earlier generation. Yet immediately the perplexities start.

One wanted, for instance, to insert 'at least' into the parenthesis about the students who form the generation's 'cutting edge'; but even the so-called average, apathetic students (all, it should be noted, born *after* the end of the war) *are* different. Their attitudes to sex, drugs, personal life and friendships, the welfare state, and authority are so much less inhibited.[1]

So why has the canvas changed? Were the various controversies of the 1967–70 era simply a response to bigger universities? Were they stimulated by the alleged failures of the Labour government? Or were they simply an inevitable response, where they occurred, to authoritarian and hamfisted university and college management? And do such emanations occur *inside* universities only when a left-wing government is in power? Was it, for example, simply coincidence that the first sit-ins occurred at the London School of Economics, which was seemingly badly administered, and at Essex University, where there was a strong emphasis on the social sciences?

When a Tory government was returned, it was interesting to note that students returned to the streets again over the issue of South African arms just as my own generation marched from Aldermaston to Ban the Bomb during the previous Tory government.

Undoubtedly, however, the atmosphere within universities has become more violent, both verbally and physically; and yet, at the same time, the supposedly 'militant' leadership of the NUS has strenuously resisted any attempt at official involvement of the Union in violent activities; and one of the cults of students today is *non*-violence.

Student violence, of course, has been a feature of universities since the last century, but the style, the form and the unity of student demonstrations since 1967 is different from the horseplay of the annual rag or the Union bar after a rugby club victory. The first publicized instance occurred at LSE on 31 January 1967, and it is graphically described by Colin Crouch.[2] He recalls the background to a meeting on the relevance of the experience of American negroes and students at Berkeley to the campaign against Walter Adams, who had been appointed Director. It was to discuss direct action, a form of violence new to British universities, and Sir Sydney Caine, the Director, decided, perhaps unwisely, to ban the meeting. Students argued with the Director, and Crouch goes on:

> The issue at stake was no longer a substantive one of whether a meeting could be held, but the formal principle of whether it should be held in the Old Theatre. It was in support of this principle that the students' mood deteriorated to one of uncontrolled anger, and they charged the doors of the theatre which were being guarded by porters. As is by now well known, Mr Edward Poole, a School porter who had a weak heart and had not been asked to help guard the doors, moved forward to help his colleagues. He collapsed and a gangway was made to carry him through the shouting and pushing melée of students. Although no direct physical assaults were being made on the porters, save pushing of the kind that is usually incurred by police guarding large crowds, Sir Sidney and Kidd were punched several times. Soon after the collapse of Poole, the students burst through the chain of porters and rushed into the theatre, which was in darkness, the Director having ordered the fuses to be removed from the lighting system.

> The scene inside the darkened theatre was extraordinary. Some students had lit candles, and small points of light illuminated agitated and gesticulating human forms as the theatre gradually filled. Several students were on the stage ready to start the scheduled meeting. Caine ascended the platform to announce that the porter had been hurt and to say that if the students would now leave the theatre there would be no victimization. The theatre continued to fill, and was very noisy. Caine returned and made a vain attempt to still the noise. 'The man has now died', he said. 'Does that satisfy you?' There were enraged screams of 'No!' from all sides of the theatre. Then the mood changed dramatically. It fell quiet, and students began slowly to leave.

> Outside the Old Theatre someone was urging us to go back and continue with the meeting; others were attempting to have the meeting reorganized in the students' union bar. It was in that direction that many of us walked, dazed and worried. Several

believed, or hoped, that Caine had lied about the porter's death in order to clear us from the theatre. In the bar Caine, to his lasting credit, was comforting weeping students, telling them they should not feel responsible. It was extraordinary how in the course of a few minutes people who had been regarding Caine with a bitter hatred could now find him a reassuring father figure. The School was closed for a day, and we all went home.

I have discussed these events in some detail because I consider they were extremely important in shaping the subsequent attitude of a minority of us towards student protest. I had been in the midst of the crowd outside the Old Theatre, and although sympathetic to its opposition to Caine's ban, I had been unable to comprehend the depth of the anger that had been aroused on the abstract question of whether the Old Theatre should be charged or whether the meeting should be in the bar. I had been standing a few inches from Poole when he collapsed, and although I saw no one actually strike him, I concur entirely with Kidd's verdict: '. . . it remains my opinion that if it had been a normal day Poole would have had his tea and gone home.'

My immediate circle of friends was for a while completely overcome by a feeling of sickness and guilt at the thought that, for the sake of a small principle, we had been prepared to join in that rampaging crowd. In 1967 students at LSE who were involved in the events reacted principally to one of two incidents. The majority reacted to the sit-in that was to follow in March, and emerged from that with an attitude of hostility to authority and an affection for direct action on the sit-in model. But for a minority of us this experience was overwhelmed by that of 31 January, which we saw as an instance of temporary mob rule.

From then on my erstwhile enthusiasm for direct action and mass participation became coloured by the image of the enraged mob. Once such an attitude is formed on the basis of a powerful incident, one continues to find evidence for it, and in this case the role of the enraged mob in history is not a flattering story. If any single incident removed me from the company of the new mass-participatory left, it was 31 January. Although subsequent events at LSE have produced nothing quite similar, nothing has occurred since to refute my image of what is likely to happen when political action seeks as its predominant channel a mass impelled by hatred and passion.

Since then the catalogue of 'violence', verbal or physical or disruptive, has grown, as the following selected summary indicates:

1967   Enoch Powell and Anthony Buck molested at Essex University.

Patrick Gordon Walker, Secretary of State, shouted down at University of Manchester Institute of Science and Technology. American Embassy officials daubed with paint at Sussex University.

1968   Mr and Mrs Patrick Wall mobbed at Leeds University.
A germ warfare lecture disrupted at Essex University.
Vice-Chancellor's office plundered at Birmingham University.

1969   Smashing of internal security gates at LSE.
MPs on the Select Committee barracked and forced to meet in private at LSE and Essex University.

1970   Attempt to set fire to Barclays Bank at Essex University.
Several sit-ins of vice-chancellors' offices during the secret files controversy.
Shouting down of Aba Pant at Kingsley Martin memorial lecture, Sussex University.
Substantial damage at Kent University after sit-in, amounting to £2,800.

Such violence has been widespread, but a series of events during the spring and summer at Keele University served to show just how far the situation had gone. The following statement was made by Dr W. A. C. Stewart, the Vice-Chancellor, on 16 June:

The recent past has seen a series of acts of hooliganism, vandalism and terrorism at Keele. Here is the dismal catalogue:

10/11 March	Break-in to my Assistant's office.
2/3 May	Excessive noise at outdoor party continuing despite appeals to stop.
3 May	Fires in Registry and Horwood General Block.
6/7 May	'Festival of peace' produces £1,000 worth of damage to Union Ballroom.
20 May	Daubings on Registry and Keele Hall.
7 June	Paint thrown through windows of the Registrar's house.
9 June	Petrol bomb thrown through windows of Architects' Department.
14 June	Three plate-glass windows in Keele Hall smashed. Glue put in locks of Walter Moberley Hall and Registry. (The Registrar and myself have also had to suffer glue inserted in the locks of our house doors.)
15 June	Eight windows broken in the Library.

The cost of repairing this senseless damage is considerable and can only reduce the amount of money available for normal University services and amenities. Only students who want to destroy rather than reform the University can be happy at this wastage of our limited resources.

These acts should be seen in relation to 'demands' made in an anonymous published motion for tonight's Extraordinary General Meeting. This motion is related to last week's motion which made similar demands, and threatened direct action if they were not met. It is difficult enough to have reasoned discussion when one side makes demands rather than proposals. It is impossible when they seek to enforce these demands by acts of destruction.

One of the demands is: 'All police off Campus', suggesting that the police are being brought in by the University to enforce its authority. In fact, of course, the police are here for two reasons: to investigate criminal acts already committed, and to deter future criminal behaviour. They have no relation to the conduct of normal University business. No one would be more pleased than myself to see the police leave the Campus. Their presence is an inevitable consequence of criminal acts by a very small group of students. The Union has already condemned these acts, and has asked students to give the police any information that might help to identify the people responsible. Giving such information would help the police to finish their investigations and leave the Campus.

One of the motions at tonight's Extraordinary General Meeting calls for the pursuit of policy through democratic and non-violent means. The other repeats the demands made at last week's meeting which threatened direct action if they were not met, and further seeks to impose on the Union the views of the Minority Report to the Exploratory Committee.

The student body has the opportunity to choose between these approaches. I believe the vast majority of students back democratic, non-violent methods and I hope they will make this clear to the small minority who are bringing deep discredit on the University in general and on the student body in particular.

After such a catalogue, it is clear that students have resorted to violence. However, the perplexities and contradictions still persist. There are nearly fifty university institutions, and the table mentions only eight as suffering violence, and the maximum has probably been only twenty. There are 225,000 university students and it is doubtful whether many more than 2,500 of these participated in the quoted incidents. So *universities*, collectively, are not suffering from violence. Nor are *students*, collectively, indulging in violent activity. Similarly, to put a fine point on it, there is a significant difference between overheated heckling, barracking, which amounts to disruption, and the violence seen sporadically at several universities. Nor does the 'violence' displayed on university campuses in Britain bear any relation to the violence initiated or approved by university students in the United States, France and Japan. Nor is society in Britain so violent as in France and the United States either in its reaction to student demonstrations or in its internal dynamic. So what we do have, perhaps, is a somewhat higher proportion than in earlier generations of students who are prepared to use violence as a tactic.

Jack Straw was President of the National Union of Students from 1970–71 He arrived at the head of the Union as the spokesman of the new student generation who were disillusioned by the Establishment image of his predecessors and the quietist, insular politics of the 1950s and early 1960s. (It is ironic, or a lesson in the British art of taming rebels, that he was the first NUS President to dine at No. 10.) Yet consider the following three reports:

NUS Head Condemns Violence

An attack on violence during student sit-ins was made last night by Mr Jack Straw, President of the National Union of Students, in a speech at Durham University to union presidents from universities and colleges throughout the country.

Dissociating himself and the student movement from 'individuals and groups with misconceived and half-baked revolutionary fantasies', he emphasized that students achieved real progress only on the basis of organized, self-disciplined, non-violent action, based on genuine grievances and supported by a majority of students.

The NUS, he said, supported individual student unions in non-violent direct action when it could be shown that four conditions had been fulfilled. These were that the issue in dispute agreed with NUS policy; meaningful negotiations, made in good faith, had failed; the intended action was non-violent, both against property and persons, and the action was actively supported by a majority of students under their union's constitution.

He said: 'I believe very strongly that in the future we should not be afraid, as I believe we have been in the past, to admit the fact that those who claim to be as radical or even more radical than we, can just as easily lead to a betrayal of our stated ideals and to the destruction of the student movement as those who attack us from the right.'

Impetuous and rash actions

Students needed the courage of their convictions not only for social and educational change and for exposing such issues as apartheid but to recognize that there were limits beyond which any action in pursuit of the ideals of the NUS became wrong in principle, undemocratic and essentially counter productive. Nor should they deny to others the rights they so fervently sought for themselves.

'We must say very clearly that every brick that is thrown actually destroys the cause in whose support it was done. We must say very clearly that those who take action of any kind that manifestly is against the will of the majority of students are acting as autocratically and undemocratically as those whom they seek to oppose . . . . We must say, too, that by their own criteria and theory, not ours, the groups who adopt these practices have failed and stand condemned, for what they manage to do almost every time, and what no revolutionary leader, neither Lenin nor Che Guevara, ever suggested, is to alienate the majority of the rest of the community by their own impetuous and rash actions.'

Students, and especially student leaders, were facing a critical moment of choice. They must opt either for a strong, organized, democratic union or decide to allow individuals and groups to act out their revolutionary fantasies, so creating more violence and alienation.[3]

Jack Straw Issues a Challenge to Society

By Our Education Correspondent

The reason for student unrest in Britain, as seen by Mr Jack Straw, President of the National Union of Students, was that events had opened their eyes and they were challenging society to live by its ideals.

This unrest could not be brushed aside as a seasonal hazard without cause or remedy, he said last night at the opening of the union's annual Easter conference at Bradford University.

It was worth pointing out to the government and the opposition, before both become totally entrenched, that the no-man's-land students were trying to cross, against intense resistance, was the unacceptable gap between the principles of politicians and their practices.

After questioning the morality of the Conservative law and order campaign and of selling arms to South Africa, Mr Straw put other questions to politicians on behalf of the 400,000 students he leads.

He asked why the government had still not announced a public inquiry into the colleges of art at Guildford and Hornsey, and why it had still not accepted the £12m. maximum claim for an improvement of student grants.

He then set about university vice-chancellors. 'One of their members, Lord Annan, of University College, London, asked why we in the NUS did not condemn those who restricted rights of freedom of speech of others', he said. 'Well, we did, and without prompting from him. . . . But if we are expected to condemn those in our midst who transgress our code of behaviour, is it not about time that at least one vice-chancellor had the courage publicly to condemn the handful of extremists in their midst?'[4]

Students Favour Peaceful Protest in Britain

Denis Taylor writes on NUS support
for the right to dissent without violence

Guns for guerrillas, a red menace and psychedelic revolution are among the ingredients fit for a thriller novel to be culled from the National Union of Students' conference which ended during the week-end at Bradford University.

But in sober retrospect this conference will probably be seen as a watershed in student affairs, with important implications for the wider political scene. For the meeting served not merely as a test case lost by the advocates of violence as a weapon of student protest.

Perhaps the most important feature was that the result of the debate on violence amounted to upholding the right to dissent at a time when this is increasingly threatened by students in the Western world, particularly in the United States.

Out of the welter of amendments and points of order emerged a clear polarization over issues, which renders the traditional political labels meaningless.

After last week it will no longer be justifiable to use traditional labels like 'Communist' or 'Socialist' when talking about student action. This is worth bearing in mind when the lowering of the voting age to eighteen means that many more students are eligible to vote. The NUS executive came out of last week's elections with a more committed membership than in the past.

But perhaps the most important new factor was the emergence of moderates like Mr Tony Lake, a determined upholder of the need for a civilized society, rather than the appearance or the elevation of left-wingers.

In the present student situation even a Communist looks almost like a member of the Establishment. For Communists are old-fashioned enough to eschew violence, and it is on this issue that the great divide is now to be found.

This was forced right into the open during the NUS conference. At first glance it might look hypocritical to reject violence at home and agree to raise money for guerrilla movements in southern Africa.

But the southern African resolution went through in that form because of the conviction that it was far too late for peaceful methods to succeed in ending apartheid.

The Bradford debate forced the recognition that a totally different situation from that in South Africa exists in Britain. The theologians of violence teach that the keeping of certain personal records on students or the financial links between universities and companies with investments in South Africa are forms of violence, and that therefore physical action to break them cannot constitute violence.

The deliberations of Bradford pronounced this doctrine a heresy. This decision has greatly strengthened the hand of Mr. Jack Straw, the NUS President. The relevant point is no longer the degree of his Socialism, but the backing he has won for supporting individual student union actions where negotiations with university administrations have failed, provided they stop short of violence.

Discontent with many features of society is shared by extremists looking for an opportunity to whip up a confrontation, and by quite serious radicals. The present burning issue happens to be the British economic stake in South Africa.

There will be plenty of other issues, and if past experience is anything to go by some of the evidence produced will be highly suspect. It will often be unfair to single out the nearest institution, the university or college, for attack. Nevertheless, the broad argument that Britain is economically involved in the home of apartheid is a strong one, and it is also the case that British business is involved in the universities.

It would be extremely naïve to imagine that there will be no more violent campus confrontations in Britain. Some delegations withdrew their support from the motion on non-violence during the conference, and it is possible that there may be some disaffiliations from the NUS.

But it is perhaps more important that Mr Straw is in a position where he can use his new mandate to add weight to the student side in his dealings with university vice-chancellors and other administrators and politicians, and more successfully isolate violence without appearing to dilute his own radicalism.[5]

Apart from confirming the previous analysis, one further point which emerges from Jack Straw's second speech is the emotional *violation* active students suffered from seeming inconsistencies of a Labour government. They expect a Tory government to sell arms to South Africa, but were not yet cynical enough not to be surprised that a Labour government should discover that office brings compromise. Hence, perhaps, the correspondingly stronger sense of betrayal, leading to an equally stronger expression of discontent, and the search for an ideology outside the traditional Labour or Communist parties or in the heroes of the Third World.

Yet the question still remains of *why* student demonstration suddenly became so much more violent, at least in some of its expression. After the first sit-in at LSE, I asked several prominent students who had been closely involved in it about their philosophies of student power, and their answers are still relevant. David Adelstein, at that time President of the Students' Union at LSE, said:

> I accept the word militancy, but it means for me that one is prepared to consider any action that will achieve one's ends, which is in accordance with one's ends. One would not rule out any mode of action because it has not been accepted in the past.
>
> I am not saying that any action is justified. I do not consider violent action justified unless it is in response to violence, and even then not always. But we do initiate unconstitutional action. We do not accept unconstitutional limits because they are undemocratic. When democracy fails, this is the only way of doing it.

Similarly, Jan Midwinter, a student at the Regent Street Polytechnic, and a leading member of the Radical Students' Association (RSA), said:

> I can approve of the Sussex paint-throwing because of my political views. I think that in cases like that the violence springs from frustration and repression, a sense of frustration at seeing that American drive away in his car completely unaffected by any views that had been expressed. So they threw paint – and what better colour than red?

Universities in Britain were also coming to the end of an era, in which student politics had concerned themselves almost exclusively with diplomacy. The aim had been to make student union politics 'respectable', to establish links with vice-chancellors and registrars, and to win the minimum right of consultation. At the time it was necessary, but the slow response of university administrations made it seem increasingly irrelevant to the new generation. The moral was summed by Dr William Boyd, Vice-Chancellor of Student Affairs at the University of California, Berkeley, and (as usual, but for the last time) ignored. Speaking at a conference in London, he said:

> Listen to students ... I mean really listen. If we do not listen they

are going to find some other way to attract our attention. There are very legitimate needs in the new student population, and if legitimate means are not found for meeting these legitimate ends, then illegitimate means will be resorted to.

Students had been lobbying and campaigning for reforms within universities throughout the 1960s. The demands were drearily familiar – representation on governing bodies, consultation about courses, reforms of teaching and examining methods, and so on – but usually they were put down as the demands of a small Union clique who, anyway, got more satisfaction from Union politics than academic work. So active students got tired of the reformers and threw weight behind the moderate and democratic revolutionaries – and Geoffrey Martin and Trevor Fisk gave way to Jack Straw. Violence, or the threat of it, succeeded instantly; and it can be argued quite convincingly that its success was the fault of the university administrators who had failed to respond sufficiently quickly to the reformist demands of the 'responsible' students throughout the early 1960s. As several radical students put it at the time:

> There is no militancy without a cause. It arises from frustration with the university environment. Agitators can raise certain issues but they cannot force people to join in. Students were not forced to sit down – they believed in it. The RSA think we can fight on grants like workers on wages – but workers can go on strike. They have real power. All students can do is to boycott lectures or stage a sit-in.[6]

One major factor in the almost instant success of the students was the influence of newspapers and television. University administrators were suddenly – and publicly – forced on to the defensive. At least in the serious newspapers, the students' case was analysed exhaustively. Neutral opinion decided that it was well argued and the groundswell of opinion led to the now-famous concordat between the NUS and the Committee of Vice-Chancellors and Principals. Student representation is now firmly established as a feature of British life. It is doubtful whether the establishment politicians of the NUS would have emerged so successfully if it had not been for the threat of violence posed from their rear – a sad commentary on many university administrations.

On the other hand, there is no doubt that the influence, especially of television but also of newspapers, was to encourage violence, often not of their own seeking. A reporter in a newspaper office got used to calls from students' unions advising him that a sit-in was about to occur. Newspapers, however, had the space to put sit-ins in perspective. Television, able or wanting to use only a few seconds of film, tended to dwell on the *visual* aspects of sit-ins – their violent elements, especially at LSE. There was one occasion when the authorities were seeking to commit students to gaol – a historic occasion. Yet the television news bulletin concentrated solely on a march by about forty students, in which the *Financial Times* was ceremonially burnt, mentioning only as an afterthought that the attempt to gaol the students had failed.

On this analysis, the use of violence by some students on the far left arose from a peculiar conjunction of circumstances: a lack of prescience by university authorities, a Labour government which failed to fulfil all its promises, and a widespread *malaise* among the young in affluent Western countries about the directions in which society is heading. Two of these factors are now missing in Britain, and it may be no coincidence that so far university life seems more quiet. There may be other reasons for the quiet. I once asked Dr Clark Kerr, the former President of the University of California, why in 1969 the university campus was relatively quiet. Two of his three reasons were relevant for Britain. The first was that staff and students had discovered how much their work was affected by the continual disruptions involved in sit-ins and their aftermath. The second was that many staff, the sort who never know quite where they stand, shrank back at the first hint of real violence on the campus. The third – the view that in California Governor Reagan was an enemy of the university and should not be offered gratuitous ammunition – may also now be relevant, since there is a significant lobby within the Tory party which wants to act severely with student protesters.

One suspects now that a distinctive phase of student protest is over. The quiet diplomacy of the early 1960s – the lobbying of vice-chancellors, MPs, and ministers and civil servants of the Department of Education and Science – was succeeded when its impetus ran out by a resort to the use of force and sanction, tinged with genuine physical violence. That phase has served its purpose – at least for the significant swathe of students who instinctively recoil from violence, but will support it if the cause seems just and other means have failed. Once that support melts away, the revolutionaries who believe in violence as a means to an end[7] are left as a small, powerless minority.

It may be that we are now entering another phase in which students, confronting authorities who know that they will use sanctions if unreasonably frustrated, will once again work to influence the Establishment and walk the corridors of power, while demonstrations against government policy are pursued outside the universities in the streets.

There is also a very real and unsentimental sense in which violence is a very un-British way of achieving radical aims. Usually they are achieved, as with the Colonies or women's suffrage, by sudden, spectacular but essentially short jolts of violence. Students in Britain just cannot claim – nor at heart, I suspect, do they inwardly believe –

that they are the victims of a violent society or of a repressive university authority, as witness the number of radical American students who find a refuge in it. The police, for instance, are unarmed and they do not fire shots at student demonstrators. Nor will they enter universities unless invited. Similarly, students in Britain enjoy much more favourable, not to say luxurious, amenities than their contemporaries elsewhere. They are supported by a generous system of grants, a staff-student ratio of one to eight and a low failure rate. Neither revolutionaries, nor the revolution, nor the use of violence, thrives in such conditions.

NOTES

1. Easily the most perceptive analysis has been made by Professor Richard Hoggart in *Higher Education, Demand and Response*, (London, 1969), pp. 217–19.
2. *The Student Revolt* (London, 1970), pp. 48–50.
3. Brian MacArthur, *The Times* (17 March 1970).
4. Ibid. (1 April 1970).
5. Dennis Taylor, *The Times* (6 April 1970).
6. John Rose (London School of Economics), *The Times* (March 1967).
7. See Paul Rock and Francis Weidensohn, 'New Reflections on Violence', in David Martin (ed.), *Anarchy and Culture* (London, 1969), pp. 114–19.

PART THREE

The Boundaries of Action

A THE STATE

XIV Policy-Making

DAVID G. T. WILLIAMS

Sir Ivor Jennings once wrote that

> democracy rests not on any particular form of executive government,
> nor upon the limitation of the powers of the legislature, nor upon
> anything implicit in the character of its penal laws, but on the fact
> that political power rests in the last analysis on free elections, carried
> out in a State where criticism of the government is not only per-
> missible but a positive merit, and where parties based on competing
> policies or interests are not only allowed but encouraged.[1]

He went on to state that the existence of a free, democratic system of
government 'creates an atmosphere of freedom which is more easily
felt than analysed, but which excludes, for instance, the use of un-
conscionable means of obtaining evidence, spying, unecessary restrictions upon freedom of movement and of speech, and, above all, any
attempt to restrict freedom of thought'.[2] In a book published in 1935
entitled *In Defence of Democracy*, which was in part an examination of
the ideas underlying Fascism and Communism, two Fellows of Balliol
College (J. S. Fulton and C. R. Morris) stressed that democracy is
possible only if all the individuals in society 'are really and effectively
free to have converse with one another, to influence and be influenced by
one another'.[3] In another work published in the same year, *The
Essentials of Parliamentary Democracy*, Reginald Bassett suggested
that democracy

> constitutes an attempt to reconcile freedom with the need for law
> and its enforcement. It may be defined as a political method by which
> every citizen has the opportunity of participating through discussion
> in an attempt to reach voluntary agreement as to what shall be
> done for the good of the community as a whole. It resolves itself, in
> practice, into a continuous search for agreement through discussion
> and compromise, and action on the basis of the maximum measure of
> agreement obtainable.[4]

Every discussion about the essence of democratic government
inevitably contains its own emphasis and its own reservations. But those
quotations from three books agree on one familiar ground: that citizens

in a democratic society ought to have the fullest opportunity of influencing their governments. Such influence can be exerted not merely at election time but throughout the life of each government, and for this reason the right of free election must necessarily be accompanied by an acceptance of the right of free speech. There is no constitutional guarantee of freedom of speech and of assembly in this country, but at least over the last century or two it has been accepted as an essential feature of our system of government. At the time of the Hyde Park disturbances of the 1860s, a former Chief Commissioner of Works expressed his belief that it is 'an essential element in the success of constitutional principles in this country that large masses of people should be able to meet together when they wished to discuss questions of public importance'.[5] In a debate in 1916 over some regulations restricting public meetings, Herbert Samuel, the Home Secretary, said that it

> is a very good thing that public opinion should be sensitive whenever there is any interference with the right of public meetings, even in time of war, for the free expression of opinion is a matter of the greatest importance, and the House of Commons is well advised to watch any measures taken by the ministry of the day which in any way threaten or impair the right of public meeting.[6]

When faced with a series of problems about meetings and demonstrations, another Home Secretary, James Callaghan, declared in 1968 that 'it is in the interests of every one of us that the right of peaceful demonstration should be preserved. To me, that is the cardinal principle which should be followed.[7]

The democratic importance of free speech and free assembly can be explained in several ways. It is clear, for instance, that minority groups must be allowed to communicate their ideas to others, especially in a society where control of the principal media of communication tends to fall into relatively few hands. Public meetings and demonstrations have the particular advantages of being speedy, inexpensive and possibly spontaneous means of communicating ideas. In some circumstances, a public meeting or demonstration is simply a means of letting off steam. Charles Bradlaugh said in the House of Commons on one occasion that 'reasonable' public meetings are 'a kind of safety-valve for the expression of public opinion';[8] and Arthur Balfour conceded a few years later, in a debate concerning the activities of anarchists, that 'there are fit and proper subjects of public discussion which, if you refuse all natural outlets of discussion, will probably breed very much more mischiefs than if you allowed them free outlet.'[9] It is, of course, easy to argue that in a democratic society people should be content with approaches through normal political channels: but it is notorious that the avenues of approach are restricted and clogged. Once it is agreed that freedom of discussion is part and parcel of democracy, it is difficult to deny that public meetings and demonstrations are proper means of expressing views and ultimately influencing representatives in the legislature. Perhaps it would be true to say that the danger raised by tactics of direct action is that the demonstrators have in effect proclaimed some measure of suspicion or cynicism about the very working of the legislative process. This point has been brought home in the debates at Stormont over the recent troubles in Northern Ireland. In April 1969, for example, John Hume had this to say:

> The first and most desirable method by which people can voice their feelings is through Parliament and their elected representatives in Parliament. But we say and we have said for some considerable time that the reason why people have gone on the streets was that their frustration pent up for many years finally burst forth and they lost faith in Parliament as a means of redress.[10]

In fact, the Cameron Report of 1969 on *Disturbances in Northern Ireland* suggested that one of the most powerful causes of the outbreaks of violence which began on 5 October 1968 was 'the continuing pressure, in particular among Catholic members of the community, of a sense of resentment and frustration at the failure of representations for the remedy of social, economic and political grievances'.[11] In a similar vein, the Kerner Commission in the United States, in seeking to explain the race riots which swept Newark, Detroit and other cities in 1967, stated that the 'frustrations of powerlessness' have convinced some Negroes that 'there is no effective alternative to violence as a means of expression and redress.' 'More generally,' added the Commission, 'the result is alienation and hostility towards the institutions of law and government and the white society which controls them. This is reflected in the reach towards racial consciousness and solidarity reflected in the slogan "Black Power".'[12]

The frustrations of powerlessness probably underlie many forms of direct action. Professor J. A. G. Griffith has recently spoken of 'the myth that ordinary men and women participate in political power and can share in deciding what shall be done',[13] and there are doubtless many who would support his rejection of traditional concepts of liberalism and Parliamentary democracy and representative government. Others would take a less pessimistic view but would nonetheless agree that much needs to be improved in our present democratic system. Brian Walden said:

> We provide democratic processes by means of which laws can be changed if necessary, and we must see that our procedures are kept

up to date and over-hauled and changed as necessary. It is a fair criticism that many of our institutions need change, and that very often the government and the governed are too remote from each other that they do not share, or do not appear to share, the same objects.[14]

The advocates of direct action, of course, are impatient of suggestions for reform in a system which they claim has invariably been unresponsive; and in calling for direct action they are fortified by the belief that this will ensure speedier and more effective change.

At the same time, it would be wrong to assume that impatience and direct action are something new in recent history. And it would be equally wrong to assume that democratic government, as it has developed in this country, is incapable of accepting some degree of direct action as a means of expression and protest. The very term 'direct action' is imprecise, and the borderline between the exercise of rights of free speech and assembly, on the one hand, and the employment of methods of direct action, on the other, is frequently obscure. It is for this reason that politicians and judges alike are driven to the position of having to re-emphasize the importance of free speech while at the same time deploring what they see as abuses of the liberty accorded by a democratic system. Take, for instance, this statement by Sir Derek Walker-Smith in a debate on law and order in the House of Commons in February 1969:

> Of course the right of freedom of expression is fundamental in a democracy. Of course we have to try to strike a fair balance between the right of the citizen to protest, on the one hand, and the duty of the State to maintain public order and preserve property, which involves the right of other citizens, on the other hand. But the violent manifestations which the government seems to be condoning go far beyond freedom of expression or constitutional protest. They are a form of legalized violence which has neither place nor purpose in a democratic society which possesses universal suffrage, free speech, a free Press and the whole apparatus of peaceful expression of opinion.[15]

In proceedings concerning the Public Order (Amendment) Bill in Northern Ireland in 1969, the Attorney-General of the province spoke of 'the recognition that, while individuals and groups of individuals should have the right to free expression of opinion in every respectable form, including by procession and assembly, this right must be reasonably, temperately and peacefully exercised'.[16] In *De Jonge* v. *Oregon*, which was decided in the Supreme Court of the United States in 1937,

Chief Justice Hughes perhaps summed up the traditional liberal approach towards protest:

> The greater the importance of safeguarding the community from incitements to the overthrow of our institutions by force and violence, the more imperative is the need to preserve inviolate the constitutional rights of free speech, free press and free assembly in order to maintain the opportunity for free political discussion, to the end that government may be responsive to the will of the people and that changes, if desired, may be obtained by peaceful means. Therein lies the security of the Republic, the very foundation of constitutional government.[17]

Throughout the 1960s, a decade of growing direct action on both sides of the Atlantic, the initial response of governments was to reaffirm the democratic belief in the virtue of dissent. The Walker Report on the Chicago riots of 1968 started by saying that the 'right to dissent is fundamental to democracy', and that the plain challenge of what happened at Chicago was how 'to keep *peaceful assembly* from becoming a contradiction in terms.'[18] After violence and threatened violence at demonstrations in London in 1968, James Callaghan, the Home Secretary, consistently urged caution and restraint as a matter of government policy. After disturbances in the West End in July, he warned against falling into the trap set by some demonstrators who, he alleged, sought 'to provoke a situation in which the right to demonstrate might have to be interfered with'.[19] The same spirit of caution is evident in the manifestos submitted to the electorate by both major political parties in the 1970 general election. The Conservative manifesto spoke of the need for changing the law 'for dealing with offences – forcible entry, obstruction and violent offences concerned with public order – peculiar to the age of demonstration and disruption' but was careful to add that a 'tolerant and civilized society must continue to permit its citizens to assemble, march and demonstrate in support of the ideals and principles they believe in'; while the Labour manifesto, after promising a vigorous pursuit of the fight against vandals and law-breakers, immediately added that 'the campaign for law and order must be linked to liberty and justice in a civilized society'.[20]

Yet the Conservative manifesto's reference to offences 'peculiar to the age of demonstration and disruption' is a reminder that neither party could possibly have had a clear solution to the problems posed by direct action at the present time. Although there are historical precedents for most forms of disorder and disruption, there are nevertheless certain important factors which have to be taken into account in interpreting the events of the 1960s and governmental reactions. One of these is publicity. Never before have the methods of protest in various countries been attended by such immediate and full news-coverage as in the decade in which television came of age. The Cameron Report on Northern Ireland suggested that it was not

> wholly accidental that events of last autumn occurred at a time when throughout Europe, as well as in America, a wave of reaction against constituted authority in all its aspects, and in particular in the world of universities and colleges, was making itself manifest in violent protests, marches and street demonstrations of all kinds. The psychological effect of this example in other countries cannot be discounted.[21]

It might be added that the example of what had occurred elsewhere was brought home most vividly through the media of communication. Because of suspicion of activities in other countries, governments have indeed been anxious to restrict the activities of visiting aliens. Lord Stonham, in a debate early in 1969 on 'Violence in Contemporary Society,' spoke of our standards of liberty being 'grossly exploited by a minority, the kind of people, whether they came from abroad or were citizens of this country, who would bring ball bearings to trip up horses, who could stick nails in horses'.[22] In the House of Commons in October 1968, a few days before the major anti-Vietnam demonstration of 27 October, the Home Secretary said that he had 'issued instructions that foreign students and other aliens with convictions for violence shall not be allowed to come here to take part in the demonstration'.[23] The feeling was so strong in some quarters that one MP was driven to claiming that the British people 'are fed up with being trampled underfoot by foreign scum', adding that there was 'seething resentment and anger of the people whom we represent at being offered as a sacrifice to alien militant agitators with no true cause'.[24] Daniel Cohn-Bendit, Rudi Dutschke, Jerry Rubin and others have all seen at first hand evidence of the reluctance of governments to give aliens a free hand in public protest; and judges for their part have not hesitated in some circumstances to recommend deportation for those convicted of offences of violence or disruption, though the Court of Appeal in the Garden House (Cambridge) riot case was disinclined to favour such a recommendation in response to one isolated offence. Suspicion of the activities of aliens is not new in this country or in any other country,[25] but the immense publicity which nowadays envelops protests and demonstrations has perhaps enchanced the suspicion.[26]

Another important factor in the 1960s, apart from publicity, was the greater opportunity now for varying or extending methods and tactics of protest. Greater mobility has led to increased international and internal travel; the expansion of higher education has undoubtedly influenced the course of events in several countries; and protesters have in many instances perhaps had ample financial assistance or resources. From the point of view of the State, it is clearly essential to take as many steps as possible to meet new methods and tactics. Sometimes the response is to provide more police or a more effective deployment of the police; on other occasions the response is to make full use of the width and flexibility of the law to seek criminal or civil remedies in the courts; or it might be deemed necessary to consider possible legislative reform of the law; but in many instances the response is simply one of sitting tight and patiently waiting for matters to improve.

The role of the police is obviously crucial if one is seeking to determine the policy of the State in relation to protest and direct action. One of the chief concerns of successive Home Secretaries has been to ensure that the morale of the police is maintained and that the conditions of service are such as to attract and retain the right men in the force. Some action has also been taken to provide training to meet new methods of protest. Experience in the United States during the past few years has revealed only too clearly the need for an intelligent and carefully thought-out use of police in the face of tactics of direct action. William Deedes has said:

> Anyone who has read the Kerner and Walker Reports on riots in America will realize that the worst of the riots sprang from exaggerated fears leading to action by authority, which exacerbated the situation. That is the principal area in which I have fear in this regard. For this, of course, the media share a considerable part of the blame. Without being smug we may turn to what we sought to do last year about the two major demonstrations for which the Home Secretary became responsible – to pacify, to give outlets to expression, to take precautions but to avoid undue repression and violent reaction.[27]

As far as possible, the approach of the authorities has been one of leaving problems of public disorder and disruption to the ordinary professional police forces. The use of stewards to keep order on private property is legal, but incidents during the South African rugby tour in 1969 and 1970 reminded the Home Secretary among others that it was perhaps unwise to exclude the police from dealing with demonstrations. The activities of stewards attached to the British Union of Fascists in the 1930s had scarcely inspired confidence in this regard. Whether a new and more difficult problem will in future be raised by the use of private security forces remains to be seen. The Home Office would almost certainly prefer to rely on the ordinary police, for the accountability of the ordinary police is more clearly established, and the methods and tactics which they adopt are likely to be controlled and restrained. But there are circumstances where, for whatever reason, the actions of the police are not sufficient – and the course of action then open to the government is that of calling in the troops. Troops were in fact called into Northern Ireland in the summer of 1969 and have remained up to the present time. Their presence coincided early on with a general reorganization of the Ulster police in the light of the Hunt Report,[28] but it is significant that the Hunt Report was firmly of the view that the Royal Ulster Constabulary 'should be relieved of its paramilitary duties and assume the character and sole function of a civil police force'.[29] In other words, despite the fact that in the view of Westminster and Stormont the events in Northern Ireland had made it necessary to use the military, action was nonetheless taken to ensure that the police were brought more into line with their colleagues in Great Britain. The Hunt Report stressed that one of the most important considerations upon which efficient enforcement of law and order depends 'must be that the control and administration of any police force should be vested in such manner as will ensure that it will not only be, but will be seen to be, impartial in every sense and that it should be accountable to the public for its actions. Furthermore, in the eyes of the public it must be seen to be civilian in nature . . .'.[30] Such a statement of principle is all the more crucial as an indication of governmental attitudes and policy, since the reorganization of the police was intended to be permanent whereas the use of troops in Northern Ireland has always been regarded as necessary only for the period of difficulty.

The immediate reaction of governments to many forms of direct action is that of seeking criminal or civil remedies in the courts. In England, the law relating to public order is unusually complex and varied in its scope. The Home Office and the office of the Director of Public Prosecutions inevitably play an important part – even if only in terms of advising local police forces as to the most appropriate means of proceeding. In face of the 'sit-in', for instance, there was no neat legal remedy to which authorities might have recourse: but out of the existing law there have emerged a number of methods of acting against organizers and participants. In face of violence and deliberate disruption in the context of demonstrations, the existing law has been much more clearly sufficient. There were those who believed that the days of riot and unlawful assembly were rapidly disappearing, but both crimes have in the last few years recovered something of the vitality which appealed to prosecutors in the 1930s. Recourse to older and major crimes of that nature would generally be had only after consultation with the Director of Public Prosecutions. On the whole, however, it would be fair to say that the usual approach is to utilize less serious crimes. Prosecutors in this country would still prefer in the vast bulk of cases to prosecute for obstruction of the highway rather than for the common law offence of public nuisance, for assaulting or obstructing the police rather than for the common law offences of riot and unlawful assembly, for threatening or insulting behaviour rather than for some more serious offence plucked from the common law or statute. This policy has the advantage from the government's standpoint of not overdramatizing particular occurrences. Just as various Home Secretaries have favoured the retention of traditional methods of crowd control, so they have encouraged the avoidance of major legal proceedings wherever possible.

But the 'law and order' reaction to events of the last few years has nevertheless stimulated an interest in the possibility that law reform might meet what are felt to be the new tactics of protest. The 'sit-in' has been at the centre of most discussions, and the Conservative manifesto of 1970 spoke of the need for an inquiry into the law relating to trespass. In his book on *The Troubles at LSE 1966–7*, Harry Kidd, former Secretary of the London School of Economics, felt that there was a definite need to change the law to deal with the deliberately disruptive sit-in demonstrations. He points out that the police have no duty at the present time to remove civil trespassers, and goes on to say:

> This is a gap in the system of law and order. In the long run the gap may need to be filled by legislation, so that the police can be called in. This does not mean that I think it will often be wise to call them in but the possibility should be there. There cannot be lawless vacuums in society.[31]

Some of those who favour improvements in the law would like to see them coupled with a comprehensive overhaul of the entire law relating to public order: so that the introduction of new procedures and new offences might at least be compensated for by the discarding of a good deal of the dead wood that continues to lie in this area. Others would wish to see any changes in the law confined to very narrow limits, and they would be reluctant, for instance, to have any *duty* imposed on the police in respect of occurrences on private property. From the standpoint of governments, it has to be recognized that any addition to the law relating to public order is notoriously open to misinterpretation by some and to the expression of misgivings by many: for laws introduced at one period of time to meet a particular problem have a habit of being adapted at a different period to meet an entirely different problem, and this is a process which over the centuries has contributed to the scope, flexibility and uncertainty of the law of public order as it is today.

To refuse to change the status and the tactics of the police, to presume in favour of less serious prosecutions, to avoid changing the law to any significant extent: these might appear to amount to a negative and passive approach to the entire problem posed by the recent methods of protest. In fact, of course, it would be misleading to assess the limits of government policy simply by reference to the tactical and legal issues. Any government in a democratic society is bound to take account of direct action by a readiness to consider genuine grievances and a readiness to institute reforms in the system of government if these are shown to be justified. This is not to suggest that there is a genuine grievance behind every case of disruption or outbreak of disorder, but it is the case that direct action in the last few years has coincided with definite efforts to improve the machinery of government – if only to ensure that the expression of grievances should be easier and less disruptive in the future. One does not have to sympathize with the more militant actions of protesters to accept, as did the Conservative manifesto in 1970, that the 'functions and powers of government have expanded so much in recent years that the traditional safeguards for the citizen no longer suffice,[32] or, as did the Labour manifesto, that the machinery of government 'must be adapted to meet new demands'.[33] Proposals for devolution in government, for more open government, for better procedures for the hearing of complaints against administrators and others, for greater participation in government, for more effective protection of individual rights, are all reflections of a view that the traditional workings of democratic government have been severely strained. These proposals would have been forthcoming without any direct action, many of the reforms actually accomplished would have been achieved without direct action, but it would be fair to say – as the situation in Northern Ireland has shown – that governments would be less than honest if they pretended that their policies and the urgency with which they are implemented are uninfluenced by persistent and widespread dissent – whatever the means of expressing that dissent.

Violence and disruption are unlikely to be tolerated, however, as a normal means of expression in a democracy. 'Throwing clods of earth and firecrackers at policemen and their horses,' declared a leading article in *The Guardian*, 'is not a basic constitutional right.'[34] 'There is no legal right to hold a demonstration when it is intended to employ force or the threat of force as a means of arousing public attention', declared a leading article in *The Times*.[35] But, as has been suggested above, the line between peaceful and violent or disruptive protest is often obscure, so any government is left with the unenviable task of having to preserve the opportunities for expressions of dissent without at the same time allowing normal democratic procedures to be side-stepped by tactics of direct action. The basic democratic approach is perhaps summed up by Justice McCarthy in a New Zealand case:

Unquestionably, freedom of opinion, including the right to protest against political decisions, is now accepted as a fundamental human right in any modern society which deserves to be called democratic.

Its general acceptance is one of the most precious of our individual freedoms. It needed no Charter of the United Nations to make it acceptable to us; it has long been part of our way of life. But democracy is compounded of many different freedoms, some of which conflict with others, and the right of protest, in particular, if exercised without restraint may interfere with other people's rights of privacy and freedom from molestation. Freedom of speech, freedom of behaviour, academic freedom, none of these is absolute. The purposes of a democratic society are only made practicable by accepting some limitations on absolute individual freedoms.[36]

NOTES

1. *The Law and the Constitution*, 5th edn (London, 1959), p. 60.
2. Ibid., p. 61.
3. J. S. Fulton and C. R. Morris, *In Defence of Democracy* (London, 1935), p. 212.
4. R. Bassett, *The Essentials of Parliamentary Democracy*, 2nd edn (London, 1964), pp. 93–4.
5. H. C. Debs, 1409 (24 July 1866) (W. F. Cowper).
6. H. C. Debs, c. 299 (12 October 1916).
7. H. C. Debs, c. 36 (22 July 1968). See also, O. Hood Phillips, 'A Right to Demonstrate?' (1970), *86 Law Quarterly Review* (1970), pp. 1–4.
8. H. C. Debs, c. 1763 (12 May 1887).
9. H. C. Debs., cc. 881 ff. (14 November 1893).
10. H. C. Debs (Northern Ireland), vol. 72, c. 846 (2 April 1969). See also, J. A. Currie, vol. 72, c. 1635 (24 April 1969).
11. Cmnd. 532 (Belfast), para. 126.
12. Report of the National Advisory Commission on Civil Disorders (London, 1968), p. 205.
13. Bernard Crick and William A. Robson (eds), *Protest and Discontent* (Harmondsworth, 1970), p. 29.
14. H. C. Debs, c. 1158 (24 February 1969).
15. Ibid., c. 1126.
16. H. C. Debs (Northern Ireland), vol. 72, c. 283 (12 March 1969).
17. 299 U.S. 353, 365 (1937).
18. *Rights in Conflict*: A Report submitted by David Walker, Director of the Chicago Study Team, to the National Commission on the Causes and Prevention of Violence (London, 1968), pp. xv, xvi.
19. H. C. Debs., c. 38 (22 July 1968).
20. 'A Better Tomorrow', p. 26; 'Now Britain is Strong Let's Make It Great Again', p. 23.
21. Cmnd. 532, para. 126.

22. H. C. Debs, c. 563 (12 February 1969).
23. H. C. Debs, c. 1598 (24 October 1968).
24. H. C. Debs, c. 1291 (23 October 1968).
25. See William Preston Jr, *Aliens and Dissenters* (*Federal Suppression of Radicals 1903–33*) (Harvard, 1963).
26. On publicity generally, see James D. Halloran, Philip Elliott and Graham Murdock, *Demonstrations and Communication: A Case Study* (Harmondsworth, 1970).
27. H. C. Debs, c. 1132 (24 February 1969).
28. Report of the Advisory Committee on Police in Northern Ireland, Cmnd. 535 (Belfast).
29. Para. 166.
30. Para. 176.
31. (Oxford, 1969), p. 133.
32. P. 26.
33. P. 20.
34. 24 October 1967, p. 8.
35. 5 September 1968, p. 9.
36. *Melser* v. *Police NZLR* (1967), pp. 437, 445.

XV The Use and Control of the Police

PETER MOODIE

There are two myths concerning the English police which, although commonly accepted, only partially represent the truth. First, that a constable is an 'officer of the Crown',[1] who nevertheless possesses 'authority [which] is original not delegated, and is exercised at his own discretion by virtue of his office';[2] and secondly, that the police are a purely responsive institution, in that they merely react to reports of crimes and do not initiate policies which themselves affect the number and nature of reported crimes. The major part of this paper is largely concerned with the second of these myths, but it is first necessary to give a brief outline of the legal and organizational constraints which affect police activity in general. To what extent are policemen able to respond with a free exercise of discretion, given the stimulus of a law-breaker, whether he be a thief or a demonstrator engaged in a riotous assembly?

It may appear self-evident that as a first major constraint upon the police they are required by the terms of the declaration made on appointment to preserve the peace 'according to law'.[3] However, the extent and clarity of this requirement is not as great as might be thought. For example, no action will normally be taken against a constable who contravenes the Judges' Rules concerning the questioning of suspected offenders, and a court which hears of a contravention will seldom disallow the evidence procured thereby.[4] Again, since the police service itself is responsible for teaching criminal law to recruits, one particular view of any disputed area of law is likely to be perpetuated; for example, there is a widespread view among policemen that an offence of shoplifting has not been committed until the offender leaves the store with the property, although this reflects the difficulty of presenting sufficient evidence to satisfy the courts rather than the substance of the criminal law.

The major organizational factor which operates as a constraint upon the discretion of the best constable is the requirement that all his actions shall be approved by his superior. Thus, in addition to specific errors being corrected, it is quite likely that if a probationary constable feels it is his duty to enforce the law so that every violator is reported, he will eventually be asked to leave the force. The corollary of this – that the decision to take no action in a particular situation should also be open to inspection by senior officers – used to be made only occasionally: that is when there was an almost complete failure to report persons for process over a period of time. The situation today has improved, at least partially, as a result of the greater penetration of two-way radio throughout the service. Since inaction is sometimes a response to uncertainty, a young constable, for example, faced with a problem such as the appropriate response to a crowd at an impromptu factory-gate meeting, can quickly obtain advice. By the same token, of course, the constable is aware that at any moment he can be checked on by an officer at headquarters.

In many ways, the influence of senior officers is more important today than it ever has been, and one must therefore ask what processes exist to check the policies adopted and promulgated through the force by the Chief Constable and his senior officers? To what extent are democratic institutions involved at a formal level in the control and disposition of the police? It is surprising that despite a Royal Commission (1962) and a Police Act (1964) the situation is far from clear. Since there is an obligation on local authorities, acting as police authority through a committee,[5] 'to secure the maintenance of an adequate and efficient police force for the area',[6] it would be reasonable to suppose that since 50 per cent of the cost of the police comes from the rates,[7] some form of control over the force rests with the elected members of the local authority. To some extent this is the case, but there are important limitations. Not all the members of the police authority are elected members of the local council. It has always been the case that county forces have been at least partially under the direction of the magistrates: the 1964 Police Act gave magistrates a one-third representation on all police authorities. The Royal Commission, which was responsible for this suggestion, based its argument on the usefulness of the close knowledge which the magistrates have of police work: 'they above all people see the fruits and nature of police work.'[8] However, the Commission also accepted the argument that control of the police by democratically elected representatives can be dangerous unless properly circumscribed: 'Under the arrangement which we are proposing, the argument that local political pressure might be brought to bear upon the police in such a way as to jeopardize impartiality in enforcing the law ceases to be tenable'.[9] Thus, one limitation upon the elected representatives is provided by the body of magistrates on the police authority. Another limitation, perhaps the greatest, is usually thought of as deriving from s. 5(1) of the 1964 Police Act which states: 'The police force maintained for a police area shall be under the direction and control of the Chief Constable.' The implication is normally accepted that, save for the power to appoint the Chief Constable and to require him to retire in the interests of efficiency, both of which powers can only be used with the approval of the Home Secretary,[10] the control exercised by the police authority is limited to hearing reports from the Chief Constable on any matters which appear to the Chief Constable not to fall into the class which 'in the public interest ought not to be disclosed or is not needed for the discharge of the functions of the police authority'; only the Home Secretary can order a Chief Constable to provide a report on any particular matter.[11] Thus, on the level of a formal legal analysis, the elected representatives on the police authority are in a far from strong position: it will be suggested at the conclusion of this chapter that advantages would be gained if police authority members did not accept the very limited legal sanctions open to them as confining the normal operational boundaries of their relationship with their police force.

These, then, are the legal provisions which are designed to ensure that the police operate effectively and in an acceptable fashion within the law. How appropriate are the provisions for attaining these objectives? The foremost requirement of any system of control, whether it be the mechanical or electronic control of an industrial process or the control of a social institution by some external body, is that accurate knowledge of the functioning of the process which is to be controlled should be directly available to the controlling agency. Without knowledge of all activity actually taking place in the process under review, it is impossible to state if and when, by reference to known standards, deviance is present in the process. Equally, of course, it is impossible to determine whether or not any given behaviour is aberrant without knowledge of how the process *ought* to be operating. At this point, the industrial quality control analogy must be abandoned, since there the control system alone can be blamed for any faulty products which escape detection, whereas in the field of social institutions both halves of the equation, both controllers and the controlled, must be examined. In other words, in the case of the police, one must question not only whether the police authorities have an adequate notion of the type and standard of policing they require (expressed in acceptable terms of police operational procedure) combined with effective means of obtaining information on the actual performance of the police; but one must also question whether there is any tendency for the police to diminish or exclude the possibility of certain types of information reaching the police authority.

The extreme example of such biasing activity would be the complete 'cover-up' operation of denying valid allegations of misconduct, but this is unlikely to be attempted and much less likely to be successful.[12] A much more typical example of such action by the police comes from outside the field of political protest, but is directly concerned with the tactical disposition of the police in all branches of their work. A new system of urban policing, designated 'unit beat policing', was devised in an attempt to recapture some of the supposed benefits of the 'village bobby' situation. The new system was given a limited trial. The first impressions were favourable, and before long many urban areas were adopting the new idea. Panda cars, the visible symbol of the scheme, spread throughout the land. In our present discussion, the important question is not so much whether this is an effective method of policing, but whether, on the assumption that the police authorities were at least asked to comment on the new scheme, the discussion of the system was undertaken on the basis of sufficient factual material to support a rational conclusion. In fact, no reliable research data was available at the time when this change was made in such a wholesale fashion.[13] Thus, whilst police opinion may have been expressed, the amount of factual information available to local authorities through their representatives on police authorities was severely limited.

A further situation in which general police procedure restricts the flow of information to the controlling and reviewing body is connected with the topic of police complaints. Whilst police authorities are obliged by s. 50 of the 1964 Police Act to 'keep themselves informed as to the manner in which complaints from members of the public against members of the force are dealt with by the chief officer of police', the effect of this requirement in practice is very much affected by the influence which the police have over the decision of what is and what is not to be categorized as a 'police complaint'. It is not necessarily very easy for even the reasonably well educated to know the procedure for making a complaint against the police, and, of course, in particular instances some policemen may make it even more difficult.[14] But this is only a minor part of the problem. An example of a much more deliberate bias introduced by the police can be seen in the handling of complaints by members of the public who were present at the Grosvenor Square demonstration of 17 March 1968. The violence which occurred during that demonstration resulted in many complaints against the police and in reports of observations made by individuals who were not themselves the objects of either unlawful or merely unwise police behaviour. Several observers from the National Council for Civil Liberties were present and had been very carefully briefed: 'We are not concerned with the objectives of the demonstration and . . . we shall in no sense be acting on behalf of the organizers or participants. . . . If incidents do occur instigated either by the marchers or the police they should be noted.'[15] In the event, the Council attributed the major blame for the violence to the demonstrators and their organizers,[16] but forwarded observers' reports of apparently questionable police tactics and behaviour to the Home Secretary as police authority for the Metropolitan Police.

There are two disturbing aspects of the Home Office's reply, dated 17 October 1968 and written after lengthy inquiries by the Metropolitan Police. First, certain points of difficulty in the police report remained apparently unquestioned by the Home Office. For example, simple denials by the police appear to be acceptable to the police authority as satisfactorily full explanations of the behaviour alleged to have taken place. One of the NCCL observers commented on how the police answered his complaint:

> The police say the allegation against PC 186 B is 'denied', but they do not say who by, and they do not offer any alternative explanation of the incident. Do they suggest that I made a mistake about his number (in fact I wrote it down while he was hitting his victim in front of me), or do they suggest that I made a mistake about his behaviour and, if so, what do they say he was doing? Do they suggest that it is more likely that I should invent the allegation or that he should deny it? Do they have any suggestions at all, or are they content with a mere denial?[17]

Thus, there appears to have been a situation in which the control system was allowed an incomplete input of information and where that system itself did not react in a fail-safe manner, such as by demanding further information in order to fulfil adequately its task of reviewing the handling of police complaints.

Important as this is, the second disturbing aspect of the inquiry into the Grosvenor Square events is perhaps more important since it displays a more general weakness in the system. Once the reports of the NCCL observers were in the hands of the police, they were processed as police complaints under the 1964 Police Act. The eventual replies to these reports show very clearly how the police interpret the phrase 'police complaint': a particular officer is being accused by a member of the public of some behaviour which is either unlawful or contrary to the police discipline regulations. All material which is not of direct relevance to this accusation and its investigation is relegated if not to the waste paper-basket, at least to a considerably lower priority of concern. There is much sense in this, since it is, of course, vital that an accused person (the policeman in this instance) should have allegations against him investigated and determined as speedily as possible in the manner for the time being enjoined by the law. However, the important disadvantage which this entails is that it is not very easy for a member of the public to comment on or to complain effectively about matters of police policy or organization which can affect his relationship with the police just as surely as any beating-up in a police cell. In the observers' reports of the Grosvenor Square demonstration, in addition to complaints against individual officers, several complaints were made about the overall police strategy and tactics for dealing with the situation. These included the use of police horses to clear the Square, the decision at one point to clear the gardens in the Square of demonstrators, and the failure to provide for adequate means of informing the crowd about intended police actions. In each of these matters, no satisfactory comment or explanation was offered in reply. On the question of the use of horses, in addition to the unreasoned statement that the horses were useful, reference was made only to the manner and style of their deployment, and the problems and difficulties associated with their use were not discussed.[18] On the second point, it was merely stated that there was 'no alternative but to enter and clear the gardens as quickly as possible'.[19] The reason for the necessity to clear the gardens as quickly as possible is not given, and in view of the reports of observers that at that stage of the events no more demonstrators were arriving and many were leaving, information as to the reason for the police decision would have been invaluable to a police authority reviewing the handling of complaints. No reference is made to the comment that the crowd were not told what the police required them to do. Altogether, it seems clear that police operational decisions as to what shall be classed and dealt with as a police complaint can be an important factor in confirming the amount of information which is readily available to the police authority in its reviewing and controlling functions.

Of course, any institution which is in some way subject to review or control by an outside agency will tend to develop procedures which reduce the effectiveness of this control: the police are not alone in this. The tendency occurs whether the institutions in question are companies compelled to provide data on their trading position, or criminals engaged in conflict with the police. In the first case, the minimum amount of information which is consistent with legality will usually be given, whereas in the second case, measures are often taken which discourage the passing of any information unless positive benefits may be obtained by a controlled leak of information. It is probable that the relationship of controller and controlled, or reviewer and reviewed, results in the most nearly undiminished flow of information where the reviewing function is exercised at least in part by an agency which, whilst organizationally distinct from the institution under review, shares certain professional or other close links with it; examples would include the Inspectorates of Children's Departments and Education Departments. However, this natural tendency to develop easing procedures is aggravated in the case of the police by two factors: first, the historical fact of the assumption by all parties that the police were established with a certain degree of independence from day-to-day control; and secondly, the increasing indications that an important current aim of the police is their own professionalization as a body.

The first point should, perhaps, not be over-stressed. Most ministers who were directly concerned with the police legislation of the mid-nineteenth century were convinced of the desirability, on grounds of efficiency, of a national police force centrally controlled by the government, and were only moved from this opinion by the realization of the strength and power of the local interests which were involved. Perhaps it was only ever in some of the smaller boroughs which had established police forces under the 1835 Municipal Corporations Act that the police felt strong enough to take an independent, even though un-orthodox, stance. Critchley cites the cases of York, where the Inspector ran several brothels and would only investigate crime complaints on the payment of a fee by the complainant, and Leominster, where the Superintendent had the perquisite of all fees derived from serving summonses and warrants.[20] Certainly today, the Home Office Circular 'advising' Chief Constables has virtually the force of law. The second point, representing a continuing concern by the police with professionalization, is of greater interest. The key features of professional status are independence and a degree of self-government, often manifested in such ways as control of the training and discipline of members of the profession. Of course, in practical terms, the degree of independence in one direction or another is likely to be limited: solicitors, for example, are not allowed to determine individually or collectively what they will charge for acting over a house purchase. Similarly, the police are free to establish a professional, independent system of crime control only so far as it remains consistent with the many legal provisions surrounding their work. Nevertheless, this gives a great scope for the adoption of policies which are not always open to the fullest degree of public scrutiny.

Such policies are not always objectionable. For example, the Juvenile Liaison Scheme, which was introduced by the Liverpool City Police and subsequently adopted in a very similar form by nearly twenty police forces, mostly in Lancashire and Yorkshire, was entirely due to police initiative.[21] It is very acceptable that in suitable cases erring juveniles should be spared a court appearance. It is even more acceptable that, in most areas, 'rules' were introduced and publicized which attempted to define the classes of juveniles and the classes of offences which would be considered suitable for handling under the scheme. This fact meant that local police authorities had a reasonable basis of knowledge to permit comment on and criticism of this police initiative. However, what was not always present was a system which enabled checks to be made on the implementation of the guiding rules in particular cases. Thus, it was not unknown for some fairly serious offences (for example, sexual offences, housebreaking by juveniles already known to the police, etc.) to be accepted under the scheme and not to result in a court appearance, whereas the 'rules' of the scheme had apparently restricted its application to first offences of a minor nature. Police officers involved in this work tend to create a further set of informal rules governing their decisions (based on such factors as their knowledge of the prior convictions of the juvenile's family and the pressure generated by their contact with other agencies such as the Children's Department) which operate outside the ambit of the original publicized 'rules'. This has the effect of reducing the possibility of adequate review, thus confirming the independence of the police in what might be termed their aspirant-professional approach to crime control.

The independent, quasi-professional organization of the police is also apparent in matters affecting public order. The Grosvenor Square demonstration of March 1968, has been referred to already. Perhaps the most significant features of the subsequent demonstration on 27 October 1968, when the possibility of violence had been widely canvassed beforehand, were its comparatively peaceful nature, and the changed police tactics which were able to maintain this peacefulness by a rejection of methods such as the unannounced clearing of the gardens and the use of police horses. It might appear from this that the complaints about police methods as opposed to complaints about specific instances of police behaviour had been effective; nevertheless, even if any causal link could be established, it is significant that any changes in tactics do not appear to have resulted from any open discussion of police problems and methods. Indeed, the Home Secretary, James Callaghan, appeared unaware of any need for discussion of particular police strategy and tactics when he stated a short time later in the House of Commons that 'the police have no intention of departing from their traditional methods when dealing with crowds and demonstrations'.[22] Were both 17 March and 27 October examples of the 'traditional methods'? If there is to be no further discussion of the undoubted problems of the use of the police during demonstrations, it appears that the police in practice have a very wide measure of independence. What is certainly clear from the Home Secretary's explanation of the organization of training for riot control ('There are at the Police College courses for senior officers which cover public order and the control of demonstrations. All officers in the Metropolitan Police District are given special training . . .'[23]) is that the effectiveness of any local review or control over strategy and tactics in the use of the police in such circumstances is very limited.

Expressions of what might be regarded as the increasing independence of the police in a political sense can be found in other areas relating to public order. For example, an interesting interchange on the prospective troubles of the 1970 white South African cricket tour occurred when James Callaghan, the Home Secretary, addressed the annual conference of the Police Federation. He explained the situation in what was, in police terms, a neutral fashion: 'We are in for a long, hot summer. You are in the middle of it. I shall continue to give you support.'[24] However, Inspector Reg Gale, Chairman of the Police Federation, adopted a stance clearly calculated to influence the political decision which had to be made by the Home Secretary when he told the Conference, 'Who will win is immaterial, but we know who will lose – the policeman standing there with orders to smile. . . . We have said that if necessary we will cope with the situation, but the pressures on the police are so great that additional pressures such as this could well be done without.'[25] Quite what direction such assumed independence might take in the future is impossible to assess. Perhaps the most significant implication of such quasi-political activity is that which it shares with the question of training for riot control: the possibility that local as opposed to national factors may become less important.

There are many ways in which the effectiveness of review and control procedures affecting the previous examples of police activity and organization could be improved, if this was thought to be desirable. One broad area of police activity, however, presents particular problems. Most, if not all, societies find it necessary to operate some equivalent of our own Police Special Branch which has particular responsibility for citizens' political activity, interpreted in a broad sense. There are two sources of difficulty: first, the delineation of types of police work for which there may be some justification for a limitation of the ambit of the review structure, and, secondly, the determination of what powers the police will be allowed to put freely into operation within the defined area. The procedure imposing the limitation on police authorities' powers is already in operation in s. 12(3) of the 1964 Police Act, which establishes that a Chief Constable may, unless the Home Secretary orders otherwise, refuse to supply a report requested by the police authority if it 'would contain information which in the public interest ought not to be disclosed'. Whilst this section by itself, of course, provides no definition of what should not be disclosed, it is in the interests of the efficiency of the review structure that police authorities should take whatever opportunities arise to ascertain where in practice the line is likely to be drawn by the other parties involved: only with such knowledge is it possible to envisage rational discussion of where the line should be drawn. An example of a situation in which one would hope the line would be drawn in favour of openness and full review concerns the case of the Cambridge students who were prosecuted and convicted after the demonstration against the 'Greek Evening' at the

Garden House Hotel in 1970. In a situation of active political protest where only a small number of participators are proceeded against, the review system should surely be able to include within its ambit the question of whether the power of selective arrest (which in the case of some Garden House demonstrators was put into operation quite a long time after the event) was based upon what ought to be termed the traditional policing criteria of the prevention and detection of unlawful violence, or whether further, political, considerations played a part in the decision of which individuals were arrested. If the response of the police to such a question from the police authority is to deny that political considerations were present in their decision, the supplementary inquiry should be pursued wherever possible: namely the question of whether in fact those arrested were amongst those most involved in the illegal, violent activity.[26]

The secrecy adopted and demanded by the Special Branch and other allied organizations is by no means always necessary, or even useful. For example, when the Committee of Privy Councillors inquiring into the problem of communications intercepted by the police, the Customs and Excise Department and the security services decided that it would be desirable to publish statistics relating to the number of warrants issued by the Home Secretary for the interception of telephone conversations, there was very considerable opposition to the suggestion.[27] The Committee nevertheless published the statistics, and thus were able to illustrate how few official interceptions took place. Their publication does not in any way appear to have rebounded on the Home Office, except, perhaps, in so far as it might have established a precedent for the framework of any future inquiry into the newer forms of electronic and other types of surveillance which may have partially reduced the need for telephone-tapping.

So far, it has been assumed that the major instruments employed in the control of the police are the police authorities constituted by the 1964 Police Act and the Home Secretary acting within the role again determined by the 1964 Act. This is certainly a realistic view of the position, and one's attention is thus drawn to the significant fact that the courts, which in many ways are the focus and arbiter of a great part of police activity, play a comparatively small part in the control of police activity. One particular way in which the courts are able to control certain types of police activity is their discretion to refuse to admit illegally-obtained evidence. This is more usually put by saying that the courts may admit illegally-obtained evidence provided that it is relevant to the charges and does not operate unfairly against the accused;[28] this certainly seems to be nearer to a description of actual practice. If policemen rate highly the securing of convictions, possibly as representing a demonstrable societal affirmation through the court of the value of their work, it is possible that they will be ready to accept any mild rebuke which may occasionally come from the court. However, it does not follow that the situation would be any more desirable if courts were encouraged to use their authority to 'punish' the police by refusing to admit such evidence on a more rigorous basis. Our magistrates and judges, whatever their undoubted merits, nevertheless form an undeniably non-democratic institution. It is possible that a certain capriciousness would develop in the exercise of the powers of discretion which might, for example, not be favourable in any hypothetical charge of conspiracy based upon the illegally-obtained documents of an activist political group. The only alternative seems to be the adoption of an exclusionary rule as is the case in the USA, under which illegally-obtained evidence is automatically excluded from the trial. Of course, there are severe difficulties in this approach, not least the consequent demoralization of the police force when they see many 'guilty' men acquitted. Improvement could be made in the present system by the oblique means of removing certain obstacles to police work which cannot in any real sense be said to preserve personal freedoms. The benefit in terms of reducing the temptations which face the police are evident from the following extract from a judgement of Lord Denning:

> No magistrate – no judge even – has any power to issue a search warrant for murder. . . . Nor to look for the axe, the gun or the poison dregs. The police have to get the permission of the householder to enter if they can; or, if not, to do it by stealth or by force. Somehow they seem to manage. No decent person refuses them permission. If he does, he is probably implicated in some way or other. So the police risk an action for trespass. It is not much risk'.[29]

It seems fairly clear that in some situations, many of which are closely related to occasions of direct action and protest, the police are used, or behave, in a fashion which is, or should be, open to question; and that the present structure of this system for the review and control of police activity either does not, or is not able to, perform adequately in all these situations. There are many possibilities for reform. Perhaps the approach which would secure most support, at least in principle, paradoxically continues the above suggestion of extending certain police powers. An example of a situation where both police and magistrates were probably put in a false position by the present law was the co-ordinated national search for fire-arms carried out on 26 August 1970. Whatever the reason for the search, whether it was based on a specific desire to check possible political extremists or was simply intended as an attempt to control the number of illegal arms at large, the requirement of obtaining individual warrants from local magistrates[30] for all the premises to be searched must inevitably have produced a tendency towards one of two possible situations. Either each individual magistrate may not have been aware of the relevant fact that the search in his area was intended as part of a nationally co-ordinated operation, or, by his knowledge of this fact, was placed under a rather unusual degree of implied pressure to conform by granting the warrant. The unreality of the situation would be more apparent should any police authority have subsequently examined the policy of the police in applying for the search warrants. Would it have been relevant information on which to arrive at a rational local policy that in the nationwide series of about one hundred raids, employing about three hundred armed detectives, 'only seventeen people were questioned and five men . . . charged' ?[31] Whether or not it would be a desirable solution to this problem to allow the Home Secretary greater powers, it seems that the present arrangement may sometimes operate against effective review of police actions. If one were to take a more detailed look at numerous other specific, statutory police powers, it is probable that detailed changes, some of which might nominally appear to give the police greater powers, would in practice make the control of their use more feasible within the present review structures.

One part of the system of review and control is at present receiving a good deal of attention; namely, the investigation of complaints against the police. A joint working-party of the Police Advisory Boards has considered the matter, and although the report itself has not been published, some of the evidence to the committee has. The recom-mendations of Justice (the British section of the International Com-mission of Jurists) were that whilst a majority of complaints, particu-larly those of a minor nature, should continue to be disposed of by the police themselves, the complainant would be entitled, if his complaint had been substantially rejected or he had been told that no action would be taken on it, to ask for the papers to be submitted to an independent investigator. These posts would be filled full-time by appointees of the Lord Chancellor working in consultation with the Home Office. There would be no appeal in most circumstances if the independent investi-gator found that the complaint was of insufficient substance to warrant action be taken on it; on the other hand, if he reported to the Chief Constable that there was evidence of an offence against the Disciplinary Code, and if the Chief Constable proposed to take action on the report, the officer would have the right to ask for the report of the investigator to be referred to a review tribunal consisting of two high-ranking police officers from another force and a 'legally qualified person of standing' as chairman.[32]

The National Council for Civil Liberties adopted a wider approach to the problem of complaints when it recommended the creation of a permanent machinery of regional tribunals to 'consider all complaints by any member of the public a) against individual police officers, and b) of dereliction of duty by the police force generally, whether or not an allegation is made against an individual'. Each tribunal would have a legally qualified chairman and at least two other members, one of whom would be a lawyer and the other a layman. If there were to be more members, the NCCL envisaged representation of the Police Federation. Somewhat naïvely, the NCCL described their suggestion as 'an extension of existing machinery specified in s. 32 of the (1964) Act'.[33] The establishment of permanent institutions would be different in kind from the present situation: the annual reports of HM Chief Inspector of Constabulary for the years following the 1964 Act indicate that on no occasion has the *ad hoc* system of local inquiries under s. 32 been utilized outside the Metropolitan Police District. And whilst the NCCL proposal reflects reality in its insistence on the importance of complaints which may not have the behaviour of one named policeman as their subject, the suggested jurisdiction of the tribunals is considerably more narrow than the area which could be covered by an inquiry under the existing s. 32, which states: 'The Secretary of State may cause a local inquiry to be held by a person appointed by him into any matter connected with the policing of any area.' It is probable that this NCCL proposal as it stands would not prove a suitable means of reviewing the existence and content of police practice in developing such patterns of operation as have been mentioned earlier.

An alternative method of review which would preserve some degree of democratic participation in the review process would be simply to encourage police authorities to take a wider view of their powers and duties under the 1964 Act – if need be by simple statutory clarification of the points which the Act leaves obscure. If a fuller part in police affairs were to be taken by police authorities, it would follow that a wider range of questions from members of county or county borough councils could be encompassed within s. 11 of the 1964 Act which deals with the nomination of a member of the police authority to be responsible for answering councillors' questions on matters relating to the discharge of the police authority's functions. The aim would not be to introduce anything approaching the issuing of directives to the police about their handling of specific cases – indeed, this would be contrary to the terms of the 1964 Act. However, by establishing a practice of detailing prior police activity and its results (for example, the number of search warrants resulting in prosecutions, or the recovery of stolen property) a body of public knowledge of operational police practice would evolve, together with the means to make effective judgements on a) the value of the practice, and b) whether or not the handling of an individual case had conformed to the current police practice. The ability to make this latter type of judgement should be inherent in any police review system. It is fallacious to assume that in a situation which allows wide powers to the police, the exercise of discretion within the legal constraints always operates in favour of the citizen who is thereby 'let off' the full rigour of the law. If 99 per cent of the people present at a demonstration – which could legitimately be referred to as an unlawful assembly – are not prosecuted, it is crucial to examine not the exercise of discretion which let the majority go free, but rather the exercise of discretion which resulted in the prosecution of the 1 per cent. The example of a demonstration is important, but in many ways atypical: a single event is there capable of establishing a 'rule' which is operated by the police, and the exceptions to the rule (the 1 per cent who are prosecuted) are self-evident. Such a situation can be expected to lead to a clearer formulation of the 'rule' of police practice, in that the reasons for the arrest of the 1 per cent should be clearly enunciated and incorporated as guidance for future practice. More typical perhaps is the situation when, over a period of time, no one in a particular district has been prosecuted for failing to have lights on a parked vehicle at night.[34] When one person is prosecuted for the offence, it may not be immediately evident to a wide public that a self-imposed rule has not been applied to a particular case. Such a situation also calls either for an acknowledgement that the particular prosecution did not conform to normal practice, or, more positively, for a reformulation of the existing 'rule' to incorporate the principle which led to the isolated prosecution – always assuming that there was a rational explanation for the 'deviant' prosecution.[35]

It might be thought that such a suggestion would involve an attempt to deny the police discretion in their job of law enforcement. This is not the case. Any such direct limitation would be not only undesirable but also impossible to achieve. Such a denial of discretion is very different from the suggestion that the exercise of discretion should be open to comment, both on matters of principle and on the application of principle to particular cases. No suggestions that a policeman must not arrest law-breaker X because the circumstances of similar offences have not previously led to prosecution could be realistically put forward and supported. All that is suggested is that, where a previously articulated principle of police discretion is not, *prima facie*, applied in a particular case, the circumstances of that particular event should be expressed with a view to the modification and refinement of the principle. Further, it is suggested that the openness which such a review system pre-supposes could probably be achieved through a reappraisal of their role on the part of existing democratic institutions without the need for any legislative changes.

NOTES

1. J. F. Garner, *Administrative Law* (London, 1970), p. 392.
2. *Attorney-General for New South Wales* v. *Perpetual Trustee Company* (155), A.C. 477, adopted by the Royal Commission on the Police (1962), p. 23.
3. Royal Commission on the Police (1962), p. 11, n. 5 (Cmnd. 1728).
4. For a consideration of the status of, and ambiguities in, the Judges Rules, see G. Marshall, *Police and Government* (London, 1967), appendix A.
5. In the case of a county, it is known as the police committee; in the case of a county borough, it is known as the watch committee; and in the case of combined or amalgamated areas, it is known by a variety of names. With regard to county forces, from their origin in 1839 until the 1888 Local Government Act, responsibility for them was vested in the magistrates. From 1888 until the 1964 Police Act magistrates constituted one-half of the police authority, the remainder being elected councillors.
6. 1964 Police Act, s. 4(1).
7. Ibid., s. 31 and the 1966 Police (Grant) Order, S.I. 1966, no. 223.
8. Royal Commission on the Police, p. 67.
9. Ibid.
10. 1964 Police Act, ss. 4(2) and 5(4).
11. Ibid., s. 12(3).
12. But see the Sheffield 'rhino whip' inquiry: *Sheffield Police Appeal Inquiry* (1963) (Cmnd. 2176).
13. See G. N. G. Rose, 'Research into Police Management and Control of Crime', paper presented at the Fourth National Conference on Research and Teaching in Criminology (Cambridge, 1970), p. 2.
14. See *The Sunday Times* (10 May 1970), p. 1, and the NCCL *Monthly Bulletin* (May 1970), for illustrations of the discouragement sometimes offered to those who might wish to complain against the police.
15. NCCL, *Report on the Demonstration in Grosvenor Square on 17 March 1968* (April 1968).
16. Ibid.
17. Addendum to a letter from Tony Smythe, General Secretary of the NCCL to the Home Office, dated 20 February 1969.
18. Letter from the Private Secretary to the Home Secretary, dated 17 October 1968, addressed to Tony Smythe.
19. Appendix to the above letter.
20. T. A. Critchley, *A History of Police in England and Wales, 900–1966* (London, 1967), p. 114.

21. J. A. Mack, 'Police Juvenile Liaison Schemes', *British Journal of Criminology*, vol. 3, p. 361.
22. H. C. Debs, c. 1548 (13 February 1969); in answer to a question asking what guidance the Home Secretary had issued to police forces on riot control.
23. Ibid. The Police College referred to is a national institution for police training.
24. *The Times* (21 May 1970).
25. *The Times* (21/22 May 1970).
26. For differing accounts of the affair, see the judgement of L. J. Sachs, in the Court of Appeal (*R. v. Caird and Others*, *The Times*, 20 August 1970), and *The Cambridge Greek Affair*, a pamphlet 'written by a group of students on the left' (Cambridge 1970). Whilst one factor which contributes to the difficulties the police find in dealing with the various manifestations of direct action is undoubtedly the ambiguous state of the substantive criminal law, this in itself can throw light on the relationship between the police and central and local government. For example, although the Chief Constable of Mid-Anglia, F. Drayton Porter, has in one sense reacted positively to the post-Garden House situation in Cambridge by attempting to initiate regular meetings between senior police officers and the committee of the students' union, it is also apparent that he regards the policy for handling demonstrations as entirely within his own domain. 'There is only one person who is responsible for law and order on the streets of Cambridge – and that's me. It was even suggested that the Home Secretary was consulted. I was subject to no pressure from anyone.' (*The Observer*, 18 October 1970). Mr Porter has also said that the Garden House affair had 'nothing to do with the police authority. Of course, I shall make a report, but it is simply a case of their sitting and listening to it.' (Telephone conversation with the writer, 27 October 1970).
27. Report of the Committee of Privy Councillors appointed to inquire into the interception of communications (1957).
28. See, for example, *Kuruma v. R.* (1955), A.C. 197; *R. v. Court* (1962), Crim. L.R. 697; *R. v. Payne* (1963), 1 WLR 637. See also, B. Livesey, *Judicial Discretion to Exclude Prejudicial Evidence* (1968), Camb. LJ 29, and, for a comparative study of the problem, Z. Cowen and P. B. Carter, *Essays on the Law of Evidence*, pp. 72–105.
29. *Ghani v. Jones* (1970), 1 Q.13. 693, 705.
30. 1968 Firearms Act, s. 46.
31. *The Times* (28 August 1970).
32. Justice, Recommendations submitted to the Police Advisory

Boards' Joint Working-Party on the investigation of complaints (January 1970).

33. NCCL, *The Police and the Citizen* (October 1969). If this description was not naïve, it may have been made in a somewhat tongue-in-cheek fashion.

34. This is not to deny the importance of the comparison over time of the handling of demonstrations. Indeed, it is crucial a) to know whether charges of unlawful assembly are becoming more prevalent, and b) to seek justification of their policies from those involved in prosecution decisions.

35. See K. C. Davis, *Discretionary Justice* (Louisiana, 1969).

XVI Political Parties and Members of Parliament[*]

GAVIN DREWRY

In terms of modern constitutional dogma as conceived by the major political parties in Britain, the idea of direct action seems to embody a paradox. On the one hand, it implies a rejection of those institutionalized means of political expression which a Parliamentary democracy provides for its members, and for which those who operate the system feel a strong sense of personal loyalty. On the other hand, the right to by-pass established channels of political influence, and indeed to question the fundamental premises on which the political system is founded, is at least as deeply entrenched in our civic culture as the idea of Parliamentary democracy itself. In practice, the reactions of party politicians to the use of direct action in a given set of circumstances depend upon a whole range of ideological and circumstantial factors, an examination of which constitutes the central purpose of this chapter.

Politicians, particularly Conservative politicians, have tended to talk about direct action simply as one aspect of the much wider issue of 'law and order' in society. To the extent that the maintenance of order is a definitive function of government, and that ultimately the authority and even the survival of a government may depend upon its ability to nip incipient revolution firmly in the bud, such a preoccupation is understandable and even laudable. But a narrow approach of this kind will hardly suffice for our present analysis. The purpose of this chapter is to examine in some detail the 'official' attitudes of the two main parties to direct action, and the reactions of individual MPs when faced with the dilemma (if it can strictly be called such) of choosing

* The author would like to thank the following people who read various drafts of this chapter and made valuable suggestions for its improvement: Dr Ivor F. Burton of Bedford College, University of London; Mr Patrick Cosgrave of the Conservative Research Department; Mr Alan Green of the Labour party's Research Department, and Professor Peter G. Richards of the University of Southampton. The author retains full responsibility for any errors of fact and for all statements of opinion.

between loyalty to party and Parliament, and involvement with movements which, even if only by implication, reject the established machinery of political influence.

Before proceeding further, it is necessary to stipulate a working definition of direct action and to suggest some criteria by which it may be distinguished from other kinds of political activity. All so-called 'pressure groups' by fairly common definition[1] act *directly* on established organs of government like Parliament and government departments. But such groups have already won the right, to a varying extent, to be ranked alongside parties as respectable representative institutions: conflict between pressure groups and parties tends to be confined to matters of demarcation, or to involve narrow issues of administration or substantive policy. The phrase 'direct action' connotes something much more positive and much less constitutionally conventional than lobbying or negotiation, which involves recognition by both sides of the legitimate status of the other. Direct action is used when negotiations have failed or where the use of conventional methods seems pointless: it entails, to a varying degree, a rejection of the efficacy or even the morality of the 'usual channels'. Whereas the lobbyist must seek official acceptance, the proponent of direct action is often courting non-acceptance, and respectability is something that he neither needs nor desires.

This does not mean, however, that acceptance by established political authority is irrelevant in the context of direct action; indeed, one aim of this chapter is to examine the extent of the tolerance towards direct action which is exhibited by MPs and by party policy-makers. Nor does it mean that those taking part in direct action are necessarily indifferent to party opinion; their main object may be to induce changes of policy, of organization, or of leadership, in a party. Other participants may be seeking to promote a satifying spectacle of alarm and despondency among those in authority. For the purposes of the present argument, the term 'direct action' will be flexibly defined to embrace various forms of activity, violent or non-violent, which signify a rejection of established political methods and institutions. This should be regarded as a statement of intention rather than a firm definition, since it is all but impossible in practice to draw a clear dividing-line between forms of political activity which are accepted and forms which are not. The rules of the political game and the attitudes of the participants have a habit of changing considerably over a period of time.

It is doubtful whether direct action really includes such phenomena as demonstrations and rallies organized by the main political parties or by pressure groups seeking either some specified advantage for their members (such as a pay increase) or some relatively narrow reform which amounts to an extension of the lobbying process rather than to an outright rejection of the 'usual channels' as a matter of principle.

However, a slight doubt might arise in the case of a mass movement like CND (discussed more fully below) which, at least in its early days, was primarily a promotional pressure group working to achieve various objectives, principally through the medium of the Labour party. There is no doubt that its supporters included many people who rejected conventional political methods and who saw themselves as doing something positive to achieve a number of pre-determined goals; but the *means* employed by the Campaign, such as mass marches, public meetings and lobbying, were the same as those used by a wide range of orthodox pressure groups. Certainly, the movement did contain a militant sub-group, the Direct Action Committee, whose members were dedicated to direct action tactics, and which eventually broke away from the Campaign to form the Committee of 100. But the phrase 'direct action' is concerned with means rather than ends: by this criterion CND remains a pressure group, and the DAC and the Committee of 100, while sharing many of the aspirations of the Campaign, were direct action movements.

Mass demonstrations of a predominantly peaceful character, intended by definition to *demonstrate* that a particular point of view enjoys wide support, are not manifestations of direct action as such, since they have by now become an accepted form of political activity. (And when political parties talk about altering the law to curb violent abuses of the right to demonstrate peacefully, they are acknowledging the respectability of demonstrations.) It may, of course, be a matter of debate, largely academic, as to the precise point at which mass movements overstep the mark and become liable to be branded as direct action movements. Most recent mass movements have in fact been hybrid to the extent that their amorphous composition has included individuals and groups dedicated to direct action: this makes accurate classification a difficult exercise. For this reason, though at some risk of fudging important distinctions still further, the term 'mass movements' will be used to include attitudinally-oriented pressure groups like CND which eschew direct action methods as such but which indulge in mass demonstrations as a major tactical weapon, together with movements expressly committed to direct action in the sense defined above.

In the context of any analysis of direct action, the nomenclature employed is of the utmost importance. There is broad consensus between the political parties about the sanctity of such ephemeral personal liberties as 'freedom of speech' and 'freedom of assembly', but there is no firm agreement about what such slogans (really they are nothing more) mean in practice. The same political demonstration may variously be described as a 'peaceful protest', a 'violent demonstration', or as a 'riotous assembly', depending very much upon the personal predilections of the observer (and often upon the view adopted by the mass media). In this context too, as we shall see, politicians are apt to use highly emotive words and phrases like 'law', 'order', 'liberty', 'mob-rule', and so on, to underline their approval or abhorrence of a particular set of events. This is not to deny, of course, that in objective terms some kinds of direct action are more violent than others, but for our present purpose, vocabulary of this kind gives little help in finding out what actually happened; though it may well give a helpful indication of a particular speaker's personal attitude towards the events in question. In examining the attitudes of politicians, it must be remembered that their own perceptions of phenomena, which cannot necessarily be tied to any particular 'objective' definition, are the determinants of their actions and statements. We should pay careful heed to the warning of Professor Bernard Crick:

> Some of our worries arise because of an inadequate vocabulary to conceptualize modern politics: opinion, pressure, threat, strike, demonstration, parade, riot, rebellion, *coup d'état*, civil war and revolution all need distinguishing as, in some way, different forces with different conventions. Until we can be a little more precise in some of these respects, defenders of the *status quo*, reformers and revolutionaries all very often confuse and alarm themselves quite as much as their opponents.[2]

Direct Action Movements and the Established Order

One might permissibly employ as one criterion for distinguishing between democratic and totalitarian forms of government their respective propensities for tolerating direct action as a means of political expression. In Western democracies, direct action, at least in its more muted forms, is widely accepted as a regular feature of political life. In totalitarian societies, genuinely spontaneous demonstrations of popular feeling are often condemned and vigorously suppressed as subversive acts; and what may appear at first sight to be a *bona fide* demonstration may turn out to have been organized by the ruling establishment either to lend weight to its claim to rule by popular acclaim or to add impetus to particular policies being pursued. Any attempt to classify political systems wholly on this criterion would be open to serious objection, but it does at least seem fair to assert that mass movements, as defined earlier, are tolerated in Western democratic cultures to an extent which would be quite unthinkable in, say, the Soviet Union, and that direct action, while it is hardly welcomed, is allowed a fairly loose rein in the interests of individual freedom.

Direct action is, by definition, the negation of party politics and a rejection of the political and social *status quo*. A more dramatic picture is painted by John Berger who argues that:

mass demonstrations are rehearsals for revolution: not strategic or even tactical ones, but rehearsals of revolutionary awareness ... any revolution which lacks this element of rehearsal is better described as an officially encouraged public spectacle .... A mass demonstration is an assembly which challenges what is given by the mere fact of coming together.[3]

Berger is treating mass demonstrations as a historical phenomenon rather than as merely the summation of individual aspirations; as a social force, a mass movement may be something far more significant than the sum of its parts. If one examines the recent history of mass movements in Britain – CND, Committee of 100, Vietnam Solidarity Campaign, Stop The Seventy Tour, Action Committee against Racialism – it becomes clear that all these movements have embraced a very wide range of disparate groups and individuals united by a common sense of disaffection with various aspects of society and seeking a temporary focus for their discontent in a comparatively simple issue.

It is no part of my present purpose to examine the extent to which direct action has, or is seen as having, some revolutionary connotations – except to the extent that this may have a bearing on the attitudes of party leaders and MPs. The parties themselves are committed to abiding by the flexibly defined rules of the Parliamentary-democratic game: as in-groups competing amongst themselves for the spoils of the system, it is simply not in their interests to become embroiled in, or even lend countenance to, potentially disruptive activity. There may, for a number of reasons which will be examined later, be important differences between the attitudes of the parties, but ultimately those who are committed to the party system have too much at stake to risk capsizing the boat.

At best, the parties will see the milder forms of direct action as healthy and harmless manifestations of democratic freedom, perhaps even serving to enhance the self-esteem of those associated with the working of so tolerant a system. At worst, even mass demonstrations of a predominantly peaceful kind may be seen as a threat to the *status quo* – as embryonic revolution to be quelled by rapid mobilization of the forces of law and order. Demonstrations are events in the course of which windows sometimes are broken, policemen are sometimes injured, and ambassadors are sometimes insulted: hence one cannot really blame politicians – who are not always to be found on the extreme right – for denouncing such activities as an aspect of democracy which is in the category of an over-expensive luxury.

A government, if it is to carry out its appointed task of maintaining an ordered society, while at the same time fulfilling its commitment to established democratic values, must navigate the tricky passage between the Scylla of abdication of proper responsibility and the Charybdis of over-zealous repression. The relationship between parties and mass movements is a shadowy one, but certainly neither side can totally ignore the existence of the other.

Mass movements are essentially *different* from political parties – in aims, in organization and in membership. The parties are coalitions of disparate views, but when it comes to a point where internal rifts on issues of principle seem to threaten the momentum of that power-seeking goal which is the *raison d'être* of party, then the cracks are papered over and amity achieved, at least in the short-term. The cohesive force derived from a party's will to attain governmental power may sometimes be strained to the limit, and this has been particularly true of the Labour party which has always managed to haul itself back from the edge of the precipice when threatened by seemingly irreconcilable divisions. Roy Jenkins once complained that:

> The will to power has always been much stronger in the Conservative party. There it is something to be pursued at all cost. The Labour party has quite rightly had a different order of priorities, but its danger is that of going too far in the other direction and thinking that it is un-socialist or immoral to desire power.[4]

This view was expressed during the same period of disillusionment and reappraisal following the Labour defeat in the 1959 election which, as will be discussed later, did much to nurture the short-lived shipboard romance between the Labour movement and CND during the 1950s. However, this does nothing to weaken the validity of the proposition that all parties, properly so called, exist for the purpose of attaining governmental power, and that as a party approaches this goal the deviant views of individuals tend to be suppressed in the interests of the general cause.

Mass movements have their own goals, but sometimes they are rather ill-defined and depend on the ascendancy of a particular group of opinion leaders at a given point in time. Certainly, these movements are not specifically committed to *displacing* the established parties as alternative governments (though in some cases they may display some of the characteristics of explicitly revolutionary groups and talk about deposing the current régime), and their aims are usually too abstract to make governing a feasible proposition. In any event, in order to achieve a measure of unity and cohesion within the movement, issues tend to become reduced to a simple common denominator: as soon as matters of detail are discussed – rules, tactics, long-term objectives and so on – the latent divisions within the movement can become all too apparent. A good instance of this is to be seen in the frequent battles that took place within CND over issues of tactics, culminating in the breaking away of the Committee of 100 to set up in business under a more militant banner. Indeed, the most damaging splits which have occurred in direct action oriented movements in recent years have been over the methodology of direct action rather than over substantive goals – a factor which lends credibility to the view that for many people participation in the activities of a mass movement serves as an end in itself rather than as a means of achieving a pre-stated tariff of specific reforms.[5] The moral of this would seem to be that, when it comes to the crunch, mass movements often lack that cohesion (stemming from a dedication to the achievement of a clearly perceived goal) which might serve to stop them tearing themselves apart.

The amorphous character of these movements also militates against the development of a close-knit organizational structure. As Frank Parkin points out:

> Mass movements have 'followings' or 'supporters' rather than members, and their characteristic mode of operation is not through committees or formal procedures but through the mobilization of supporters in public demonstrations or similar techniques which by-pass the orthodoxies of the political process and democratic machinery. . . . Mass politics is usefully thought of as the polar opposite of bureaucratized politics – one of the features in fact which often contributes to its appeal.[6]

Certainly, for practical reasons, CND's organizers felt the need to avoid the Campaign becoming too formally organized. In part this was because it was felt that 'members' with 'rights' might precipitate endless squabbles by trying to assert those rights at conferences and elsewhere: it was also because CND, as a formally constituted body, would immediately have been proscribed by the Labour party, 'with the consequent disappearance of all MPs from its stationery and all Labour party members from its committees'.[7]

The fact that mass movements tend to be amorphous in membership and in aims and lacking in a formal bureaucratic structure not only serves to underline the extent to which they differ from established parties and pressure groups but also has an important practical bearing upon their relationships with the parties. In the first place, they are not seen as *rivals*, though they may be perceived as a general threat to the *status quo* in which the parties have a major stake and, as the case of CND shows, they may on rare occasions be used by party members in an attempt to bring pressure to bear upon the party leadership. There is nothing logically inconsistent in such party members joining mass movements, though there is inconsistency in their taking part in direct action which expressly rejects the party system.

Secondly, groups which lack formal structure would find it difficult to parley with the parties at an official level, even if they wished to do so. Although mass movements invariably have their executive committees, the latter are not always bound by collective responsibility and it is usually difficult to discover the extent to which their views represent those of the rank and file. Remoteness from grass-roots opinion is not, of course, a monopoly of mass movements, but lack of formal organization does tend to exacerbate an already serious difficulty in establishing a coherent dialogue with a movement which is made up of a large number of factions.

Finally, it is difficult for the parties to proscribe an individual's associations with a mass movement as being incompatible with party membership, since such movements, as we have seen, often avoid committing their supporters to formal membership, and 'belonging' can mean no more than attending a few public meetings. Formal disciplinary sanctions can only be applied when a party member's association with the movement gives rise to distinct political consequences such as ignoring a three line whip, or involves the member in overtly subversive activity. Groups organized on a more formal basis are a sitting target for party sanctions. The Labour party can add their names to its already formidable list of proscribed organizations, while the Conservatives have more discreet, but equally effective methods of advertising official disapproval via the party grapevine.

Inevitably, occasions do arise when mass movements become entangled with the established parties. Sometimes there is an overlap of membership. Sometimes the organizers of such a movement may attempt to further its ends by interfering with party activities; by disrupting public meetings, heckling at conferences, sponsoring rival candidates, and so forth. While such activities do not come within our definition of direct action, they sometimes come very near to it. The parties themselves, not unnaturally, tend to frown heavily upon attempts at infiltration or manipulation, and take steps to deter those of their followers who look like becoming seriously involved in such activities, though the limits of possible remedial action are often circumscribed by circumstantial factors. In the case of CND, for example, the involvement of members of the Labour movement was on such a vast scale that it is difficult to conceive what steps the party leadership could have taken without precipitating a major crisis within the party.

This review of factors which may have a bearing upon the relationships between the established parties and mass movements has raised at an abstract level a number of issues which will be looked at more closely in the next section. There we shall examine, in particular, the relationship between the Labour party and the unilateral disarmament movement, with special reference to issues of direct action arising in this context.

Mass Movements and the Political Parties

In Britain, the major political parties epitomize the solid virtues (and vices) of a political system within which barely distinguishable élite groups continually jostle one another, in a more or less gentlemanly manner, for the spoils of governmental power. Mass movements, while often exhibiting some of the characteristic features of parties – issuing policy manifestos, putting up candidates at general and local elections, etc. – fight a very different kind of battle, with different objectives, in different arenas, and according to rules which the parties would regard as unacceptable and would probably find incomprehensible.

The parties themselves tend to tolerate such groups, even when they indulge in direct action, partly because they do not normally constitute a credible threat to the existing system, and partly because precipitate attempts at repression would conflict with fundamental ideas about social liberty to which all the main parties are firmly committed.

In recent years, direct action movements have tended to be associated more with the far left than with the far right, and in consequence have tended to have a greater impact upon the Labour party than upon the Conservatives. The Liberals too, having in recent years been faced with the increasingly radical demands of a vigorous youth movement within the party, found themselves unwittingly (if not unwillingly) associated with Peter Hain's Stop The Seventy Tour movement which attracted support from all parts of the political spectrum, though predictably more from the left than from the right. Within the Liberal party (and this is particularly true of the Young Liberals), there is a vocal element, regularly denounced by the party leadership, which considers that, since the party stands no hope under present circumstances of obtaining substantial representation in the House of Commons, it should seek fresh pastures in the field of 'community action'. Were this to happen, we might either have to reconsider further our preconceived ideas about the boundaries of 'accepted forms of political activity', or to accept that the Liberals had crossed that indistinct boundary which separates parties from other kinds of politically active groups.

The Conservative party too have not been wholly immune from attack by methods akin to direct action: during the 1950s, the party was harassed by the activities of the League of Empire Loyalists which demanded a return to the halcyon days of British imperialism and which took every opportunity to impress its views on the Conservative government (and on the country at large) by such means as vigorous organized heckling at party meetings and conferences. These nuisance tactics reached a *crescendo* in 1958 when members of the League infiltrated the party conference at Blackpool with the purpose of interrupting the Prime Minister's address, and were ejected with a considerable show of violence. After this, in the words of one commentator, 'pressure was applied to many sympathetic members [of the party] either to leave the League or to face the political consequences. By the end of that year, continued association with the Empire Loyalists meant political death to any Tory who still had political ambitions left.'[8] One Empire Loyalist featured prominently in the much-publicized 'Nigel Nicolson affair' in the constituency of Bournemouth East and Christchurch during the late 1950s.[9] This case shows, among other things, that the power wielded by constituency organizations outside Parliament can be quite distinct from that which is wielded by the leadership of the party inside Parliament. It would be quite misleading to treat either of the main parties as being synonymous with that small part of their organization which operates within the Palace of Westminster.

The most interesting, and in many ways unique illustration of the kind of relationship that can develop between a mass movement and a major political party is the case of the Labour party and the unilateralist movement in the period spanning the mid-1950s and the mid-1960s. The story of the Campaign for Nuclear Disarmament which, under the restraining hand of its chairman, Canon Collins, managed (at some cost) to avoid involvement in direct action, and of its militant offshoot the Committee of 100, shows the extent to which, in very special circumstances, a mass movement may be employed as a lever to manipulate a political party: it also demonstrates the speed with which such a situation may be transformed by changes taking place within the party, within the movement and in the surrounding political circumstances. The account which follows is written essentially from the outsider's viewpoint; it should be read in conjunction with the personal accounts in the earlier chapters by George Clark and Peter Cadogan.

The history of CND and of Labour's involvement with it can conveniently be divided into three overlapping phases. The first was in the middle and late 1950s when a succession of organizations opposed to the manufacture and stockpiling of nuclear weapons (and ultimately, in 1958, CND itself) came to be established; when official party attitudes towards nuclear defence strategy were crystallizing; and during which period the conflict between 'fundamentalists' and 'revisionists' within the Labour movement ebbed and flowed, finally reaching the highwater mark in 1960 at the party's Scarborough conference. The second phase came immediately before, during and after the Scarborough conference, culminating in the victory of the unilateralists at the conference followed by Gaitskell's successful fight to reassert his authority. The final phase was the split in the unilateralists' ranks following (though not necessarily caused by) the establishment of the Committee of 100 in 1960 and the increasing use of militant forms of direct action. This coincided with a rising tide of optimism within the Labour party (encouraged by a change in leadership and a simultaneous decline in the fortunes of the Conservative government) and culminated in 1964 in the advent of a Labour government, with all that this meant to the supporters of a party which had languished in opposition for thirteen years.

Members of the Labour movement played a prominent part in the unilateralist campaign from the very beginning. Men like Anthony Greenwood and Fenner Brockway were very much to the fore in 1954 in organizing the short-lived Hydrogen Bomb National Campaign Committee which called for an international disarmament conference. And in February 1958 when CND itself was formed, of nineteen elected and co-opted members of the first Executive, 'ten at least', according to Christopher Driver, 'had been publicly associated with the Labour party'.[10] Among Labour Parliamentarians who were prominent in the campaign at this time were Michael Foot, Frank Beswick, Stephen Swingler, Frank Allaun, Sydney Silverman, Anthony Greenwood and Barbara Castle.

The proportion of the Parliamentary Labour party which overtly supported CND is difficult to calculate with any degree of precision, particularly since, as we have seen, the Campaign eschewed any formalities associated with registration of membership. According to Driver, when Victory for Socialism was revived in 1957 as a left-wing ginger group whose principal aim was to sponsor a Labour campaign against the Bomb, its Parliamentary membership 'oscillated around forty MPs'. 'This compares', says Driver, 'with the figure of about seventy MPs, including twenty-five actual pacifists, in the 1959–64 Parliament who were prepared to support unilateralism in the House of Commons, usually by abstaining on official Labour defence motions or amendments; and to these should be added another thirty or so who on some issues, like the British H-Bomb tests in 1958, sided with the unilateralists.'[11]

In July 1965, by which time support for CND among Labour members had declined very considerably from its initial level, Neil Marten (Cons.) initiated a motion in the Commons regretting 'the influence which the supporters and policies of the Campaign for Nuclear Disarmament have upon the government's policies.' In the course of his speech, he asserted that just under one-third of Labour MPs 'have shown themselves as being sympathetic to CND'.[12] Parkin suggests that this figure is certainly an over-estimate: the Campaign itself in its journal *Sanity* claimed after the 1964 election that thirty-seven MPs were 'in close touch' with the Campaign, and that thirty-six were in some agreement (a phrase which could mean almost anything).[13] But by this time, of course, several of the leading Labour disarmers had themselves been disarmed in the most effective way possible by accepting posts in the government: thus Castle, Cousins, Gardiner, Greenwood, Stonehouse and Swingler were now bound by the shackles of collective responsibility. Moreover, now that a Labour government was at last in power, back-bench supporters of CND had much to lose by nailing their colours to the mast of what had by now become a sinking ship and, thanks to the efforts of the Committee of 100, one of increasingly dubious respectability in the eyes of the authorities. This did not mean, of course, that members of the Parliamentary Labour party simply forgot their old allegiance to the unilateralist cause: a considerable number of left wing back-benchers such as Emrys Hughes, Hugh Jenkins, Anne Kerr, Michael Foot and Sydney Silverman (to name only a few) continued to prod the government on issues of defence and nuclear policy. In March 1965, *Tribune* reported that thirty-four Labour MPs and one Labour peer had issued a letter supporting CND's Easter march: and at the CND rally in Trafalgar Square at Easter in 1966, a *Guardian* reporter counted seventeen Labour back-benchers among the demonstrators. But with a Labour government in office, unilateralist members of the PLP shifted the main platform of their campaign away from the mass rallies of CND into Westminster and the Parliamentary party itself.

The issue of nuclear strategy (and of support for NATO) was just one element in the fundamentalist-revisionist quarrel which threatened to tear the Labour movement apart during the 1950s and early 1960s. Within the party, says Professor Samuel Beer, 'the hard core of the opposition on foreign policy was much the same as that on domestic policy.'[14] The commitment of so many members of the party to the cause of unilateralism cannot be explained in isolation: it must be seen as part of a complex framework of beliefs about the nature of Socialism, and examined in the context of the position of the party at that time.

During the 1950s all the conditions were ripe for the development of a symbiotic relationship between Labour's disillusioned left-wing and an ideologically congenial extra-Parliamentary movement like CND. The parties themselves were slow in deciding how to cope with the tactical implications of nuclear weapons, and the Labour party equivocated to such a degree that, in the end, the vote at Scarborough was not on unilateralism as such which by now (since the cancellation of Blue Streak earlier in 1960) the party had broadly accepted in principle, but about Britain's future commitment to NATO. Ideologically, unilateralism was attractive to many members of the PLP (and not just to the traditional pacifist element), and for their own part most supporters of CND saw the party as the only possible 'official' channel through which nuclear neutrality could be achieved. As Kingsley Martin wrote in the *New Statesman* (2 July 1960):

I know of no way of obtaining a non-nuclear Britain except by converting the Labour party. Unless they work through the Labour movement, nuclear disarmers are simply marching about to satisfy their own consciences.

It seems clear, however, that many non-party supporters of CND during the period of the Scarborough crisis became irritated by the behaviour of those Labour left-wingers who exploited the Campaign as a device to embarrass Gaitskell, and no doubt this accelerated the growth of the rift between the party and the Campaign in the months that followed. Moreover, several prominent unilateralists in the party such as Michael Foot and Anthony Greenwood had incurred the wrath of CND supporters by urging Gaitskell to accept a pro-NATO compromise resolution in an attempt to unite the party after the events at Scarborough.

With the advent, in February 1963, of Harold Wilson as certainly the most acceptable leader of the party that the left-wingers could reasonably have hoped for in the circumstances, much of the old anti-revisionist sentiment which had actuated many Labour disarmers during the 1950s evaporated. Moreover, the growing involvement of the disarmers with direct action tactics, post-1960, was hardly calculated to enhance the popularity of CND within the party.

Since its foundation in 1958, CND had co-existed, rather uneasily, with the Direct Action Committee led initially by, *inter alia*, Michael Randle and Pat Arrowsmith, who advocated the use of Gandhi's tactics of non-violent civil disobedience. The DAC had been the initial driving force behind the first Aldermaston march and while the Campaign's Executive (and in particular its chairman, Canon Collins) was opposed to the use of militant tactics, it was also very anxious to avoid dampening the invaluable zeal of activists working for the cause of disarmament. So long as the DAC remained a junior partner in the movement, co-existence was possible, but the alliance became increasingly uneasy once Lord Russell and his fellow founders of the Committee of 100 presented the disarmers with a straightforward choice between using civil disobedience as a declared tactical weapon or of opting for the quieter life with Canon Collins and the rump of CND.

From the beginning, there had been bitter wrangles within the movement about tactics, and the DAC had alienated many Labour unilateralists in the later 1950s by advocating a 'voters' veto',[15] directed against Labour candidates who were not prepared to espouse the unilateralist cause. Such activities, though not in practice pursued to very great lengths, tended to force party members into a clash of loyalties – between party and principle; and, certainly as far as members of the PLP were concerned, such tactics could only have the effect of closing the ranks of party supporters. The formation of an Independent Nuclear Disarmament Election Committee[16] to sponsor unilateralist candidates produced a similar effect on Labour supporters and, in any event, INDEC was promptly added to that formidable list of organisations proscribed by the party. INDEC was, however, sufficiently closely associated with CND to be a considerable source of embarrassment to the Campaign.

It hardly comes as a surprise to find the Labour party ill-disposed towards an organization whose declared purpose was to split the radical vote on the issue of disarmament. But what steps, if any, did the party take to exclude CND supporters from the ranks of Labour candidates? The answer seems to be that the matter was generally left in the hands of individual constituency organizations – and, in his study of the selection of Parliamentary candidates, Dr Michael Rush remarks that the most frequent questions asked of would-be Labour candidates at selection conferences during early 1960s were 'Are you a member of CND?' or 'Do you support the party's nuclear policy?'[17] Rush also cites two instances of the party's National Executive Committee refusing to endorse candidates who were supporters of CND, though one cannot be absolutely certain that this was the decisive factor, since no reasons are given for such refusals.[18] The general conclusion seems to be that, particularly during the party's rather jittery mood of the early 1960s, supporters of CND may have been at a disadvantage when seeking nomination in some constituencies, but that the NEC took no formal steps to intervene in the selection process. Certainly, no overt attempt was ever made to unseat sitting Members because of their unilateralist beliefs.

Just as it is impossible to explain the affinity between the Labour movement and unilateralism other than by reference to the combined effects of a whole range of diverse factors, so there is no simple explanation as to why the nuclear disarmament movement went into a decline during the 1960s. A marked improvement in the fortunes of the Labour party, divisions in the ranks of the disarmers, the partial Test-Ban Treaty, a shift in the focus of public concern from the rather abstract concept of a nuclear holocaust to the much more immediate horror of the Vietnam war – all these factors undoubtedly had a marked bearing upon the direction and momentum of political protest.

It is particularly significant in the light of subsequent events that the unilateralists, and, in particular, the Committee of 100 which grew out of the DAC and eventually merged with it in 1961, ultimately fell foul of party opinion on the issue of law and order arising out of the use of increasingly militant tactics. As the disarmers ceased to conceive of the Labour party as their chosen instrument, and as at the same time the disruptive activities of the Committee of 100 began to hit the headlines with increasing frequency, Labour supporters of unilateralism reacted sharply against the new militancy:

> . . . not only because their own standing with Transport House and the public suffered damage by association with extremism, but because as active politicians they could not accept that CND could achieve anything outside the context of party politics. . . .[19]

Labour MPs could still be heard from time to time complaining that the law was being invoked against protesters in an unfair or over-harsh manner. Thus late in 1959, thirty-eight Labour MPs had tabled a motion protesting against the imprisonment of six leading members of the DAC for threatening a breach of the peace in connection with an impending demonstration at Harrington. In October 1961, Anthony Greenwood raised in the adjournment debate the question of police behaviour at the Trafalgar Square demonstrations, and in the following month, during the committee stage of the Expiring Laws Bill, both Michael Foot and Emrys Hughes protested against the refusal of the Home Office to renew the visa of Ralph Schoenman, a prominent figure in the Committee of 100.

But while condemning the repressive actions of the public authorities, several former PLP supporters of CND took the opportunity on a number of occasions to condemn the new forms of militant direct action. In the adjournment debate on the Trafalgar Square demonstrations, Anthony Greenwood began by saying: 'I want to emphasize that I strongly disapprove of civil disobedience as a method of political expression. I believe equally strongly however that every citizen should be protected from any abuse of police powers.'[20] In another debate, nearly eighteen months later, about the prison conditions encountered by arrested protesters, Greenwood remarked: 'Whatever one may think of civil disobedience – and I am as passionately opposed to it as anyone in this House. . . .'[21] And in the debate on the Schoenman case, another founder-member of CND, Michael Foot, said: 'It so happens that the civil disobedience activities with which he [Schoenman] has been occasionally concerned are run by a body [the Committee of 100] with which I disagree. . . .'[22]

In 1963, Victory for Socialism was wound up. Both Greenwood and Foot, together with Judith Hart, declined to stand for re-election to CND's National Council. Subsequently, during the Labour government's term of office, the left wing of the party retained its role as a fundamentalist ginger-group, reserving the right to dissent on issues of principle. But although there were a number of important back bench revolts, many of the old schisms were successfully papered over. CND itself moved out of the headlines; unilateralism was displaced by the Vietnam war as the central target for direct action, and new protest groups arose which continued the kind of militant crusade formerly associated with the Committee of 100.[23] Once the Labour government had refused to condemn American involvement in Vietnam, the tendency of direct action movements to reject the efficacy, and even the morality, of established political institutions became still more pronounced. Although violence as such was used only by a minority of protesters, mass demonstrations became increasingly a matter of much-publicized confrontations between hordes of police and hordes of protesters – with both main parties committed to the maintenance of 'law and order', though disagreeing about its meaning in particular circumstances.

The Law and Order Question

Whereas the Labour party *malgré lui* found itself the proud father of a vigorous direct action movement born on its own doorstep, and nurtured eagerly by the party's dissident back benchers, the Conservatives have generally kept themselves aloof from such activities. (This is not, of course, to say that CND attracted no Conservative supporters, or that no members of the party have ever associated themselves with non-militant direct action.) CND was unique, however, and the general differences between the two main parties on the issues arising out of direct action can best be illustrated by reference to the vexed question of law and order.

The Conservative party enjoys a homogeneity and a cohesive quality which is often seen to be lacking in the Labour party. True, Conservatism does embrace a wide spectrum of opinion, but there are no identifiable factions (corresponding, for example, to the Labour party's Tribune Group) which can be counted upon to defy the whips time after time on issues of principle: the Bow Group and the Monday Club have a real existence, but they do not constitute caucuses in the House of Commons. 'Powellism' may be more than a myth, but it is less than a mass movement in any coherent sense. Some individual Conservatives may show themselves to be more 'liberal' than others in relation to specific issues, but the traditional left-right dichotomy is of little assistance when it comes to analysing the present-day structure of the party.[24] There are thus no pre-defined breakaway groups within the Conservative movement which might conceivably be attracted *en masse* to any ideologically and politically congenial mass movement. It should also be added that the organization of the party is founded upon firm and authoritative leadership from the top, cemented by a high degree of social homogeneity within the ranks of the party: leaders of the Labour party (with its emphasis upon mass participation in decision-making) particularly when the party is in opposition, are much more exposed to movements in rank and file opinion, a factor of which would-be manipulators are apt to make good use.

The stance adopted by the Conservative party towards direct action has been strongly conditioned by its ideas about law and order and the need for social stability. This is not to say that Conservatives take no notice of the substantive issues which are a target of direct action: indeed, it is essential to realize that what may apparently be an attack by the party on the *means* used by demonstrators to express their views may in fact be part of a more general antipathy towards the *goals* of direct action. Thus although the debate early in 1970 about the South African cricket tour was conducted very largely in the vocabulary of law and order, by implication this was also closely bound up with party views about the rights and duties of a British government in taking, or refraining from taking, action against a foreign government pursuing racialist domestic policies. It must be remembered too that debates of this kind, particularly as an election is drawing near, become part of the inter-party dog-fight: this was particularly true in the present instance since the Conservative party, at the 'Selsdon Conference' of the Shadow Cabinet, had committed itself to making law and order a central issue in its election campaign.

These *caveats* notwithstanding, it seems fair to say that a speech made by Reginald Maudling, then Shadow Home Secretary, in an adjournment debate in the Commons on the South African tour in May 1970, embodies the essence of the Conservative view of law and order in the context of direct action. Mr Maudling said:

> I believe our basic principle must be that any man is entitled to do what is lawful and to expect that the State will protect him from unlawful interference. . . . Once a man is denied the right to do what is lawful because other people at home or overseas may disagree with his views, it would be striking at the roots of freedom under the law. Once we admit the right of people to enforce their views by violent means with impunity – and there are many examples in the world today – democracy is at risk.[25]

Mr Heath had spoken on much the same subject a few weeks earlier in a speech to the Society of Conservative Lawyers. After talking about the growth of organized crime and increases in crimes of violence in our society (the juxtaposition of these phenomena with direct action has been a significant feature of many Conservative speeches in this field) he continued:

> But more than that, society itself is challenged. That challenge comes from those willing and anxious to promote violence and disruption to further their political and social ends. They wish to make use of freedom in order to destroy that society which provides

it for them. It is a challenge to politicians as well as to people. Indeed it is the first duty of government to protect the freedom, dignity and security of the citizen against the abuse of freedom and toleration.[26]

Finally, a leading article in the *Spectator*, following the enforced cancellation of the South African tour, represents a further facet of the Conservative case – the need to show determination in the face of organized disruption:

> ... Once you have paid him the Dane-geld, you never get rid of the Dane. ... A government's duty when confronted by an overt challenge from the new militants is plain. It is to resist any attempt to diminish the ordinary liberties of the country. It is to assert the supremacy of the elected representatives of the people over self-appointed bands who believe that if they shout and threaten enough they may get their way. It is to show with determination that freedom to undertake lawful activities will not be curtailed under duress.[27]

These rather lengthy quotations usefully illustrate three different but closely related aspects of the Conservative attitude. These are: first, the duty of a democratic State to safeguard individual freedom against the tyranny of a disruptive minority; secondly the essentially (and deliberately) destructive character of militant direct action; and thirdly, the dangers of 'giving in' to 'unlawful' pressures. The first of these is probably the most fundamental aspect of the Conservative case and is, in a sense, a product of the second. The third stems from a belief in strong and authoritative government.

Ultimately, however, the stance adopted by the parties depends upon their perception of a particular set of events, and this in turn is conditioned by a complex set of psychological and ideological factors. Certainly all politicians conditioned to working through the Parliamentary system have a threshold of tolerance beyond which direct action is reclassified as mob-rule – and, of the two main parties, the Conservatives have consistently taken a more authoritarian line. Contrast Reginald Maudling's speech with that of Reginald Prentice in the same debate:

> I hope that no hon. Member would suggest that there should be any doubt cast upon the rights of people to protest and demonstrate peacefully simply because there might, on the fringe of that demonstration, be an element of violence. Peaceful demonstrations and protests have a long and honourable tradition in this country and many of our basic liberties spring from the fact that people did protest in many ways in the past, sometimes in ways which involved great sacrifice to themselves.[28]

– or with that made by the liberal Conservative Sir Edward Boyle who had himself protested (peacefully) against the South African tour:

> I believe that one mark of a civilized community – the sort of community in which most of us in this House believe – is that every now and then in our society a larger section than usual should wish to protect itself by means of peaceful protest. . . .[29]

Three able and respected politicians, all talking about the same set of events, are yet unable to agree on their interpretation of these events. Is mass demonstration destructive of democratic freedom or the embodiment of such freedom? Are demonstrators outlaws, or law-abiding citizens indulging in legitimate protest? Do demonstrations represent mob violence, or are they peaceful occasions, marred by isolated acts of violence by a fringe element? Granted, facts are confused in these circumstances and that it *is* difficult to determine the extent to which violence is involved in demonstrations, particularly as, to a much greater extent than was the case with CND, more recent protests have come to involve *ad hoc* coalitions of groups with widely divergent aims and tactics. Granted too that debates on these occasions involve a good deal of party flag-waving. But can this entirely explain the fact that, on the Conservative side of the House, speaker after speaker (Sir Edward excepted) talked about threats to liberty and about violence and mob-rule, while successive Labour speakers insisted on seeing matters in quite a different light: a pattern which, with variations, can be found repeated time after time in those pages of *Hansard* recording debates on matters related to direct action? In one sense, this is no more than a matter of differing emphasis since ostensibly the parties are agreed in principle on the need for law and order, but the consistent direction of the emphasis reflects important ideological differences between the parties.

The ideological position of the Conservatives on the issue of law and order and direct action was succinctly summarized by Norman St. John-Stevas, Conservative Member for Chelmsford. Writing in *The Times* he said:

> No law, no liberties is as true as no bishop, no king. Hence there is nothing Eldonine about Tory distrust of demonstrations, no panic fear, but a hard-headed assessment of a position where extremists are using the right of demonstrations not to reform institutions or to extend liberties but to destroy them. Conservatives recognize more clearly than some that today the barbarians are not outside the walls but within the city, seeking to destroy those unwritten traditions of civility on which liberty in a free society must ultimately depend.[30]

Within these three sentences, St. John-Stevas has managed to encapsulate the ingrained mistrust which Conservatives seem to have for unconventional, untraditional or unconstitutional activity. The party has from its beginnings sustained a belief in the excellence of what has gone before; it has a long history of holding power and long experience of working both for and within 'the system': is it really surprising, therefore, that Conservatives should see as barbarians those who so often seem to reject everything that Parliamentary democracy and political parties stand for?

Although the Labour party is, today, as firmly committed as the Conservative party to the Parliamentary-democratic system, it has always retained a lingering commitment to social revolution: the party, says Beer, 'thought of itself not just as a party but as "the movement".'[31] The old revolutionary fire may have died down, but the party cannot entirely reject its past: how can a movement which itself was born out of the direct action of Socialist militancy turn too fiercely on those who wish to make use of the self-same democratic right? And, at a purely practical level, how can a party condemn activities in which so many of its members may have participated – perhaps seeking solace for a revolutionary past that never quite happened.

The dilemma re-emerged in an acute form during the stormy debates on the Conservative government's Industrial Relations Bill early in 1971. The cry of outrage that arose from virtually every section of the PLP, not merely at the substantive provisions of the Bill itself but, more particularly, at the imposition of a guillotine at its committee stage in the Commons, led to a temporary breakdown of those 'usual channels' (including pairing arrangements) so essential to the smooth conduct of Parliamentary business. At one stage, a group of thirty-nine Labour left-wingers (later dubbed 'half-cock martyrs' by Norman Shrapnel, writing in *The Guardian*) staged a noisy, if unproductive, 'demonstration' on the floor of the Commons: even in this instance, the Members concerned took care not to proceed so far beyond the rather nebulous limits of Parliamentary propriety as to run the risk of disciplinary sanctions or of having their gesture dubbed 'unconstitutional'. The careful replacement of the Mace which became dislodged during the course of the demonstration was a gesture of considerable symbolic significance. Although this piece of direct action received no overt backing from the Shadow Cabinet, it was clear that the Labour leadership was only too glad to welcome growing evidence of unity among back-benchers still smarting from the aftermath of electoral defeat.

Outside Parliament, trade unionists waxed indignant about the Bill and threats came from several quarters to sabotage it by a policy of non-cooperation after it became law: there were also a number of token strikes. For its own part, the Labour party promised, rather ambiguously, to repeal the Act when it returned to power. Predictably, both the trade unions and the parties reacted vehemently against the kind of murderous extremism evidenced by a bomb attack on the home of Robert Carr. Taken as a whole, this case study serves to reinforce the view that, even in opposition, Labour MPs, however strong their ideological commitment, are anxious to remain securely within the fold of the Parliamentary-democratic system.

Direct Action and the Law

The concern of the Conservatives about law and order has led them to promise firm action against militant demonstrations. The 1970 Conservative manifesto promised to:

> ... change the law so that the demonstrator who uses violence or the criminal who causes personal injury [note once again the juxtaposition of the two] will be obliged to compensate his victim in addition to fines or other punishments imposed by the courts.

And it continued in familiar vein:

> A tolerant and civilized society must continue to permit its citizens to assemble, march and demonstrate in support of the ideals and principles they believe in. Our purpose is to protect the citizen against the disruption of lawful activities and, to that end, we will immediately institute an inquiry into the law affecting trespass. Such a reform of the law would in no way inhibit the peaceful use of the right to demonstrate or strike.

Clearly, such a promise is consistent with those Conservative views already discussed, though the right to demonstrate peacefully was not given the same degree of emphasis in the speeches and statements quoted earlier – and to this extent perhaps the wording of the manifesto may even reflect a victory by a hitherto latent liberal element in the party hierarchy, though this is pure speculation.

Before the election, Sir Peter Rawlinson, subsequently appointed Attorney-General, was given the task of studying, *inter alia* (here I am quoting Edward Heath), 'whether we should create an offence of malicious or criminal trespass which will provide better redress against the wilful interruption of business or pleasure'.[32] When Sir Peter, who is on record as favouring a review of the law as it affects demonstrators,[33] became a member of the government, the issue ceased to be a party matter as such. It is on the cards, however, that even if there were a satisfactory way round the legal difficulties in defining an enforceable law of 'malicious trespass', opposition might well be encountered from those liberal constitutionalists within the party who see grave risks in tampering with fundamental civil liberties to which the party has, despite everything, remained firmly committed.

Certainly the legal difficulties involved in such an undertaking are themselves formidable enough. There are already in existence a number of statutory and common law offences (under, for example, the 1861 Malicious Damage Act,[34] and the 1936 Public Order Act) which circumscribe the legitimate limits of the right to demonstrate. There are too a whole range of offences against the person, ranging from common assault to murder:[35] and, as the demonstrators at the Wethersfield Base found to their cost in 1961, the Official Secrets Acts of 1911 and 1920 provide, *inter alia*, for a sentence of up to two years' imprisonment for unlawful entry into a prohibited place within the meaning of the Acts. The real difficulty lies not so much in framing a jurisprudentially satisfactory offence of malicious trespass (though one would have to be very careful, for example, when it came to defining 'malice' in a context where no measurable damage was being done) but in enforcing it. Politicians sometimes forget that demonstrations are contained, not by threat of penal sanctions but by the mutual good sense and self-restraint which has been shown by a large majority of police and demonstrators on all but a very few occasions. Trespass is traditionally a preserve of the civil law. The police do not need more statutory powers – they already have many powers which they hardly ever invoke – they need more policemen.

Conclusions

So long as British society continues to embody a system of libertarian values which permit free expression of political beliefs (within the rather arbitrarily defined limits thought necessary for the maintenance of an ordered society), direct action will continue to be a recurrent phenomenon. Direct action is a primitive form of political activity which pre-dates the existence of anything remotely resembling the modern party system: and the parties themselves have had to learn to live with a vocal segment of society which totally rejects almost everything that they stand for and refuses to have any truck with established political institutions.

While conventional pressure groups usefully complement the function of political parties in acting as mediators between the centre of governmental power and the peripheral public, direct action movements tend to play a very different role by providing *alternative* lines of political communication and by speaking a language of deeds rather than words. Supporters of the traditional game of politics would probably argue that the existing machinery is adequate to meet all reasonable demands placed upon it, while advocates of direct action seem to hold the view that the political system is composed of a series of devices for fobbing off embarrassing grass-roots demands and for masking the procrastination and dishonesty of political leaders. It is no part of my present purpose to comment upon these points of views except to remark that they are part of a syndrome of mutual non-comprehension which characterizes the relations between parties and direct action movements.

The established political parties and direct action groups inhabit totally different worlds, and the lack of a common language or a common set of values inhibits any serious attempts at communication between them. As Elizabeth Vallance argues in an earlier chapter, '. . . direct action . . . [sins] against the rules of the political language-game in a number of ways'. Both sides tend to reduce one another to a set of elemental symbols: the issue becomes a struggle between bureaucrats and imperialists, on the one hand, and anarchists and trouble-makers, on the other. It is perhaps for this reason that the parties sometimes seem to treat mass demonstrations as if they were no more than an abstract problem of police logistics. And such a situation gives rise to a circle of self-fulfilling expectations where confrontation between hostile policemen and hostile demonstrators gives rise to the trouble which everyone had predicted.

It is important to realize that mutual rejection is a definitive ingredient of direct action. Once parties and direct action movements come to *understand* one another, a mass movement tends to become just another 'respectable' pressure group. Perhaps this goes some way towards explaining the difficulties experienced by CND in sustaining its momentum as a grass-roots protest movement, while trying to fulfil a self-imposed role as a ginger-group at the fringe of the Labour movement. The preoccupation of party politicians – particularly Conservatives – with law and order is a product of a sincerely held belief that the key to democratic government is to be found within the party system and that attempts to by-pass the established political channels must *by definition* be a threat to society: and, indeed, it *may* be a threat to society in the sense that they conceive of it.

It seems unlikely at the present time that either of the main parties will attempt to suppress direct action altogether, though they may from time to time try to redefine its boundaries by changing the law. The problem is one of all or nothing. Once one acknowledges the existence of a fundamental right to demonstrate peaceably, it becomes all but impossible to dictate to determined dissidents precisely what form their protest must take.

Most divergences between parties have involved matters of line-drawing. There seems to be a broad consensus among party politicians about the desirability of enhancing the quality and extent of political awareness and of promoting an already deep-rooted belief in the virtues of Parliamentary democracy based upon tolerance and free expression. At the same time, the basic terms of any social contract demand that governments must exercise some controls to prevent, as far as possible, any serious disruption of orderly social life. While there is some ideological disagreement about the nature of this 'orderly' life (for example whether it entails preservation at all cost of existing property relationships), the parties, all too often donning an ill-fitting disguise as radical social innovators, have shown themselves in their true colours as guardians of the *status quo*.

But while direct action movements reject that same *status quo* in so far as it asks them to have recourse to conventional political institutions, this does not mean that direct action itself is necessarily bound up with radicalism; indeed some of its most frightening manifestations in this country and elsewhere have come from the far right. In Britain in recent years, however, the most spectacular direct action has tended to have its roots in the ideological left of the political spectrum. In terms of active membership, the broad-issue movements like CND have attracted a disproportionate number of middle class intellectuals; but some of the most 'personal' direct action tactics – such as squatting by or on behalf of homeless and the various community-rooted protest movements in Golborne and elsewhere – have thrived upon the active involvement of deprived working-class participants.

The party system and the bureaucratic edifices of the mass parties themselves have not been able to adapt satisfactorily to changing social conditions and to changing attitudes in society. An age when the morality, and even the legality, of governmental action in waging 'defensive' warfare or accumulating weapons of mass destruction has come increasingly to be questioned, has witnessed the growth of intellectually-based mass movements (particularly among the young) which wholly reject the methods and the standards adhered to by 'government', of which all parties properly so-called are considered a part. At another level, the same 'government' has become increasingly active in ways which directly and adversely affect the quality of life enjoyed by many individuals; major planning decisions are a case in point. Small wonder then that a distrust and downright dislike of so much that is associated with government should impel people to turn towards more satisfactory and more directly expressive means of obtaining redress or of bringing about change. Political alienation translated into direct action is a product of our age, and the extent to which the political system has been able to accommodate and even in some cases almost to institutionalize this phenomenon is perhaps a tribute to the ingrained values of political tolerance and to the flexibility of traditional institutions. But the fact remains that the continuing and increasingly extensive use of direct action is a standing rebuke to the limitations of conventional political methods and one which the parties can neither repress nor ignore.

NOTES

1. The terminology generally used in this field has become so idiosyncratic that one almost hesitates to talk about 'pressure groups'. In this context, I am referring simply to organized groups which exert pressure on government in order to achieve some determinate object. CND was a pressure group employing 'direct action'.
2. Bernard Crick and William A. Robson (eds), *Protest and Dissent* (Harmondsworth, 1970), introduction, p. xiii.
3. 'The Nature of Mass Demonstrations', *New Society*, 23 May 1968.
4. 'British Labour Divided', *Foreign Affairs* (April 1960), p. 494. Quoted by Frank Parkin in *Middle Class Radicalism* (Manchester 1968), p. 35. Cf. Richard Crossman's oft-quoted opinion (stemming from the same vintage period of Labour disillusionment) that 'the prime function of the Labour party . . . is to provide an ideology for nonconformist critics of the establishment.' *Fabian Tract* (June 1960), no. 325, p. 5.
5. This view is supported by Parkin, op. cit., p. 36, in his study of CND supporters and their backgrounds and attitudes. The respondents whom he questioned invariably put the *principle* of demonstrating before the achievement of specific objectives: they also put the principles of Socialism before the attainment of power by the Labour party.
6. Ibid., p. 10.
7. Christopher Driver, *The Disarmers: A Study in Protest* (London, 1964), pp. 64 ff.
8. George Thayer, *The British Political Fringe* (London, 1965), p. 60.
9. After the local Conservative Association had elected to discard the Member then sitting for the constituency because of his opposition to the government's Suez policy, it found, to its acute embarrassment, that the candidate selected to replace him, a Major Friend, was a member of the League. See Peter G. Richards, *Honourable Members*, 2nd edn (London, 1963), p. 19.
10. Driver, op. cit., p. 44.
11. Ibid., pp. 84–5.
12. H. C. Debs, vol. 716, cc. 291 ff.
13. Parkin, op. cit., p. 137 fn. See *Sanity* (September and November 1964).
14. Samuel Beer, *Modern British Politics* (London, 1965), p. 226. This work also contains a useful account of the 'revisionist' – 'funda-

mentalist' split during the 1950s (see pp. 219–28). See also Stephen Haseler, *The Gaitskellites* (London, 1969), *passim*.

15. See Driver, op. cit., pp. 67–9.
16. The founder of INDEC, Michael Croft, fought Twickenham in 1964 and obtained 1,073 votes. The Radical Alliance has, more recently, drawn support and inspiration from INDEC – and has enjoyed the same lack of electoral success.
17. Michael Rush, *The Selection of Parliamentary Candidates* (London, 1969), p. 239.
18. Ibid., p. 140.
19. Driver, op. cit., p. 66.
20. H. C. Debs, vol. 646, c. 155 (17 October 1961).
21. H. C. Debs, vol. 673, c. 1269 (12 March 1963).
22. H. C. Debs, vol. 649, c. 372 (15 November 1961).
23. The history of events during the 1960s, and particularly those leading up to the anti-Vietnam war demonstrations in 1968, are conveniently summarized in Halloran *et al.*, *Demonstrations and Communications: A Case Study* (Harmondsworth, 1970), chap. 3.
24. See Anthony King, 'The Changing Tories', *New Society* (2 May 1968). Also a short article by Julian Critchley on the Bow Group, 'The Tory Left', *The Times* (30 July 1970). The obsolescence of the traditional left-right labels was clearly demonstrated by the cross-voting in the Commons in December 1969 on the issue of abolishing capital punishment. See Peter G. Richards, *Parliament and Conscience* (London, 1970), p. 62.
25. H. C. Debs, vol. 801, c. 1484 (14 May 1970).
26. Speech to the Society of Conservative Lawyers at the Waldorf Hotel, London, on 16 March 1970.
27. *The Spectator* (30 May 1970).
28. H. C. Debs, vol. 801, c. 1488 (14 May 1970).
29. Ibid., c. 1501.
30. 'The Basic Principles of Conservatism', *The Times* (16 June 1970).
31. Op. cit., p. 135.
32. Speech to the Conservative Lawyers, *supra*.
33. Writing in the *Daily Express* (5 February 1970), Sir Peter Rawlinson said:

> Why should not the financial burden of the cost of police and the damage which results from disorder be contributed to by those who organize or encourage demonstrations which might well lead to damage? At present the cost is borne by those whose lawful activity is the target for the demonstrator and by the law-abiding citizen out of his rates and taxes.
>
> At the very least, hooliganism and violence must be shown not to pay and the criminal elements which infiltrate into

sincere demonstrations should be dealt with by trial or indictment. The present law of trespass, forcible entry, malicious damage and public order should be examined and if necessary strengthened so as fairly to retain the balance between reasonable protest and violence.

A tolerant and civilized State must continue to permit citizens to assemble, march and demonstrate. The demonstrator may stand for freedom but the rioter stands for tyranny. It is a weak State and a State poorly served which permits anyone to take the law into his own hands.

34. In a report entitled 'Criminal Law Report on Offences of Damage to Property' (1970–1, H.C. 91), the Law Commission proposed a simplification of the law in the field covered by the 1861 Act. This was implemented in the 1971 Criminal Damage Act.

35. The law in this area is reviewed in a pamphlet entitled *Public Order* produced by a committee of the Society of Conservative Lawyers and published by the Conservative Political Centre in September 1970.

XVII The Role of the National Council for Civil Liberties

TONY SMYTHE

Introduction

Charged with patrolling the boundaries between the rights and freedoms of citizens and the limitations imposed on them by the authorities, the NCCL occupies a curious no-man's land which, without even the brittle mandate of a UN peacekeeping force, is constantly exposed to misunderstanding, criticism or deliberate misrepresentation. Our only basis for being there is that thoughtful opinion desires it. Our public support depends on our ability to identify principles and distinguish them clearly from the different social or political interests which converge in any human rights situation. Our reputation and influence, as opposed to acceptance, rest on a determined response to evident injustices, the capacity to secure redress for the victims and the ability to communicate. Every demand for help must be approached without illusions, without pre-judgements and with as much objectivity and integrity as we can muster.

Before examining the NCCL's precise role in relation to direct action, it must also be made clear that we have other functions which could be prejudiced if civil liberties were to be regarded as merely ancillary to political protest. In serving the community as a whole, we must seek both to preserve a climate of tolerance and, wherever possible, to extend civil liberties by achieving more personal freedom and improving measures for its defence. Furthermore, most individuals who complain of injustice can in no sense be described as political. They are usually people who, for one reason or another, cannot cope with the system and need some other agency to fight their battles for them. With our limited resources, the underprivileged or the uninformed, the hopeless and the helpless should, in my view, have first call on our casework machinery before those whose inclination or ability to protest gives some initial advantage. Put more graphically, it could be that the old lag beaten-up on arrest, or the patient in a mental hospital seeking representation for a tribunal appeal, would come higher on our waiting-list than the veteran demonstrator with complaints arising out of yet another scuffle with the police.

In preserving the NCCL's 'watch-dog' role, there is at least one further complication. Although we exist to research, to educate, to refer and to define (or re-define) the essence of the civil liberties concern, we are ourselves on occasion the initiators of protest activities. Admittedly this is (almost) invariably on behalf of someone else, but unless handled carefully there is always the risk of causing a distorted view of ourselves in the eyes of the authorities and thereby losing credibility and opportunities for the access to the decision-makers on which effective pressure, in our terms, is based. If, however, we are over-cautious, we risk losing the trust, and therefore the co-operation, of those who may come to us for help. The balance is hard to maintain and it is easy to make mistakes. For example, I now think we were wrong to join with other groups in organizing a protest march against the 1968 Commonwealth Immigrants Act. At the time it did not seem that there was anyone else with the necessary resources to do the job. But the right to demonstrate in general can be defended more effectively by a disinterested group which does not seek to exercise that right on its own behalf.

The intermediary role of the pressure group is quite distinct from the committed role of a trade union, a political party or a protest organization. They exist to take sides and to engage in conflict. The pressure group need not identify totally with the victims of injustice until the point is reached where their interests and the general issue at stake merge in the face of an obdurate refusal to concede the remedy. By standing apart from the conflict initially, the pressure group aims at being in a position to establish any common ground which may exist between both sides but which has been overlooked. It may oppose what authority does, but starts off by assuming that authority may accept a basis for discussion, if not its own interpretation of what should be done. When the NCCL is finally forced to protest and actively contest an issue, it is best limited to conventional methods such as direct representations, lobbying, publicity or legal action through the courts.

Demonstrations

The NCCL's unwavering policy on demonstrations has been stated many times, for example in our Annual Report for 1970:

> It is not our function to judge the aim of a particular demonstration or the success or failure of the methods employed. We are solely concerned with preserving the right to peaceful protest within the law. Violent protest cannot claim our help. Our support for the right to protest non-violently and within the law – reasonably defined – is absolute. Those who choose to go beyond this point must recognize that they have stepped outside a workable context for civil liberty. The consequences are theirs to face, although a

different NCCL involvement remains – the upholding of legal rights in relation to the machinery of law enforcement.

In the introduction to our Report 'Public Order and the Police' issued after the Trafalgar Square demonstration in September 1961, we stated: 'The NCCL does not support the policy of civil disobedience which was practised at both these demonstrations, but it is concerned to see that freedom of expression is not infringed.' Bald policy statements, however, cannot adequately describe the impact which protest has made on the development of the NCCL nor the full range of its response. In fact, the NCCL was conceived out of protest when, in 1934, a group of lawyers, journalists and the public personalities, who act as the clothes-pegs for the washing-lines of voluntary endeavour, decided to 'observe' the police handling of the hunger marchers. A letter to *The Times* signed by Kingsley Martin, C. R. Attlee, A. P. Herbert, Harold Laski, D. N. Pritt and H. G. Wells said that a vigilant committee would be present to keep a watch on the behaviour of both marchers and police. According to Kingsley Martin in his autobiography: 'It was generally believed that the knowledge that responsible and well known people were on the watch had something to do with the restraint shown by the authorities on this occasion. This technique of arranging for public figures to be present at working-class demonstrations became part of our regular routine.' It has remained so ever since.

I have no means of knowing whether the NCCL's founding fathers envisaged the permanent organization of immense scope which the NCCL has become, or its recognition as a bastion of traditional tolerance and liberal values even by those who would plunder our freedoms if they could. If they had such pretensions they were not to be easily realized; for institutions are built, not merely on conscious decisions, but on the circumstances in which they operate. It was the pioneering concern of the NCCL for the rights of the unemployed that brought support from the Labour movement. This was quickly entrenched by a necessary involvement in the aftermath of the 1928 Trades Disputes Act, which until its repeal seriously threatened basic trade union rights. Add to this the deep-rooted (and justified) fear of Fascism sweeping Europe at the time, which was often expressed through the condemnation of the assaults on human rights taking place in Germany, Italy and Spain, and it can be seen that the NCCL's role as an impartial arbiter was unlikely to go unchallenged. Those who then spoke publicly for the NCCL took immense pains to express their universalist approach, but they were not entirely successful at a time when political labels were easier to adopt than to shed.

If the NCCL was portrayed then as a creature of the left, the picture took on flesh as the illusion grew, and support from the left flourished. Fear of Communist domination led the American Civil Liberties Union (ACLU), the counterpart of the NCCL, to exclude Communists from membership. The result was a breakaway movement and a rift which only recently has begun to recede in importance. The liberal element in the NCCL, while not prepared to submit to exploitation by the Communists or any other political formation, did not, to its credit, commit the same fundamental error. With the passage of time, the balance was restored. Fascism and essentially Labour movement issues became less central in a programme which embraced every aspect of civil liberties. The campaign for the rights of mental patients in the 1950s was devoid of party political content, while in the 1960s it became clear that the rights of middle-class members of CND and the tribulations of ethnic minorities did not appeal to the 'left' in the same way as the experiences of the unemployed in the 1930s. The Communist smear died a slow death. But today, while the main target of the NCCL's criticism is invariably the government of the day, civil liberty issues cut right across party allegiances and leave little room for questioning our ideological independence.

The Influence of Political Events

It was, perhaps, even more difficult for a young NCCL to escape the political pressures of the time than for the long-established American Civil Liberties Union to ignore the impact of the Vietnam war on every facet of American society. A senior official of the ACLU wrote:

> The time has come for the ACLU to acknowledge publicly that the war in Vietnam . . . is the immediate cause for the wholesale denial of civil liberties in the United States. . . . Virtually half the work of the Union over the past three years has related directly to public action taken to protest against the war . . . under present conditions, the assault on civil liberty and repression of dissent, already well-rooted, may expand into wholesale disregard of personal freedoms. The reason for the present precarious state of civil liberties and the immediate threat of still greater sanctions against their exercise is underlined because of the war. The danger to civil liberty, therefore, will abate only if and when the war is ended. As long as the war continues, civil liberty is in jeopardy.

This assessment could hardly be denied by anyone who had examined the ACLU's handling of issues in recent times. Its problem, as was the NCCL's in the 1930s, is how to maintain the balance on the point of the utmost effectiveness when one issue, one receptacle for the fears and lost hopes of a generation, engulfs every other political reality. It is hard to criticize the same writer when he added: 'It is imperative, therefore, that the ACLU denounce the war in those terms.' In effect, some American civil libertarians are being blasted out of their traditional stance based on the operation of the Constitution because, they say, the State has acted unconstitutionally in pursuit of its foreign policy, and this betrayal is visibly eroding the fabric of society, including the preservation of citizens' rights.

A political cataclysm of similar magnitude in Britain could well provoke a similar response. It would be the height of political naïveté for the NCCL to insist on a purely mediatory role and to carry on as usual if, as in the United States or Northern Ireland, there no longer existed a minimal consensus opinion which recognized the basic principles of civil liberty. There are occasions when one must take sides so that, while one may respect the perseverance of the Civil Liberties League in South Africa, it could be argued that the existence of that organization is not only irrelevant but counter-productive.

We are, I believe, nowhere near such a situation in Britain in spite of increased opportunities for radical confrontation and the polarization of attitudes between young and old, white and black, traditionalist and direct-actionist. This conclusion may lose us superficial radical sympathy but life goes on for the mass of ordinary people who have problems enough in grappling with everyday complexities and the insatiable appetite of authority for instant obedience. Even if the worst were to happen, there would be an intermediate stage where activists could well find it necessary to promote civil rights activity in defence of their own interests. This would, I believe, be a more satisfactory alternative than forcing the NCCL to adopt a role which would exclude it from intervening effectively throughout the full range of civil liberty issues. But what if there were during this decade, as some predict, a massive swing to the right? What if the legislators, backed by Powellite public opinion, embarked upon a programme of stark repression? What if the NCCL's supporters were to experience a basic confrontation between ideology and objectivity? In a world where many, if not most, societies are caught up in this dilemma, the possibility cannot be discounted. Then the NCCL, like other social pressure groups, would have to choose between alternative roles; it could remain an unbiased and essentially defensive pressure group or become a militant movement on the offensive in a desperate campaign for human rights. Perhaps a reasonable balance can only be maintained when problems are tractable in terms of reform rather than radical change. An alliance with America in fighting an imperialist war or the re-introduction of conscription would inevitably transform the NCCL or provoke a mass exodus into movements committed to direct action and militant confrontation.

Intermediary Role

The NCCL's central task in relation to the preservation of political freedoms is to provide the back-drop to the stage where the political dramas are enacted with occasional sallies from the wings. The players may be moderate or extreme, traditionalist or way-out, right or left. In upholding the rights of any one group, we shall always risk identification with the aims and philosophy of that group, rather than the principles which should be universally applied. To take two mild examples, when the NCCL opposed arbitrary immigration controls on scientologists, the opponents of the cult suspected that we had been naïve or simply taken over. Our defence of a landlady, whose rejection of coloured would-be tenants was filmed by the BBC without her consent or knowledge, brought criticism from sections of the race relations lobby and the proponents of absolute freedom for the Press. But the more glaring issue from our point of view was privacy, not race.

A more difficult situation arises when the freedoms at stake are claimed by groups which do not profess the slightest concern for civil liberties and which actively oppose the very policies which the NCCL pursues, for example in areas such as immigration control and race relations. When, in the 1930s, the NCCL provided the focus for much anti-Fascist opinion, only a civil libertarian of unsullied purity could have advocated the *active* defence of Mosley's right to hold public meetings, although, to be fair, NCCL spokesmen at the time claimed no more than equal rights for anti-Fascists. All the same, in more recent times and in spite of growing racial tension, we have been able to operate a defence of the traditional free speech issues for all groups, no matter how much we may deplore their views. Most notably, advice was given to the right-wing leader Colin Jordan following his arrest. Later we publicly condemned a decision by Birmingham Corporation to bar Mr Jordan from using public meeting facilities. The hypothesis that he was likely to commit an offence under the penal section of the Race Relations Act, or that his presence on a public platform would provoke public disorder and damage to property, was not in our view relevant to the immediate issue at stake.

Fortunately in Britain we may assume, as a basis for the NCCL's intermediary role, that the power structure and public opinion are still, to a greater or lesser degree, responsive to the idea of civil liberty as it relates to political freedom. This does not, of course, mean that the majority will look sympathetically on the activities of minority groups or that decision-makers will allow their policies to be influenced by their demands.

Cases and Issues

The NCCL's central task is to preserve and extend the climate of political freedom. In addition, we must respond to the general threats to civil liberties which arise through legislation, public hysteria or judicial decisions. We must fight arbitrary curbs or the harassment of organizations, journals and demonstrations, help individuals who allege a denial of rights arising from political activity. We must make a continuing analysis of all political activity and its impact, so that we are free to comment when particular activities run the risk of provoking a repressive reaction.

We may help the individual protester by providing information on rights (thus in many cases helping him to avoid conflict with the law), by advising in particular situations, explaining legal procedures, taking up complaints against the police, prisons and courts, and by pursuing issues of general importance such as police discretion in charging or magistrates' discretion in refusing legal aid. It is evident that this need not be a one-way process, particularly as far as the individual is concerned. The political protester provides the NCCL with an invaluable source of information on standard civil liberty problems which affect accused persons of all types. Much of this kind of case-work does not differ essentially from case-work with no political content. But, whilst the habitual delinquent will accept the régime, however bad, and get round it as best he may, the articulate protester is more ready to identify and complain about deficiencies in the conditions and the rights afforded to the accused. Nevertheless, it remains true that even the majority of protesters are appallingly ignorant of their rights and the procedures that operate between arrest and trial; and this situation is unlikely to change without reform in the educational system to ensure that everyone emerges into the adult world with a working knowledge and understanding of his legal, social and welfare rights.

Apart from the granting of rights, the arrest, even perhaps of an innocent person, does not necessarily involve any civil liberty issue, provided it can be assumed that he will be treated fairly before and during the trial. The assumption cannot always be made. It is easier to stand on your rights in a police station than to receive them, and some courts have a remarkable propensity for exercising their discretion against the accused in granting bail, legal aid or adjournments. Communication when in custody, either in a police station, prison or remand centre, is never easy in spite of any theoretical state of innocence until a court has held otherwise. These are the realities which provide the justification for the NCCL's role as a service organization and as a perpetual watch-dog.

It is perhaps necessary here to separate the ordinary run of cases from those where the person concerned consciously decides to use the denial of his or her rights to illustrate and, hopefully, amend a more widespread injustice or establish a right which is contested or un-recognized. The archetypal direct-actionists were the conscientious objectors of the First World War. By their willingness to go to prison, or even face execution on the battlefield, they had the remarkable distinction of establishing a new right to refuse military service either unconditionally or in exchange for alternative service of a civilian nature. The operation was not an unqualified success, for many, including the writer many years later, were to reflect in prison that the claiming of a right and the granting of it are two very different matters.

In the style of the Gandhian practitioners of civil disobedience, the conscientious objector stood aloof and took whatever was doled out. A civil liberty case could then be made for what the law should be. In contrast, the Committee of 100, acting as a mass movement rather than adopting the individual idealism of the conscientious objectors, under-took a form of direct action which involved breaking the law but which no one suggested should lead to a change in that law. It would have been easier for the NCCL to come to their defence if the laws they were breaking had been directly connected with the point of their protest. Many direct-actionists since have tried to use the courts as an essentially political platform. While in the NCCL's view it would not be in the interests of justice for the courts to become the stamping-ground for fringe politicians not inventive enough to get a hearing elsewhere, it would be a denial of civil liberties if there were indeed political or civil rights issues at stake which were only permitted expression by the prosecution. This is precisely what has happened most notably in the Wethersfield Official Secrets trial of the members of the Committee of 100.

In spite of some 'consumer' resistance, the NCCL may have to concede that political trials do not take place in Britain. On the other hand, the customary appeals from the bench to the jury to forget the political background and concentrate on the substance of the charges, have the unmistakable stamp of polite fiction when measured against the opportunities afforded the prosecution. Evidently there *are* political *prosecutions*. The police decide whether to bring charges. The Director of Public Prosecutions, responsible to the Attorney-General, decides whether to prosecute. The charges themselves, particularly under the Official Secrets Acts, may be unmistakably political. The Special Branch, which is a political police force, may give evidence, and a political appointee, the Attorney-General, may be found leading the prosecution case. A whole prosecution may take place to the accompani-ment of expressions of public or governmental disquiet about particular activity, even perhaps those which had not hitherto met with legal sanctions.

The civil liberties' concern in such situations is to ensure a fair trial, but as always a number of problems arise. The defence of a principle during the course of a particular case will not always be considered by his legal advisers to be in the interests of the defendant. The defendant may consciously take the risk, but there are more numerous examples where human rights issues have gone by default. Political activists, whether they be men of principle or masquerading under a cloak of idealism, rarely invoke the tolerance and understanding of the public or the courts. Disapproval of their aims or methods may well submerge the merits of the case in a welter of prejudice which is hard to prove or to quantify without an exhaustive study of all public comment, transcripts (which are expensive to obtain), and minute by minute observation of every gesture and inflection of the *dramatis personae* in court. The *sub judice* rule, however necessary in the interests of justice, may inhibit comment when it is most pertinent while the broader concept of contempt has, even in the most deserving cases, placed judges virtually beyond criticism.

Faced with problems like these, the NCCL's service in individual cases is pitifully inadequate. We do, however, have a full-time legal staff and a large panel of voluntary, but qualified, legal advisers who can provide initial advice, draft any representations which should be made, interview witnesses and prisoners, and distil the civil liberty issues at stake. These and other volunteers may act as court observers and participate in research projects. A civil liberties legal defence fund exists, to finance appropriate test cases. Above all, in liaison with other voluntary agencies, the NCCL can provide a central clearing house for all information and case histories likely to be useful in the assessment of current civil liberty problems.

The State of Public Order Law

The failure to achieve success in so many political cases poses funda-mental questions concerning the extent to which the interests of freedom and justice have been served by the judiciary, police and lawyers as well as by the content of the law itself. True, the law must be administered as it is found by those who enforce it. But public order law is so vague as to leave much to the discretion of the courts; and in the absence of adequate definitions as to what does and does not constitute acceptable political activity, the protection of civil liberties must depend too heavily on the judges' observance of their grave responsibility never to act with that expedient arbitrariness which the law makes possible. A similar anxiety focuses on the conduct of the police, whose considerable powers furnish no automatic immunity to fashionable prejudice but prove, on the contrary, to be a disturbingly versatile weapon especially in dealing with unfashionable minorities; one thinks particularly of the search powers made further available under the 1967 Dangerous Drugs Act. As any complaint against the police is still investigated by the police themselves, a corrective review is unlikely and individual remedies extremely rare. It goes without saying that socially-conscious lawyers willing to exercise creative ingenuity as well as procedural vigilance in cases where civil liberties issues are at stake are in urgent demand. They are few and far between: simply not enough lawyers are prepared to deal with criminal cases in general and civil rights cases in particular. In comparison with their American counterparts, the vast majority of British lawyers are uninterested in the law as it affects personal freedom.

It is ironic that recent expressions of public disquiet on all aspects of crime and particularly on breaches of public order have included demands for a strengthening of the law while individual prosecutions have shown that the law can be used with almost infinite severity in dealing with political offenders. The NCCL has always maintained that if the authorities ever chose to draw from the arsenal of powers available to them under both common law and statute, political freedom as we know it could not survive. As it happens, their powers have been used with moderation laced occasionally with exemplary toughness. Such a policy can be maintained for as long as the State does not feel itself to be seriously threatened or is not politically overwhelmed by a public outcry against disruptive, minority elements.

Recent developments, however, have indicated that the time has come to examine public order law in the light of the obvious threat it poses for civil liberties. The prosecution tactic, in cases which go back to the Committee of 100 days, has included the use of catch-all charges carrying penalties of varying degrees of severity. Furthermore, a defendant may find himself facing one or two charges at committal but with a much longer list shortly before he comes to trial. This enables the prosecution both to intimidate and to engage in the kind of bargaining which will ensure guilty pleas on one count in exchange for other charges being dropped. After the Greek Embassy occupation in 1967, more than forty non-violent demonstrators were faced with the specious charge of riotous assembly with the result that they were forced to plead guilty to unlawful assembly. Three defendants received exemplary prison sentences ranging from six to fifteen months.

The prosecuting authorities have some sixty offences to choose from in dealing with any behaviour likely to occur through protest activity. The common law offences of conspiracy, unlawful assembly, riot, affray and even sedition, all carrying unlimited penalties of fines or imprisonment, are available as a useful alternative to the wide range of public order offences which normally carry lesser penalties. Overt violence can be dealt with under a variety of enactments covering firearms, malicious damage and explosive substances. The maximum penalties for these are severe and may include fourteen years to life imprisonment.

Many of these powers have been used in recent times and seem likely to become even more fashionable in the future. Sedition is a possible exception. This, according to Archbold, 'embraces all those practices, whether by word, deed, or writing, which fall short of high treason, but directly tend to have for their object to excite discontent or dissatisfaction.' If the authorities were to respond to the law-and-order lobby by using sedition, it can be seen that no political activist could engage in any protest without the constant threat of prosecution and imprisonment.

However, as the situation stands, sedition remains a reserve power while the police and the courts are still experimenting with marginally lesser charges. The Cambridge students' trial coupled with those trials arising out of the Queen Frederika demonstration in 1963, the Greek Embassy occupation, the South Africa House demonstration in 1969, and the Senate House demonstration in 1970, should be treated as warning signals which could herald a period in which the law will be used as a bludgeon to discourage political protests and to isolate the more militant groups.

If student or single-issue protest, mainly thought to be the province of middle-class youth, were to give way to the more threatening prospect of mass action by the trade union movement, I have little doubt that we should see an escalation of public order prosecutions. Before such a situation is allowed to develop, the government and law enforcers should take note of the conclusions contained in a report by a committee of the Society of Conservative Lawyers, which on the surface did not appear to differ substantially from the views expressed consistently by the NCCL:

The provisions of the law, in the sense of the prescription of offences, are generally adequate in the field of public order.

These provisions, however, in respect of demonstrations or manifestations of violence with a political content or purpose tend to be scattered, diverse, and in some cases archaic and lacking in clarity. It would be well, therefore, to review the law with a view to its simplification and clarification, which, in addition to assisting the authorities, would give participants and potential participants in such activities a clearer indication of their rights and liabilities under the law.

I would add that in a review to be undertaken the legislators should bear in mind that the law is not merely 'generally adequate' but in theory, if not in practice, far more repressive than can be tolerated in a democratic society. Unfortunately, the law-and-order myth is self-perpetuating. If the courts make a direct association between serious charges and less serious behaviour, it is the charges and the sentences rather than the reality which will serve as the measure of protest activities in the public mind. In one breath there will be those who argue that charges should be used as a deterrent while at the same time demonstrating their lack of faith in the deterrent by calling for even more serious charges to be imposed. I do not believe that idealistic minorities can be deterred in this way. As protesters and law enforcers engage in an eye to eye confrontation, escalation, with all the social damage it will bring, seems inevitable. I would also foresee governmental resistance to simplification or clarification because they would prefer to leave the law as vague as possible and allow themselves plenty of room for manœuvre. The NCCL's reply to the Conservative Lawyers would therefore be that the provisions of the law are more than adequate and that if any consolidation is to take place, it could only be on the basis of leaving less discretion to the prosecuting authorities and radically reducing the penalties for all offences which do not involve serious assault on persons or property.

Handling Demonstrations – Observers

Since its first undertaking, observing at demonstrations has remained a crucial aspect of the NCCL's broader function in relation to political events. The scope and effectiveness of this activity has increased over the years.

Demonstrations constitute a test of the freedoms of speech and assembly in circumstances which may carry a latent threat to public order. The NCCL's capacity both to defend these freedoms against attack and to assess any irresponsible exploitation of the right to demonstrate is based on the reports of volunteer observers carefully selected for their impartiality and reliability. Their written accounts are used to provide the basis for an overall assessment which may be submitted to chief officers, the Home Secretary, MPs and the Press. They may also be asked to act as witnesses in police complaints or in court proceedings, and it is often necessary to follow up observation at demonstrations with observation in court.

If the observer's role is one of central importance, it is not without its risks: on occasions, exaggerated suspicion on the part of the police has led them to give isolated observers a bad time. For this reason, some effort has to be made to assure the police that they are not being subjected to one-sided snooping designed to catch them out; though the fact that the NCCL remains a critical observer, not an ally, of the State means that such risks can never be entirely discounted.

The constructive impact of efficient observing is well-illustrated by two major demonstrations in Grosvenor Square in 1968. Twenty-five accredited observers were sent to the first one which took place on 17 March. A subsequent report to the Home Secretary made a number of points, amongst which the following were included:

> Organizers of demonstrations should not evade their responsibilities and should communicate their objectives both to participants and police. . . . Violence seems more likely at the point of confrontation between large numbers of demonstrators and police.
> The following comment arose because the police sealed off a narrow street already filled by the mass of demonstrators. Complaints about using police horses for crowd control have been made by this organization many times in the past. This occasion conclusively demonstrated the problems they caused. They are an unnecessary provocation to demonstrators and help to create an atmosphere conducive to violence. On pavements and roads they are a danger to their riders as to everyone else in the vicinity. On grass, as in the centre of the square, their riders do not seem to be able to control them effectively. On this occasion the crowd were so infuriated by the conduct of mounted policemen that one or two were dragged from their saddles. The use of horses (and dogs) for maintaining public order should stop . . . truncheons should never be drawn except on the orders of a senior officer. Their widespread use could lead to demonstrators arming themselves in the future. Such escalation must be prevented. Those who used truncheons indiscriminately should be reprimanded.

In their replies, the Metropolitan Commissioner and the Home Office tended to dismiss the general points as well as the individual complaints.

However, the second demonstration on 27 October, although the object of much public disquiet encouraged by certain newspapers beforehand, produced a very different response. On this occasion some 200 observers were in attendance and operated in groups of three. In our final report to the Home Secretary, we were able to say:

> In (previous) reports we criticized certain police tactics involving the use of cordons, horses and truncheons. On 27 October most of the causes of friction from the police side were removed and the general strategy was not only more appropriate to the handling of such a large demonstration, but was in the event more successful in promoting good order. Clearly the police and, as our report shows,

the demonstrators and their organizers share the credit for the absence of serious disorder . . . the change of police tactics was wholly successful as far as the main march was concerned . . . the behaviour of individual police officers, with very few exceptions, was exemplary . . . the good humour of the demonstrators and the determination of their organizers to prevent disorder made the occasion a responsible and peaceful protest.

A change had occurred and I find it difficult to believe that the NCCL was without influence in this. In his reply, the Home Secretary expressed his appreciation to the Council's observers for the trouble they had taken to make known their observations on the conduct of the demonstration and the fairmindedness of their tributes to the police. Clearly, as far as James Callaghan was concerned, the value of observing had struck home: when out of office he was to ask the new Home Secretary to arrange for an all-party team of MPs to observe the Orange Day Parades in Northern Ireland.

The history of the NCCL contains many examples where the same basic principles and methods were applied. One of its unsolved problems, as the Springbok rugby tour highlighted, is that of supplying sufficient numbers of observers, at short notice, outside London.

Conclusion

I have not attempted in this paper to disguise the conflicts which are basic to the civil liberty approach. Civil liberty provides a meeting-point for elements which in any other context would conflict: conservatism, including the practice of generally agreed principles, classic liberalism and the kind of radicalism which does not distinguish between fundamental change and reform. I would not attempt to deny that inconsistencies emerge when dealing with the irreconcilable. Some believe that if the Establishment fails to put its principles into practice this can be put down largely to administrative failure. But time and again the argument gets politicized because such failures can be traced to the wrong financial and social priorities. Justice is not seen as a priority. Accordingly, in contesting the failure of legal aid to provide equal rights before the law or the unending list of deficiencies in the prison system, we run the risk of shirking solutions which imply fundamental change. There again, should we be influenced by protestations of goodwill and humanity from people who in practice permit themselves to be implicated in the polite repression of underprivileged minorities and nonconformist individuals? In a way I admire the honesty of an Enoch Powell or a Peregrine Worsthorne who wrote with reference to the Dutschke affair:

What the Conservative leaders fail to recognize is that the case against liberal values . . . is becoming both strong and respectable. It may be necessary for the advanced Western nations if they are to protect themselves against the forces of disruption . . . to behave in a way that flouts the liberal conscience. I suspect that this is the direction in which the Western world is inexorably moving, and that governments will become more and more involved in actions that contradict the rule of law. . . . Increasingly Home Secretaries and Foreign Secretaries will find themselves acting arbitrarily, the former in fields that have to do with the maintenance of order in the streets, campuses and even factory floors, and the latter in fields having to do with the maintenance of order overseas.

Is there room for liberalism in the modern world where government is often in the hands of mediocrities or brutes, where the lust for power engulfs concern for human values, where irrationality passes for necessity and where lies are as essential to political systems as the ballot box or the party card? Liberalism can only be sustained by an acute intellectual and moral toughness and the ability to get results. Its advantages are that it may be uncluttered by the mythologies of the radical right and the radical left which have had an anaesthetizing impact on those who, in reaching for the unattainable, find excuses for not undertaking the possible. Direct action is a last resort and must be directed to the right issues at the right time. Its use will become increasingly important as technology adds efficiency to governmental and commercial power. Liberals may warn that computerized data-banks containing personal information will be used as a source of immense commercial and political power and provide the foundation of an entirely manipulated society where the individual counts for nothing. They may propose rules and procedures to prevent the abuse of data-banks but, ultimately, they may have to turn to the direct actionist because it is inconceivable that those in a position to increase their power through technology will relinquish it without a struggle.

My experience as an official at the NCCL and my study of its activities over the years leads me to some very tentative conclusions about direct action as distinct from protest in general. I take direct action to mean a method which enables individuals or groups to stop, dramatize or protest against what they may regard as a social or political evil by their own actions and without resort to the usual intermediaries and institutions. It can be conducted within the law (for example strikes, squatting) or outside the law, whether violent or non-violent tactics are employed. It may involve mass action as in a sit-down demonstration, small group action as with squatting or hijacking, or individual action as when a conscientious objector chooses prison rather than

K

induction into the forces. Stripped of effective power over his environment, the individual is left in the last analysis with nothing more than the ability to say no, withdraw his labour, or to lay his mind or body before the bulldozers of the State. On this basis, direct action has occupied an honourable place in the history of social change and the fight for political, welfare and industrial rights in this country. It is normal for government to resist change and for the majority of the public to support it, feeling perhaps that anything is better than the unknown. Nevertheless, important problems do arise which find the traditional institutions unprepared to take the strain of new ideas and reform. In situations like this, direct action is often advocated and sometimes successful. In practice, it has perhaps proved more useful in provoking debate or in uncovering problems which are tacitly ignored than it is in influencing decision-making and bringing about major changes of policy. Successful direct action has tended to be quite explicit in its aims, while the direct action philosophy which is solely concerned with bringing about the millennium, or in popular terms 'the revolution', tends to relapse into irrelevance and destroy itself and its advocates through sheer frustration.

Clearly the State has a duty to prevent serious disorder or damage to persons and property. Clearly it will defend itself and the vested interests it represents from fundamental change and the destruction of its institutions or power structure. But can it deal with real or imaginary threats without resorting to methods which would effectively destroy the rights and freedoms which have been traditionally enjoyed by citizens in this country? I cannot feel that a reasonable balance has been achieved, although I would not like to suggest, nor do I think it possible, that political protest should be merely tolerated and institutionalized after the fashion of the totalitarian States which bring out their obedient citizens to acclaim their own establishments and heap calculated hostility on the governments of other nations. All the same, the British power structure has been heavy-handed and highly selective in its treatment of opponents. On occasions the law has been bent to deal with protest on the correct assumption that the public and those who operate the system will tolerate a certain measure of injustice.

In recent times, the 'law and order' lobby has used fairly transient problems, like squatting or opposition to the South African tours, to raise the toleration level of injustice. The NCCL's central task is to lower it while, at the same time, raising the level of social consciousness. To do this, we need to understand protest, its motivations and methods, and wherever possible to build bridges of understanding. As conventional institutions like Parliament and the political parties become more incapable of coping and responding to the fears and aspirations of idealistic minorities, so opinions will polarize and the NCCL's inter-

XVIII Direct Action, Democratic Participation and the Media

NICHOLAS GARNHAM

The contents of this chapter are necessarily tentative. In the present state of media study, it seems to me not only more useful, but also more honest, to ask questions, to hesitantly suggest possibly fruitful areas of inquiry rather than to attempt definitive answers. Many people are only too ready with opinions on the effects of the media, but in general their opinions are only equalled in slickness and superficiality by the media themselves. Many who write and talk about the media become infected by the endemic disease of those who work in the media – the worship of the new. They therefore lack a historical perspective. To come to any firm conclusions on the role played by the media in the relationship of direct action to democratic participation would require a deep knowledge of the history of direct action, and of the effectiveness of such action, in the absence of modern media. I am even more aware than usual of my lack of such knowledge when compared with many of the contributors to this book.

Let me give one example of how such a historical perspective can significantly alter conclusions in this field. D. Halloran, P. Elliott and G. Murdock in their by now classic *Demonstrations and Communication*[1] came to the conclusion that media coverage of the 1968 Vietnam demonstration was structured, in both Press and television, as a self-fulfilling prophecy: that the media set up a context of expected violence and then fitted their 'news' into that prepared context. The implication of this study, it seems to me, is that the role of television and the Press in a democracy can be reduced to a question of professional ethics: that if only we could change the inferential structure within which journalists work all would be well. But what is overlooked is that this inferential structure has no specific connection with journalism. As G. Rudé points out in *The Crowd in History*, violence has been the prevailing stereotype for crowd action since at least the eighteenth century. This view, although unsupported by the historical facts, has been propagated by Burke and Taine and is now firmly entrenched at the centre of academic, never mind popular, mythology. Those in power see those who disagree with them as a threat. As Rudé puts it:

mediary role become more difficult. We cannot always draw ba
criticizing those institutions merely to preserve access to them

The political parties, the trade unions and certainly conv
pressure groups like the NCCL must give up the idea that they l
sole monopoly of the political stage. If we don't like militant
disorder or violence, we must give minority groups much
opportunities to express themselves particularly through tl
media. As far as law enforcement is concerned, we must give
idea that 'anything goes' where members of minority gro
concerned. Above all, we should learn to listen. World and
problems are serious and urgent enough for them not to be le
to the young and the disaffected. We run the risk as a society of r
into a state of vegetable conformity willing to collaborate with
where this is seen as desirable to preserve the *status quo*. Man
people have become so disturbed by these possibilities that th
elevated protest not merely to the level of political activity l
total life style. We would do well not to ignore them, to recogn
democratic institutions cannot be perfect and to understand th
action in the form of non-violent civil disobedience occupies
portant place in the democratic system.

'For as long as no serious attempt was made to probe the deeper aspirations of the poor, their periodic outbursts in riot or rebellion were liable to be attributed to the machinations of a political opponent or a "hidden hand".'[2] We know how true that still is of the way in which politicians of both parties and the media talk of strikes. The point I am making is that the existence of the media has not significantly altered the ideological stance of those in power. The media merely reflect that stance. But if we wish to change that stance we must look, not to changes within the media, but to changes in society as a whole.

So we should not be surprised that the media are biased against direct action. I am indeed always amused by that naïve liberal shock that greets any evidence of such bias. But does this bias make any significant difference? Is it not at least possible that the media are quite simply irrelevant to direct action? Halloran and his co-authors clearly do not think so, for one of their conclusions is this: 'the point is, that, even with an exclusive concern for the "what", television bulletins emphasize and interpret only those aspects of events which conform to the basic pattern of news angles which originally made the event news. This must throw considerable doubt on the possible effectiveness of media-reported demonstrations as a form of political communication with society.'[3] This makes the colossal assumption that media-reported demonstrations both could and should be an effective form of political communication. It seems to me that many people involved with direct action have fallen into this media-oriented trap. They have begun to believe the media's own myths about itself. Jerry Rubin's book is the most notable recent example of the way in which certain radicals have become so caught up by the illusion of media that they can no longer see the realities of political communication.[4] People who stage demonstrations in order to obtain media coverage have been persuaded by the media to forget what direct action is all about. For surely one of the basic motives behind direct action is just to escape from the image and substitute for it a concrete reality, an action. Direct action is a revolt against the use of language in political communication. Instead of talking or writing about democratic participation, it acts it out, and by so doing it cuts down the manipulative possibilities inherent in any language. It says in effect 'let's cut the cackle. Instead of the illusion of oppression and the hypocrisy made possible by that illusion let us see real naked physical oppression, so that everyone can see it for what it is.'

'See it for what it is' is here the crucial notion. For we have been led astray by the media to the extent that we believe that through them we see things as they are. The most disturbing finding in *Demonstrations and Communication* is that the study of viewer reaction revealed a widespread faith in the unbiased nature of television coverage. The belief that the camera cannot lie remains very persistent. It has led leaders of demonstrations to hope that if only television viewers can see the police hitting them over the head, governments will fall. Of course, governments do not fall that easily. But, apart from that, one can see why this has always been a temptation to anyone concerned in direct action. Surely they ask, if one of the chief motives of direct action is to bear witness to the evil of authority, and if through the media many millions can be made to bear witness to this evil, then direct action will have been that much more effective. But unfortunately, technology enables us to have the illusion of witnessing without its deeper physical and emotional implications. Even if we assume for the moment widespread and unbiased coverage of a demonstration (although this rarely occurs: for instance, a study undertaken by ABC television shows that only 1 per cent of their 1968 Chicago Convention coverage showed police violence), the experience of watching it on television or reading about it in the newspapers is radically different from actually being there. It is similar to the difference that has so concerned Norman Mailer between bombing North Vietnamese from 50,000 feet and fighting them hand to hand. The latter is an existential experience. For better or worse, it alters your whole being because your whole being is involved and so you cannot avoid some moral commitment. If you are on a street where a demonstration is taking place, it is impossible to be uninvolved. Even the decision to be apparently uninvolved is a conscious act. So however you react, you will have certain physical and emotional responses that involve the real you in a real event. But if you see it on television, you can enjoy the illusion of involvement without either the pain or the exhilaration. People are not converted by demonstrations on television, not because television fails to discuss the underlying issues, but because people are not forced to choose and thus to examine their position. Let me give two examples that perhaps indicate the irrelevance of media coverage in assessing the effectiveness of a demonstration. The rioting at the Chicago Convention was widely seen on television. Most people who were present seem to have been horrified and revolted by the police behaviour. But most people who watched it on television merely affirmed their support for Mayor Daley. The Paris riots, demonstrations, etc. of May 1968 were remarkably effective as political communication, that is the unrest spread throughout France and the government was seen to wobble, and yet all this happened in a country where television and radio were firmly in government hands.

So it seems probable that the effect of media coverage on direct action is similar to its effect on party politics. Certain demonstrators and certain politicians share the same illusions. These illusions are described by J. G. Blumler and D. McQuail in *Television in Politics*:

impressions of politicians are no more susceptible to media influence than are attitudes towards the parties. Nevertheless, the reputation of television as a medium which is suited to the projection of personality may influence the stress which is put in a party's publicity on the appeal of its leader. Also a leader's relative power *vis-à-vis* any would-be rivals in his own party, may depend in part now on his reputation for using the medium effectively and confidently or ineffectively and uneasily.[5]

If media reportage is an illusory extension of the use of direct action for political communication, how true is the related proposition that the media help to open up society and by widening the range of imagined possibilities for each individual citizen make central political control more difficult? On this proposition theorists of the left like Enzensberger meet with demagogues of the right like Spiro Agnew. They both see the media as liberating, anarchic forces threatening the established political power structure. The unsophisticated version of this view is the often heard "all these demonstrations, riots and strikes. All this political violence. It is all the fault of television." At the same time, we should ask whether this view is compatible with the other view widely held, at any rate on the left, that the media are a force for quiescence, that they peddle a reassurance that reinforces established authority, that the power they wield is concentrated in the hands of small economic and political power groups who can use that power to manipulate populations. At its most extreme, this view becomes the Orwellian vision of Big Brother. Can both these apparently mutually contradictory propositions be true?

There seems to be a good deal of evidence to link the development of efficient communication systems with the development of more open, democratic societies. Indeed, the participation of large numbers of people in the political process would have been impossible without printing, the railways and the postal service. Moreover, even the desire to participate depends upon an awareness of the wider political context in which one is asking to participate. Until you realize that the decisions taken in Westminster affect you in Bradford, you have no reason for wanting to control those decisions. It is the fear of this process that makes many in South Africa oppose the introduction of television and that delayed its introduction in Israel. But I think two points need to be noted from the outset. The previous advance in communication aided political freedom in so far as they were either open to all, that is roads, railways and the postal service, or could be controlled by radical forces, that is newspapers and pamphlets. (It is significant that one of the most successful manifestations of direct action in English history was the Rebecca Riots in 1843 which were directed against the erection of turnpike toll bars.) Neither of these conditions holds for television and radio nor does it hold for the mass-circulation newspapers. It seems therefore, likely that just as radical forces had to fight for freedom of the Press against government monopolies, stamp duty, etc., so now radical forces will have to fight to free radio and television and to re-liberate the Press. We should remember that the use of scarce communications resources as a tool of government control has a long history. Lévi-Strauss documents extensively the use of writing as a weapon in primitive South American cultures, and in Europe literacy itself was for a long time confined, quite consciously, to the ruling classes.

The present structure of radio and television has similarities with another historical use of communications systems, the military road and rail system which enabled central governments to move force quickly to where it was required. It is the absence of such systems that has aided the formation of separatist movements in East Pakistan, Biafra or Katanga. Network radio and television remind me of nothing so much as the pacification of the Highlands or Bismarck's railway system. But here we can learn a lesson from Vietnam. American air-power with the refined use of the helicopter is the modern equivalent for the electronic age of those old military systems. The Vietcong have shown that you can defeat such power by refusing to fight on its terms. In a media-dominated society, local guerrilla operations, such as the Squatters movement, are more likely to be successful than a mass political movement. Perhaps ignoring the media is the name of the game.

The most authoritative inquiry so far into the causes of civil disturbances was made by the Kerner Commission which was set up in July 1967 by President Johnson in response to a wave of riots in Negro ghettos right across the country from Newark to Watts. In examining the charge that the media helped to cause disturbances, they came to this conclusion:

We do not conclude that the media are a cause of riots, any more than they are the cause of other phenomena which they report. It is true that newspaper and television reporting helped shape people's attitudes towards riots. In some cities people who watched television reports and read newspaper accounts of riots in other cities later rioted themselves. But the causal chain weakens when we recall that in other cities people in very much the same circumstances, watched the same programmes and read the same newspaper stories, but did not riot themselves. The news media are not the sole source of information and certainly not the only influence on public attitudes. People obtained their information and formed their opinions about

1967 disorders from the multiplicity of sources that condition the public's thinking on all events. Personal experience, conversation with others, the local and long-distance telephone are all important as sources of information.[6]

This seems to me an eminently sensible conclusion and a valuable corrective to the McLuhanite nightmare. As the Kerner Commission showed, the race riot has a long history without the aid of mass media. In this country, the Luddites, Captain Swing, and the Chartists all spread widely and rapidly without the aid of any medium. Indeed, media coverage, to the extent that it may speed up the process, may also weaken its effect. We may well see here a social effect similar to the personal effect I have already noted of the media actually lessening involvement and therefore effectiveness. The longer a civil disturbance takes to spread, the more chance it has of changing people's consciousness. If popular dissatisfaction is brought to a head too quickly, it may, like an infection, burn itself out too fast. Certainly these days we see a debilitatingly rapid cycle of fashionableness affecting both the aims and methods of direct action. Once you have had a massive media-covered demonstration or riot, the long, hard, patient political and educational work may well seem anti-climactic. I felt this with the TUC demonstration against the Industrial Relations Bill in December 1970. It was at the time, certainly for anyone present, an impressive and massive display of peaceful defiance. But not only was there nowhere else to go, but was seen wrongly as a substitute for effective direct industrial action. After the demonstration, too many people seem to have felt that they had done their bit, and the fact that this bit was totally ineffective escaped notice.

When deciding whether the media help to liberate or pacify, the location of effective political control seems to be crucial. What Israel and South Africa feared was outside influence. But their fears were cultural rather than directly political. All the evidence shows that television has a shattering effect upon sheltered, conservative cultures. To take a simple example, if Arab women watch the programme *I Love Lucy* regularly, they will soon stop wearing the veil. Of course, in the long term such cultural changes will have their political repercussions, but they may well not be liberating. On the contrary, they may lead to domination by Yankee imperialism. I think South Africa's political fears are unwarranted. The African population already know the score. There is nothing more that television can teach them. They are held down by good old-fashioned force and television will not change that.

Where television can have a liberating political influence is where political power is located outside the area illuminated. This, I believe, did happen for a time with the American Civil Rights movement in the Deep South and is happening in Ulster. Media coverage of the Montgomery bus boycott in 1955 was significant but not in spreading Martin Luther King's message of non-violent action to his fellow Negroes. The subsequent sit-in movement across the Deep South would have been fuelled anyway by a grass-roots spread of information. But what media coverage did do was to communicate to Northern whites some inkling of what segregation was about. It was finally the image of Bull Connors on national television herding Negro women and children with a cattle prod in Birmingham, Alabama, in 1963 that inspired widespread white involvement in the Civil Rights movement – an involvement that reached its apogee with the Selma march in 1965. But once again, media were giving people conscience on the cheap. All this very fashionable Northern white liberal indignation helped to achieve very little in the end on the political level. Why? I think the process went something like this. To begin with the Civil Rights movement generated considerable momentum at the federal level because it confined its actions to the South, but the overwhelming voting power was in the North. It was, therefore, easy for northern politicians and those who voted for them to wax indignant, to ask: 'How can such things happen in this great country of ours?' It was this pressure that led to the use of federal troops to impose school desegregation. But, as H. J. Gans has noted, 'sympathy for the Civil Rights movement disappears when demonstrations take place outside the Deep South'.[7] When Negroes started rioting in the Northern ghettos, the feeling that had been aroused among Northern whites was seen for the superficial thing it had always been. So I believe that the media did help things along in the South by opening to view the practices of a small, entrenched and conservative power structure and allowing the Northern voters to support political action that did not affect them.

We can now see the same process at work in Ulster. It was not the Unionist power structure that was shaken by the Bogside riots, but, thanks in part to media coverage, the Westminster power structure. The sight of B-Specials in action, the revelation to English voters of the primitive religio-political rites of Northern Ireland and the social inequality that stemmed from them, allowed the voters, who were not going to be affected by any gains won by the Catholic minority, to support action that they might well not tolerate on their own doorstep, for example a coloured Civil Rights movement in Birmingham. As the effective political power lies in Westminster, where the Northern Ireland electorate wields little influence, it was safe for Westminster politicians to back reform measures, such as the disarming of the B-Specials, in the confident knowledge that their electorate would back them. Things can never, as a result, be the same again in Ulster. The Unionist cat is well and truly out of the bag, and the media undoubtedly helped to release it. That this is true is attested to by the fury of the Ulster politicians that television has now escaped from their iron grip. The BBC in Northern Ireland was until recently an arm of the Stormont government. The pressure of direct action has undoubtedly succeeded in loosening that relationship. The complaints about IRA gunmen being allowed to appear on the programme *24 Hours* are symptoms of that healthy situation.

But if, as happened in America, the Ulster Civil Rights movement began direct action in Britain, I think you would see the attitude of the media change rapidly. If the established power structure in this country was threatened, the media, on their record, would rush to its defence. The most notable example of this was the BBC's behaviour during the General Strike in 1926. In the debate on BBC bias against the unions, this story should not be forgotten, for after all the strike is a form of direct action that is almost respectable, even in this country. In this story the image of broadcasting as the modern equivalent of the military road network is particularly apt. Asa Briggs[8] in his authoritative history of the BBC, writes of their performance during the General Strike: 'The BBC not only spread intelligence during the strike: it reinforced authority.' In Briggs's view, even the apparently impartial intelligence function helped the government. 'By providing a steady and regular supply of news and announcements for all parts of the country, the Company (this was before the BBC became a public corporation) greatly assisted the government of the day.' It is worth noting here in passing that the Kerner Commission found that media coverage of disorder was more helpful to the law enforcement authorities in giving them time to take pre-emptive measures than it was in fuelling the riots. In 1926 the then Managing Director, John Reith (later Lord Reith), always felt that the BBC had to be, as he put it, 'for the government in the crisis'. When it was over, he took great pains to defend his position in a confidential memorandum to his senior staff. The following quotations are from that document[9] and they delineate accurately the position the BBC still occupies in the political system, and the attitude, now almost unconscious, of the BBC hierarchy towards political unrest. Reith wrote:

There could be no question about our supporting the government in general, particularly since the General Strike had been declared illegal in the High Court. This being so, we were unable to permit anything which was contrary to the spirit of that judgement, and which might have prolonged or sought to justify the Strike. . . . Since the BBC was a national institution and since the government in this crisis were acting for the people the BBC was for the government in the crisis too.

One of the failures for which the BBC had been criticized was in not allowing a labour spokesman to broadcast. To give Reith his due, he had fought for this, but the question of importance in view of the prevailing myth of the BBC's political independence, is how hard he fought. His view was that he could not run the risk of being taken over by the government.

Had we been commandeered we could have done nothing in the nature of impartial news, nor could we have in any way helped inspire appreciation of the fact that a prolongation of the stoppage was a sure means of reducing the standard of living.

This quotation makes clear the strict limits of the BBC's impartiality. During the strike, Reith had issued a directive that 'Nothing calculated to extend the area of the strike should be broadcast.' It is difficult to see what difference the commandeering of the BBC would have made.

Social attitudes have of course changed since 1926 in ways that make this traditional BBC stance more difficult to maintain, or at least defend in such frank terms, but it still remains true that with the present structure within which our limited broadcasting frequencies are organized, the BBC and ITV (which in this sense was created in the image of the BBC) have an almost symbiotic relationship to the Westminster power structure. The controlling hierarchies of these organizations move so constantly in their corridors of power, sit so frequently at the dinner-tables at which policy is discussed, that their value judgements take on an authoritarian colour. To act responsibly becomes, of course, a moral imperative, and responsibility is unconsciously defined as that which supports the *status quo*. They are so deeply enmeshed constitutionally within the established democratic structure that to threaten one is to threaten the other, and, like all élites, the broadcasters will in the last analysis defend their own power base above all else.

This defence is, of course, disguised, as it was in Reith's day, by an assertion of impartiality; what Charles Curran calls 'tolerance'. I think they really believe that this tolerance allows all voices to be heard. Indeed, in a speech Charles Curran described the BBC, with the support of quotations from Edmund Burke, as the very centre of a free society in which all voices met in rational debate. We have seen in Reith's statement the real limits of this impartiality. But besides these ideological and political limits, the claimed impartiality of radio and television and indeed the sincere attempt to exercise that impartiality has, I think, serious consequences for those engaged in direct action, for those who do not see our present universal franchise, representative democracy, as the last word in political freedom. The consequences are, first, that impartiality on a medium that is catering overwhelmingly for majority audiences, will be the impartiality of the consensus. It will inevitably give maximum weight to the established views of the majority at the expense of those minorities who challenge the *status quo*. In the words of Robert MacNeil, in his book *The People Machine*, 'television journalism appears anxious to sell the chief commodity of entertainment television . . . reassurance'.[10] The second consequence is the development of political alienation. Impartiality, as Curran himself saw, depends as a principle upon a view of politics as a rational activity. If it means anything, its virtue is that all voices will be heard, that as voices they are equal and after rational consideration the most reasonable of those voices will be upheld. But unfortunately, the expectation of rationality thus aroused cannot be satisfied by those media that arouse it. Many practitioners and commentators have attested to the fact that television and to a lesser extent radio, whatever their virtues, are not good at giving reasons. They concentrate on the 'what' rather than the 'why' and upon a fairly narrow range of 'what' at that. I think there is no practitioner who would seriously argue otherwise. It seems to me that this sharp conflict between the expectation of rationality and the experience of irrationality must have helped the growth of political alienation. Blumler and McQuail found that 32 per cent of the population were sceptical about politics. Similar figures have been produced in the United States. Blumler and McQuail attribute this to 'what has been called "meaninglessness" or a feeling that an election is without meaning because . . . an intelligent and rational decision is impossible because the information upon which such a decision must be made is lacking.[11] As this study also found that television was the primary source of political information, the media must, I think, play a considerable part in this alienation process.

To the extent that direct action is a response to this feeling of alienation, the media can be said to have encouraged it. But can we also go on from there with Anthony Wedgwood Benn and say that lack of access to the media, the narrow way in which impartiality has been defined, encourages direct action? Is direct action, now that we have universal suffrage, no longer the voice of the disenfranchised, but the means of expression of those denied a say on the media? Would a widening of access therefore discourage direct action, and is it desirable that it should? Benn said of student demonstrators against the Vietnam war:

in part they are protesting against the very denial to them and others of any real access of their views on mass media. . . . If law and order were ever to break down, in part or in whole, in Britain, the policy

of restricted access and unrestricted coverage, would have to bear a
very considerable part of the burden.[12]

This is, as I hope I have by now made clear, in my view a gross exag-
geration, but it does echo a concern also voiced by the Kerner Commission.

> The Commission's main concern with the news media is not in riot
> reporting as such, but in the failure to report adequately on race
> relations and ghetto problems. . . . In defining, explaining and
> reporting the broader, more complex and ultimately more funda-
> mental subject, the communications media, ironically, have failed to
> communicate.[13]

Benn and the Kerner Commission see this process of communication
as part of the conventional political process. Benn is quite frank
about it:

> it is not a question of balance between Labour and Conservatives
> that matters. It is the BBC's failure to provide the means by which
> the true complexity of affairs can be explained, without which the
> gap between political leaders and people will inevitably tend to widen
> and widen.[14]

Behind Benn's concern lies an image of politics that I would have
thought it was the concern of direct action to break up, an image of a
few political leaders and a large number of people with whom these
leaders communicate. The media constitute a significant part of that
image. But it is an image that fails to tackle the central issue of how you
transform words into deeds. For behind the myth of impartiality lies
not only the concept of rational discourse, but the expectation that the
result of this discourse will be action. Direct action is a response to the
denial of that expectation. It affirms the existence of real grievances and
real conflicts of interest that will not disappear just by being talked
about. So those who believe in the need for direct action must not
delude themselves that a transformation in the structure of media
will transform society. The opposite is nearer the truth.

This does not mean that such a structural change in the media is
not desirable and should not be fought for. Democracy is not something
that should be confined to conventional politics. The battle for real
democratic participation must be fought on all fronts, and even small
victories within the media might have a powerful exemplary effect. As
Raymond Williams writes in *The Long Revolution:* 'The situation can
be held as it is, not only because democracy has been limited at the
national level to the process of electing a court but also because our
social organization elsewhere is continually offering non-democratic

patterns of decision.'[15] We who are interested in a participatory democracy must stop playing our opponents' game by regarding the media as an integral part of the established political system. They assume that its political role is as an extension of that system and that if, for instance, the broadcasting networks are under the control of Parliament, they are democratically controlled. Nothing could be further from the truth. We must regard the media as a totally separate structure within which the widest access and accountability are desirable for their own sake, just as workers' control in industry is desirable for its own sake, independently of the wider political structure in which they operate.

Exactly how this access and accountability will work will be discovered and refined in practice. Workers' control itself will only be desirable as a transitional phase, because otherwise it will result in marginally widening and then more firmly entrenching the present unrepresentative and unresponsive élite. Any development of democracy in the media will entail changing our notions of the nature of art and of the role of the artist and the intellectual. Within the existing structure, the possibility of certain immediate advances should be looked at. These should include the election of the BBC governors and the Board of the IBA, the control of local radio by representative listeners' councils and of the regionally based ITV companies in the same way. Within the Press and broadcasting industries the unions must steel themselves to take on the responsibility of control in a tightening financial and confused technological situation. The greatest barrier at the moment to democratic control of the media is the élitism of the unions involved, an élitism founded upon a solid base of prestige and high pay. But if this battle can be won within the unions, the media are extremely vulnerable to direct action; run as they are by a small, highly-skilled group of workers with a product susceptible to unavoidable daily sabotage. Such direct action would, of course, be resisted in the name of impartiality and a free Press by the economic and political forces that at present control the media. As a rehearsal for this defence, the condemnation of the print workers who in 1970 stopped the *Evening Standard* because of a critical JAK cartoon was revealing. But such a confrontation could have the most interesting consequences. As Wilkes replied, when asked in 1763 by Madame de Pompadour how far the liberty of the Press extended in England, 'I do not know. I am trying to find out.'

NOTES

1. J. D. Halloran, P. Elliott and G. Murdock, *Demonstrations and Communication: A Case Study* (Harmondsworth, 1970).
2. G. Rudé, *The Crowd in History* (Chichester, 1965), p. 215.
3. Op. cit., p. 237.

4. Jerry Rubin, *Do It* (London, 1970).
5. J. G. Blumler and D. McQuail, *Television in Politics: Its Uses and Influences* (London, 1968), p. 262.
6. *Report of the National Advisory Commission on Civil Disorders* (Kerner Commission) (US Government Printing Office, 1968), p. 203.
7. Herbert J. Gans, 'Some Changes in American Taste and Their Implication for the Future of Television', in Stanley T. Donner, *The Future of Commercial Television*, Report of the Stanford University Television Seminar, 1965, p. 43. Quoted in '*The People Machine*' by Robert MacNeil (London, 1970), p. 7.
8. Asa Briggs, *The History of Broadcasting in the United Kingdom:* vol. 1: *The Birth of Broadcasting* (Oxford, 1961), p. 384.
9. Quoted in Briggs, ibid., pp. 364–6.
10. Robert MacNeil, op. cit., p. 58.
11. Blumler and McQuail, op. cit., p. 290, quoting Murray B. Levin, *The Alienated Voter* (Holt, Rinehart and Winston, 1962), p. 62.
12. Anthony Wedgwood Benn in a speech at a Labour party meeting in Bristol, reported in *The Guardian* (19 October 1968), quoted in Halloran *et al.*, op. cit., p. 22.
13. Kerner, op. cit., p. 210.
14. Wedgwood Benn, quoted in Halloran *et. al.*, op. cit., p. 21.
15. Raymond Williams, *The Long Revolution* (London, 1961 and Harmondsworth, 1965), p. 339.

XIX Protest and Democracy

TREVOR SMITH

Militant protest in various forms has been a regular though not constant feature of British political life since the medieval foundations of civil society, as Victor Kiernan demonstrates in Chapter I. The concern of the present chapter is to consider in very broad terms the nature of what passes for contemporary protest in this country.

Modern political protest embraces a variety of activities which can be delineated easily enough for analytical purposes but which in practice are less readily identifiable. It is possible, that is to say, to claim that protest encompasses three distinct forms of activity, namely, political violence, direct action, and the operations of the more militant kinds of pressure groups. It is more difficult, however, to pin-point with much accuracy where one type of activity stops and another begins. Moreover, it is even more hazardous to trace how one form of protest interacts with another and how, both individually and collectively, they all relate in the wider context to the general conduct of public affairs. And yet these are among the main considerations involved in any attempt to understand the recent manifestations of protest in Britain.

The main focus of this book is on direct action as a political form and deals only *en passant* with the extremes of political violence, on the one hand, and the more conventional kinds of pressure group activity, on the other, which run the gamut of extra-Parliamentary politics. The term 'direct action', however, is not a very useful one in view of the blurring, overlap and interaction between the three categories of protest politics. Our political vocabulary has not yet been extended to accommodate with elegance and economy the new vehicles of radical expression which direct action and its contiguous associates represent. 'Riot', 'strife' and 'rebellion' are clearly archaisms – outside Ulster – while 'demos', 'happenings', 'sit-ins' and other such linguistic innovations are equally infelicitous. What is lacking is a suitable generic term. Anthony Wedgwood Benn calls these burgeoning activities 'the new politics', but this perhaps overstresses their novelty and too readily subsumes them under the idea of politics – at least as it is conventionally understood. There is, then, no easy way of conveying the meaning and nuance of contemporary protest.

Limitations of vocabulary, however, have not inhibited many explanations from being offered which endeavour to account for the latest upsurge of protest in Britain and elsewhere – most notably in the United States and France. In so far as it has attracted the young, the biological fact of earlier maturation has been seen as a causal element in the situation. In similar vein, it has been argued that the rise of more democratic child-rearing patterns and the general softening of authority relationships in both family and school have increased the radical propensities of the post-war generation. Again, the extension of higher education in general, and the development of the social sciences in particular, have been construed as engendering a fundamental change in the political socialization of a significant minority of young people which has attracted them towards radical activism. The mass media, particularly television, has been identified also as contributing to the new wave of unrest, often for very different reasons, ranging from the portrayal of violence to the rapid transmission of news both between and within countries; while others have argued that this unrest stems from the increasing sense of alienation fostered by the living and working conditions of urban society.

In Britain, at any rate, it is most unlikely that any of these factors can be regarded as being the prime causes of protest though undoubtedly, to a greater or lesser extent, they have helped to shape the direction and the style which it has taken in recent years. As in the past, some forms of protest have originated in a sense of grievance or threat: the Ulster crisis, the 'work-in' among Upper Clyde Shipbuilders and the objectors to an inland site for London's third airport arose as defensive responses to grievances, actual or threatened, felt by people. Again, as in the past, other forms of protest have been inspired not by the determination to defend immediate self-interests but by the desire to advance and implement certain values or beliefs: CND, the Stop The Seventy Tour and the activities of the Welsh Language Society are examples of ideologically-based protest. But what, perhaps, is new about the present situation is the range rather than the types of protest. It is not so much that there is more protest than before but rather that protest now seems to encompass a wider spread of issues. It is not readily apparent how one would quantify it, but it seems likely that protest has covered more issues from 1955 to 1970 than any other previous fifteen-year period in British history. And it is this phenomenon which needs explaining. Clearly, for example, television has played a part both in highlighting the identification of issues and even more in publicizing the recourse to protest in different countries and in different parts of the same country – not always to its advantage, as Nicholas

Garnham shows in Chapter XVIII; though the effects of other influences, biological, educational or environmental, are less immediately obvious.

If one had to single out the primary reason for the latest growth of protest, one would probably locate it in the steady decline in the activity of politics as conventionally defined – not least because its decline pre-dates the new wave of protest.[1] Attention has been focused on the rise of protest precisely because it is highly visible and consciously dramatic relative to the erosion of the traditional activity of politics and the implications this has for the conduct of public affairs.

In the mid-1950s, when the decline set in, there was, it is true, an awareness of the fact: indeed it was welcomed by the *cognoscenti* as an index of political maturity. There arose a widespread view that modern society – called variously by such terms as 'post-industrial' or 'post-capitalist' – was one whose politics were characterized by an absence of ideological fervour and the abatement of class conflict. Social engineering, piecemeal reform, or incrementalism resulting from the bargaining of interest groups (reflecting divisions of status rather than those of class), together with the application of new skills and techniques would determine the content of public policy. In future, civil society would be ordered by the pursuit of reason carried on within a broad consensus about means and ends rather than by the clash of rival doctrines tempered by the vicissitudes of circumstance. The good society needed no longer to be striven for, since in the West, at least, it had already been achieved: history had come to rest provided that the balance of nuclear terror could contain international conflagration until the remainder of mankind reached the same final state of harmony.

The 'end of ideology' thesis seemed to fit the facts of mid-century prosperity and the soporific quality of public debate. The withering away of ideology, if not the State, became accepted as the prevailing conventional wisdom and was reflected *inter alia* in Gaitskellite revisionism and the naked hedonism of Tory electioneering in 1959. Having been quickly established, it was soon forgotten for the most part, leaving as its legacy the operational ideal of 'consensus politics' to which fashionable thought enthusiastically subscribed.

Under the umbrella of 'consensus', the occupants of governing roles and those who aspired to them – by definition they no longer merited being called 'politicians' – together with their intellectual fellow-travellers, turned their attentions to matters of social engineering. In the event, this meant little more than calling in economics to fulfil the role which politics had been made to vacate. (It was in this way, rather than in the socialization of the young, that the social sciences, or a branch of them, fully asserted themselves.) Now a belief in the virtue of 'consensus' provided no hints for action, although it did allow full room for the display of technocratic enthusiasms: and thus it happened that economic growth and improved efficiency in government were decreed to be the over-riding goals of public policy. Since these goals were themselves vague and open-ended they were to be 'firmed up' by reference to international statistics dealing with relative growth rates, productivity indices, investment schedules and patterns of industrial training. And the elevation of the international reference group as a determinant of the nation's psychology, inherent in this remorseless cross-national comparison, gave in turn added impetus to the decision to seek admission to the EEC.

The unprecedented degree of institutional innovation in the machinery of government, which began in the late 1950s and gathered pace in the following decade, was an earnest of the commitment to the new goals of policy. Economic growth and the quest for efficiency were to be served by the NEDC, the DEA, the PIB, the IRC, the CIR, the CSD, and other such agencies whose creation apparently was constrained only by the upper limits of human ingenuity and of alphabetical juxtaposition. But these outward and visible signs, including the formation of the Government Economic Service, did not represent a *coup d'état* by a new breed of technocrats. Such a move had been pre-empted by those in governing positions, the erstwhile politicians, who, though lacking formal qualifications and therefore unable to be regarded as technocrats themselves, had nevertheless co-opted the technocratic caste of mind. Elizabeth Vallance demonstrates in Chapter IV how 'politicians' assimilate the language of technocracy and make it their own.

This assimilation, however, is not costless. The adoption of 'consensus' and its concomitant technocratic ethos extracted an exorbitant price in terms of the erosion of democratic politics: the adoption of the one necessarily meant the exclusion of the other for, as Jean-Paul Sartre has remarked, 'statistics can never be dialectics'.

Consensual technocracy provided a debilitating formula for the exercise of government. Its least disastrous attribute was that it failed its own tests for the most part, spectacularly so in the case of economic growth which fell, rather ungraciously, to zero by the end of the 1960s. Initially oversold in highly hortatory terms, the subsequent failure of consensual technocracy could only exacerbate the widespread disenchantment with what the populace, without being alerted to the contrary, continued to believe were politics and politicians. The advent of technocracy had been camouflaged by the continual use of the forms of liberal democracy, and at elections the doctrinal residues of party conflict, while the substance had all but atrophied. The oscillations recorded by opinion-polls, the dramatic reverses at by-elections and municipal elections, and the ephemeral appearance of Celtic nationalism were in the 1960s all manifestations of a bewildered and frustrated electorate, while those who sought a more positive response resorted to protest.

But of more profound significance than its immediate failures was that consensual technocracy set in train what has since become an established feature of public policy – the enunciation and pursuit of boundless goals which preclude the restoration of politics as the means for regulating society. An unrelenting quest for economic growth, governmental efficiency, enforcement of law and order, or competition by abandoning the 'lame ducks' of industry are poor surrogates for alternative political programmes which order priorities in a reasonably specific and finite way. Boundless goals are exhausting to pursue and difficult to evaluate: how much is 'enough' in the case of growth or efficiency or law enforcement or competition? The pursuit of such goals resembles nothing so much as the antics of Schnozzle Durante searching for the lost chord. Inevitably, what are properly second order considerations, such as efficiency and the development and application of techniques to policy-making, are promoted to act as first order ones: and thus means rather than ends assume over-riding importance. Moreover, the emphasis placed on technique in such circumstances puts an excessive premium on novelty as officials seek to feed the insatiable appetite of boundless goals. And it is this which accounted for the wholesale importation of foreign forms and procedures and the swift succession of new techniques which has been so marked a feature of Whitehall in recent years.

The substitution of administration for politics which, in short, is the fundamental change which has been wrought by consensual technocracy, promoted apathy and cynicism among the masses and provoked anger and frustration among what previously would have been the politically active minority. Like the erstwhile politicians, the activist minority rejected the idea and practice of liberal democracy which, in their view, had led to consensual technocracy: and one result of this is to be seen in the continuing decline of the individual memberships of the political parties since the mid-1950s. In retreating from the parties, the activists resorted to protest in order to give expression to their convictions and aspirations. Chapter X by Peter Cadogan and Chapter XI by George Clark offer personal testimonies as to why they abandoned traditional political activity in favour of protest. Wherever political imagination still flickers, protest may seem a preferable alternative to consensual technocracy; but whether it may lead to a more democratic ordering of society is less obvious.

Although protest can be identified as a reaction to consensual technocracy, it by no means constitutes a unified movement of radical, dissenting opinion, though some protesters may cherish the thought that it may later emerge as such. At best, it represents a rather disparate set of activities ranging from violence, through direct action, to militant pressure groups. Although parallels can be found for most of them in British history, in their current manifestations they borrow heavily from recent American and Continental experience; this is particularly true of student protest in the universities, public demonstrations which seek confrontation with the authorities, and much of what is called community action. Violence, Ulster excepted, has for the most part been eschewed.

In Britain, then, modern protest is to be seen largely as a reaction to the newly-installed technocratic order, inspired by foreign experience, and in the event a pale reflection of what has occurred in other countries. Neither here nor elsewhere has it been nourished by much theoretical speculation; indeed the lack of theory is seen by many, particularly in France, to be one of its strengths.[2] Despite the absence of a coherent intellectual framework, it is possible to tease out some of the main assumptions which underlie the more extreme forms of contemporary protest and which to a lesser extent influence its more moderate forms.

First, as has been said, it is motivated by the feeling that representative democracy has somehow failed and needs either to be replaced or, more moderately, complemented by the spread of direct democracy which involves those most immediately affected by whatever the issue may be: the principle operating here is the classical syndicalist one that the smaller the unit the more democratic it will be. Secondly, and allied to the first, is the need to encourage individual participation. Thirdly, to do this, issues must be selected which are close at hand. The world has become too complex for any individual to cultivate his own macro-cosmic view of it which might guide his actions and possibly those of others; the only solution is to avoid such lofty considerations and concentrate one's energies instead at a level of society and within a range of issues which one can fully comprehend. Even then it is in action rather than in reflection that one's consciousness will be extended. At its most ambitious this, or something like it, provides the impetus for the retreat into the commune and the vision of founding an alternative society, and which offers also some sort of rationale for the other, more sporadic forms of protest. The distinguishing feature of modern protest perhaps lies in its commitment to *proximity* rather than *priority*. That is to say, instead of starting from a critical analysis of society which indicates the desired sequence of change, whether by revolutionary or constitutional methods in the manner of the more traditional revolutionary or social democrat, the modern protester rejects society as given; and by activating widespread 'grass-roots' renewal seeks its replacement in an ultimate form which it would be both too early and too authoritarian for him to specify.

In so far as this is not too gross a caricature of the basic assumptions behind the more extreme forms of protest, it is by no means clear how protest is preferable to consensual technocracy, for both commit the modern heresy of espousing boundless goals and of stressing means rather than ends. Both, for that matter, are prone to the distractions of fashion and trend; the serial passions of cost-benefit analysis, account-able management, and output budgeting in Whitehall, have as their counterparts Suez, the Bomb, Vietnam, the Springboks, and Biafra in the field of protest. The one is the mirror image of the other and both faithfully reflect the climate of the times, which they nourish in turn.

At the beginning of this chapter it was suggested that the newer kinds of militant pressure groups which have mushroomed in recent years should be included within the ambit of modern protest, not so much in spite of but because of the difficulties of definition and overlap. I is accepted that it is hard to draw fine distinctions between the more militant pressure groups and direct action, on the one hand, and, on the other, between the more militant and the more conventional kinds of pressure groups. Mothers in Action, for example, display a versatility in their activities which span direct action, militant lobbying and the more conventional approaches to applying pressure. Shelter, which has the attributes of both a conventional and militant pressure group is helped in its chosen task, fortuitously or otherwise, by the activities of the direct-actionist London Squatters with whom it now has formal links. Similarly, the success of the Stop The Seventy Tour, which Peter Hain chronicles in Chapter XII, was a militant pressure cum direct actionist group which, arguably, was aided by those more extreme and violent elements outside STST which 'upped the ante' by daubing cars with paint and threatening to tear up cricket pitches. And, further-more, the tactics of both enhanced the role played by the more moderate anti-Springbok group led by David Sheppard and Lord Boyle. Such 'parasitical benefits', if so they may be termed, are not the prerogative of protest: the Confederation of British Industries enjoys these benefits and is able to appear moderate and responsible as a result of the more extreme attitudes espoused by the Industrial Policy Group, the Institute of Directors, Aims of Industry and the Economic League in advancing the cause of private enterprise and the business community. Flying kites and hoisting storm-cones are old dodges in the tactical repertoire.

But blurred boundaries and interaction are not the only reasons for including militant pressure groups under the heading of protest. Another reason for doing so is because their dramatic rise derives from the same impulses which have inspired the recourse to direct action and, to the limited extent it has occurred, violence. They represent the retreat from party and impatience with, but not outright rejection of, established Parliamentary institutions and procedures, and form part of the reaction to consensual technocracy. And they provide, along with the more extreme manifestations of protest, a harbour for those whose attention can no longer be sustained at the national level of public affairs and who choose to settle for a more limited horizon which is at least within their understanding.

There are circumstances where a case can be made out for protest as one of the available resources of the democratic system. Its legitimacy can be established fairly easily in those situations where the socio-political system withholds *de facto* rights and opportunities to whole categories of citizens and where, without protest, concessions are unlikely to be yielded as in the case of Catholics in Ulster, blacks in America, and women almost everywhere. But, if one is not an outright revolutionary or anarchist, to remain effective protest must be used sparingly in a democratic system of government. The Pavlovian recourse to widespread protest in recent years cannot be justified and indeed it is ultimately destructive of the aims of its participants.

Extensive protest plays into the hands of government in two ways. First, faced with a multitude of protest movements, the government can apply the principle of selective legitimacy. That is to say it can go some way to accommodate to the demands of the more moderate ones, thus appearing responsive, while isolating the more radical ones and labelling them as extremist or irresponsible. It is the old divide-and-rule tactic. Secondly, direct action and violence is not the exclusive preroga-tive of radical opinion; the State, too, has always been ready to meet like with like and usually more effectively because of its superior resources. Harassment, politically inspired prosecutions, deportation, and internment without trial have been and are still used by the State. Such action by the State can only be ultimately countered if the cause in question is one that can attract over time a large measure of public sympathy. But the climate created by widespread protest makes it easier for the State to justify its actions and correspondingly much more difficult for a particular cause to mobilize public opinion on its own behalf.

A third criticism of the widespread use of protest is that radicals cannot reasonably object if reactionaries emulate them. To subscribe to the participatory democracy of protest is to declare open season for any group to organize itself and advance its beliefs. And, historically, in Britain at least, the right has been better able to organize itself than the left.

But the basic weakness of extensive protest is that its various mani-festations cannot be summed or placed in any kind of rank order of importance – and it is this which makes it, literally, mindless.[3] It comprises a welter of more or less diverse pressures which, whatever their common sources of inspiration, can in no way be brought together to form a coherent basis for concerted national action. In the context of protest, no means are available for the aggregation of interests, for the emphasis is placed exclusively on the articulation of interests. The more moderate protesters (that is those who claim to aim not at the overthrow of Parliamentary democracy but rather to seek to complement it and make it more effective) would presumably argue that the aggregative function remains where it has traditionally been with the political parties and the executive branch of government. Such an argument, however, is disingenuous in so far as protest in all its forms represents a retreat from the party. Having done their best to divert the energies of activists away from the parties, having argued that a major part of the rationale of protest is a response to the failings of the parties, and having sought directly to place a bewildering array of issues on the public agenda, moderate protesters are expecting a lot of the parties in such circumstances to continue as effective instruments for aggregating interests. Assailed both by protest and technocratic fervour it is not surprising that the policy forming, interest aggregation role of the parties has been severely eroded.

Other, more radical protesters might argue that to say that no means have yet emerged for aggregating interests within the world of protest is not to say that they will not be forthcoming in the future. Against such an expression of faith, there can be no direct answer except to say that it is extremely unlikely. The parochial loyalties which have to be mobilized within a protest movement, if it is to be even minimally successful, cannot easily be transformed to accommodate wider considerations without doing violence to the unity of the movement.

Extensive protest might merit more sympathy if it could be shown to have increased the number of activists and to have sustained their support. Its achievement seems more likely to have been to spread their number more thinly over a wider number of issues and, in particular, to have deflected them away from seeking to advance their aims within the framework of the political parties. To this extent, protest has made its full contribution to the erosion of democratic politics without offering anything like a reasonable alternative. The public interest, or what passes for it, remains an amalgam of technocratic enthusiasms and the bargains made between government and the established pressure groups; by contrast, the influence of protest in moulding the substance of public policy has been minuscule. Consensual technocracy triumphs while radical opinion is trapped in the *cul-de-sac* of protest.

NOTES

1. This point is elaborated in my *Anti-Politics: Consensus, Reform and Protest in Britain* (London, 1972).
2. Cf. Alfred Willener, *The Action-Image of Society* (London, 1970), p. 294.
3. Cf. T. B. Bottomore, *Critics of Society* (London, 1967), chap. VIII *passim*.

INDEX

ABC Television, 294
Acheson, Dean, 166
Acland, J. H. B. *Lt.-Col.*, 176
Action Committee against Racialism, 252
Acton, *Lord*, 64
Adams, Walter, 204
Adelstein, David, 212
Adjustment Action Society, 155
Africa, 131, 154, 196
Agnew, Spiro, 295
Aims of Industry, 311
Aldermaston marches, 167, 170, 173, 178, 180, 181, 183–4, 186, 203
Algeria, 103, 104
Ali, Tariq, 173, 174, 175
Allaun, Frank, 258
Alliance Party (*Northern Ireland*), 130
Alton Locke, 35, 47n.
American Civil Liberties Union, 114, 278–9
Amritsar Massacre, 43, 44
Anarchists, 220
Angry Brigade, 53
Annan, *Lord*, 210
Anti-Defamation League (US), 114
Anti-Fascism, 50, 54, 55, 57, 58, 280
    Thurloe Square meeting (1936), 57
Anti-Semitism, 53, 54, 57–8, 59
Anti-Vietnam War Movement, 224, 273n., 301–2, 311 (*see also* Vietnam Solidarity Campaign)
Argyle, *ninth Earl of*, 29
Army, British, 139, 165, 173, 226
Arrowsmith, Pat, 167, 168, 170–1, 260
Asians in Britain, 160
Atomic Weapons Research Establishment, Aldermaston, 166–7
Attlee, C. R., 277
Attorney-General, 282

BBC, 280, 299–300, 302, 303
B-specials, 139, 140, 298–9
Baldwin, James, 85n.
Balfour, Arthur, 220
Bandaranaike, S. W. R. D., 131
Barwick, *Dr* John, 29, 46n.
Bassett, Reginald, 219, 229n.
Beer, Samuel, 259, 272–3n., 267
Belfast, 137, 138, 140
    Shankill Road, 140
Belgium, 39

Benn, Anthony Wedgwood, 301–2, 304n., 305
Bentham, Jeremy, 64
Berger, John, 251–2, 272n.
Berlin Wall, 169
Beswick, Frank, 258
Bevan, Aneurin, 180
Bevanites, 164, 165
Beveridge Report (1942), 163
Bevin, Ernest, 164
Beyond Counting Arses, 170
Biafra, 296, 311
Bidwell, Sidney, 154
Bienen, H., 104, 108n.
Birmingham, 156
    Bull Ring riots, 34
Birmingham Corporation, 280
Birmingham Immigration Control Committee, 144
Birmingham University, 206
Birmingham, Alabama (US), 298
Bismarck, Otto Edward Leopold von, *Prince*, 296
Black Panthers (GB), 155–6
Black Panthers (US), *see* United States
Black Power (GB), 150–61
Black Power (US), *see* United States
Black Power Party, 155
Black Stonerangers (*Chicago*), 159
Black Unity and Freedom Party, 155, 156–8
Blackshirts, *see* British Union of Fascists
Bleak House, 45, 48n.
Blue Streak, 259
Blumler, J. G., 294–5, 301, 304n.
Boer Wars (1899–1902), 42, 48n.
Bournemouth East and Christchurch, 257
Bow Group, 263
Boyd, William, 212
Boyle, *Sir* Edward, 266, 311
Bradford University, 209, 210
Bradlaugh, Charles, 220
Brecht, Bertolt, 166
Briggs, Asa, 299, 304n.
Bristol, 34
British Council for Peace in Vietnam, 173
British Union of Fascists, 44, 51–9, 225